COMMODORE-64 DATA FILES

A BASIC Tutorial

COMMODORE-64 DATA FILES

A BASIC Tutorial

David Miller

A RESTON COMPUTER GROUP BOOK
Reston Publishing Company, Inc.
A Prentice-Hall Company
Reston, Virginia

Library of Congress Cataloging in Publication Data
Miller, David
Commodore 64 data files.

"A Reston Computer Group Book."
1. Commodore 64 (Computer)--Programming. 2. Basic (Computer program language) I. Title. II. Title: Commodore sixty-four data files.
QA76.8.C64M55 1984 001.64′2 83-26926
ISBN 0-8359-0797-X
ISBN 0-8359-0791-0 (pbk.)

Editorial/production supervision and interior design by Barbara J. Gardetto

10 9 8 7 6 5 4

Printed in the United States of America

Honor thy father and thy mother. . . .
Deuteronomy 5:16

To our parents: Harold and Frances Miller and Emily Mark for their continued encouragement and support.

contents

acknowledgments

I would like to express my sincere appreciation to Dave Stewart, Mark Stewart, and Scott Bridston of Quality Computer Service for their patience and assistance. They are an excellent Commodore dealer. Rob Tyler and Forrest Kendall provided useful timely suggestions and support. Ron and Elli Busch have courageously served as helpful testers on this and on previous books. Finally, Bill Sanders, author of *Elementary Commodore-64* et al. and a close friend from high-school days, gave needed encouragement to proceed with this book as my first priority.

What exercise is to the body,
Programming is to the mind.
D. M.

preface

The purpose of this book is to take some of the misery and mystery out of learning to use the Commodore-64's file structure. The book is aimed at people who would like to learn to use the computer to assist them at home or at work by using the file capabilities of the Commodore-64 personal computer. *Commodore-64 Data Files: A BASIC Tutorial* is designed as a step-by-step tutorial. The book explains some things that, without adequate manuals, take many painful hours of trial and error to learn. Progress has been made in creating better file-handling techniques and an explanation of some of these techniques is included.

Upon completion of the book, you should fully understand what files are and how to use them. You will be able to create your own sequential or random access files. Examples of both of these file types are included throughout the book. Program examples include creation programs for: the stock market, mailing lists, inventories, drill and practice, and medical records.

There are some very good data-base programs available commercially. If your needs require an elaborate data base structure, you should probably use one of those programs or pay a programmer to create one for you. Reading this book will not make you capable of creating complete commercial data base programs, but with practice, you will be able to effectively create and use any type of file you want.

I really enjoy programming and creating programs for my own use. I like the freedom programming gives me, because I can easily change or add to what the program does. I hope this book conveys some of that enjoyment and freedom.

David Miller

Books . . . (should) be read
as deliberately and reservedly
as they were written.
H. D. Thoreau

introduction

No book is magic in that, by possessing the book, you possess the knowledge of that book. Yet I have tried to make it relatively easy for ANYONE to learn to meaningfully use the Commodore-64 personal computer.

No single book will suffice for everyone, and this book makes no claim to being the exception. But I have attempted to make it useful for the beginner as well as the more experienced Commodore-64 BASIC user. The program examples cover the areas of home, education, business, hobby, or investment.

Computer vocabulary has been introduced very gradually. Readers somewhat knowledgeable about the vocabulary may find the process repetitious at first, but I have found this to be the best method for acquiring a working knowledge of the multitude of "jargon."

The "system" approach has been used so the reader would not be overwhelmed with a large number of different application programs. The programs presented are intended to be useful as well as instructive. The programs build upon themselves so that something that may appear awkward to an experienced programmer is used to help explain a concept needed in later chapters.

Information for the more experienced BASIC user includes a thorough discussion of DIF files with application programs. Other items are: random (relative) access files, automatic, initial use, file-creation techniques, and tape files.

You cannot just absorb this information. You must read the book and plan to re-read and/or study the text and programs of parts that are at first unclear. Invest time in learning how to get the most out of the Commodore-64. Experienced BASIC users may find that they can either skip parts or proceed quickly through certain sections. I would encourage everyone to finish the book.

Finally, a two-diskette set containing all the programs presented in the book is available. You can make the diskettes yourself by typing in all the programs, but if you just want to see the programs in operation, then you may want to purchase the two diskettes. I sincerely hope you enjoy the book and find it instructive.

Commodore-64 keyboard

Everyone seems to have difficulty with at least some aspect of using a keyboard to communicate with a computer. It does not seem to matter which computer it is or even how much typing experience a person has. And until better methods of human to machine communications are developed, we are stuck with learning to effectively use the keyboard. This initial learning process is often very important. Some people have become convinced that they cannot work with computers when, in fact, they are simply having difficulty with the keyboard. Therefore, it is imperative for new computer users to become as familiar with the keyboard as possible.

The Commodore keyboard is laid out in a manner very similar to a standard typewriter keyboard. The Commodore keyboard contains all the standard keys plus some keys designed specifically for the computer. When the computer is first turned on, the screen will display all typed keys in upper case mode. This means that all letters typed will appear as capital letters. All keys that have two characters on the key tops will display the lower character when the key is pressed by itself. The upper character will be displayed when the SHIFT key is pressed and held and the key containing the desired upper-portion character is also pressed. In other words, to display the $ symbol on the screen, the SHIFT key must be pressed and held while the key containing the characters $ and 4 is also pressed. Keys that do not contain two characters on the key top but do contain graphic characters on the front of the key will display the graphic character that appears on the right side of the key whenever the SHIFT key and that key are pressed.

The blinking box (called the cursor) can be moved around the screen with the use of the CRSR keys and the SHIFT keys. Pressing the left/right arrow CRSR key by itself will move the cursor to the right. Pressing the SHIFT key and the left/right arrow CRSR key will move the cursor back to the left side of the screen. In either direction, when the cursor comes to the end of the line, the cursor will move to the opposite side of the screen and either up or down a line. Pressing the up/down arrow CRSR key by itself will move the cursor down the screen. With the SHIFT key, the up/down arrow CRSR key moves the cursor up the screen but this time it will not go beyond the top of the screen. Pressed by itself, the CLR/HOME key immediately "homes" the cursor to the top left hand corner of the screen. Used with the SHIFT key, this key clears the screen and then homes the cursor. The INST/DEL key by itself will delete characters to the left of the cursor. Used with the SHIFT key, the INST/DEL key will insert spaces to the right of the cursor.

To place the computer into the lower case mode, the Commodore key, in the extreme lower left hand corner of the keyboard, and SHIFT key must be pressed. While in lower case mode, the keyboard functions very much like a typewriter keyboard. The SHIFT key and a letter key will produce a capital letter. Without the SHIFT key, letters are displayed in lower case. Keys with two characters on the key tops work in the same way they did in upper case mode. The CRSR, CLR/HOME, and INST/DEL keys also function in the same way they did in upper case mode. The left side graphic character is displayed by pressing the Commodore key and the key containing the graphic symbol.

Of particular importance is the SHIFT/LOCK key. This key can be used to display a number of characters that require the SHIFT key, but should NOT be depressed when the RETURN key is used. The RETURN key is used to inform the computer that the user has finished entering a line of instructions/information. This key is the single most used key on the keyboard and the key that frequently causes beginning computer users to wonder why the computer is not doing what the user wants the computer to do. Most of the time, the RETURN key will need to be pressed after you have finished typing a line even if the line only has a few characters on it. The RETURN key informs the computer that the user is finished and wants the computer to do something. But if the SHIFT/LOCK key is depressed, the RETURN key does not function as a RETURN key. It does not inform the computer that the user is finished. This quirk of the Commodore keyboard has caused many people to wonder if their computer was not broken. The "quick fix" has been to unlock the SHIFT/LOCK key and then press the RETURN key. The RUN/STOP key and the RESTORE key sequence can be used to stop certain programs or certain operations.

Finally, new users may experience problems with the auto repeat feature of some keys. Depressing those keys (the SPACE BAR for one) for more than a fraction of a second causes the key to automatically repeat itself. For certain keys, this feature can be very useful. But until you get used to it, the auto repeat feature may cause a few problems.

Although the standard Commodore BASIC interpreter allows 80 characters on a line, it was necessary in the printing of this book to limit the number of characters to approximately 57 per line. That is the reason you will see words split in two. When you are typing in a line from a listing given in the book, it is preferable to continue typing the line for as many characters as the BASIC interpreter will allow, regardless of where the break occurs in the listing given in the text. And since the Commodore screen display is normally only 40 characters per line, the break in the text listing will not match the point at which you will actually be typing on the next line. The point is that you do not need to break the line according to the text listing if the line is longer than 57 characters. Therefore, do not expect the screen listing to look exactly like the listing given in the book.

■ An Important Note About the Program Listings

There are two types of Program Listings: (1) Listings that appear within chapters, and (2) Listings that appear at the end of the chapters. The first type of listings, *i. e.*, those that appear within the text of a chapter, have been typeset and are NOT taken directly from a computer printout. Since these listings have been typeset, the position of characters and spaces relative to other characters and spaces may not match the actual position of characters and spaces when entered into the computer. However, the second type of listing, *i. e.*, listings that appear at the end of chapters, do come directly from a computer printout. These listings have been photocopied directly from my program listings. Therefore, in all matters, the listings at the end of the chapter should be regarded as authoritative since they come directly from working programs.

I printed these listings using a very good letter quality printer but, unfortunately, one that did not have a printwheel with a slash through the zero, two distinct characters for the lower case L and the number one (1), or a true up-arrow. Therefore, it is imperative that you read the text and look closely at the printouts and determine which character to type when entering these programs. The up-arrow appears in the printouts as the ^ (raise to the power of) character. The inadequacy of the printwheel was one of the reasons the listings within the chapters were typeset.

bookware

The programs in this book are available on two diskettes. Additional file programs and documentation are also included. To order your two-diskette set, please send $25 ($27.50 outside North America) to: C-64 FILES, AEN, 9525 Lucerne St., Ventura, CA 93004. California residents, please add 6% sales tax. Please be certain to specify C-64 FILES!

1 introduction to the Commodore-64® file types

There are as many definitions of the word file as there are kinds of files. You can quickly become confused if your understanding of the term differs from an author's intended use, and dictionary definitions are of little use in the computer world of today. Before becoming involved with the computer, my understanding of a file was limited to information that was kept in a folder in a file cabinet. I think we often learn best by trying to fit that which is new into something we already understand. Therefore, following this idea, I will try to explain Commodore-64 file structure in terms of a file cabinet.

In a four-drawer file cabinet, one drawer might be for accounts payable, while another could be for accounts receivable, a third for personnel information, and the fourth for inventory information. These are used only as examples to show that each drawer might contain different file types. The file cabinet just as easily can contain game instructions in one drawer, receipts in another, name and address information in a third, and medical records in the fourth. The idea is of a file cabinet containing different types of information. *The Commodore-64's file cabinet is the disk drive and diskette* (or for those without a disk drive, the *datassette recorder* and *cassette tape*. The majority of this book will be directed toward the reader with one or more disk drives, but the first part of the book will include information

---

Commodore 64® is a registered trademark of Commodore Business Machines, King of Prussia, Pa.

relevant to the reader with the *datassette recorder*). One type of file is a BASIC program file. A second file type contains only data. Other file types are identified by a three-character *extension* to their file names. Therefore, each diskette you use is like a file cabinet. It is set up to accept and classify many types of files.

How do you know what files are on your diskettes? We will begin the tutorial part of this book by going through all the steps necessary in order to find out just what files are on your diskette. (If you are already acquainted with the procedure used to start up the computer and disk drive, sometimes called *booting the system,* you can skip the rest of this paragraph.) First, turn on the disk drive. Second, turn on the computer. Third, if you have not yet turned on the monitor or TV, do so now. Fourth, take your TEST/DEMO diskette and insert it into the disk drive with the label side face up and last to go into the drive. Do *not* touch the cutout area on the diskette. (If you have more than one drive, make sure to put the diskette into the drive with a direct connection to the computer.) Make sure the drive door is closed properly with the handle down. At this point, you should see the following message displayed (the message may vary slightly due to different production runs):

```
**** COMMODORE 64 BASIC V2 ****
64K RAM SYSTEM 38911 BASIC BYTES FREE
READY.
```

Fifth, type:

```
LOAD "$",8
```

Sixth, after you have finished typing, press the key marked RETURN on the right side of the keyboard. The red light on the disk drive should come on. The screen will display the message:

```
SEARCHING FOR $
```

Then:

```
LOADING
```

Soon the disk drive will stop, and the light will go out. The statement READY should appear. (If you have not been able to get to this point with the computer, try another diskette, preferably the diskette marked TEST/DEMO. If switching diskettes does not work, you will need to check the manuals for your particular system.)

At this point, type:

```
LIST
```

or

```
list
```

Remember to press the RETURN key when you have finished typing. The Commodore's operating system will recognize either upper case or lower case letters. You will see a list with three things on each line of text:

1. A number representing the size of the file,
2. The name of the file,
3. A three-character file designator or extension.

The extension will indicate what type of file it is: PRG for a BASIC program file, SEQ for a file containing only data in sequential order, USR for a user file, and REL for a file containing only data in random or relative order. The name, consisting of letters and/or possibly numbers, is the actual name of the specific file. The size of the file is given as the decimal number of blocks or sectors (sections) in that file. In our file cabinet example, this is the same information that might appear on each folder. You might label each folder with (1) a name for the information within the folder, (2) an extension indicating which drawer it goes in, and (3) how much information it contains.

Most file cabinets do not have a list of all the files stored within them. It would be a time-consuming job to update that list every time you added, changed, or threw away a file, but Commodore-64's file-management system does just that and does it automatically. The diskette's list of everything in the file cabinet is what you get when you type LOAD "$",8 and then LIST. *Typing this sequence shows the list previously created by the file management system.*

How are these files used? What are they? How are they different? Returning to the file cabinet, the person in charge of that cabinet might put some rules or locks on the drawers. In other words, he or she might say that the PRG file could be used only in a certain way or only by certain people. The same could be true of the other file types or drawers. This is exactly what Commodore-64's file-management system has done. Each file type is used differently and can be used only in certain specific ways. *PRG files are instructions (also called programs) to the computer to do something.* Examples of such instructions would be:

```
40 IF NUMBER = 5 THEN 5000
50 GOTO 200
100 PRINT "HELLO"
```

Most SEQ and REL files are not computer instructions but contain information of value to people, such as names, addresses, zip codes, payroll deductions, pay rates, or book titles. Often SEQ and REL files are just lists of such information. Such lists, of course, would not make sense as instructions to the computer.

It should be clear that Commodore-64 files are used to store information just as you or I use a filing cabinet, that there are different types of files, and that they are used for different purposes. In the next chapter, we will look more closely at the file types and how they are used. In subsequent chapters, we will look at two of those file types, SEQ and REL data files, and examine how information is kept, how that information is used, and how those files are created. The latter, creating files, is the main emphasis of this book and will occupy the remaining chapters. If you want to know how to create the BASIC files (programs), you will need to learn programming. Effectively using the data files requires some knowledge of how to program in BASIC. The programs discussed in this book will be BASIC programs, and the discussion will be such that anyone willing to try the examples should learn to program, as well as learn to create and use data files. In other words, although the main emphasis of this book is on data files, you will learn a certain amount of programming—BASIC program files, in order to be able to create, display, and change data files. And I repeat, *Anyone willing to try all the examples, and read carefully through the discussion of the examples, can and will learn to program and thus make effective use of data files*. Individuals, no matter what their ages, backgrounds, or experiences, can learn the information presented in this book. Programming and file manipulation are a matter of learning how to give instructions to the computer in a manner the computer can understand; or, more simply, programming is learning how to talk to the computer and tell it what you want it to do.

QUESTIONS

1. How are Commodore-64 file types identified?
2. What extension is used to identify BASIC program files?
3. What extensions are used to identify data files?
4. Which file type will this book emphasize?
5. What sequence should you type in order to see a list of the files on a diskette?
6. Which files contain instructions to the computer?
7. Which files contain information of value to people?
8. What information is shown when you ask to see a list of the files on a diskette?

ANSWERS

1. By the extension to their file names
2. PRG
3. SEQ or REL data files
4. Data files
5. LOAD "$",8
   LIST
6. BASIC or other program language files
7. Data files
8. The size of the file, the file name, and the extension to the file name (or file type)

2 BASIC program files

In this chapter, we are going to take a closer look at the first main file type. This would be the same as opening our file cabinet's top drawer for a quick look at what is kept inside.

We begin with what is probably the most common type of file, the BASIC file. Some of you might already be confused because you have always referred to BASIC "programs" rather than files. In reality, they are both. Suppose one drawer in the file cabinet is used for games. Each folder contains the rules or instructions for playing a different game. Most of the time, you would simply refer to the folders as games, not files, yet they are really both games and files. When you have taken one folder out of the file cabinet and are using the instructions to play the game, it is not a file; however, when you are finished with the game and want to put it back in its place, it becomes a file, one of many game files.

The same is true of BASIC program files. The top drawer contains only BASIC programs or computer instructions (rules). When the computer is using the instructions in one of those BASIC "folders," the instructions are a program, but when the computer is not using the instructions, the instructions are stored as files. The important thing to understand is that BASIC files contain only computer instructions (programs). Some of those files contain larger or longer sets of computer instructions than others, but a BASIC file can only be a set of instructions for the computer or, therefore, a computer program. The second limitation of the top drawer, or "PRG" file, is that it can only be a certain kind of computer program, a BASIC computer program, not a FORTRAN computer program or a COBOL computer program. (FORTRAN and COBOL are two other computer languages, just as BASIC is a computer language.)

Let's look at the rules for using these BASIC computer program files. In our mythical office, we have two main secretaries that can use BASIC program files. Secretary number one can only go and get the file (LOAD). Secretary number two can only put the file away (SAVE). *These two secretaries or commands do not have access to other drawers or file types.*

Secretary number two (SAVE) can only put the file (program) currently in the computer's memory in the file cabinet (disk).

Secretary number one (LOAD) is only able to get the file (program) from the file cabinet (disk) and put it on the boss's desk (in the computer's memory). The load command goes to the diskette and gets a specific file. In order to know which file to get, the LOAD command must be given the specific name of the file: LOAD "MATHDRILL",8 or LOAD "CHECKER",8. The quotation marks indicate the beginning and ending of the file name. The number 8 represents the disk drive. The disk drive is device number 8. (The keyboard is device number 0, the cassette recorder, device number 1, modems are assigned device number 2, the screen is device number 3, printers are device numbers 4 or 5, usually 4, and disk drives are device numbers 8 through 11, usually just number 8. Nobody knows what happened to device numbers 6 and 7!)

If the file name is not spelled exactly the way it is spelled in the list of all the files on the diskette (in the file cabinet), then the LOAD command or secretary will not be able to find the file and will come back and tell you "FILE NOT FOUND ERROR". (The LOAD command will add the extension PRG and look for the file name with that extension.) On the other hand, if the LOAD command does have the exact name, it will go to the disk and get a copy of the file. Notice the use of the word "copy." The LOAD command does not actually go and remove the file from the diskette, as a secretary would remove a file from the file cabinet. The LOAD command takes only a copy so that the original always remains on the diskette. The copy of the file is loaded into the computer's memory, similar to a secretary getting a file and putting it on the boss's desk. You, the boss, must then decide what you want to do with the file. If you want to open it and look at it, you use some form of the LIST command. (Type LIST or LIST 100-200, etc.) If you want to see the program in operation, type RUN.

Secretaries, or BASIC file commands, must be given a specific file name. Usually, after using the LOAD command, you will want to look at the instructions (LIST) and perhaps change, add, or remove some instructions. When you have finished, you may want to keep what you have done by giving the file to secretary number two (SAVE) and telling the secretary the exact name you want this file kept under. If you have made changes but still want to keep the original currently on the disk, then the secretary must be informed of a new file name. If the secretary uses the same file name as the file currently on the diskette, the red light on the disk drive will begin blinking and the revised file will *not* be saved (unless you have provided additional information indicating that you do want the old file replaced). This may not be what you want, so be careful what name you use (the SAVE command).

Let's actually try some of these commands. You will need the TEST/DEMO diskette and a new diskette. If you do not have a new diskette, you should: (1) wait until you do have a new diskette before doing the next steps, or (2) use a diskette that you know has some room on it and skip the first step below, or (3) use an old diskette that contains information you no longer need. Use the information from Chapter 1 to get the computer working; i.e., to boot the system. (Review the procedure in Chapter 1, if necessary.) If you have the TEST/DEMO diskette in the drive, *remove the TEST/DEMO diskette and insert a blank or new diskette*. If you do not remove the TEST/DEMO diskette, you can destroy the information on it. When you get the READY prompt on the screen and have chosen and inserted your blank diskette, type the following carefully. (Remember to press the key marked RETURN after each entry. You can use either upper case or lower case.)

```
OPEN 15,8,15
```

You should see:

```
READY
```

Then, with a blank diskette in the disk drive, type the following exactly as shown—without spaces:

```
PRINT#15,"NEW0:FORM.10-20-84,84"
```

Remember to press the key labeled RETURN to indicate to the computer that you have finished typing the above line. The disk drive makes a noise and the red light comes on. The computer is transferring numerical information onto the diskette to enable the computer to later find locations on that diskette. In about a minute, the disk drive will stop and the red light will go out. *Remember, this first step destroys any existing information on an old diskette*. This step is used to format a new diskette or reformat an old diskette so that the diskette can store files. The FORMAT command is usually used only once on each diskette. A *second use erases whatever is currently on the diskette*.

All the characters you have typed in this formatting sequence have a specific meaning. The OPEN command instructs the computer to open communication to whatever file, device, and channel are specified by the numbers that follow it. In the above instruction, file number 15 is used to coincide with the assigned (and therefore nonarbitrary) *command channel* number. The first 15 could have been any number between 1 and 255. But since the third number had to be a 15, it seems logical and perhaps less confusing to use the same number for both the file number and the channel number. As we saw previously, the device number (the middle number in the OPEN statement) for the disk drive is usually 8. Therefore, the command OPEN 15,8,15 instructs the computer to initiate communication through file number 15 on device number 8 over (command) channel number 15.

The PRINT instruction has more strict syntax. No space may exist between the T in PRINT and the # symbol. The comma and opening quotation mark are also required. The word NEW instructs the computer that a new diskette is to be formatted. This instruction may be abbreviated with just the first letter N. The zero that follows the NEW instruction is the drive number of device 8 (the disk drive). Zero is used for the first drive and 1 may theoretically be used for a second drive. (Use of the 1 is not possible with two 1541 drives. An alternative for a second drive is to change the device number to some number other than 8. The 1541 *User's Manual* gives instructions on changing the default device number 8 by either typing in some instructions or by physically opening the case and cutting a wire.)

After the zero, a colon is used to initiate the separation of the diskette's actual name from all the other parameters. Here, the user has some choice in the name. The name may be only sixteen characters in length and some control, escape, or graphic characters may not work properly. But any combination of the twenty-six letters of the alphabet and/or ten digits 0 through 9 should work without a problem.

The final part of this sequence is another unique feature to the Commodore line of computers. First, a comma is used to indicate that the diskette's name has been entered. Then, a two-digit code is allowed. This code is used throughout the formatting of the diskette so that the computer can always know if diskettes have been changed since the last diskette access. Therefore, no two diskettes should have the same two-digit code. The reason for this seeming complexity is the great flexibility the Commodore-64 possesses. A large number of devices or *peripherals* may be connected to the Commodore-64 with few external connections to the computer itself. Persistent and careful programmers may completely control the access to any diskette. The price for this type of flexibility is a greater degree of programmer knowledge and persistence.

Commodore has provided a degree of help by way of the DOS (Disk Operating System) Wedge or the DOS Support Program. This utility program makes it easier to use the BASIC file commands, or secretaries, and provides additional commands. To load the DOS Wedge program, remove your newly formatted diskette and insert the TEST/DEMO diskette. Then type:

```
LOAD "C-64 WEDGE",8
```

When the READY prompt returns, type:

```
RUN
```

You should see:

DOS MANAGER V5.1/071382

BY BOB FAIRBAIRN

(C) 1982 COMMODORE BUSINESS MACHINES

READY

(Some of your numbers may be different depending on when you received your copy of the DOS Wedge.)

After loading the DOS Wedge, the LOAD and SAVE commands will work the same as before, but less syntax is required to achieve the same results. By loading the DOS Wedge, we have instructed the computer that we are going to be primarily using the disk drive. In other words, we have put the computer into a disk drive default mode so that it is not necessary to use the disk drive device number 8. It is also not necessary to type the characters LOAD or SAVE in order to accomplish those tasks. The following chart may make the point clearer.

Purpose	*Before DOS Wedge you had to type:*	*After DOS Wedge you only type:*
To load a program:	LOAD "TEST",8	/TEST
To save a program:	SAVE "PROGRAM",8	←PROGRAM
To list the files on a diskette:	LOAD "$",8 LIST	@$
To format diskette:	OPEN 15,8,15 PRINT#15,"N0:FILE NAME,XX"	@N:FILE NAME,XX
To run a program directly from diskette:	(No single step is available before DOS Wedge)	↑ MY PROGRAM

Because the DOS Wedge makes things easier and even provides us with additional commands, throughout this book, wherever possible, *all programs presented will use the DOS Wedge syntax instead of the syntax necessary without the DOS Wedge.* This means that you will need to load the DOS Wedge before using any of the programs presented in this book or that you will need to translate the syntax given in the programs into the required syntax for programs to work without the DOS Wedge. If you did not receive a copy of the DOS Wedge on your TEST/DEMO diskette, or did not get a TEST/DEMO diskette with your disk drive, I would suggest that you return to your dealer and ask for a copy of the DOS Wedge or the TEST/DEMO diskette.

Now, let's actually try some of these commands. Remove the TEST/DEMO diskette (or whatever diskette you used to load the DOS Wedge) and insert your newly formatted diskette (the diskette named FORM.10-20-84). Now type:

```
NEW
10 PRINT
20 PRINT "HELLO"
40 PRINT "I AM THE COMMODORE-64"
```

Check your typing to be sure you have typed everything exactly the way it is shown above. The word NEW (in this case) erases any BASIC program that is already in the computer's memory. It does not do anything to the diskette or any information stored on a diskette. The numbers 10, 20, and 40 are line numbers in a BASIC program. Line numbers can be any number from 0 to 65535. Usually, the numbers chosen are not consecutive in order to allow other lines to be added, if necessary. The word PRINT instructs the computer to display on the screen whatever follows it and is between the quotation marks. So, since nothing follows the word PRINT in line 10, a blank line will be displayed. Line 20 will cause the computer to display the word "HELLO". Now, type the word RUN and press the RETURN key. Below the word RUN, you should see: (1) a blank line, (2) the words between the quotation marks followed by a blank line, and (3) the READY prompt.

```
HELLO
I AM THE COMMODORE-64

READY
```

You have just written and executed a BASIC program. The program is still in the computer's memory, but if you were to turn off the computer now, you would lose that program. It would be lost because it has not been permanently saved on tape or diskette. We will take care of that with our next step.

The third step is to transfer (SAVE) the program in the computer's memory out to a file on the diskette (or tape). This is easily accomplished by giving the file to the SAVE secretary and letting the secretary do all the work. For those using a disk drive and the DOS Wedge, simply type:

```
←HELLO
```

Or, for those using tape:

1. Type SAVE "HELLO"
2. Follow the screen instructions

A message similar to "SAVING HELLO 00,OK,00,00" should appear on the screen. You do not have to add the file type indicator since this command, or secretary, knows to add the standard indicator of PRG for BASIC programs. The secretary or SAVE command has transferred a copy of the contents of the computer's program memory to the diskette (or tape) and stored it in the file called "HELLO". If you want to see the names of the files on the diskette while working under the DOS Wedge, you need to type the command:

```
@$ (or >$)
```

You should see:

```
0 "FORM.10-20-84   " 84 2A
1      "HELLO"                    PRG
663 BLOCKS FREE
```

To see what is in the computer's memory, type:

```
LIST
```

The display should show:

```
10 PRINT
20 PRINT "HELLO"
40 PRINT "I AM THE COMMODORE-64"
READY
```

LIST is similar to @$ under the DOS Wedge in that @$ shows what is on a diskette, and LIST shows what is in the computer's memory. Now, type:

```
NEW
LIST
```

The program is now gone and there is nothing in the computer's memory. To bring it back, follow the directions for your particular system. For DOS Wedge disk drive users, type:

```
/HELLO
```

For tape users:

1. Rewind tape.
2. Type: LOAD "HELLO"
3. When the screen returns and displays the message "FOUND HELLO", press either the space bar, CTRL key, or the Commodore key in the lower left hand corner.

Then for everyone when the screen displays "READY", type:

LIST

The program is back. Immediately after the /HELLO, the disk drive comes on for a brief time. The computer is instructed to go to the diskette, bring in a copy of the file called HELLO, and store that copy in its memory. When you type LIST, you are telling the computer to show you what it has in its memory. Therefore, the program now actually exists in two places: (1) in the computer's memory, and (2) as a file on the diskette (or tape). Type carefully and add a fourth line like this:

60 PRINT "I AM A SMART COMPUTER"

Then, for disk drive users, type:

←HELLO2

For tape users:

1. Type SAVE "HELLO2"
2. Follow the screen instructions.

For disk users, in order to see this new file on the diskette, type:

@$

Now, the list shows:

```
0 "FORM.10-20-84       " 84 2A
1      "HELLO"              PRG
1      "HELLO2"             PRG
662 BLOCKS FREE
```

There are two files on the diskette. Both are BASIC program files (programs written using the BASIC language). After you type ←HELLO2 (i.e., give the HELLO2 file to the SAVE secretary), the disk drive comes on briefly while the computer transfers a copy of the contents of its memory to the diskette. The command @$

shows the new list of files on the diskette. Finally, type:

NEW
LIST

The program is gone. Type:

↑ HELLO2

and the screen shows:

HELLO
I AM THE COMMODORE-64
I AM A SMART COMPUTER

READY

Now, type:

LIST

and the full program is back. Type:

RUN

(since the instructions are already in memory, a file name is not necessary), and you should get the same message.

First, you erase the program in the computer's memory (NEW), and then ask to see if there is anything left in the computer's memory (LIST) in order to verify what you did. Next, ↑ HELLO2 tells the computer to access the diskette, load the file called HELLO2 into its memory, and begin operation according to the file's instructions. LIST shows that the program is back in memory. To prove it, RUN tells the computer to again operate according to the program's instructions.

Let's review from the viewpoint of the secretaries and file cabinet. Remember, so far we have two main secretaries (and with the DOS Wedge we get at least one more): number one (LOAD or /), number two (SAVE or ←), and number three (LOAD and RUN or ↑). Remember that there is no comparable single-word command outside the DOS Wedge that loads a file from diskette and immediately begins execution of that program. For these secretaries to do anything, they must be given a file name:

/MATH.DRILL	(loads MATH.DRILL into the computer's memory from diskette)
↑ CHECKERS	(loads CHECKERS into the computer's memory from diskette and immediately begins execution of the program's instructions)

←ANYTHING (save the contents of the computer's program memory out to the diskette with the file name of ANYTHING)

BASIC file commands and DOS Wedge commands must be given a specific file name.

There are other BASIC and DOS Wedge commands that can be used with files. The following chart summarizes these commands:

Purpose	*Before DOS Wedge you had to type:*	*After DOS Wedge you only type:*
To load a program:	LOAD "TEST",8	/TEST
To save a program:	SAVE "PROGRAM",8	←PROGRAM
To list the files on a diskette:	LOAD "$",8 LIST	@$
To format diskette:	OPEN 15,8,15 PRINT#15,"N0:FILE NAME,XX"	@N:FILE NAME,XX
To run a program directly from diskette:	(No single step is available before DOS Wedge)	↑MY PROGRAM
To change the name of a file:	OPEN 15,8,15 PRINT#15,"R0:FILE2 = FILE1"	@R:FILE2 = FILE1
To make a backup copy of a file on the same diskette:	OPEN 15,8,15 PRINT#15,"C0:FILE2 = 0:FILE1	@C:FILE2 = FILE1
To scratch (delete) files from a diskette:	OPEN 15,8,15 PRINT#15,"S0:FILENAME"	@S:FILENAME
To switch diskettes (i.e. initialize a change of diskettes):	OPEN 15,8,15 PRINT#15,"I"	@I

These additional commands are generally less used but are good to have when you need them.

I have used the concept of secretaries for a specific reason. I believe it gives the impression that BASIC file commands and DOS Wedge commands are there to help you. In the examples, the secretaries are really BASIC file commands. BASIC file commands do certain things for you that a number of personal secretaries might do. The only limitation is that you must be exact and specific with the secretaries (commands). File commands must be used with a specific file name.

We have covered a lot of new information in this chapter. If something is not clear, you should review it and use the Commodore-64 personal computer and disk drive to better understand these concepts.

QUESTIONS

1. *True or False:* BASIC programs are stored on diskette as files.
2. What DOS Wedge command is used to show a list of files on a diskette?
3. What does DOS stand for?
4. How many main DOS Wedge commands are used with BASIC program files?
5. Which DOS Wedge command gets the program from diskette and immediately begins execution or operation of the program?
6. Which DOS Wedge file command stores programs on the diskette as files?
7. *True or False:* The LOAD command actually removes the program from the diskette and loads it into the computer's memory.
8. What happens when you save back to diskette a program you have changed, and you save it under the same name?
9. *True or False:* LIST shows what is on the diskette.
10. What DOS Wedge command is used to prepare a new diskette to receive files?
11. *True or False:* BASIC programs are never files.
12. Explain what NEW (by itself) does.

ANSWERS

1. True
2. @$
3. Disk Operating System
4. 3
5. ↑ with a file name
6. ← with a file name
7. False, it takes a copy.
8. The previous version is not erased and replaced with the new version unless you have added the REPLACE character.
9. False
10. @N:FILENAME,XX
11. False
12. Erases whatever is in the computer's memory

3 data file introduction

Using the analogy of the file cabinet example in the last two chapters, this chapter is a quick look inside the DATA file drawer and a superficial look inside the two different kinds of file folders in this drawer. We will examine the characteristics that are common to both kinds of DATA files and look at how you can access those files.

Of the different types of files, we have seen that one type contains instructions (called programs) for the computer: BASIC program files. One of the other types usually contains information for people rather than machines. By this, I do not mean that the computer cannot make use of the information, but that the information usually is not in the form of direct instructions for the computer. An example of an instruction for the computer is:

```
20 PRINT "HELLO, HOW ARE YOU?"
```

An example of information that is not in the form of a computer instruction would be:

Title: Commodore-64 Data Files: A BASIC Tutorial

Author: David Miller

Publisher: Reston Publishing Co.

Address: Reston, Va.

This last example is the kind of information usually kept in a data file. Before we get into the process of actually storing and retrieving data files, we need to understand the main difference between the two kinds of data files.

Data files have two ways of storing and retrieving information. (Remember that the information really stays on the diskette and we are just getting a copy of the information!) These two ways of storing and retrieving information are *sequential access* and *random access*. A sequential access data file basically means that the information stored in the file is kept in sequential order. A random access data file usually means that each part of the file is divided equally and can be reached directly and at random instead of going through all previous records. The process of looking at each record in order (sequence) to decide if it is the record you want is a characteristic of sequential files and can require more time than the direct method of random access files.

Commodore refers to random access files as *relative* files. But the term "relative" in the computer world often means "in relation to" and can be misleading when used as the name of the method for *directly* accessing records within a file. To further confuse matters, Commodore also provides a subset of their *relative* files which they call *random* files. Since Commodore's random files are basically an elementary version of their relative files, we will not cover them in a direct way. Anything that can be done with Commodore's random files in the BASIC language can be accomplished with relative files and in a much easier way. Therefore, any mention in this book of random files is meant to refer to Commodore's relative files, not Commodore's random files. In other words, whenever I use the term "*random access,*" I am talking about the same thing that Commodore is when they refer to relative files. And, after checking with individuals at Commodore, I have decided to use the term "random" rather than use Commodore's term of "relative" because, in the long run, readers of this book will be less confused by a correct application of the appropriate term.

The basic difference between sequential data files and random data files is somewhat like the difference between a cassette tape and a phonograph record. If I want to find a specific song on a cassette tape, even using the best available tape deck, I must begin at the current location of the tape and proceed either forward or backward, passing over all intervening songs until I have found the song I want. The process proceeds in sequence, one song after another. For example, if I want to play only the fourth song on the tape, I would have to advance the tape through the first, second, and third songs until I get to the fourth one. On the other hand, if the songs are on a phonograph record, all I would have to do to play the fourth song would be to place the phono cartridge containing the needle at the start of the fourth division instead of at the start of the first song. I can do that because I am able to clearly see the divisions between songs and because those individual songs are directly accessible. I do not have to go through the grooves of the first three songs to get to the fourth. And moving the needle by hand takes only seconds. So imagine that the data drawer contains two basic divisions: the first division contains files that operate in a way similar to cassette tapes, while the second division contains files that operate like phonograph records in the way described.

But these two kinds of data files do have things in common, just as tapes have things in common with phono records. The most obvious common characteristic is that they both usually contain information that is not in the form of instructions for the computer. In other words, they contain information like lists of things, addresses, receipts, and inventories. Second, both files make use of some of the same BASIC file commands, but with different parameters.

Because these data files are not computer instructions, they cannot be used in the same manner as BASIC program files. In other words, you cannot RUN a data file, SAVE, or LOAD it. Those three commands, when combined with a file name, are the computer's means of access to BASIC disk files. The obvious question, then, is that if you cannot use RUN, SAVE, or LOAD with data files, how does the computer get the information on the diskette in a data file or back off the diskette from a data file?

To gain access to data files, you must use certain BASIC file commands in specific ways, depending on the kind of data file you are accessing. Both sequential and random access data files primarily use four types of commands: (1) OPEN, (2) CLOSE, (3) some way of reading the file (INPUT# or GET#), and (4) some method of writing to the file (PRINT#). Future chapters will examine in detail how each of these is to be used for either of the two kinds of data files. For now, you only need to understand the essential task of each command.

Again, the example of the filing cabinet is useful. In much the same way that a secretary must open a file folder removed from the filing cabinet before making use of any information contained in the file, so also must all data files be opened before the information they contain can be put to use. And as the secretary should properly close the file folder before replacing it in the filing cabinet, all data files should be closed before ending the program or turning off the computer. If a secretary does not close the file folder, some information might drop out and get lost. The same is true if data files are not properly closed. This is usually only the case after new information has been written to the file and the file not closed. Loss of information should not occur after a data file has only been read and not closed.

INPUT#, PRINT#, or GET# are the main processes by which information is either read from or written to the file. If you only want to see information already in a data file, the BASIC file commands INPUT# and GET# are the commands you would use. If you want to add information to the file or create a new file, use the BASIC file command PRINT#.

At this point, let's try out some of this information on the computer. Turn on the computer and the disk drive. (Refer to Chapters 1 and 2 if you are not sure what to do.) When the cursor (blinking box) and the READY prompt appears, take the TEST/DEMO diskette, insert it in the disk drive, and type carefully, remembering to press the RETURN key after each entry. Below the READY prompt, type:

```
LOAD "C-64 WEDGE",8
```

Remember, you can use either upper case or lower case letters. The disk will come on, and after a short time you will see the READY prompt. Then type:

```
RUN
```

You should see:

```
            DOS MANAGER V5.1/071382
                BY BOB FAIRBAIRN
      (C) 1982 COMMODORE BUSINESS MACHINES
      READY
```

The numbers may be different depending on which version you are using, but a similar message should appear. The READY is the BASIC prompt indicating that the system is ready for you to use. Remove the TEST/DEMO diskette, take the diskette that you formatted in the last chapter, and place it in the disk drive. Now, type:

```
@$
```

You should see:

```
0 "FORM.10-20-84       " 84 2A
1     "HELLO"              PRG
1     "HELLO2"             PRG
662 BLOCKS FREE
```

Remember, @$ shows the names of the files on the diskette. Now, type:

```
NEW
```

This clears the computer's memory.

```
100 REM ***--DATA FILE EXAMPLE--***
110 :
120 :
130 REM **--FILE OUTPUT ROUTINE--**
140 OPEN 2,8,2, "0:ADDRESS FILE,SEQ,WRITE"
150 PRINT#2,"COMMODORE-64 IS A BRIGHT COMPUTER"
160 CLOSE 2
```

For those using tape, the program should read:

```
100 REM ***--DATA FILE EXAMPLE--***
110 :
120 :
130 REM **--FILE OUTPUT ROUTINE--**
140 OPEN 2,1,1,"ADDRESS FILE"
150 PRINT#2,"COMMODORE-64 IS A BRIGHT COMPUTER"
160 CLOSE 2
```

Check your typing very carefully. If you make a mistake, you can use the edit keys (the CRSR keys and the INST/DEL key) to correct the mistake, or type the entire line over again. The computer will place the line in the proper sequence. Once your program matches the program above, type:

```
←EXAMPLE
```

Or, for tape users:

```
SAVE "EXAMPLE"
```

and follow the screen prompts!

The program is now saved on the diskette (or tape) under the name EXAMPLE. Disk users should type:

```
@$
```

And you now see:

```
0 "FORM.10-20-84      " 84 2A
1      "HELLO"            PRG
1      "HELLO2"           PRG
1      "EXAMPLE"          PRG
661 BLOCKS FREE
```

Next type:

```
LIST
```

just to see that the program is still in the computer's memory.
Then, type:

```
RUN
```

The disk drive comes on, but little happens on the screen. Once again, type:

```
@$
```

This time you get:

```
0 "FORM.10-20-84      " 84 2A
1     "HELLO"              PRG
1     "HELLO2"             PRG
1     "EXAMPLE"            PRG
1     "ADDRESS FILE"       SEQ
660 BLOCKS FREE
```

We have created a data file! Even though you did not actually see the data file being written to the diskette, that is exactly what happened immediately after you typed RUN and pressed the RETURN key. The reason you did not see anything on the screen is that our BASIC program told the computer to print our information to the disk (or tape) rather than to the screen.

We will look at this program to see what each line does and what the correct syntax for each should be. Line 100 provides a name for this program. It is a good practice to make the name of the program similar to the file name under which the program is saved on disk. The one problem is that the file name cannot be more than sixteen characters long, while there is no limit to the length the program name can be. REM is a BASIC reserved word meaning remark, indicating that what follows is only a comment by the programmer and will not be executed by the computer. The characters and words ***--DATA FILE EXAMPLE--** are the actual comment. Lines 110 and 120 contain colons that can be used to help separate sections of programs. Line 130 names the routine to follow. Again, it is a good idea to identify, with a REM statement, what it is that you are about to do. The remark in this case indicates that we are creating a routine to write information to the disk (or tape).

Line 140 tells the computer whether we are going to use the disk or the tape. For disk, the syntax is OPEN 2,8,2, and for tape, the syntax is OPEN 2,1,1. The first number represents an arbitrary number between 1 and 255 (usually between 1 and 127) for the number of the file we are going to be using. This number can change from program to program even though we are accessing the same physical file. In other words, the file number is not written to the diskette with the file name. It is just a number we temporarily assign to the file so that we can refer to that file by number rather than by name. The second number, either an 8 or a 1, refers to the number of the device we are using to save the data file. The disk drive's number is 8, and the tape drive's number is 1. These are usually unchanging numbers and should be memorized as such for future use.

The last number represents two different things, depending on the device being referenced. The number following the 8 (*i.e.,* 2) is a channel number on which the data will be transmitted to the disk. This number is usually between 2 and 14. Since it does not matter which channel we use, it is often recommended that the channel number be the same number as that used for the file number (if the file number is between 2 and 14). For tape users, the number following the 1 (the device number) does not represent a channel number. Instead, it represents the type of operation we will be performing on this data file. If the number is a 0 (zero), the computer knows to read information from the data file. If the number is a 1 (as in our current program), the computer is instructed to write information to the data file and place a special marker, called an End-Of-File marker (EOF), at the end of the information, indicating that all information has been written. If the number is a 2, then the computer is instructed to do the same as with a 1, but to place an End-Of-Tape (EOT) marker instead of the End-Of-File marker.

We are going to open a file called "ADDRESS FILE". Notice the quotation marks. These quotation marks must be included in the program statements. That is how the computer understands where the specific file information begins and ends. The 0: indicates the drive numbers 0 for the first drive, 1 for drive 2 (not physically possible on the 64 equipped with two 1541 drives. Instead, the device number of one of the 1541s should be changed according to the instructions given in the 1541 *User's Manual*). Next, we tell the computer what type of file we want ADDRESS FILE to be: SEQ (for a SEQuential access file). Finally, we must instruct the computer how we are going to be using that file: WRITE, meaning that we are going to write information into the file rather than read information from the file.

Then, we tell the computer that we are going to be adding information to the file with the PRINT#2 statement. Line 150 also tells the computer what information to put in the data file. Anything between the quotation marks will be written to the data file on the diskette. The PRINT statement in this line does not print the string (the information between the quotation marks) on the screen when the program is RUN, as would normally be expected. This PRINT statement contains the file number telling the computer to print to the diskette rather than to the screen. Line 160 contains the computer instruction to CLOSE the file whose number is 2.

We have now put information onto a diskette. The next task is to be able to read back from the diskette what we wrote. There are a number of different ways that we can read back the information, but for now we will use the single-program approach and add more lines to the program that wrote the information to the diskette. Type:

```
LIST
```

The program should still be in the computer's memory. Add the following lines carefully:

```
170 :
180 :
190 REM **--FILE INPUT ROUTINE--**
200 OPEN 2,8,2,"0:ADDRESS FILE,SEQ,READ"
210 INPUT#2,LINE$
220 CLOSE 2
230 :
240 :
250 REM **--DISPLAY ROUTINE--**
260 PRINT CHR$(147):REM CLR/HOME
270 FOR I = 1 TO 5
280 PRINT CHR$(17);:REM CURSOR DOWN
290 NEXT I
300 PRINT LINE$
310 END
```

For tape users, line 200 should read:

```
200 OPEN 2,1,0,"ADDRESS FILE"
```

And add line 185:

```
185 INPUT "REWIND TAPE. PRESS RETURN ";L$
```

All the other lines are the same.
Check your typing. Then, type:

```
SAVE "@0:EXAMPLE",8
```

Or, using the DOS Wedge syntax:

```
←@0:EXAMPLE
```

Tape users do not need to use the @ (replace) symbol. Disk users must use the @ (replace) symbol, since the disk will not write over an existing file without that symbol. This replaces the previous and shorter version of our program. Finally, type:

```
RUN
```

No file name is necessary since the program, besides being on the diskette (or tape), is also still in the computer's memory. This time the disk drive will come on for a brief time; then the screen will go blank, and the words "COMMODORE-64 IS A BRIGHT COMPUTER" will be printed five lines from the top of the screen.

Let's examine each line of the additional program lines. Lines 170 and 180 provide a separation between the *file output routine* and the *file input routine*. Line 190 names the next routine. Line 200 informs the computer that we want to open the file called "ADDRESS FILE" in order to be able to read the contents of that file. We need to reopen the file in order to start at the beginning of the file so we can read from the file what we have just written. We also want the computer to identify that file as our number 2 file. We can use the number 2 since we closed the original number 2 after we finished writing our information to it. Line 210 then tells the computer to bring in, from that number 2 file (INPUT#2), a copy of the first (and in this case the only) piece of information in the file and store that information in the string variable memory location we have labeled LINE$.

A string variable is identified in BASIC by a letter or letters followed by the dollar sign, $. Variables are names assigned to locations in the computer's memory. String variables can contain just about any value (*i.e.*, numbers, letters, punctuation, and so forth). They are referred to as "variables" because their values may vary within a program; i.e., they are not constant. An example of a string variable might be NAMES$, where the first value of NAMES$ is "ANDY", the second value is "MARY", the third value is "PAUL", and the fourth value is "JANE". Therefore, we are storing the contents of the first and only piece of information in the ADDRESS FILE file in the computer's memory location labeled LINE$.

Line 220 is the same as line 160. We close the file before proceeding to the display routine. Lines 230 and 240 again provide the separation between the various parts of the program, while line 250 names the next portion of the program.

Line 260 instructs the computer to clear the screen by printing the value of CHR$(147). The value of the CLEAR SCREEN/HOME instruction as set by the code for all characters is 147. The code used in the Commodore-64 and most micros is called ASCII. It sets a decimal and hexadecimal value for all characters used. If you look on page 136 of the Commodore-64 *User's Guide* and go down the page under the column PRINTS until you find the key marked with CLR above the word HOME, you will find a column to the right with the number 147. Therefore, the value of the CLR/HOME key is 147. The reserved characters CHR$ can be used with parentheses and a decimal value to display nonalphanumeric characters on the screen.

Commodore provides another method by allowing you to actually enter non-alphanumeric characters into a program line. These characters are then displayed as graphic symbols both on the screen and in a printed listing. I will avoid using these graphic symbols because they are not descriptive of their function. In addition to remembering the purpose of the function (*i.e.*, CLR/HOME means clearing the screen and placing the cursor in the upper left hand corner of the screen), the use of graphic symbols requires pure memorization of which symbol goes with which function. The same can be said for the decimal values of these nonalphanumeric keys. In the next chapter, I will show a method that can make use of CHR$ values in a descriptive way.

One other major problem occurs with the use of Commodore's graphic symbols. Many printers will not actually display these symbols properly. Unless you have the Commodore printer or a printer with the right interface (equipment that translates information from the computer to the printer), you are likely to get a variety of strange characters and/or sounds. Even those with either the Commodore printer or a printer with the right interface find it difficult to "read" a printed program listing and harder still to type such a listing into their computer. Entering such a listing also requires remembering the exact sequence of key strokes needed to obtain the graphic symbol for these keys—the CLR/HOME key for example. Therefore, whenever possible, I will use the ASCII value for various functions that do not have a BASIC reserved word already established to accomplish the purpose of the function.

Lines 270, 280, and 290 are a similar situation. There is no BASIC reserved word to vertically position the cursor on the screen. If we want a statement to appear on the fifth line from the top of the screen, we must either use the graphic symbol for cursor down five times, or print five CHR$(17) instructions. We will discuss the meaning of lines 270 and 290 (called a FOR–NEXT loop) in the next chapter, so for now, simply understand that this is one method of spacing down five lines from the top of the screen when executed immediately after a PRINT CHR$(147)—CLR/HOME—instruction. Lines 270–290 position the cursor five lines from the top of the screen and in the first column of that fifth line.

Finally, line 300 provides the instructions necessary to display the contents of the string variable LINE$. Line 300 prints the value contained in memory location LINE$ on the screen five lines from the top. The computer prints this information on the screen because we have not told it that we want the information to go anywhere else. The screen is the default for PRINT statements. Default in this case means that a certain value, the screen, has been predetermined, and unless the value is specifically changed, the predetermined value is taken as the desired value. Since we have closed our data file and not used a file number in the PRINT statement, the computer understands that we want the information printed on the screen.

This program is merely to give a brief explanation of the main file commands used with either sequential or random access data files. It is not intended to be a meaningful or useful program in any other sense. Such programs will begin in the next chapter. Please review this chapter and the program example with explanation until you are confident you fully understand what each of the BASIC data file commands, OPEN, CLOSE, INPUT#, and PRINT#, does.

Finally, let's "clean up" our diskette so that we can put some serious programs on it in the next chapter. By following the instructions given below, you will gain practice in the use of two other BASIC file commands and learn about the two modes in which the computer can operate. If you do not wish to erase these programs, you can skip what follows and start Chapter 4 with a fresh diskette, provided you remember to first format the new diskette. (Refer to Chapters 1 and 2 if necessary.)Type:

```
@$
```

The list shows:

```
0 "FORM.10-20-84       " 84 2A
1      "HELLO"              PRG
1      "HELLO2"             PRG
2      "EXAMPLE"            PRG
1      "ADDRESS FILE"       SEQ
659 BLOCKS FREE
```

Now, carefully type just the following:

```
@SCRATCH:ADDRESS FILE
```

Then, type @$ again. And ADDRESS FILE should be gone! Next, type:

```
@SCRATCH:HELLO
@RENAME:HELLO=HELLO2
```

We have erased (SCRATCHed) one more file and changed (RENAMEd) the name of another one. As the last step, type:

```
/HELLO
@SCRATCH:HELLO
←HELLO

/EXAMPLE
@SCRATCH:EXAMPLE
←EXAMPLE
```

This step puts HELLO and EXAMPLE back as the first two files on the diskette. If you have followed these instructions carefully, the list of files should show:

```
0 "FORM.10-20-84       " 84 2A
1      "HELLO"              PRG
2      "EXAMPLE"            PRG
661 BLOCKS FREE
```

(If you want to see why I recommend use of the DOS Wedge, try the preceding steps using all the procedure and syntax necessary under the standard operating system; i.e. without the DOS Wedge.)

All the steps you have just taken have been done in what is called the *immediate mode,* in which what you type is acted upon immediately after the RETURN key is pressed. The immediate mode (sometimes called the *direct mode*) can be very helpful in determining what errors exist in your programs. But most of the work we will be doing will be in what is called the *deferred mode* (sometimes called the *indirect mode*)—deferred because the computer does not follow the program instructions immediately. Rather, it waits until it is told to RUN the program. It defers action until it is specifically told to act. This is the reason for the line numbers in programs. Line numbers tell the computer the exact sequence by which the computer is to follow the program instructions. In the next chapter, we will create our first useful program.

QUESTIONS

1. Name the type of file that usually contains lists of information, rather than computer instructions.
2. Give the two kinds of data files.
3. Which kind of data file is similar to a cassette tape?
4. How many characters may a file name contain?
5. *True or False:* You can RUN a data file just as you RUN a BASIC program.
6. Give the number of modes in which the computer can operate and name them.
7. Name the four operations usually used with data files.
8. What does REM stand for?
9. What three-character file type designator is used for sequential files?
10. Explain what the BASIC reserved word INPUT, without a file number, does.
11. What symbol is used to designate string variables?
12. What are variables?

ANSWERS

1. Data files
2. Sequential access, direct access (random/relative access)
3. Sequential access
4. 16
5. False
6. 2; immediate and deferred
7. OPEN, CLOSE, some method of writing to the file (PRINT#), and some method of reading from the file (INPUT# or GET#)
8. Remark
9. SEQ
10. Brings information into the computer from the keyboard
11. $
12. Names of locations in the computer's memory where values can be stored

Program for DATA FILE EXAMPLE

```
100 REM ***--DATA FILE EXAMPLE--***
110 :
120 :
130 REM **--FILE OUTPUT ROUTINE--**
140 OPEN 2,8,2,"0:ADDRESS FILE,SEQ,WRITE"
150 PRINT#2,"COMMODORE-64 IS A BRIGHT COMPUTER"
160 CLOSE 2
170 :
180 :
190 REM **--FILE INPUT ROUTINE--**
200 OPEN 2,8,2,"0:ADDRESS FILE,SEQ,READ"
210 INPUT#2,LINE$
220 CLOSE 2
230 :
240 :
250 REM **--DISPLAY ROUTINE--**
260 PRINT CHR$(147):REM CLR/HOME
270 FOR I = 1 TO 5
280 PRINT CHR$(17);:REM CURSOR DOWN
290 NEXT I
300 PRINT LINE$
310 END

READY.
```

Program for EXAMPLE.TAPE

```
100 REM ***--EXAMPLE.TAPE--***
110
120
130 REM **--FILE OUTPUT ROUTINE--**
140 OPEN 2,1,1,"ADDRESS FILE"
150 PRINT#2,"COMMODORE-64 IS A BRIGHT COMPUTER"
160 CLOSE 2
170 :
180 :
185 INPUT "REWIND TAPE. PRESS RETURN ";L$
190 REM **--FILE INPUT ROUTINE--**
200 OPEN 2,1,0,"ADDRESS FILE"
210 INPUT#2,LINE$
220 CLOSE 2
230 :
240 :
250 REM **--DISPLAY ROUTINE--**
260 PRINT CHR$(147):REM CLR/HOME
270 FOR I = 1 TO 5
280 PRINT CHR$(17);:REM CURSOR DOWN
290 NEXT I
300 PRINT LINE$
310 END

READY.
```

4 creating sequential files

We begin to get into the heart of our study with the first part of our examination of sequential data files. First, let's briefly review. We have seen that there are different types of files: BASIC program files, FORTRAN or COBOL (or any other language) program files, and data files. You should now understand that program files are files that contain specific instructions for the computer. Data files usually contain only lists or data, not computer instructions. We have also seen that there are two kinds of data files: sequential data files and random access data files. The difference between these two kinds of data files lies in the way the information within them is accessed, sequential requiring access one after the other, and random allowing access to any record directly and immediately. In the last chapter, you were introduced to a new set of BASIC file commands common to both sequential and random data files. Now, we are ready to put some of this knowledge to work and create some useful programs.

We will begin by taking another look at the program given in Chapter 3 and modifying it.

```
100 REM ***--DATA FILE EXAMPLE--***
110 :
120 :
130 REM **--FILE OUTPUT ROUTINE--**
```

```
140 OPEN 2,8,2,"0:ADDRESS FILE,SEQ,WRITE"
150 PRINT#2,"COMMODORE-64 IS A BRIGHT COMPUTER"
160 CLOSE 2
170 :
180 :
190 REM **--FILE INPUT ROUTINE--**
200 OPEN 2,8,2,"0:ADDRESS FILE,SEQ,READ"
210 INPUT#2,LINE$
220 CLOSE 2
230 :
240 :
250 REM **--DISPLAY ROUTINE--**
260 PRINT CHR$(147):REM CLR/HOME
270 FOR I = 1 TO 5
280 PRINT CHR$(17);:REM CURSOR DOWN
290 NEXT I
300 PRINT LINE$
310 END
```

This is the program from Chapter 3. Start the computer. When the cursor appears, insert the TEST/DEMO diskette. Type:

```
LOAD "C-64 WEDGE"
RUN
```

Remove the TEST/DEMO diskette, take the diskette that you have been using, and place it in the disk drive. Then, type the following to see the program instructions:

```
/EXAMPLE
```

Or without the DOS Wedge:

```
LOAD "EXAMPLE",8
LIST
```

Type:

```
RUN
```

Again, you should see the screen clear, and five lines from the top, the following will appear:

```
COMMODORE-64 IS A BRIGHT COMPUTER
```

Type:

@$

And you should see that ADDRESS FILE is back! Then, change line 150 to:

```
150 PRINT #1,"COMMODORE-64 IS OK"
LIST
```

to make sure the change was made. Then, type:

```
RUN
```

Yes, again! You should see:

```
COMMODORE-64 IS A BRIGHT COMPUTER
```

Why didn't we get our new message: COMMODORE IS OK? The reason lies with the need to indicate to the computer that we want to replace our old data file with a data file that has the same name but different data. As indicated in Chapter 3, the replace character @ must precede the file name. So, add this replace character to line 140.

```
140 OPEN 2,8,2,"@0:ADDRESS FILE,SEQ,WRITE"
```

Now, RUN the program again. This time you should see our new message five lines from the top of the screen. It includes everything the ADDRESS FILE now contains. Reopening a sequential data file with the replace character @ destroys the original contents of the file. In some cases, this may be exactly what you want, but in other situations you may not want to destroy the original contents; instead, we might want to add to the file. Some BASIC languages provide a word for just such additions to sequential files: APPEND. Commodore BASIC does not use APPEND. Instead, we will need to add to the file once the file is in the computer's memory and then use the replace character to write the larger file back out to diskette. Now, we can begin on the programs for the Mailing List System.

MAILING LIST SYSTEM

I am not going to get involved in the discussion over flow-charting or structured programming, but, as in building anything, you should have a plan. In this Mailing List System, we will need several programs. The first program should create the file. That first program should probably have at least three different parts: an input routine, a correction routine, and a file creation routine. With this minimum plan, let's begin. We start with what might be called the initialization statements. Type:

```
NEW
100 rem ***--mail.create--***
110 :
120 :
130 rem **--initialization--**
```

At this point, do not worry about making mistakes in your typing. We will go back and make corrections later. But please notice, I have switched into the upper/lower case mode on the computer. I have done so in order to use a mixture of upper/lower case characters in my screen displays for two reasons: (1) To give the screen displays a professional look, and (2) so that program users will be able to enter lower case letters when they type in their names and addresses. The upper/lower case mode is obtained by pressing down on the Commodore key, the key in the extreme lower left hand corner of the keyboard, and at the same time pressing the SHIFT key. You can shift back and forth by holding the Commodore key down and alternately pressing and releasing the SHIFT key. From this point on, most of the programs will be presented as written in this upper/lower case mode. All the listings will also be displayed in lower case letters so that you will be able to easily understand which characters should be entered as upper case characters.

Most COMMODORE program listings given in books or magazines display the listings in upper case and use some procedure to indicate when an actual upper case character is desired (such as underlining characters or words that actually are upper case, or placing a special character before those characters that are upper case). It is not necessary to follow this procedure, and I believe that it is actually much easier to enter programs from a listing that will exactly match the listing once it is entered in the computer. So from here on, in addition to loading the DOS Wedge when you turn on the computer, you should shift into the upper/lower case mode immediately. I know that this may at first prove awkward. But the benefits of using lower case within programs far outweigh the initial awkwardness of shifting from the normal upper case only mode into upper/lower case mode.

Lines 140 through 220 provide the method for using descriptive chr$( ) values to obtain functions not directly developed in Commodore BASIC (*i.e.*, with reserved words). Enter the following:

```
140 home$ = chr$(147):rem clr/home
150 ::cd$  = chr$( 17):rem cursor down
160 ::cu$  = chr$(145):rem cursor up
170 ::cl$  = chr$(157):rem cursor left
180 ::cr$  = chr$( 29):rem cursor right
```

```
190 :blk$   = chr$(144):rem black
200 :ylw$   = chr$(158):rem yellow
210 :wht$   = chr$( 5):rem white
220 :rvs$   = chr$( 18):rem reverse video
230 :
```

The colons are used to help format the listing so that the lines are all straight and easy to read. Each line sets a string variable equal to a specific chr$ ( ) function. The string variables defining colors will be used to set different colors for text at certain points throughout the program. Continue typing:

```
240 dim line$(20)
250 poke 53272,23:rem upper/lower case
260 poke 53281,0:rem set bkgrd to black
270 :
280 :
```

Line 240 uses the dim (dimension) statement to reserve space in the computer's memory for 20 lines of up to 255 characters per line. This number of lines will be more than enough for a starter program. (In fact, a dim statement is not necessary unless you will have more than 10 lines of information for any single set of information-lines.)

Line 250 introduces a new BASIC statement, *poke*. POKE is used to place some value directly into the computer's memory. In this line, the decimal value of 23 is placed into memory location 53272. When this memory location contains the value of 23, the computer switches into the upper/lower case mode. (A value of 21 switches the computer back to the upper case only mode.) The computer contains many such "switches" that can be "set" using the poke statement.

Line 260 refers to another of these special memory locations. This location (53281) is used to establish the color of the background. The value poked into 53281, (0), sets the background to black instead of the dark blue that is present when you turn on the computer. There are sixteen colors available for the background, border, and text, each of which can be set to a different color. This "feature" on the Commodore-64 is one of its best. Such versatility and flexibility are unusual even for more expensive computers. At the same time, misuse of color can be harmful to proper operation of the program. Misuse will not hurt the equipment, but program users may experience eye strain at the very least. Type the following:

```
300 rem **--keyboard input routine--**
310 k = 1:rem line counter
320 print home$:rem clr/home
330 print tab(5)
340 print rvs$;:rem reverse
```

```
350 print "INSTRUCTIONS"
360 print ylw$:rem yellow
370 print "Type name and address as if"
380 print "addressing an envelope."
390 print "Do not use a comma or colon!"
400 print "Press ";wht$;"RETURN";ylw$;
410 print " after each line."
420 print
430 print "Type the word ";wht$;"END";ylw$;" when finished."
```

Upper case is achieved with either the SHIFT key or the SHIFT LOCK key. Line 300 labels the routine and line 310 uses a counter "k" to keep track of the information-lines used. Line 320 uses the now-defined string variable home$—chr$(147)—to clear the screen and place the cursor in the upper left hand corner. Line 330, print tab(5), provides for spacing five spaces from the left side of the screen. The "print rvs$;" in line 340 indicates that the computer is to display the following line in reverse video. This techique is common for screen titles but should be used sparingly. The title is given in line 350 and is also displayed in upper case letters. Line 360 informs the computer to use the yellow color for the text that follows. Lines 370–400 provide instructions to the person entering information: in this case, names, addresses, and phone numbers. All these lines are optional, but I have included them because they help the user to enter the information correctly. And, of course, the instructions themselves can be reworded to your own preference.

Line 400 first displays the word "Press" and a blank space using the previously established color for text (yellow). But then the computer is instructed to switch to white for the following word. The word "RETURN" in line 400 and the word "END" in line 430 are, therefore, printed in white on a black background. Immediately after the printing of these words, the text color is returned to yellow (ylw$). Throughout the book, I will attempt to similarly "highlight" keys or characters the program user should press or type. Such highlighting helps the program user to specifically follow the instructions given. Again, conservative and appropriate use is best.

Line 410 contains a space immediately after the quotation mark, because, without that space, the "a" in "after" would be placed right next to the "N" in "RETURN". The semicolon following the ylw$ variable instructs the computer to leave no space between the last displayed character and the next displayed character.

```
440 print
450 print "Type in line ";k;":"
460 poke 19,32:rem disable input ?
470 input line$(k)
480 print
490 if line$(k) = "end" or line$(k) = "END" then 540
```

```
500 if line$(k) = "" then print "We need some information.":goto 440
510 k = k + 1
520 goto 440:rem go back for more
530 :
```

These lines are the heart of the keyboard input routine. Line 450 instructs the user which line is being entered. The first print (in line 440) prints a blank line. Next, the phrase "Type in line" is displayed. The semicolon instructs the computer to print the value of the numeric variable "k" immediately following the quotation mark. Line 460 is another of those special locations that can be set in different ways. Normally, the "input" statement displays a question mark. But line 450 does not contain a question. Instead, this line is instructing the user what to do. Consequently, I would rather not have a question mark displayed. Memory location 19 controls the prompt on an input statement. Altering that location, this time with a value of 32, eliminates the question mark. Line 470 (input) accepts whatever is typed in and stores it in line$( ), the reserved memory, depending upon the value of "k". Remember that we told the computer to reserve space for 20 possible lines of line$. (Reserving multiple space for a variable creates an ARRAY for that variable.)

The regular "input" statement does not allow certain punctuation to be entered. That is the reason for the specific instructions regarding the comma or colon in line 390. Line 490 checks what was typed in to see if it equals the word "END" or "end". Since the user could type in either upper case or lower case, we should check for both. If it does equal either form of the word, the computer is instructed to jump ahead to line 540 immediately. If it does not equal either an upper or lower case form of the word "END", this line is ignored and the computer goes to the next instruction in line 500.

Line 500 checks for a response that contains no information. Since it is possible for a new user to accidentally press the RETURN key more than once, we should make it impossible to do so. Without the check in line 500, such a mistake would result in a number of blank information-lines. Once more, if the condition is not met, this instruction is ignored and control passes to the next instruction. Line 510 is a method of increasing the line count. The first time through, k will equal 1, so the formula really is: k = 1 + 1 or 2. Once we have increased our line count, we want to go back and get another line, which is exactly what line 520 does.

Next, type the following:

```
540 line$(k) = "*":rem separator for phone number
550 k = k + 1
560 print home$:rem clr/home
570 cd = 3:rem 3 lines down
580 gosub 9000:rem cursor down routine
```

```
590 print "PHONE: ";:print "Press ";wht$;"RETURN";ylw$;" if
    none."
600 input line$(k)
610 if line$(k) = "" then line$(k) = "NONE"
620 k = k + 1
630 line$(k) = "!":rem separator between sets of information
640 :
650 :
```

These may be the most confusing lines to understand. In order to easily separate the name and address from the phone number, I have included a separator, "*", on a line by itself. The reason for separating the phone number from the rest of the information is that now we can use the first part of our information to produce mailing labels. I have also included a separator, "!", to easily differentiate between the name, address, and phone number of one person and the name, address, and phone number of the next person. Therefore, line 540 sets the kth line of line$ equal to "*". At this point, if the first line contains the name; the second line the address; and the third line the city, state, and zip code; then the fourth line will contain the word "END", and k will be equal to 4. By making the fourth line equal to "*", we have actually accomplished two tasks: eliminating the word "END" and establishing a one-character separator before the phone number. We could have required the user to type the "*" when he or she finished entering the name and address, but I prefer to have the user type something natural within the context. Line 550 increases the line count by one for the phone number.

Lines 560–580 are the instructions used to (1) clear the screen and home the cursor, and (2) position the cursor three lines from the top of the screen. Line 570 uses a common variable that specifies the number of cursor down (cd) moves to be made. Then, line 580 transfers control to a subroutine beginning at instruction-line 9000. This subroutine will be explained in more detail at the end of the program. Essentially, it is the same routine used in the EXAMPLE program to display the message.

The GOSUB instruction in conjunction with the RETURN instruction allows a programmer to transfer control from one location in a program to another location, process the instructions in that subroutine, and then return control to the instruction that follows the GOSUB statement. This instruction is especially useful for often-used subroutines. These often-used subroutines can be located at the end of a program and then *called* from various locations within the program. Once again, this flexibility can be misused—and often is. A program that contains many un-documented GOSUBS can be very difficult for even the original programmer to "read" and/or decipher later.

Line 590 gives instructions about typing in the phone number with the word "RETURN" displayed in white. Line 600 accepts whatever format the individual uses to type in the phone number and stores the information in the string reserved memory. If the user just presses the RETURN key, then line$(k) is set to equal the word "NONE". Line 620 again increases the count by one, this time for the separator between sets of information. Line 630 makes the kth line of line$ equal to "!". If the fourth line of line$ is "*" and the fifth line is the phone number, then k would be 6 and the sixth line would equal "!". This concludes the input routine.

The correction routine is next. Type:

```
660 rem **--correction routine--**
670 print home$:rem clr/home
680 cd = 3:rem 3 lines down
690 gosub 9000:rem cursor down routine
700 print "Do not change the line with the ";wht$;"*";ylw$;"."
710 print "This symbol is used as a separator."
720 print
```

These lines explain what the routine is, set the format for the correction routine, and give instructions to the user about the separator "*". Line 660 labels the routine; lines 670–690 clear the screen and place the cursor in the upper left hand corner three lines from the top. Lines 700 and 710 print the instructions for the user. Line 720 prints a blank line after the instructions.

```
730 for i = 1 to k - 1
740 print i;" ";line$(i)
750 next i
```

Lines 730–750 make a loop used to get the information stored in the string reserved memory and print that information on the screen. Line 730 is the first line of a FOR–NEXT loop. It uses a counter (i) that starts with the value of 1 and counts to the value of k minus 1. In our example above, the sixth line was the last line and so was set equal to "!". Since that line should not be changed, there is no reason to display the line. Therefore, the counter only goes to k − 1 or 5. Line 740 prints the current value of the counter, a blank space, and then the information contained in line$(i) stored in the computer's memory. Line 750 increases the counter by one until the counter equals the value of k − 1. The instructions between the FOR instruction and the NEXT instruction are executed the number of times specified in the FOR instruction. To conclude the correction routine, type:

```
760 print
770 print "Change any line? ";
780 gosub 8000:rem y/n input routine
790 print
800 if yes$ = "y" then 850
810 if yes$ = "n" then 830
```

```
820 :
830 goto 3000:rem file creation routine
840 :
850 print:input "Change which line? ";ln
860 print
870 if ln > k - 1 then print "Number too large!":goto 850
880 if line$(ln) = "*" then print "Line";ln;"is the *":goto 850
890 print "Line";ln;"now is:"
900 print line$(ln)
910 print
920 print "Line";ln;"should be:"
930 input line$(ln)
940 goto 660:rem correction routine
950 :
960 :
```

These lines are fairly standard correction routine lines. Line 760 prints a blank line before the question in 770. Line 770 asks the necessary question and provides instructions for answering it. Control is transferred to the Y/N (yes/no) subroutine beginning at instruction-line 8000. In this subroutine, the user's response is stored in the string variable yes$. When the user has responded with some form of either a "y" or "n", control is returned to the instruction following the GOSUB instruction. Line 800 checks the answer, stored in yes$, to see if it equals "y". If it does, the computer is instructed to jump to line 850 and proceed. If it does not equal "y", the computer goes to the next instruction in line 810. Line 810 checks for the negative response of "n". If the value stored in yes$ equals "n", control is passed to the instruction in line 830. Since the computer will not reach this point until the value of yes$ is either a "y" or "n", no further checking need be done. With a negative response, the computer is instructed to go to line 830. Since a negative response indicates that the typist believes all the information-lines are correct, the instruction in line 830 directs the computer to the file creation routine. A positive response to the question in line 770 indicates that at least one of the information-lines needs changing. Therefore, the computer is instructed to jump to the instruction in line 850, which asks the user to indicate which information-line needs changing.

Line 850 requests the number of the line that needs changing and stores that value in the variable "ln". Notice that there is no dollar sign following ln. This indicates that this variable is a numeric variable rather than a string variable. Numeric variables can only contain numbers.

Line 870 checks to see if the user has typed a number larger than the total number of lines displayed. If that is the case, a message is printed and the computer returns to line 850 to ask again for the number of the information-line to be changed. Line 880 makes certain that the typist does not change the line with the "*". Line 990 prints the originally typed line, and line 930 waits for the user to type in the correct information. Finally, line 940 returns to line 660 to begin the correction process over again. The correction process will be repeated until the user answers the question in line 770 in the negative, indicating that all information-lines are correct. A number of other lines or checks could have been included, but for our present needs these lines are sufficient.

The third and last major part of the program is the file creation routine. Type:

```
3000 rem **--file creation routine--**
3010 :
3020 rem *-pointer file-*
3030 open 2,8,2,"0:adrs-ptr,seq,write"
3040 print#2,k
3050 close 2
3060 :
3070 rem *-data file-*
3080 open 3,8,3,"0:adrs-data,seq,write"
3090 for i = 1 to k
3100 print#3,line$(i)
3110 next i
3120 close 3
3130 :
3140 :
```

For tape users, the only lines that are different are lines 3030 and 3080:

```
3030 open 2,1,1,"adrs-ptr"
3080 open 3,1,1,"adrs-data"
```

We are finally down to the actual file-handling routine. As you can see, the routine is quite short. The key to filing system programs is often in proper planning. If you have tried to anticipate and provide for all possible requirements, present and future, your data files can become very powerful and useful. If you are not careful in your planning, however, you may find that some of the information you thought you had in the file has been overwritten, lost, or is practically unavailable. This is the reason for including the two single-character separators and the reason for lines 3020–3050 in this routine. Line 3030 opens a file called "adrs-ptr" in the "write" mode so that this file can receive information. This file is also identified as #2. This first data file will be used to keep track of the number of information-lines we have in the second data file. This data file provides a pointer value for the "adrs-data" file. That is the reason for the name of this data file: "adrs-ptr."

Line 3040 prints the current value of k, which, in our example, should be a "6." This is done to keep track of the total number of information-lines that will be kept in "adrs-data" so that we know how many lines to read back into the computer with other programs. There are other ways to keep track of this number, but with sequential files this is one of the easiest and clearest. Commodore provides a useful reserved word (ST, for STATUS) that actually lets us know when the end of the file has been reached. We will be making use of this handy feature in some of our later programs. But at this point it is important to know the number of information-lines and the process for obtaining that number.

Line 3080 opens the second data file also in the "write" mode and readies it to receive our information. Lines 3090 through 3110 are essentially the same loop as lines 730 to 750, but this time the information is printed to the diskette instead of just the screen. Here, we do want to print the separator "!", so the counter goes from 1 to the value of k. Finally, we close the file in line 3120.

One additional comment needs to be made. Lines 3040 and 3100 print information to the diskette rather than to the screen because the word print is immediately followed by the # symbol (*without an intervening space!*), a number, a comma, and the information that is to be written to the specific file. This is the method the computer uses to distinguish between information that is to be sent to the disk instead of the screen and, therefore, is absolutely necessary! If a file name has not previously been identified with the number, an error will occur. If an incorrect number is specified, information can be sent to the wrong file or be lost. It is very important to keep the numbers consistent with the file names.

The only remaining lines that need be discussed are the two subroutines and a routine to end the program. We will accomplish this with the next lines to enter. Type:

```
5000 rem **--end routine--**
5010 end
5020 :
5030 :
8000 rem **--y/n input routine--**
8010 print "Type a ";wht$;"Y";ylw$;" or ";wht$;"N";ylw$;" :";
8020 poke 19,32:rem disable input ?
8030 input yes$
8040 print
8050 if yes$ = "y" or yes$ = "Y" then yes$ = "y":return
8060 if yes$ = "n" or yes$ = "N" then yes$ = "n":return
8070 print
8080 print rvs$;"Incorrect Choice!";ylw$
8090 print
8100 goto 8000:rem ask again
8110 :
8120 :
9000 rem **--cursor down routine--**
9010 for i = 1 to cd
```

```
9020 print cd$;
9030 next i
9040 return
```

These three short routines (or two subroutines and one routine, if you want) actually reduce the amount of program instructions necessary in the entire program. As indicated above, the "y/n input routine" and "cursor down routine" are "called" by "gosub" statements in previous instructions. Control is transferred to the subroutines until certain conditions are met or certain instructions are followed. Once the task of the subroutine is finished, the "return" statement transfers or returns control back to the instruction that directly follows the gosub instruction. The "end routine" must be placed between the "file creation routine" and the two following subroutines in order to stop the computer from again executing those routines. Entering such a subroutine without the gosub statement will cause a "return without gosub error" and cause the program to completely stop. In this situation, such an error would not hurt anything since we are finished anyway, but it is not good programming to allow such an error to occur.

Line 8010 instructs the user what to type. This line can be "read" and understood by someone with a small amount of previous instruction. It will also be understandable to the original programmer six months from now. It says: Print (or display on the screen) the words "Type a " in the already set color for text (yellow). Immediately follow that with a white capital "Y". Switch back to yellow for the word " or " with a space on each side. Still on the same line, use white to display a capital "N" followed by a final switch back to yellow, a space, and a colon. The method used in line 8010 is far more descriptive than either of the following two forms of this line:

```
8010 print "Type a ";chr$(5);"Y";chr$(158);" or " ;chr$(5);"N";chr$
     (158);" :";
```

or the method that would place graphic symbols in place of the chr$( ) portions of this instruction line.

Line 8020 is the already discussed way of disabling the question mark prompt used for input statements. The user's response is stored in the string variable yes$ (line 8030). Line 8050 checks the answer stored in yes$ to see if it equals "y" or "Y". If it does, the computer is instructed to store a lower case "y" in yes$ and then "return" to the line following the gosub statement. If it does not equal "y" or "Y", the computer goes to the next instruction in line 8060. Line 8060 checks for the negative responses of "n" or "N". If the value stored in yes$ matches one of those, the computer is instructed to store a lower case "n" in yes$ and then "return" to the line following the gosub statement. If it does not match one of those negative responses, the computer ignores this instruction line and proceeds to the following instruction-line. If the computer ever reaches these next lines, lines 8070–8100, we know that the individual has typed something other than either a "y", "Y", "n", or "N". Anything but one of these responses, in this situation, can be viewed as an incorrect response. Therefore, the instruction in line 8080 tells the user that he or she has typed something wrong. Line 8100 sends the computer back to line 8000 to inform the user to type some form of a "y" or "n". Although in this program this subroutine is used only once, when we expand the program, this subroutine will come in very handy.

The cursor down subroutine is basically a loop that extends for the number of times specified in the numeric variable "cd". Notice that we can have a numeric variable that uses the same characters as a string variable, with the only difference being the $ that specifies a string variable. In this subroutine, cd$ equals the cursor down function or chr$(17), while cd equals the number of cursor down moves we want to make. Once the specified number of cursor down moves has been made, control is transferred (returned) to the instruction following the gosub routine. The computer keeps track of which instruction originated the transfer and thus can return to the instruction that follows it.

If you have been following along and typing in the program, you can edit and make corrections to the program by using the cursor keys on the right of the keyboard. Once a correction has been made, pressing the RETURN key saves the corrected version in the computer's memory. When all corrections have been made, you should save this program on diskette (or tape) by giving it a name such as "mail.create". Remember that to save a program, you type the word "SAVE" and the program file name or, under the DOS Wedge, the left arrow and the program file name, like this:

```
SAVE "mail.create",8
or
←mail.create
```

Now type the @$ and see if the file name is listed. It should be listed like this:

```
0 "form.10-20-84        " 84 2a
1     "hello"                prg
2     "example"              prg
1     "address file"         seq
12    "mail.create"          prg
648 blocks free
```

At this point, you can run the program and enter your own name, address, and phone number if you wish. If you do not get the results given below, you will need to check over the program listing to see that what you have typed is entered exactly as given in this chapter. This checking process is often referred to as debugging a program (*i.e.*, finding the mistakes that have somehow found their way into the program). Often the mistakes result from unfamiliarity with the particular keyboard. The more one uses the keyboard, the fewer the number of mistakes there will be. Persistence and careful checking will eventually result in a program operating correctly. The exhilaration associated with finally getting a program to operate correctly is well worth the frustration *all* programmers go through in creating programs.

But, I repeat—type carefully! This program has been thoroughly tested and checked for errors. As listed in the book, the program is fully operational. If you get an error message after you are finished typing in the program and have tried to RUN the program, the most likely problem is with the typing, *not the program logic or any misprint of the listings!* I cannot emphasize enough the aspect of careful typing and reading for mistyped instructions. An example is the typing of a 1 (the number one) instead of l (the lower case letter l). And for those who do not want to spend the time keying in all these instructions, a diskette containing all the programs is available. (Information on ordering the diskette is given at the beginning of the book.)

One last note. I have added *'s and -'s as a personal preference to help set off certain remarks. In addition, I purposely left out line numbers between 960 and 3000 to indicate that the line numbers do not need to have any specific sequence or pattern and because future programs will add routines within this range of lines.

My preference is to begin with line 100 for the program name. Furthermore, I like to have each part or section of the program begin on some round number, 100, 300, 500, 1000, 3000, etc. with each line number some multiple of 10. This numbering system is not always possible, and without a renumbering program it is more trouble than it is worth. But if you have access to a utility program that can renumber your program (such as SYSRES™ from Solidus International)*, I have found that it helps the readability to number by 10 beginning with line 100 and jump to round numbers for major routines. The main point here is not to introduce the numbering system I feel most comfortable with, but to stress the importance of having a numbering system that you *consistently* follow whenever possible. Careful attention to small details, like a consistent numbering system and program format, can make life for any programmer much easier. Such attention to detail can also help develop thinking patterns that aid in creativity and logical solutions to difficult problems.

When you type the word "RUN", you become the *user* of the program. As the user, you should see the screen clear and five lines down the message from lines 350–450 will appear. Type in a name and press the RETURN key. You are then told to type in line number 2. If you want to type in a title for the name in the first line, you can. If no title is needed, then type in the street address and press RETURN. This process should continue until you type in the word "END" or "end." When you do type some form of the word "END," you will be asked for the phone number

---

** Copyright 1982 by Solidus International Corp., North Vancouver, British Columbia, Canada.*

and told that, if there is no phone number, you should just press RETURN.

After the phone number has been typed, you are shown a list of the lines you have typed and asked if you wish to change any of those lines. If you want to change a line, you must answer the question with a "Y" (or a "y"). If you do not want to change a line, either type an "N" or "n". If you need to make changes and have typed a "Y" (or "y"), you will be asked which line number you want to change. Respond with one of the numbers on the screen. You will be shown the originally-typed line and asked for the correct information for this line. After typing in the new line and pressing RETURN, you will be shown the list of lines again with the new line in place of the old line this time.

You can make as many changes as you wish. When you are satisfied and do not wish to make any more changes, a response of "N" (or "n") to the question about changes will instruct the computer to write the information out to the disk. The disk drive will come on for a few seconds, and the "ready" prompt will reappear. (If you are using tape, the message "Press Play & Record" will appear. After you press those keys on the recorder, the screen will go blank for some time. Eventually, the "ready" prompt will reappear.) Now, for disk users, if you type "@$", in addition to the previously created files, you should see:

```
0      "form.10-20-84    " 84 2a
1        "hello"              prg
2        "example"            prg
1        "address file"       seq
12       "mail-create"        prg
1        "adrs-ptr"           seq
1        "adrs-data"          seq
646    blocks free.
```

Two additional files have been created with this one program: "adrs-ptr" has been created to store the number of information-lines now in "adrs-data". In other words, the first file keeps track of the amount of information in the second file.

But several questions present themselves at this point. How do I add more names to this file? And how do I actually see what is in the file? As you may have realized by now, there are a number of possible answers. One answer would be to add more lines to this program so that the program reads back what it just wrote to disk. Another answer is to write a separate program and possibly a program menu that would be able to switch easily between programs that write information and programs that read the information. In the next chapter, we will explore a number of these possibilities and see a little of what can be done with the information once it is safely and correctly on disk.

QUESTIONS

1. *True or False:* Information in a sequential access file can be overwritten by additional information.
2. What BASIC reserved word is used to initiate a sequential data file?
3. Name the three main parts (or routines) in the "mail.create" program.
4. What does reserving multiple space for a variable create?
5. What symbol did we use to separate sets of information?
6. What does DIM stand for?
7. "FOR I = 1 TO K" is the first line in what kind of loop?
8. The program user's response is tested by what kind of BASIC statement?

ANSWERS

1. False; opening a sequential file with the REPLACE character (@) erases the entire contents of any file with the same name. Without the REPLACE character, opening a sequential file that already exists and attempting to write to that file produces an error condition.
2. OPEN
3. INPUT, CORRECTION, and FILE CREATION routines
4. An ARRAY
5. !
6. Dimension
7. A FOR–NEXT loop
8. An IF . . . THEN statement. Check lines 490, 500, 610, 800, 810, 870, and 880.

Program for MAIL.CREATE

```
100 rem ***--mail.create--***
110 :
120 :
130 rem **--initialization--**
140 home$ = chr$(147):rem clr/home
150 ::cd$ = chr$( 17):rem cursor down
160 ::cu$ = chr$(145):rem cursor up
170 ::cl$ = chr$(157):rem cursor left
180 ::cr$ = chr$( 29):rem cursor right
190 :blk$ = chr$(144):rem black
200 :ylw$ = chr$(158):rem yellow
210 :wht$ = chr$(  5):rem white
220 :rvs$ = chr$( 18):rem reverse video
230 :
240 dim line$(20)
250 poke 53272,23:rem upper/lower case
260 poke 53281,0:rem set bkgrd to black
270 :
280 :
300 rem **--keyboard input routine--**
310 k = 1:rem line counter
320 print home$:rem clr/home
330 print tab(5)
340 print rvs$;:rem reverse
350 print "INSTRUCTIONS"
360 print ylw$:rem yellow
370 print "Type name and address as if"
380 print "addressing an envelope."
390 print "Do not use a comma or colon!"
400 print "Press ";wht$;"RETURN";ylw$;
410 print " after each line."
420 print
430 print "Type the word ";wht$;"END";ylw$;" when finished."
440 print
450 print "Type in line ";k;":"
460 poke 19,32:rem disable input ?
470 input line$(k)
480 print
490 if line$(k) = "end" or line$(k) = "END" then 540
500 if line$(k) = "" then print "We need some information.":
    goto 440
510 k = k + 1
520 goto 440:rem go back for more
530 :
540 line$(k) = "*":rem separator for phone number
550 k = k + 1
560 print home$:rem clr/home
570 cd = 3:rem 3 lines down
580 gosub 9000:rem cursor down routine
590 print "PHONE: ";:print "Press ";wht$;"RETURN";ylw$;" if
    none."
600 input line$(k)
```

```
610 if line$(k) = "" then line$(k) = "NONE"
620 k = k + 1
630 line$(k) = "!":rem separator between sets of information
640 :
650 :
660 rem **--correction routine--**
670 print home$:rem clr/home
680 cd = 3:rem 3 lines down
690 gosub 9000:rem cursor down routine
700 print "Do not change the line with the ";wht$;"*";ylw$;"."
710 print "This symbol is used as a separator."
720 print
730 for i = 1 to k - 1
740 print i;" ";line$(i)
750 next i
760 print
770 print "Change any line? ";
780 gosub 8000:rem y/n input routine
790 print
800 if yes$ = "y" then 850
810 if yes$ = "n" then 830
820 :
830 goto 3000:rem file creation routine
840 :
850 print:input "Change which line? ";ln
860 print
870 if ln > k - 1 then print "Number too large!":goto 850
880 if line$(ln) = "*" then print "Line";ln;"is the *":goto 850
890 print "Line";ln;"now is:"
900 print line$(ln)
910 print
920 print "Line";ln;"should be:"
930 input line$(ln)
940 goto 660:rem correction routine
950 :
960 :
3000 rem **--file creation routine--**
3010 :
3020 rem *-pointer file-*
3030 open 2,8,2,"0:adrs-ptr,seq,write"
3040 print#2,k
3050 close 2
3060 :
3070 rem *-data file-*
3080 open 3,8,3,"0:adrs-data,seq,write"
3090 for i = 1 to k
3100 print#3,line$(i)
3110 next i
3120 close 3
3130 :
3140 :
5000 rem **--end routine--**
5010 end
5020 :
5030 :
8000 rem **--y/n input routine--**
```

```
8010 print "Type a ";wht$;"Y";ylw$;" or ";wht$;"N";ylw$;" :";
8020 poke 19,32:rem disable input ?
8030 input yes$
8040 print
8050 if yes$ = "y" or yes$ = "Y" then yes$ = "y":return
8060 if yes$ = "n" or yes$ = "N" then yes$ = "n":return
8070 print
8080 print rvs$;"Incorrect Choice!";ylw$
8090 print
8100 goto 8000:rem ask again
8110 :
8120 :
9000 rem **--cursor down routine--**
9010 for i = 1 to cd
9020 print cd$;
9030 next i
9040 return

ready.
```

5 appending sequential files

Before we get into the subject of this chapter, a few comments are necessary. When you first turn on your computer, if you have a disk drive, you should load the DOS Wedge. And regardless of the hardware used to store and recall files (disk drive or cassette recorder), you should switch into the upper/lower case mode as soon as possible. Please note that although the discussions in this chapter, and those that follow in the sequential access section, are directed at disk users, Commodore-64 owners with the Commodore cassette tape unit can use all these programs by changing the "open" instruction-lines to the specific parameters necessary for tape use. A list of all such lines within each program is given at the end of the chapter. I would also recommend that tape users *(but not disk users)* store their programs on one tape and use another tape on which to save their data. Regardless, tape users must keep track of the exact location of their data file and remember to rewind or exchange tapes *before* running any program. Besides the additional time needed to load programs and data into the computer, tape use requires manual file management operations that the Disk Operating System handles automatically.

Now the fun begins. We have created a file, but as you will soon see, the creation is one of the easiest parts of file manipulation. There are two things we would immediately like to do with this file: add to the file, and read what is in the file. Both tasks are easy to do, but because the job of reading is simpler to explain and more rewarding, we will go over a short program to read the file first.

Type the following:

```
100 rem ***--mail.reader1--***
110 :
120 :
130 rem **--initialization--**
140 home$ = chr$(147):rem clr/home
150 ::cd$ = chr$( 17):rem cursor down
160 :ylw$ = chr$(158):rem yellow
170 :
180 poke 53272,23:rem upper/lower case
190 poke 53281,0:rem set bkgrd to black
200 :
210 :
220 rem **--new lines for reader--**
230 print home$:rem clr/home
240 cd = 5:rem 5 lines down
250 gosub 9000:rem cursor down routine
260 print ylw$;"ONE MOMENT PLEASE!"
270 :
280 :
```

Lines 100 through 280 should be familiar. These are many of the same instructions (with different line numbers in some cases) that we had in the "mail.create" program. They perform the same functions in this program that they did in the "mail.create" program. If you do not understand any of these instructions, refer back to Chapter 4 for a thorough discussion of each line. The only new instruction is line 260. This line displays the message contained inside the quotation marks in yellow; *i.e.*, yellow characters on a black background (line 190).

The next section of programming code brings the contents of the data file into the computer's memory. Enter the following:

```
290 rem **--file input routine--**
300 :
310 rem *-pointer file-*
320 open 2,8,2,"0:adrs-ptr,seq,read"
330 input#2,rec
340 close 2
350 :
360 rem *-data file-*
370 dim tlines$(rec)
380 open 3,8,3,"0:adrs-data,seq,read"
390 for i = 1 to rec
```

```
400 input#3,tlines$(i)
410 next i
420 close 3
430 :
440 tk = rec:rem total k = # of lines
450 :
460 :
```

Line 320 tells the computer that we want to use the disk and that we want to open the "adrs-ptr" file as file #2 in order to bring in the number of information-lines stored in our main data file. Remember, file numbers can go from 1 to 255 with most numbers used under 127. Remember also that the number chosen is simply an arbitrary assignment and in no way indicates the actual number of files in use at any one time. I avoid using the number 1 for a file number since disk drive channel numbers only go from 2 to 14. Line 380 opens that main data file called "adrs-data" as our second file. This instruction-line also opens the file in such a way (read) that information can only be read from the file, not written to the file.

Line 330 brings in, from file #2, the value for the number of lines we wrote to the diskette in our file creation program. If you are not clear on this, check back to the explanation of lines 3010 and 3030 in the previous chapter. We are simply reading back the number written in those lines. Line 370 reserves space in the computer for the information we will be bringing in from the diskette. Since we are not sure of the exact number of lines and the number will change every time we add information, we should use the variable "rec", which will always equal the number of lines (or records) that have been written.

Now, we can bring in a copy of the information contained in the file. Lines 390, 400, and 410 bring in those data. Line 390 establishes the boundaries for the loop we want. We want the count to go from the first to the last line of information as represented by the variable "rec". Because we have identified the file by its number, the computer understands that the input statement in line 400 refers to the disk and not the keyboard. This instruction line tells the computer to go to the diskette and obtain a copy of the information contained in the information-line specified by the variable i.

The operation is on the same principle as the logic of lines 3090 to 3110 in our file creation program. But this time we are bringing information into the computer from the diskette instead of transferring information from the computer to the diskette. Now, the information physically exists in two locations. One location is in the computer's memory, and the other location is still out on the diskette. By bringing the information into the computer, we have not erased that information on the diskette. Merely reading a file does not disturb the contents of that file. Finally, line 420 closes the file.

If you run this program, you are not likely to see anything happen except the appearance of the word "ready". We need a routine that will display the information.

We will become deeply involved in different ways of displaying our information a little bit later, but for now the following routine will get the job done.

```
1000 rem **--display routine--**
1010 print home$:rem clr/home
1020 for i = 1 to tk
1030 print i;" ";tlines$(i)
1040 next i
1050 :
1060 :
```

Our input routine can be used in a number of different programs to bring in all the information from the file, but our display routine will not be functional in very many situations. We will alter this routine later to make it more usable (see Chapter 6). To conclude, type in two short routines already discussed:

```
5000 rem **--end routine--**
5010 end
5020 :
5030 :
9000 rem **--cursor down routine--**
9010 for i = 1 to cd
9020 print cd$;
9030 next i
9040 return
```

Save the program now as "mail.reader1", then type @$ to see the list of files now on the diskette. Type:

```
←mail.reader1
@$
```

and you should see:

```
0    "form.10-20-84    " 84 2a
1        "hello"            prg
2        "example"          prg
1        "address file"     seq
12       "mail.create"      prg
1        "adrs-ptr"         seq
1        "adrs-data"        seq
4        "mail.reader1"     prg
642 blocks free
```

For tape users:

1. Lines 320 and 380 need to be changed to:
   320 open 2,1,0,"adrs-ptr"
   380 open 3,1,0,"adrs-data"
2. Insert the program tape and type:
   save "mail.reader1"
3. Follow the screen prompts.
4. Then insert the data tape and rewind if necessary.

Finally, for everyone, type:

```
run
```

The information you provided when you used the "mail.create" program should be displayed on the screen. If it is not, you need to check back over your programs to see that they are entered exactly as given in this book.

So far, you have created a file, "adrs-data", and written the first group of lines containing information to that file. Now, you have read that information back and displayed it. Next, we need to be able to add more information to the file. If you run the file creation program again and use a different set of information-lines, what would happen? Would the new information be added to the file? Would the old information be replaced? If you do not know for certain what would happen, look at the explanation on page 33 concerning reopening a sequential data file. Every time this program is RUN, the computer is instructed to open two new files, "adrs-ptr" and "adrs-data", before writing any new information. But both files already exist, so you will get a "file exists" error. Nothing will happen to the first set of information-lines already on the diskette if you try to use this program to add a second set of information-lines, but the information you just typed in will be lost due to the error.

So, we need a third program to add more lines of information to our "adrs-data" file. (For those of you itching to put all these programs into one large program, have patience. I will eventually explain how these programs can be tied together without actually existing as one large program.) This third program is really just a modification of the file creation program. The modification needs to be done or, as we have seen, the results will be worthless. The modification is relatively simple if you closely follow the instructions given below.

Down to line 260 of the "mail.create" program (see the complete listing at the end of Chapter 4), the new program can be the same with one minor change. So, first load the "mail.create" program; then list it to see a complete listing of the instructions in this program. Type:

```
/mail.create
list
```

All the program will not fit on the screen at one time. The first instructions disappear from view off the top of the screen. In BASIC, you can list to a certain instruction-line number, or from a certain instruction-line number to the end of the program, or from one line number to another, like this:

```
list - 200
list 350-
list 100-800
```

Line 100 should be changed to read:

```
100 rem ***--mail.adder1--**
```

Except for that one change, the "mail.create" program works fine down to line 260 for our new "mail.adder1" program. Be certain to make that change before continuing.

The next lines essentially come from our "mail.reader1" program. The numbering of the lines must be changed in order to fit these lines in between instruction-line 270 and instruction-line 300. Type:

```
265 :
266 :
270 rem **--new lines for adder--**
271 print home$:rem clr/home
272 cd = 5:rem 5 lines down
273 gosub 9000:rem cursor down routine
274 print ylw$;"ONE MOMENT PLEASE!"
275 :
276 :
277 rem **--file input routine--**
278 :
279 rem *-pointer file-*
280 open 2,8,2,"0:adrs-ptr,seq,read"
281 input#2,rec
282 close 2
283 :
284 rem *-data file-*
285 dim tlines$(rec + 100):rem add up to 100 new lines
286 open 3,8,3,"0:adrs-data,seq,read"
287 for i = 1 to rec
288 input#3,tlines$(i)
289 next i
290 close 3
```

```
291 :
292 tk = rec:rem total k = # of lines
293 :
294 :
```

For tape users:

```
280 open 2,1,0,"adrs-ptr"
286 open 3,1,0,"adrs-data"
```

There are three basic parts to the code presented above.

1. Lines 270–274 instruct the computer to clear the screen and display a message five lines from the top of the screen.
2. Lines 279–282 bring into the computer the number of information-lines (records) that the "adrs-data" file contains.
3. Finally, lines 284–290 dimension the string array tlines$() and bring the data into the computer from the diskette. Line 285 informs the computer that it needs to reserve space (dimension) for a certain number of information-lines—the number of records already in the file, plus the maximum number of information-lines a user can enter at any one time before writing the information back out to the file. Lines 286–290 bring the information into the computer. Without the ability to physically add to the file on the diskette (there is no APPEND command), it is necessary to bring all the information into the computer's memory, add the new information to the previous information, and then write the combined total information back out to the diskette.

Between lines 300 and 960 of "mail.create", only one line needs to be changed for the "mail.adder1" program. Line 830 still sends the computer to the routine at 3000, but now that routine is called "file addition routine" instead of "file creation routine".

```
830 goto 3000:rem file addition routine
```

The logic for the placement and numbering of these next two routines will become clear a little later. For now, add these lines:

```
2000 rem **--repeat routine--**
2080 print home$:rem clr/home
2090 cd = 3:rem 3 lines down
2100 gosub 9000:rem cursor down routine
2110 print "Do you want to add more information?"
2120 gosub 8000:rem y/n input routine
```

```
2130 if yes$ = "y" then run
2140 if yes$ = "n" then 5000
2150 :
2160 :
```

Line 2000 names the routine. Line 2080, as we have seen, clears the screen, and lines 2090 and 2100 space down the screen three lines. Line 2110 prints the question about additional information, and line 2120 transfers control to the "y/n input routine" at 8000 and waits for a response from the user. The computer knows to wait for the response from the keyboard in the "y/n input routine" because we have not identified a file number with the input statement (line 8030). Lines 2130 and 2140 check the response. If the response equals "y", the computer is instructed to "run" the program again. If the response is negative, control is transferred to the instruction at 5000, the end routine. Line 5010 tells the computer to end this program.

Neither of these choices writes anything to the diskette. That is the reason we need another routine, our file addition routine. This file addition routine is very similar to the file creation routine, but the changes are essential! First, we must add the new information-lines to the existing information-lines; that is, we add the number of information-lines already in the file to the number of newly-entered information-lines for a revised information-line total. Type:

```
3012 rem *-add new lines to exist. file lines-*
3013 for i = 1 to k
3014 tlines$(tk + i) = line$(i):rem tk + i, not tk + 1
3015 next i
3016 tk = tk + k
3017 :
```

Line 3014 is the heart of the routine. The string array, tlines$(), contains the information from the diskette. The string array, line$(), contains the new information that has just been entered from the keyboard. Line 3014 combines the two sets of information by adding the information from line$() to the end of the information in tlines$(). It is essential that the subscript read "tk + i" and not "tk + 1". If it were to add only one, then only the last piece of new information would be combined to the existing file. Finally, line 3016 totals the number of information-lines from the diskette (tk) and the number of new information-lines entered from the keyboard (k) to get a new total for tk. The logic for this line is the same as for our now-standard "k = k + 1" lines. If you are not clear about this logic, it is best to just accept that this is one way the computer totals things.

You must be careful about the choice of variable names. Variables that contain (or are) reserved words must not be used. This is the reason we do not use totalines$ for our string array. Check your selection of variable names very carefully.

Now, the only thing left is to change five lines in the "mail.create" program for our new file addition routine.

Old line:	3030 open 2,8,2,"0:adrs-ptr,seq,write"
New line:	3030 open 2,8,2,"@0:adrs-ptr,seq,write"
Old line:	3040 print#2,k
New line:	3040 print#2,tk
Old line:	3080 open 3,8,3,"0:adrs-data,seq,write"
New line:	3080 open 3,8,3,"@0:adrs-data,seq,write"
Old line:	3090 for i = 1 to k
New line:	3090 for i = 1 to tk
Old line:	3100 print#3,line$(i)
New line:	3100 print#3,tlines$(i)
For tape users:	3030 open 2,1,1,"adrs-ptr"
	3080 open 3,1,1,"adrs-data"

The changes in each line are all small changes but are very necessary if the "mail.adder1" program is to work. Line 3100 is changed to write the information contained in the string array tlines$() instead of the contents of line$(). This last is a very important change and will mess up the file badly if it is not made. The @ symbol is the replace symbol. With the addition of this character, the two existing files are replaced by the updated files.

This procedure accomplishes what we want it to, but it is a somewhat dangerous practice. For example, if the power goes out at the moment the newly updated files are being written to the diskette, we might lose not only the information just entered, but all our previous information as well. A better procedure is to rename the old "adrs-data" file to something like "adrs-backup" and then write the updated file out to the diskette. This practice is not possible with tape. It is also not needed if the user does not rewind the tape before writing out the newly updated file.

One more line must be added to this new file addition routine:

```
3125 goto 2000:rem repeat routine
```

Once the information has been written out to diskette, control is transferred back to the "repeat routine" to find out if any more information is to be added to the file. The flow of logic in this program is from the keyboard input routine to the corretion routine, from the correction routine to the file addition routine, from the file routine back to the repeat routine. At the repeat routine, the user is asked if additional information is to be added. If more information is to be added, the program is instructed to "run" itself again. If no more information is to be added at this time, the program is concluded by transferring control to the end routine (lines 5000–5040).

We are finished with the program to add more information to our "adrs-data" file. You should now save this new program to the diskette as "mail.adder1".

```
←mail.adder1
```

You can check your typing by going over the complete listing of the program given at the end of this chapter. Please remember that it is very important to be following along by typing the necessary lines on your Commodore-64.

We have three complete programs: "mail.create", "mail.reader1", and "mail.adder1". The combination of these programs will create a file, add information to the file, and read information back from that file. The three adequately demonstrate the procedures used to accomplish these tasks. But the programs are not really very useful or practical as they now exist. For instance, every time you run the "mail.reader1" program you will read the entire file and display the entire file. This happens even if you want only one name and address. After just a few names and addresses are added to the file, the list begins to disappear off the top of the screen during display. It is quite obvious that more modification needs to be done in order to make these programs useful. If you are already a good programmer in BASIC, you probably have some ideas about "features" or changes you would like to see in one or more of these programs. If you have little experience in programming, you will soon become much more experienced.

I am going to add a few "features" to these programs and fully explain each additional step. So, if you would like to include these things and become more experienced at programming, especially with file information data, follow closely with the different programming lines and explanations given. If you don't need these features or want to create your own, you might want to skip ahead to the chapters on advanced sequential data file manipulation. Or, if you have had enough of sequential data files, you might want to jump immediately to the chapters on random access (*i.e.*, direct access/relative access) data files. We will be using some of these same routines in the chapters on random access, but I will not go into the same explanatory detail as in these chapters. Let's begin adding features to our three programs and making them more useful.

MAIL.ADDER2

We will begin by modifying the "mail.adder1" program. If you have used this program to enter a number of names and addresses, you will have noticed that the disk operates every time you have accepted a set of information-lines as correct. This disk operation may not bother you if you are somewhat slow in typing or are in no hurry to enter a large number of names and addresses, but there is no reason that the disk needs to operate after every name. Why not write the information out to disk only after we have finished entering all our information-lines for the current session? Such a change is clearly a preference feature that proponents and opponents often argue about. In this situation, I prefer to enter all of my information before writing any of it to the diskette. Even before typing in a second set of information-lines, I may want to print a mailing label of the information I have just entered. This is obviously a preference feature and will do little good if you do not have a printer. If you do not have a printer, the routine may still be of interest because we will be formatting our display in a new way.

So, the first two additional routines will be to the "mail.adder1" program. The first routine will consist of adding lines of computer instructions to allow the user to print out a mailing label of the information just entered. The second routine includes the computer instructions necessary so that the information will be written to the diskette after all information for the current session has been entered and corrected. The additional computer instructions necessary to include both of these features are fairly small in number.

PRINT LABEL ROUTINE

We will begin with the print label routine. Add the following lines to the "mail.adder1" program remembering that if the "mail.adder1" program is not already in memory, you must load it into the computer's memory from the diskette or tape:

```
1000 rem **--print label routine--**
1010 print home$:rem clr/home
1020 cd = 3:rem 3 lines down
1030 gosub 9000:rem cursor down routine
1040 print "Would you like to print a"
1050 print
1060 print "mailing label now?"
1070 print
1080 gosub 8000:rem y/n input routine
1090 if yes$ = "y" then 1120
1100 if yes$ = "n" then 2000
1110 :
1120 print home$:rem clr/home
1130 cd = 3:rem 3 lines down
1140 gosub 9000:rem cursor down routine
1150 print "Please make sure the printer"
1160 print
1170 print "is on and ready to use."
1180 print
1190 print "Are you ready to begin printing?"
```

```
1200 print
1210 gosub 8000:rem y/n input routine
1220 if yes$ = "n" then 1000
1230 :
1240 rem **--printer channel--**
1250 open 4,4,7
1251 :
1252 rem first 4 = file #
1253 rem second 4 = printer device #
1254 rem 7 = command for upper/lower case
1255 :
1260 for i = 1 to k
1270 if line$(i) = "*" then i = i + 1:goto 1300
1280 if line$(i) = "!" then 1300
1290 print#4,line$(i)
1300 next i
1310 close 4
1320 :
1330 :
```

Change lines 100 and 830 to:

```
100 rem ***--mail.adder2--***
830 goto 1000:rem print label routine
```

With these few additional instructions, we can now print a mailing label of the information just entered.

Line 1000 gives title to the routine. Lines 1010–1030 clear the screen and place the cursor three lines from the top. Lines 1040 through 1060 print (display on the screen) instructions for the user. Line 1050 prints a blank line so that any user instruction that follows will not come immediately below the last line. Line 1060 prints the question, while line 1080 sends the computer to the "y/n routine" to wait for the response from the keyboard. Lines 1090 and 1100 check the response. If the response is positive, which indicates that a printed label is desired, the computer is instructed to jump over the next two lines and go on to the rest of the routine. Line 1100 is only reached if the response is a negative response, indicating that the user does not want a printed label. Negative responses end the routine and transfer the computer to the instruction at line 2000 for the repeat routine. Lines 1120–1220 provide additional information to the user and check to see that everything is ready to print. If not, or if the user changes his or her mind, control is returned to the original question.

Line 1250 opens the printer channel using the standard printer device number of 4 and the command of 7 (indicating the desire to use both upper and lower case in the printout). The instruction in line 1260 is the now-familiar beginning of the loop.

Lines 1270 and 1280 are different from anything we have had so far. Line 1270 checks the contents of each line$() string for the "*" symbol. If, and only if, it locates that symbol, it instructs the computer to add 1 to the value of the variable i and then to proceed to the instruction at line 1300. The reason for this is simple but hard to explain. When the computer comes to an asterisk, we do not want that asterisk printed, nor do we want the phone number printed in a mailing label. So, we skip printing the asterisk and the phone number by adding one to the counter (i) and jumping to the end of the loop, line number 1300. Line number 1300 increases the counter by one more line, so we have skipped two lines in the file: the lines that contained the separator symbol "*" and the phone number. I think this will become clear, if it is not already so, when you type in and try the routine.

Line 1280 does much the same thing. It tells the computer to jump over the print statement and go to the instruction that increases the counter. We have the effect, then, of skipping over the "!" separator symbol and not printing it either. Line 1290 does the printing. It prints to the printer the contents of every string in the line$() array that is not either a "*", "!", or phone number, unless the phone number has been typed in before the "*" symbol. The information is sent to the printer instead of the screen because we have: (1) previously opened output to the printer as file number 4, and (2) used the # symbol with a file number in the print statement. In the next chapter, we will see how we can send information to either the printer or the screen with just one line of code, but for this routine the print#4 statement is sufficient.

Line 1300 increases the counter. When the loop is finished, when all lines of information have either been printed or skipped and the i counter has reached the value of k, the computer can go on to the next instruction "outside" the loop. Line 1310 is the first instruction outside the loop, and because we are finished printing, we need to close the channel that we opened for the printer. It is especially important to do this before attempting to do anything else, since strange things occur with the Commodore-64 and an open channel to device 4. We are now finished with the print label routine and control passes to the repeat routine.

REPEAT ROUTINE

The new repeat routine is even shorter and easier. Do the following very carefully:

1. List lines 3010–3017
   list 3010–3017
2. Use the cursor keys to:
   change the line numbers 3010–3017,
   so that they go from 2010 to 2070.

Lines 3010–3017 were:

```
3010 :
3012 rem *-add new lines to exist. file lines-*
3013 for i = 1 to k
3014 tlines$(tk + i) = line$(i):rem tk + i, not tk + 1
3015 next i
3016 tk = tk + k
3017 :
```

Those lines now become:

```
2010 :
2020 rem *-add new lines to exist. file lines-*
2030 for i = 1 to k
2040 tlines$(tk + i) = line$(i):rem tk + i, not tk + 1
2050 next i
2060 tk = tk + k
2070 :
```

3. Delete lines 3012–3017 by:

a. typing each line number

b. then pressing the {RETURN} key.

```
3012 {RETURN}
3013 {RETURN}
3014 {RETURN}
3015 {RETURN}
3016 {RETURN}
3017 {RETURN}
```

(line 3010 can stay as a separator)

4. Change line 2130 to:
2130 if yes$ = "y" then 300

5. Change line 2140 to:
2140 if yes$ = "n" then 3000

6. Delete line 3125
3125 {RETURN}

7. *Optional! For disk users only.*
If you want to, add:
3075 @ "rename: adrs-backup = adrs-data"
and eliminate the @ from line 3080.

They look like such small changes, but when viewed by the computer, the changed and added instructions make quite a difference in the way the program works. The program now becomes more practical. We have moved seven lines of code: 3010, 3012, 3013, 3014, 3015, 3016, and 3017. These lines are now part of the repeat routine instead of the file addition routine. By moving these lines, we have made it possible to continue to add more lines of information before writing all the information out to the diskette or tape. Once these lines have been moved to the repeat routine, they must be deleted from the file addition routine. Then, lines 2130 and 2140 need to be altered to reflect the change of direction we want the computer to take. We now have the flow of logic in order. The two subroutines that occur after the end routine are "called" from various points within the program, but control is always returned to the point of the originating gosub instruction. It may not always be posssible to have every program proceed in order through the program instructions, but it is a desirable goal. Proceeding in order makes the flow of logic much easier to understand. This *top-down* approach to programming is one of the reasons the "mail.adder1" program needs alteration and the reason line 3025 must be deleted from this "mail.adder2" program. Line 3025 directs the flow of logic to a previous routine, which asks if the user wants to add more information. In the "mail.adder2" program, the logic flows from the keyboard input routine to the correction routine to the repeat routine and back again, until the user indicates that he or she is finished entering information. Then, the logic drops from the repeat routine (2000–2160) to the file addition routine (3000–3140) and to the end routine (5000–5030).

The transferred lines need some further elaboration. Line 2030 is the start of a loop. Again, the logic is fairly easy. We are going to keep the contents of the string array line$() in the string array tlines$() also. Then, since we have the information stored in two locations in the computer, we can use the line$() string array over again. In other words, we have moved the information from one memory location to another memory location. We have moved it from line$(1) to tlines$(tk + 1), and from line$(2) to tlines$(tk + 2), and so on. The instruction at 2060 helps us to keep track of all the lines that are typed in. Tk (which may stand for total k) is a cumulative total of all the lines of information. For the first set of additional information-lines, the value of tk is the number of records already in the file. After the first set of information-lines, tk becomes the value of tk plus the number of lines of information just entered (k). And in the loop, we have moved the contents of the second line$(i) to tlines$(tk + i), after tk has been updated by tk = tk + k, and so on. This process can continue until we have accumulated 100 lines of information, or more if you have dimensioned tlines$() to more than 100. You can make this number smaller or larger. The number 100 was a completely arbitrary choice. If you are adding more lines of information, 2130 must direct the computer to begin again by proceeding to the keyboard input routine.

In the next chapter, we will add some features to our display program and combine all our programs so that they can operate together. When you have made the necessary changes, be sure to save this new version. There are several ways of saving a new version of the same program. But for now, type the following:

```
←mail.adder2
```

Then, type @$ and you should see:

```
0      "form.10-20-84    " 84 2a
1          "hello"           prg
2          "example"         prg
1          "address file"    seq
12         "mail.create"     prg
1          "adrs-ptr"        seq
1          "adrs-data"       seq
4          "mail.reader1"    prg
15         "mail.adder1"     prg
18         "mail.adder2"     prg
609 blocks free
```

INSTRUCTIONS FOR TAPE USERS

Instruction lines that should be changed:

mail.reader1

320 open 2,1,0,"adrs-ptr"
380 open 3,1,0,"adrs-data"

mail.adder1

280 open 2,1,0,"adrs-ptr"
286 open 3,1,0,"adrs-data"

3030 open 2,1,1,"adrs-ptr"
3080 open 3,1,1,"adrs-data"

mail.adder2

280 open 2,1,0,"adrs-ptr"
286 open 3,1,0,"adrs-data"

3030 open 2,1,1,"adrs-ptr"
3080 open 3,1,1,"adrs-data"

QUESTIONS

1. *True or False:* Running the "mail.create" program a second time with new information does no harm to the first information stored in the "adrs-data" file.
2. Give the name of the BASIC command that allows a programmer to place a value directly into the computer's memory.
3. To what does line 3080 in the "mail.adder1" program print the information?
4. What is the BASIC word used to tell the computer to jump to a certain line number?
5. Give the purpose of the symbols ←, /, and ↑ under the DOS Wedge.
6. What is the procedure we used to add information to an existing sequential data file?

ANSWERS

1. True
2. Poke
3. Disk or diskette
4. GOTO
5. ← = SAVE
   / = LOAD
   ↑ = LOAD and then RUN with the equivalent of pressing the RETURN key after each command
6. (1) Bring the contents of the existing file into the computer's memory.
   (2) Add additional information to the information now in the computer's memory.
   (3) Write the now combined information out to the diskette, replacing the old file (or renaming the old file and then creating a new file with the original file's name).

■ *Program for MAIL.READER1*

```
100 rem ***--mail.reader1--***
110 :
120 :
130 rem **--initialization--**
140 home$ = chr$(147):rem clr/home
150 ::cd$ = chr$( 17):rem cursor down
160 :ylw$ = chr$(158):rem yellow
170 :
180 poke 53272,23:rem upper/lower case
190 poke 53281,0:rem set bkgrd to black
200 :
210 :
220 rem **--new lines for reader--**
230 print home$:rem clr/home
240 cd = 5:rem 5 lines down
250 gosub 9000:rem cursor down routine
260 print ylw$;"ONE MOMENT PLEASE!"
270 :
280 :
290 rem **--file input routine--**
300 :
310 rem *-pointer file-*
320 open 2,8,2,"0:adrs-ptr,seq,read"
330 input#2,rec
340 close 2
350 :
360 rem *-data file-*
370 dim tlines$(rec)
380 open 3,8,3,"0:adrs-data,seq,read"
390 for i = 1 to rec
400 input#3,tlines$(i)
410 next i
420 close 3
430 :
440 tk = rec:rem total k = # of lines
450 :
460 :
1000 rem **--display routine--**
1010 print home$:rem clr/home
1020 for i = 1 to tk
1030 print i;" ";tlines$(i)
1040 next i
1050 :
1060 :
5000 rem **--end routine--**
5010 end
5020 :
5030 :
9000 rem **--cursor down routine--**
9010 for i = 1 to cd
9020 print cd$;
9030 next i
9040 return

ready.
```

■ Program for MAIL.ADDER1

```
100 rem ***--mail.adder1--***
110 :
120 :
130 rem **--initialization--**
140 home$ = chr$(147):rem clr/home
150 ::cd$ = chr$( 17):rem cursor down
160 ::cu$ = chr$(145):rem cursor up
170 ::cl$ = chr$(157):rem cursor left
180 ::cr$ = chr$( 29):rem cursor right
190 :blk$ = chr$(144):rem black
200 :ylw$ = chr$(158):rem yellow
210 :wht$ = chr$(  5):rem white
220 :rvs$ = chr$( 18):rem reverse video
230 :
240 dim line$(20)
250 poke 53272,23:rem upper/lower case
260 poke 53281,0:rem set bkgrd to black
265 :
266 :
270 rem **--new lines for adder--**
271 print home$:rem clr/home
272 cd = 5:rem 5 lines down
273 gosub 9000:rem cursor down routine
274 print ylw$;"ONE MOMENT PLEASE!"
275 :
276 :
277 rem **--file input routine--**
278 :
279 rem *-pointer file-*
280 open 2,8,2,"0:adrs-ptr,seq,read"
281 input#2,rec
282 close 2
283 :
284 rem *-data file-*
285 dim tlines$(rec + 100):rem add up to 100 new lines
286 open 3,8,3,"0:adrs-data,seq,read"
287 for i = 1 to rec
288 input#3,tlines$(i)
289 next i
290 close 3
291 :
292 tk = rec:rem total k = # of lines
293 :
294 :
300 rem **--keyboard input routine--**
310 k = 1:rem line counter
320 print home$:rem clr/home
330 print tab(5)
340 print rvs$;:rem reverse
350 print "INSTRUCTIONS"
360 print ylw$:rem yellow
370 print "Type name and address as if"
380 print "addressing an envelope."
```

```
390 print "Do not use a comma or colon!"
400 print "Press ";wht$;"RETURN";ylw$;
410 print " after each line."
420 print
430 print "Type the word ";wht$;"END";ylw$;" when finished."
440 print
450 print "Type in line ";k;":"
460 poke 19,32:rem disable input ?
470 input line$(k)
480 print
490 if line$(k) = "end" or line$(k) = "END" then 540
500 if line$(k) = "" then print "We need some information.":
    goto 440
510 k = k + 1
520 goto 440:rem go back for more
530 :
540 line$(k) = "*":rem separator for phone number
550 k = k + 1
560 print home$:rem clr/home
570 cd = 3:rem 3 lines down
580 gosub 9000:rem cursor down routine
590 print "PHONE: ";:print "Press ";wht$;"RETURN";ylw$;" if
    none."
600 input line$(k)
610 if line$(k) = "" then line$(k) = "NONE"
620 k = k + 1
630 line$(k) = "!":rem separator between sets of information
640 :
650 :
660 rem **--correction routine--**
670 print home$:rem clr/home
680 cd = 3:rem 3 lines down
690 gosub 9000:rem cursor down routine
700 print "Do not change the line with the ";wht$;"*";ylw$;"."
710 print "This symbol is used as a separator."
720 print
730 for i = 1 to k - 1
740 print i;" ";line$(i)
750 next i
760 print
770 print "Change any line? ";
780 gosub 8000:rem y/n input routine
790 print
800 if yes$ = "y" then 850
810 if yes$ = "n" then 830
820 :
830 goto 3000:rem file addition routine
840 :
850 print:input "Change which line? ";ln
860 print
870 if ln > k - 1 then print "Number too large!":goto 850
880 if line$(ln) = "*" then print "Line";ln;"is the *":goto 850
890 print "Line";ln;"now is:"
900 print line$(ln)
910 print
```

```
920 print "Line";ln;"should be:"
930 input line$(ln)
940 goto 660:rem correction routine
950 :
960 :
2000 rem **--repeat routine--**
2080 print home$:rem clr/home
2090 cd = 3:rem 3 lines down
2100 gosub 9000:rem cursor down routine
2110 print "Do you want to add more information?"
2120 gosub 8000:rem y/n input routine
2130 if yes$ = "y" then run
2140 if yes$ = "n" then 5000
2150 :
2160 :
3000 rem **--file addition routine--**
3010 :
3012 rem *-add new lines to exist. file lines-*
3013 for i = 1 to k
3014 tlines$(tk + i) = line$(i):rem tk + i, not tk + 1
3015 next i
3016 tk = tk + k
3017 :
3020 rem *-pointer file-*
3030 open 2,8,2,"@0:adrs-ptr,seq,write"
3040 print#2,tk
3050 close 2
3060 :
3070 rem *-data file-*
3080 open 3,8,3,"@0:adrs-data,seq,write"
3090 for i = 1 to tk
3100 print#3,tlines$(i)
3110 next i
3120 close 3
3125 goto 2000:rem repeat routine
3130 :
3140 :
5000 rem **--end routine--**
5010 end
5020 :
5030 :
8000 rem **--y/n input routine--**
8010 print "Type a ";wht$;"Y";ylw$;" or ";wht$;"N";ylw$;" :";
8020 poke 19,32:rem disable input ?
8030 input yes$
8040 print
8050 if yes$ = "y" or yes$ = "Y" then yes$ = "y":return
8060 if yes$ = "n" or yes$ = "N" then yes$ = "n":return
8070 print
8080 print rvs$;"Incorrect Choice!";ylw$
8090 print
8100 goto 8000:rem ask again
8110 :
8120 :
9000 rem **--cursor down routine--**
```

```
9010 for i = 1 to cd
9020 print cd$;
9030 next i
9040 return

ready.
```

Program for MAIL.ADDER2

```
100 rem ***--mail.adder2--***
110 :
120 :
130 rem **--initialization--**
140 home$ = chr$(147):rem clr/home
150 ::cd$ = chr$( 17):rem cursor down
160 ::cu$ = chr$(145):rem cursor up
170 ::cl$ = chr$(157):rem cursor left
180 ::cr$ = chr$( 29):rem cursor right
190 :blk$ = chr$(144):rem black
200 :ylw$ = chr$(158):rem yellow
210 :wht$ = chr$(  5):rem white
220 :rvs$ = chr$( 18):rem reverse video
230 :
240 dim line$(20)
250 poke 53272,23:rem upper/lower case
260 poke 53281,0:rem set bkgrd to black
265 :
266 :
270 rem **--new lines for adder--**
271 print home$:rem clr/home
272 cd = 5:rem 5 lines down
273 gosub 9000:rem cursor down routine
274 print ylw$;"ONE MOMENT PLEASE!"
275 :
276 :
277 rem **--file input routine--**
278 :
279 rem *-pointer file-*
280 open 2,8,2,"0:adrs-ptr,seq,read"
281 input#2,rec
282 close 2
283 :
284 rem *-data file-*
285 dim tlines$(rec + 100):rem add up to 100 new lines
286 open 3,8,3,"0:adrs-data,seq,read"
287 for i = 1 to rec
288 input#3,tlines$(i)
289 next i
290 close 3
291 :
292 tk = rec:rem total k = # of lines
293 :
294 :
```

```
300 rem **--keyboard input routine--**
310 k = 1:rem line counter
320 print home$:rem clr/home
330 print tab(5)
340 print rvs$;:rem reverse
350 print "INSTRUCTIONS"
360 print ylw$:rem yellow
370 print "Type name and address as if"
380 print "addressing an envelope."
390 print "Do not use a comma or colon!"
400 print "Press ";wht$;"RETURN";ylw$;
410 print " after each line."
420 print
430 print "Type the word ";wht$;"END";ylw$;" when finished."
440 print
450 print "Type in line ";k;":"
460 poke 19,32:rem disable input ?
470 input line$(k)
480 print
490 if line$(k) = "end" or line$(k) = "END" then 540
500 if line$(k) = "" then print "We need some information.":
    goto 440
510 k = k + 1
520 goto 440:rem go back for more
530 :
540 line$(k) = "*":rem separator for phone number
550 k = k + 1
560 print home$:rem clr/home
570 cd = 3:rem 3 lines down
580 gosub 9000:rem cursor down routine
590 print "PHONE: ";:print "Press ";wht$;"RETURN";ylw$;" if
    none."
600 input line$(k)
610 if line$(k) = "" then line$(k) = "NONE"
620 k = k + 1
630 line$(k) = "!":rem separator between sets of information
640 :
650 :
660 rem **--correction routine--**
670 print home$:rem clr/home
680 cd = 3:rem 3 lines down
690 gosub 9000:rem cursor down routine
700 print "Do not change the line with the ";wht$;"*";ylw$;"."
710 print "This symbol is used as a separator."
720 print
730 for i = 1 to k - 1
740 print i;" ";line$(i)
750 next i
760 print
770 print "Change any line? ";
780 gosub 8000:rem y/n input routine
790 print
800 if yes$ = "y" then 850
810 if yes$ = "n" then 830
820 :
```

```
830 goto 1000:rem print label routine
840 :
850 print:input "Change which line? ";ln
860 print
870 if ln > k - 1 then print "Number too large!":goto 850
880 if line$(ln) = "*" then print "Line";ln;"is the *":goto
    850
890 print "Line";ln;"now is:"
900 print line$(ln)
910 print
920 print "Line";ln;"should be:"
930 input line$(ln)
940 goto 660:rem correction routine
950 :
960 :
1000 rem **--print label routine--**
1010 print home$:rem clr/home
1020 cd = 3:rem 3 lines down
1030 gosub 9000:rem cursor down routine
1040 print "Would you like to print a"
1050 print
1060 print "mailing label now?"
1070 print
1080 gosub 8000:rem y/n input routine
1090 if yes$ = "y" then 1120
1100 if yes$ = "n" then 2000
1110 :
1120 print home$:rem clr/home
1130 cd = 3:rem 3 lines down
1140 gosub 9000:rem cursor down routine
1150 print "Please make sure the printer"
1160 print
1170 print "is on and ready to use."
1180 print
1190 print "Are you ready to begin printing?"
1200 print
1210 gosub 8000:rem y/n input routine
1220 if yes$ = "n" then 1000
1230 :
1240 rem **--printer channel--**
1250 open 4,4,7
1251 :
1252 rem first 4 = file #
1253 rem second 4 = printer device #
1254 rem 7 = command for upper/lower case
1255 :
1260 for i = 1 to k
1270 if line$(i) = "*" then i = i + 1:goto 1300
1280 if line$(i) = "!" then 1300
1290 print#4,line$(i)
1300 next i
1310 close 4
1320 :
1330 :
2000 rem **--repeat routine--**
2010 :
```

```
2020 rem *-add new lines to exist. file lines-*
2030 for i = 1 to k
2040 tlines$(tk + i) = line$(i):rem tk + i, not tk + 1
2050 next i
2060 tk = tk + k
2070 :
2080 print home$:rem clr/home
2090 cd = 3:rem 3 lines down
2100 gosub 9000:rem cursor down routine
2110 print "Do you want to add more information?"
2120 gosub 8000:rem y/n input routine
2130 if yes$ = "y" then 300
2140 if yes$ = "n" then 3000
2150 :
2160 :
3000 rem **--file addition routine--**
3010 :
3020 rem *-pointer file-*
3030 open 2,8,2,"@0:adrs-ptr,seq,write"
3040 print#2,tk
3050 close 2
3060 :
3070 rem *-data file-*
3080 open 3,8,3,"@0:adrs-data,seq,write"
3090 for i = 1 to tk
3100 print#3,tlines$(i)
3110 next i
3120 close 3
3130 :
3140 :
5000 rem **--end routine--**
5010 end
5020 :
5030 :
8000 rem **--y/n input routine--**
8010 print "Type a ";wht$;"Y";ylw$;" or ";wht$;"N";ylw$;" :";
8020 poke 19,32:rem disable input ?
8030 input yes$
8040 print
8050 if yes$ = "y" or yes$ = "Y" then yes$ = "y":return
8060 if yes$ = "n" or yes$ = "N" then yes$ = "n":return
8070 print
8080 print rvs$;"Incorrect Choice!";ylw$
8090 print
8100 goto 8000:rem ask again
8110 :
8120 :
9000 rem **--cursor down routine--**
9010 for i = 1 to cd
9020 print cd$;
9030 next i
9040 return

ready.
```

6 displaying sequential files

In this chapter, we will begin to put together a *system* of programs and improve our display program. When you want to use the "mail.reader1" program, you must type: ↑ mail.reader1 if you have first loaded the DOS Wedge (if not, the following sequence is necessary: load "mail.reader1",8 [RETURN] run [RETURN]). And when you are ready to add to the file, you need to type: ↑ mail.adder2 (or "1" depending on your preference). For occasional use, that amount of typing is not a problem, but if you are going to use the programs quite often, the necessity of typing a specific syntax and the file name can become bothersome. Besides, the computer can help eliminate the need to type that, so why not let it do so? All that is needed is another program. You will still have to type ↑ and the name of this new program. The difference is that when properly set up, you may need to do the typing only once, and then you will be able to switch back and forth between programs with little typing other than a number. You will then have a *system* of programs that work together and are controlled by one *master* program.

Unfortunately, for tape users, this method depends upon the storage device being able to access any of the programs in any order. Such access virtually eliminates tape because of its sequential nature. A possible alternative is to combine all these programs into one large program and, therefore, retain all parts within the computer's memory. Separately, these programs contain between 20 and 25 K (kilobytes: a kilobyte is roughly equivalent to a thousand characters) of program code, which leaves approximately 13 to 18 K for data.)

Let's see how this can work. Make sure any program currently in memory is saved on diskette, and then type the following:

```
new
100 rem ***--mail.menu--***
110 :
120 :
130 rem **--initialization--**
140 home$ = chr$(147):rem clr/home
150 ::cd$  = chr$( 17):rem cursor down
160 ::cu$  = chr$(145):rem cursor up
170 ::cl$  = chr$(157):rem cursor left
180 ::cr$  = chr$( 29):rem cursor right
190 :blk$  = chr$(144):rem black
200 :ylw$  = chr$(158):rem yellow
210 :wht$  = chr$(  5):rem white
220 :rvs$  = chr$( 18):rem reverse video
230 :
240 poke 53280,14:rem border = lt.blue
250 poke 53272,23:rem upper/lower case
260 poke 53281, 6:rem set bkgrd to blue
270 :
280 :
```

These lines are essentially the same instructions used in the "mail.create", "mail.adder1", and "mail.adder2" programs. The differences occur in lines 100, 240, and 260. Line 100 indicates the name for this program, "mail.menu". Line 260 sets the background color to dark blue instead of the black color used in the other programs. Different color backgrounds can be used to indicate different functions. Line 240 is used to set the color of the border. In this menu program, we do not need to dimension any string variables and can replace that instruction contained in the other programs. Since Commodore's BASIC does not have a delete instruction (an instruction that allows a programmer to delete a range of lines), it is just about as fast to re-enter these program lines as it is to load one of the other programs, make the necessary changes, and then line by line delete instruction-lines that will not be needed in this "mail.menu" program. Regardless of the method you choose, the next group of program lines displays the choices available. Enter the following carefully:

```
500 rem **--menu--**
510 tb = 5:rem tab value--5 spaces rt.
520 print home$:rem clr/home
530 print wht$
540 print tab(tb + 3)
550 print rvs$;
560 print "MAIL PROGRAM MENU"
570 print
580 print ylw$
590 print tab(tb)
600 print "1. FILE CREATION PROGRAM"
610 print:print tab(tb)
620 print "2. FILE ADDITION PROGRAM"
630 print:print tab(tb)
640 print "3. FILE DISPLAY PROGRAM"
650 print:print tab(tb)
660 print "4. FILE CORRECTION PROGRAM"
670 print:print tab(tb)
680 print "5. LIST OF FILES"
690 print:print tab(tb)
700 print "6. END"
710 print:print tab(tb)
720 poke 19,32:rem disable input ?
730 input "Which Program Number? ";nu$
740 number = val(nu$)
750 :
760 if number = 1 then 1000
770 if number = 2 then 2000
780 if number = 3 then 3000
790 if number = 4 then 4000
800 if number = 5 then 5000
810 if number = 6 then 6000
820 :
830 rem *--incorrect choice message--*
840 print:print
850 print tab(tb)
860 print rvs$;"Incorrect Choice!"
870 print
880 print tab(tb)
890 print "Press ";wht$;"RETURN";ylw$;" to continue:";
900 gosub 19000:rem return key routine
910 goto 500:rem menu--check again
920 :
930 :
```

Line 540 uses a new BASIC statement—tab. This tells the computer to horizontally tab over a certain number of spaces (the number stored in the numeric variable tb) and then display the contents of the next print statement. I use a variable so that I have to change only one instruction line (line 510) if I don't like the positioning on the screen.

Line 740 uses the first of several instructions available to manipulate string variable information. Instruction-line 730 stores the user's response in the string variable nu$. Line 740 then takes the numeric value (val) of the string—(nu$). Lines 760 to 810 check this value, now stored in two different memory locations, number and nu$, and direct the computer to jump to the appropriate program location. If the value of number is not between 1 and 6, the computer proceeds to the "incorrect choice message" routine. After displaying the message, the computer is directed to go to the subroutine located at line 19000. The full explanation of this subroutine will be given in the proper sequence, but once the user has pressed the RETURN key, control is returned to line 910, which sends control back to line 500, the instruction that once again begins the menu routine.

```
1000 rem **--file creation prog.--**
1010 print home$:rem clr/home
1020 cd = 2:rem 2 lines down
1030 gosub 9000:rem cursor down routine
1040 print tab(15)
1050 print rvs$;
1060 print "WARNING!"
1070 print:print
1080 print "If the 'adrs-data' file already exists,"
1090 print
1100 print "do NOT run this program!"
1110 print
1120 print "Do you want the file creation program?"
1130 print
1140 gosub 8000:rem y/n input routine
1150 if yes$ = "n" then 500:rem menu
1160 print:print
1170 print "Are you sure? Type ";wht$;"YES";ylw$;" if you are:";
1180 input yes$
1190 if yes$ = "YES" or yes$ = "yes" then 1210
1200 goto 1000:rem check again
1210 file$ = "MAIL.CREATE"
1220 gosub 7100:rem new program routine after question
1230 ↑ "mail.create":rem load & run
1240 :
1250 :
```

Most of this routine is not necessary but does provide the user with enough information and/or escape hatches so that, if line 1230 is finally reached, we can be certain that the instruction has not been reached by accident. The purpose for including so many checks is to indicate the necessity on the part of the programmer to attempt to protect the user from making a disastrous mistake with files. The other options do not contain the same potentially disastrous possibilities and, therefore, the following routines do not need to provide the same level of error checking.

```
2000 rem **--file addition prog.--**
2010 file$ = "MAIL.ADDER2"
2020 gosub 7000:rem new program routine
2030 ↑ "mail.adder2":rem load & run
2040 :
2050 :
3000 rem **--file display prog.--**
3010 file$ = "MAIL.READER2"
3020 gosub 7000:rem new program routine
3030 ↑ "mail.reader2":rem load & run
3040 :
3050 :
4000 rem **--file correction prog.--**
4010 file$ = "MAIL.CORRECTION"
4020 gosub 7000:rem new program routine
4030 ↑ "mail.correction":rem load & run
4040 :
4050 :
5000 rem **--list of files routine--**
5010 print home$:rem clr/home
5020 @"$":rem wedge/diskette directory
5030 print cu$;chr$(13):rem 13 = rtn
5040 print "Are you ready to return to the menu?"
5050 print
5060 gosub 8000:rem y/n input routine
5070 if yes$ = "y" then 500:rem menu
5080 goto 5000:rem check again
5090 :
5100 :
6000 rem **--end routine--**
6010 poke 19,0:rem restore input prompt
6020 print home$:rem clr/home
6030 cd = 5:rem 5 lines down
6040 gosub 9000:rem cursor down routine
6050 print tab(tb)
```

```
6060 print rvs$;
6070 print "That's all for this session!"
6080 print:print:print
6090 print tab(tb + 5)
6100 print rvs$;
6110 print "See you next time."
6120 print ylw$
6130 cd = 10:rem 10 lines down
6140 gosub 9000:rem cursor down routine
6150 end
6160 :
6170 :
```

In the routines at 2000, 3000, and 4000, the first line titles the routine. The second line sets the string variable file$ equal to the appropriate program name. The third line transfers control to the new program routine, which is used to display the action the computer is taking when the fourth line executes. This fourth line uses the DOS Wedge syntax to load the specified program file and then begin execution according to that program's set of instructions. The symbol used by the DOS Wedge to load and run a program is the up arrow. This character is often printed out as ^ rather than ↑. (Although it is not impossible to load and run one program from another without the DOS Wedge, it is certainly more complicated and, at this stage, more confusing.) In other words, we simply instruct the computer to go to the diskette, load, and then run the new program. Control is transferred to the new program, and the computer receives and follows the instructions contained in that program. Such transfer of control erases the "mail.menu" program from the computer's memory, replacing those instructions with the instructions in the selected program. That is why it is *very important* to SAVE this "mail.menu" program to diskette before RUNing it. Even though we are not finished with this program, the fourth instruction in each of these routines is operational and will transfer control to the appropriate program, erasing all your typing if you have not saved the program lines to the diskette. The instructions will only become operational if the program is RUN.

The list of files routine and the end routine contain little that is new. Again, each of these routines can be accomplished with fewer lines of programming code, but the additional lines give the user a more pleasing, easier program. You should note that when used within a program the DOS Wedge syntax is a little different—a difference I could not find documented anywhere. In the immediate mode, there is no need for quotation marks surrounding the file name. Yet, within a program or in the deferred mode, the quotation marks are essential. Therefore, to display a list of files on a diskette, @$ (without quote marks) works fine from outside a program, but @$ gives a syntax error if used within a program. Inside a program (as an instuction-line with a line number), the syntax must be: @"$". The same rule also applies to other DOS Wedge commands used from within programs.

The routine at 8000 (y/n input routine) and 9000 (cursor down routine) are the same routines presented in earlier programs. The code can also be found in the complete listing of the "mail.menu" program given at the end of this chapter. The routines at 7000 (new program routine) and 19000 (return key routine) are new and will be covered in some detail. Neither of these routines is necessary since, in some cases, single line instructions can accomplish the same thing. The inclusion of these routines, though, makes the entire "mail.menu" program a much more "professional" looking program.

```
7000 rem **--new program routine--**
7010 print home$:rem clr/home
7020 cd = 2:rem 2 lines down
7030 gosub 9000:rem cursor down routine
7040 print "You have selected the ";file$:print:print "program."
7050 print:print:print
7060 print "Is this the program you want?"
7080 gosub 8000:rem y/n input routine
7090 if yes$ = "n" then 500:rem menu
7100 print home$:rem clr/home
7110 cd = 5:rem 5 lines down
7120 gosub 9000:rem cursor down routine
7130 print tab(tb)
7140 print rvs$;
7150 print "Please wait!"
7160 print:print:print
7170 print tab(tb + 5)
7180 print rvs$;
7190 print "I'm loading. . . ."
7200 print:print:print
7210 print tab(tb + 10)
7220 print rvs$;
7230 print file$
7240 poke 19,0:rem restore input prompt
7250 return
7260 :
7270 :
```

The main purpose of this routine is to notify the user that the computer is changing programs. Some programs take a while to load from the diskette, and rather than have the user sit with a blank screen, the program should inform what action is being taken. The only action instruction comes in line 7240. Location 19 is restored to the original value before the computer changes programs. It is a very good idea to try to leave things in their original form when you leave a program. The same principle can apply to the colors used for text, background, and border. But since information is still being displayed, it is acceptable to leave the color settings and allow the next program to change the colors if necessary.

```
19000 rem **--return key routine--**
19010 poke 198,0:rem clr kbrd buffer
19020 for i = 631 to 640
19030 poke i,0:rem no value
19040 next i
19050 x = peek(197):rem store key press
19060 if x = 1 then 19080:rem 1 = rtn
19070 goto 19050:rem if not 1 go back
19080 poke 198,1:rem allow for cursor
19090 poke 631,0:rem clr kbrd
19100 nu$ = "":rem clr string variable
19110 return
```

The entire purpose of this routine is to check for the press of the RETURN key. When the question mark used for the input prompt is disabled with a poke 19,32, the actual input routine in the operating system is changed. Sometimes the changes are desirable, and other times the changes require considerable code to fix. The latter is the case in this situation. Location 198 is used to inform the computer of the number of characters waiting in the keyboard buffer. Locations 631 to 640 are the actual keyboard buffer area. These locations are cleared by the code in lines 19020 to 19040. Memory location 197 stores a value for each key pressed. Unfortunately, this value is *not* the same value used in determining the code for all characters (*i.e.*, ASCII). This value, stored in location 197, is a Commodore value derived from the location of the keys on the keyboard. Furthermore, it is a rather complicated calculated value. The best advice is to simply memorize the values of desired keys or establish a *table* (list of values) of all the keys. A list of the values obtained when each key is pressed is included in the appendix. The value of the return key is one. Therefore, when the numeric variable x equals 1, we know that the return key has been pressed. The keyboard buffer must be cleared prior to the check (the loop in lines 19020–19040), or x might pick up a previous return key. When x does equal 1, the computer can proceed to the end of this subroutine. Lines 19080, 19090, and 19100 restore values and prepare the computer to leave the routine. Line 19110 returns control to the instruction following the origination instruction.

When you have all the program lines typed in, save it to disk as "mail.menu".

```
←mail.menu
```

The "mail.menu" program should take up 17 blocks and leave the diskette with

592 blocks free. Now, all that is needed to run any of our programs is: ↑ mail.menu. Then, choose a number and let the computer do the rest. Please notice that I have included a choice for a program that we do not yet have, that is, *file correction program* (lines 690 and 4000–4030) and an update to the "mail.reader1" program called "mail.reader2" (lines 3010 and 3030). But we still do not have a system of programs. What will happen, for example, when you are finished adding information and the information has been written out to the disk? Will the program return you to this new "mail.menu" program? If you are not sure, check any of our previous programs to see if they contain instructions to load and run this "mail.menu" program. Instead, each program contains an instruction-line, line 5010, that ends the operation of the program. That is the reason we must include instructions to run "mail.menu" in each of our previous programs. We can add the necessary lines to each program by loading the respective program into the computer's memory, adding the appropriate line numbers, and then saving each program back to the diskette under its same name. Type:

```
/mail create
```

The return to menu routine is:

```
5000 rem **--return to program menu--**
5010 poke 19,0:rem restore input prompt
5020 rem clr/home cursor down routine
5030 print home$:cd = 5:gosub 9000
5040 print tab(5)
5050 print rvs$;
5060 print "LOADING THE MAIL.MENU PROGRAM"
5070 ↑ "mail.menu"
5080 :
5090 :
```

When you have finished, type:

```
←@:mail.create
```

Follow the same procedure for "mail.adder2". Type:

```
/mail.adder2
```

Now, instead of retyping the above instructions, use the cursor up key to go to the 5 in line 5000. If you press the RETURN key on each of the line numbers between 5000 and 5090, those lines will be added to the "mail.adder2" program just as if you had retyped them. Again, when you have finished, remember to save the corrected version. Type:

```
←@:mail.adder2
```

If you display the directory, you will see that the "mail.adder2" program has increased the number of blocks it uses by one to a total of 19. That increase thus decreases the number of free blocks to 591. We now have a system of programs that work together and are controlled by one master program. There is no need to go through all the antics that are sometimes involved in building one large program. In addition, it is much easier to make changes to individual programs than to change something in a large program that might have an unnoticed effect. This borders somewhat on programmer preference, but I have found this method to be easy.

We now have a system that will create a file, add to that file, and, in a primitive way, read the file. Two main tasks are left: (1) improving the display features of the "mail.reader1" program, and (2) creating a program that will change and delete information in the file. One other feature that we will add within our display program is the reformatting of our data with the possibility of creating a new file for these reformatted data. We will begin with the program to increase our display options.

MAIL.READER2

Our present program displays every line in the "adrs-data" file, including the two separator symbols. You don't really want to see those symbols, so eliminating them should be one of the first tasks in creating a new display program. What else would be nice or useful to have in this display program? The computer could display a list of just the names of the individuals in the file. How about a list of the names and addresses without the phone numbers? Can we get a display of a single name, address, and phone number? How about a single name and address, without a phone number? What about an alphabetical list? Can we have a range of names and addresses displayed rather than just the entire list or a single individual? The answer to all these questions is "yes," we can do these things and others also. With all these possibilities, the obvious solution would be to have a menu for these choices.

There are several ways to go about creating a program that uses the same routines as other programs. The most obvious is to rekey in all the instructions (*i.e.*, type everything in again). A far better (and faster) method is to use a programmer's utility program that allows the merging of program segments. If you have such a utility (such as the aforementioned SYSRES program), operational routines can be saved separately on a diskette that contains a *library* of such routines. Then, when you are creating a new program, these routines can be incorporated directly into the new program without the necessity of retyping the instructions and with the certain knowledge that the routines will operate correctly (if you have been consistent and careful in the choice of your variable names, *etc.*). If the routine needs to be placed at a different point in the new program, a renumber utility program can alter the line numbers of the routine so that the routine will fit within the desired program. The use of such utility programs is widespread among professional programmers and may help explain why a programmer's work will look similar from program to program.

Without a utility program, you can approximate the library of routines by loading a program that contains many of the routines you will be using, changing instruction-lines and line numbers that need changing, deleting lines that will not be used, and adding instruction-lines that are needed. This method is certainly more time consuming than if you had access to a good utility program, but it is also less expensive. The results, if you are careful, should be the same. I will give the specific instructions necessary to change the "mail.adder2" program into our new "mail.reader2" program. But if you become confused or lost, you can always turn to the end of this chapter and type in the full listing of this "mail.reader2" program directly or obtain the diskette. The instructions may sound complicated or time consuming, but I assure you that the instructions will work if followed exactly. I have tested these instructions to make certain that they do not contain errors.

First, load the "mail.adder2" program (but make certain that you have saved any program in memory and/or that you have loaded the DOS Wedge program). Type:

```
/mail.adder2
```

Change line 100 to:

```
100 rem ***--mail.reader2--***
```

Add line 225:

```
225 :bnk$ = chr$( 10):rem blank line
```

Change line 240 to:

```
240 poke 53280,14:rem border = lt.blue
```

Change line 260 to:

```
260 poke 53281, 2:rem set bkgrd to red
```

Change line 270 to:

```
270 rem **--user message--**
```

And finally, change line 285 to:

```
285 dim tlines$(rec),nd$(rec),u(rec),r(rec),ad$(rec),zi$(rec)
```

Down to line 300, these are the only additions or changes that need to be made. Beginning at line 300, we have a large number of instructions that are not needed in "mail.reader2". If we could delete a range of lines, we would want to delete everything from line 300 through line 960. Since we cannot, the next best thing is to type the unnecessary instruction's line number and immediately press the return key. The sequence of typing a line number and immediately pressing the return key causes the computer to erase the previous instruction associated with that line number and replace it with the new instruction. Since there is no new instruction, the line number has no value and, therefore, ceases to be a part of the program. We have *deleted* that line number and its unnecessary instruction. As troublesome as it may sound, this delete sequence must be followed for all lines from 300 to 960. Since all the numbers are in increments of ten, we need not check the actual numbers used. I found that the process takes about two minutes and has less chance of error than re-entering all duplicate instruction-lines from scratch. But type carefully. A misplaced digit can result in the wrong line being eliminated.
{RETURN} indicates that the RETURN key is to be pressed.

```
300 {RETURN}
310 {RETURN}
320 {RETURN}
330 {RETURN}
340 {RETURN}
       .
       .
       .
(all intervening numbers)
       .
       .
       .
920 {RETURN}
930 {RETURN}
940 {RETURN}
950 {RETURN}
960 {RETURN}
```

When you have finished deleting the lines, list 300–960 in order to make certain that all lines have been deleted. In the same way, delete all line numbers from 2000 through 2160 and 3000 through 3140.

The next group of instructions are the ones most likely to cause confusion. The intent is to change the line numbers in the currently titled "print label routine". By changing the line numbers, we will transfer the instructions in this routine to a routine called "display routine" that will exist beginning with line number 10000. First, list lines 1000 to 1100 by typing: list 1000–1100. Second, use the SHIFT key and the cursor up/down key to move the cursor up to the 1 in line 1000. Third, using just the cursor left/right, position the cursor on the second digit of the line number (the first 0 in this case). Fourth, use the SHIFT key and the INST/DEL to insert one space between the 1 and the first 0. Fifth, type the number zero (press the 0 key). Sixth, press the RETURN key to accept the line as correct. The computer now has a line 1000 and a line 10000. The cursor should be blinking on top of the 1 in line 1010.

You should repeat steps three, four, five, and six for the remaining lines. Then, list line numbers 1110 to 1230 and begin with the second step. Again, steps three, four, five, and six should be followed for each of these listed lines. When you are finished, you will have the beginning of our new "display routine".

You now have two routines that are the same except for their line numbers. We no longer need the instructions that exist between 1000 and 1330, so use the method described above to delete these lines. Once again, although somewhat tedious, this procedure is probably less prone to error than retyping all the instructions between 1000 and 1230. Please notice that you are to renumber only through line 1230 but should delete the entire "print label routine" (including lines 1251, 1252, 1253, 1254, and 1255) once the appropriate lines have been copied to lines 10000 to 10230.

A few lines in this "display routine" must still be changed. Change line 10000 to:

```
10000 rem **--display routine--**
```

You can accomplish this change either by editing the existing line or typing the line over again. If you want to make the change by editing the existing line, first list line 10000 by typing: list 10000. Second, use the SHIFT key and the cursor up/down key to move the cursor up to the 1 in line 10000. Third, using just the cursor left/right key, position the cursor on the character *p* in the word *print* and type: display routine. Fourth, use the cursor left/right key to place the cursor on the first right-side dash. Fifth, use the INST/DEL key to delete the now duplicate letters *e n i t* (reading from right to left in the same manner the DEL key functions). Sixth, press the RETURN key to accept the corrected version of this instruction line. This same procedure can be used to edit, correct, or change any existing instruction line.

Continuing with the necessary changes in the new display routine, change line 10040 to:

```
10040 print "Would you like a paper print out?"
```

Delete lines 10060 and 10070:

```
10060 {RETURN}
10070 {RETURN}
```

Change the indicated lines to:

```
10080 gosub 18000:rem y/n input routine
10090 if yes$ = "y" then 10120:rem prnt
10100 if yes$ = "n" then 10300:rem scrn
10210 gosub 18000:rem y/n input routine
10220 if yes$ = "n" then 10000
```

Finally, add the following lines:

```
10240 rem *-printer display-*
10250 file    = 4
10260 dvic    = 4
10270 cmnd = 7
10280 goto 10500:rem open instruction
10290 :
10300 rem *-screen display-*
10310 file    = 3
10320 dvic    = 3
10330 cmnd = 1
10340 goto 10500:rem open instruction
10350 :
10360 :
10500 rem *-open instruction-*
10510 open file,dvic,cmnd
10520 return
10530 :
10540 :
10550 :
```

This new display routine allows us to use one print statement in each of our different display options. The output will go to either the printer (device number

4) or to the screen (device number 3), depending on the response given to the question displayed by line 10040.

Two more routines need to be moved. List lines 8000 through 8120. Use the procedure presented above to renumber these lines so that they are lines 18000 through 18120. First, list lines 8000 to 8120 by typing: list 8000–8120. Second, use the SHIFT key and the cursor up/down key to move the cursor up to the 8 in line 8000. Third, use the SHIFT key and the INST/DEL key to insert one space before the 8. Fourth, type the number one (press the 1 key). Fifth, press the RETURN key to accept the line as correct. Steps three, four, and five should be repeated for each of the listed lines. When all the lines have been changed, the routine still at 8000 needs to be deleted. Carefully delete lines 8000 through 8120 in the manner described above: 8000 {RETURN}, 8010 {RETURN}, *etc*. Finally, the newly renumberd "y/n input routine" has one line that must be changed and one line that should be added. Change line 18100 to:

```
18100 goto 18000:rem begin again
```

Add line 18130:

```
18130 :
```

The addition of this line is purely aesthetic. The longer the program, the more space between routines is needed. Now list 5000 to 5090. Move the cursor up to the 5 in 5000. Type a number 8 in place of the 5 and press the RETURN key. Continue to change each of the listed lines. Once all the lines have been changed, delete lines 5000 to 5090. For aesthetic reasons, add 9050 : and 9060 :. To be sure that all lines have been deleted, list 300–8000. If you have followed these directions exactly, the only line that should show on the screen is line 8000.

To finish, we need two brief subroutines: the "return key subroutine" and the "return-to-menu subroutine".

```
19000 rem **--return key routine--**
19010 poke 198,0:rem clr kbrd buffer
19020 for i = 631 to 640
19030 poke i,0:rem no value
19040 next i
19050 x = peek(197):rem store key press
19060 if x = 1 then 19080:rem 1 = rtn
19070 goto 19050:rem if not 1 go back
19080 poke 19,0:rem restore input prompt
19090 poke 198,1:rem allow for cursor
19100 poke 631,0:rem clr kbrd
```

```
19110 nu$ = "":rem clr string variable
19120 return
19130 :
19140 :
19150 :
20000 rem **--menu return routine--**
20010 print#file
20020 close file
20030 print
20050 print "Press ";wht$;"RETURN";ylw$;" to go to Display Menu:"
20060 gosub 19000:rem return key routine
20070 print
20080 goto 400:rem display menu routine
20070 print
20080 goto 400:rem display menu routine
```

The "return key routine" is the same one used in the "mail.menu" program. The "return to menu routine" closes the file so that the user can decide differently on every part of the program. Line 20080 returns the user to the menu.

With this last change, we have concluded the modification of the "mail.adder2" program. The program in the computer's memory is the "skeleton" of the soon-to-be "mail.reader2". You may want to save this portion of the eventual complete program out to either the diskette or tape. Line 100 should be changed to reflect the correct name of this "program."

```
←shell
```

The "shell" program should be 12 blocks long, leaving 579 blocks free. There are two reasons for saving an incomplete program. First, you might want to save an incomplete program just to be certain that you do not lose many hours of work in case the power should go out. Second, an incomplete program can serve as a "shell" for other programs. This shell might be used to help create the correction program for example.

Now, we need to fill in the "shell" with the remaining structure of the "mail.reader2" program. We will begin with a menu of the options available. Type carefully and add the following lines:

```
400 rem **--menu routine--**
410 tb = 5:rem tab value--5 spaces rt.
420 print home$:rem clr/home
430 print wht$
440 print tab(tb + 3)
450 print rvs$;
```

```
460 print "DISPLAY MENU"
470 print ylw$
480 print:print tab(tb)
490 print "1. INFORMATION--ORIG. ORDER"
500 print:print tab(tb)
510 print "2. NAMES ONLY"
520 print:print tab(tb)
530 print "3. INFORMATION--NO PHONE"
540 print:print tab(tb)
550 print "4. SPECIFIC NAME"
560 print:print tab(tb)
570 print "5. SPECIFIC NAME--NO PHONE"
580 print:print tab(tb)
590 print "6. INFORMATION--RANGE"
600 print:print tab(tb)
610 print "7. INFORMATION--ALPHABETICAL"
620 print:print tab(tb)
630 print "8. RETURN TO PROGRAM MENU"
640 print:print tab(tb)
650 input "Which Number Please ";nu$
660 number = val(nu$)
670 :
```

If you have been following along with our programs, these lines of code should now be easy to understand. We are doing the same sequence of programming we did when we created the "mail.menu" program. We format the menu display and request a number. The next series of program lines is familiar also.

```
680 if number = 1 then 1000
690 if number = 2 then 2000
700 if number = 3 then 3000
710 if number = 4 then 4000
720 if number = 5 then 5000
730 if number = 6 then 6000
740 if number = 7 then 7000
750 if number = 8 then 8000
760 :
```

Now, you have the basic structure for the rest of the program. All that is necessary is to fill in the code for each routine. But what happens if the user enters a character other than a number between 1 and 8? This possibility is the reason for the incorrect choice message routine that follows. If the number does not contain a value between 1 and 8, the computer will not branch to any of the major routines. Immediately after the computer has checked the value of the number against the constant value of 8 (line 750), the computer will proceed to the next instruction. Type the following:

```
770 rem *-incorrect choice message-*
780 print:print tab(tb)
790 print rvs$;"Incorrect Choice!"
800 print:print tab(tb)
810 print "Press ";wht$;"RETURN";ylw$;" to continue:";
820 gosub 19000:rem return key routine
830 goto 400: rem menu--check again
840 :
850 :
860 :
```

This small routine displays a message whenever the user enters a number that is not between 1 and 8. After the Incorrect Choice message (line 790) has been displayed, the user is told to press the RETURN key (line 810) in order to again be given the opportunity to enter a valid number (line 830). Once the user has entered a valid number, control passes to the desired routine.

NOTE: The routines get progressively more difficult to follow, and it really is not the intent of this book to teach the concepts behind routines such as sorting and searching. But it is within its scope to present examples of such routines so that readers can make use of these routines in their own file-manipulation programs.

■ *Original Order Routine*

```
1000 rem **--original order routine--**
1010 gosub 10000:rem display routine
1020 rem clr/home cursor down routine
1030 print home$:cd = 3:gosub 9000
1040 for i = 1 to tk
1050 if tlines$(i) = "*" then 1080
1060 if tlines$(i) = "!" then print#file,bnk$:goto 1080
1070 print#file,tlines$(i)
1080 next i
1090 goto 20000:rem menu return routine
1100 :
1110 :
1120 :
```

If you look closely, this routine is very similar to the original "mail.reader1" display routine (lines 1000 to 1040). All this routine does is display all the information lines in the file in the order they were entered. But with lines 1050 and 1060, we have eliminated the display of the separator symbols "*" and "!". There are two additional lines that are new. Lines 1010 and 1090 direct the computer to separate routines used by each of the main routines. Line 1010, as indicated by the rem statement, will be the code that asks if the user wants the information displayed on a printer or on the screen. This instruction uses a GOSUB statement which directs the computer to go to the instructions that begin at line 10000 and follow those instructions until the computer encounters a RETURN statement. At that point, the computer returns to the instruction following the GOSUB instruction. Line 1090 is the instruction that directs the computer to the routine that returns the user to the DISPLAY MENU when the user is ready.

■ *Name Only Routine*

```
2000 rem **--name only routine--**
2010 gosub 10000:rem display routine
2020 print home$:rem clr/home
2030 for i = 1 to tk - 1
2040 if tlines$(i) = tlines$(1) then 2080
2050 if tlines$(i) = "!" then 2080
2060 goto 2150
2070 :
2080 rem *-line up numbers-*
2090 if i < 10 then print tab(3)
2100 if i > 9 and i < 100 then print tab(2)
2110 if i > 99 then print tab(1)
2120 :
2130 if tlines$(i) = tlines$(1) then print#file,i;tlines$(1)
2140 if tlines$(i) = "!" then print#file,i + 1;tlines$(i + 1)
2150 next i
2160 goto 20000:rem menu return routine
2170 :
2180 :
2190 :
```

This routine should not be very difficult to understand. We want to print only those lines that follow the "!" separator. We print those lines because those are the lines that should contain the names of the individuals. We need the instruction at 2040 because there was no separator for the first name. We use tk − 1 because we do not want to get to the last "!" separator since there is no name to follow it yet. The instructions in lines 2080 to 2110 provide for the alignment of the number that precedes the name. This number is the number for the first line of information in each set of information-lines.

No Phone Routine

```
3000 rem **--no phone routine--**
3010 gosub 10000:rem display routine
3020 print home$:rem clr/home
3030 for i = 1 to tk
3040 if tlines$(i) = "*" then i = i + 1:goto 3070
3050 if tlines$(i) = "!" then print#file,bnk$:goto 3070
3060 print#file,tlines$(i)
3070 next i
3080 goto 20000:rem menu return routine
3090 :
3100 :
3110 :
```

This routine should look completely familiar. It is practically the same routine we used to print a label in "mail.adder2" (lines 1260 to 1300 in that program). The effect is the same here also. We can print a mailing label for every person in our file with this routine. Because just about every type of printer handles things differently, you will probably need to add some code to this routine to get the labels spaced properly. One method of spacing would be to find out the number of lines on the label and between labels and then adjust the routine to always space just exactly that number of lines regardless of the number of lines to be printed. That method would always start the printer at the top of the label and not center the material on the label, but it is probably the easiest method to develop.

Search Routine

```
4000 rem **--search routine--**
4010 gosub 10000:rem display routine
4020 print home$:rem clr/home
4030 print "Type the word ";wht$;"END";ylw$;" when finished."
4040 poke 19,32:rem disable input ?
4050 print:input "Name to find: ";find$
4060 if find$ = "END" or find$ = "end" then 4240
4070 print
4080 for i = 1 to tk
4090 if tlines$(i) = find$ then 4110
4100 goto 4210
4110 if tlines$(i) = "*" then 4210
```

```
4120 if tlines$(i) = "!" then 4210
4130 print#file,bnk$
4140 print#file,tlines$(i)
4150 print#file,tlines$(i + 1)
4160 print#file,tlines$(i + 2)
4170 if tlines$(i + 3) < > "*" then print#file,tlines$(i + 3)
4180 if tlines$(i + 4) = "*" then 4200
4190 print#file,tlines$(i + 4):goto 4210
4200 print#file,tlines$(i + 5)
4210 next i
4220 print
4230 goto 4030:rem repeat until done
4240 goto 20000:rem menu return routine
4250 :
4260 :
4270 :
```

The routines begin to get more difficult now. To this point, we have not really made any assumptions about the number of lines of information in each set. But with this routine, we make the assumption that there are a maximum of five lines containing information in any set. If you want a greater maximum, then additional code will have to be added to print out those other lines. The additional code would follow the pattern of 4170 to 4200. We begin in the same way with 4000, 4010, and 4020 (our routine name, gosub display routine, and clear screen lines). Line 4040 gives instructions to the user to type the word "END" when the user is finished looking for a specific name. Line 4050 requests the name from the user and stores that name in the string variable "find$". Line 4060 checks the contents of "find$" to see if it contains the word "END" or "end". If it does, the computer is directed to go to line 4240, which further directs the computer to go to the "menu return routine". One might logically ask why 4060 does not instruct the computer to go directly to the "menu return routine". The reason lies in the necessity of structuring the various routines in the same way so that any programmer can locate the exit point of the routine easily. There are a number of GOTO statements in this routine, but all of them direct the computer (and any programmer) to various lines within this routine. In following the logic of this routine (and all the other routines also), one never needs to look outside the routine, except for the display routine and exit routine, which are common to all other routines. The idea is to keep the flow of logic in one place as much as possible. You enter at the top of the routine and exit at the base of the routine. This is the case for all the routines.

Lines 4080 to 4210 are the heart of this routine. They are also the boundaries of the loop used to find and print the information associated with a specific name. Line 4090 checks the contents of tlines$(i) to see if it equals the contents of find$. If it does, the computer is instructed to jump over the next instruction. If it does not, the next instruction is executed. Line 4100 is reached only if the contents of tlines$(i) and find$ do not match, and 4110 is reached only if they do match. Lines 4110 and 4120 check for the separators and skip them when they are found. At this point in the routine, we have found the name we are looking for and now want to print out the information associated with this name. We assume that the first three lines will not contain a separator and, therefore, will automatically print those lines. Lines 4140, 4150, and 4160 accomplish this task. Lines 4170 through 4200 are lines of code that require some thought. If the fourth information-line does not contain the separator "*", then we want to print this line also (4170); but if it does contain the separator, we do not want the fourth information-line printed. Rather, we know that the fifth information-line contains something to be printed (the line following the "*" will have the phone number if there is a phone number). Line 4190 prints the fifth information-line. Line 4180 first checks the fifth information-line to see if it contains the asterisk separator. If it does contain the separator, then we need to jump over 4190 (the instruction that prints that fifth information-line) and, instead, print the sixth information-line (4200). Go back through the explanation if you are not certain you understand. We use this same routine, combined with the previous one, for our next routine.

Search Routine, No Phone

```
5000 rem **--search routine/no phone--**
5010 gosub 10000:rem display routine
5020 print home$:rem clr/home
5030 print "Type the word ";wht$;"END";ylw$;" when finished."
5040 poke 19,32:rem disable input ?
5050 print:input "Name to find? ";find$
5060 if find$ = "END" or find$ = "end" then 5250
5070 print
5080 for i = 1 to tk
5090 if tlines$(i) = find$ then 5110
5100 goto 5220:rem next i
5110 if tlines$(i) = "*" then i = i + 1:goto 5220
5120 if tlines$(i) = "!" then print#file,bnk$:goto 5220
5130 print#file,bnk$
5140 print#file,tlines$(i)
5150 print#file,tlines$(i + 1)
5160 print#file,tlines$(i + 2)
5170 if tlines$(i + 3) <> "*" then print#file,tlines$(i + 3)
5180 if tlines$(i + 3) = "*" then i = i + 1:goto 5220
5190 if tlines$(i + 4) = "*" then i = i + 1:goto 5220
5200 print#file,tlines$(i + 4):goto 5220
5210 print#file,tlines$(i + 5)
```

```
5220 next i
5230 print
5240 goto 5030:rem repeat until done
5250 goto 20000:rem menu return routine
5260 :
5270 :
5280 :
```

I included this routine for a number of reasons. First, it is a very useful routine because, with a printer, one can print out a specific mailing label. Second, it shows how two routines can be combined into a third routine. This latter point is the most important reason. Very few programs will do everything anyone could ever want of them, but if a person understands these separate routines, combining two or more to form others should be possible. Quite a number of combinations are possible and might be useful to some people.

As you can see, this routine is exactly the same as the previous one down to the instruction at 5110. The only difference is that when we find the "*" separator, we add one to *i*, thus skipping the phone number. Lines 5130 through 5170 are the same instructions as 4120 through 4170. The instructions at 5180 and 5190 are the only different instructions. Both of those instructions are simply checking to see which information-line contains the separator symbol and then advancing the counter by one. The end of the routine is the same as the end of the previous routine.

With the routines at 4000 and 5000, you have the ability to search for a specific name and display that name, either with the phone number or without the phone number. But both of these routines require that you know and type in the exact spelling of the name, including spaces. That presents a reason for our next routine, the range routine. With this routine, you will only need to know the starting and ending information-line numbers to be able to display the information you want. You can obtain those numbers from the "names only routine". I will present the range routine only, but you might want to combine this routine with the "names only routine" and possibly some others also.

Range Routine

```
6000 rem **--range routine--**
6010 gosub 10000:rem display routine
6020 rem clr/home cursor down routine
6030 print home$:cd = 3:gosub 9000
6040 input "Type beginning line number please: ";bg
6050 print:print
6060 if bg < 1 then print "Number too small!":goto 6040
6070 input "Type ending line number please: ";ed
```

```
6080 print
6090 if ed > tk then print "Number too large!":goto 6070
6100 for i = bg to ed
6110 if tlines$(i) = "*" then i = i + 1:goto 6140
6120 if tlines$(i) = "!" then print#file,bnk$:goto 6140
6130 print#file,tlines$(i)
6140 next i
6150 goto 20000:rem menu return routine
6160 :
6170 :
6180 :
```

Line 6040 asks for the beginning information-line number. Remember that you can check the numbers first by using the "names only routine" or by actually including that routine at the beginning of this one. Line 6060 checks the number typed to see if it is less than 1, the number of the first information-line. If it is too small, a message is printed and the user is again asked for a beginning number. Line 6070 requests the ending information-line number and goes through the same checking process, this time for a number larger than the maximum number of information-lines. Then comes our loop (6100 to 6140). I have included the code for printing the information without the phone number (6110), thus providing a routine that can print out a selected range of mailing labels.

I have tried to show how you can take various routines and combine them in just about any way you might want. With the addition of each new routine, the number of possible combinations of routines increases so much that no single programmer could include all possibilities within one program, but, with a minimum of understanding, everyone can create combinations of routines to meet their needs.

■ *Alphabetical Order Routine*

We come now to the most complex of our routines. I will not even attempt to explain the logic involved in all parts of this alphabetizing routine since complete books have been written on various sorting techniques. The sort method I am including is sometimes called the *Quicksort* technique. There are a number of other public domain sorting routines that I could have used, such as the bubble sort or the Shell–Metzner sort, but I decided on the Qucksort because it is very efficient and somewhat less publicized. I modified the sort to enable it to work with string variables. Otherwise, the sort subroutine is a standard routine that can be used in a number of different ways to order lists composed of numbers or letters. For example, if you want to display the information in the "adrs-data" file in zip code order, you first need to access the zip codes and then use the Quicksort subroutine to arrange the zip codes and their associated information-lines in either ascending or descending order. The creation of such a routine would require that you completely understand another feature of this routine: the flexibility possible with string variables and the manner of utilizing that flexibility. Again, I will not try to fully explain the logic or programming power behind the BASIC statements of LEFT$, MID$, or RIGHT$. I strongly encourage you to learn as much as possible about these BASIC statements and how they can be used to take string variables apart and put them back together in just about any way you want.

This alphabetizing routine will be presented in two sections. The first section makes use of this string variable flexibility to: access the last section of characters in that first information-line; reverse the order of that information-line, placing the last section of characters first; (*i.e.*, David Miller becomes Miller, David); and then combine all other information-lines associated with this first line into one long string variable, ad$(i). The second section alphabetizes the list now stored in the string variable nd$(j).

```
7000 rem **--alphabetical order routine--**
7005 rem clr/home cursor down routine
7010 print home$:cd = 5:gosub 9000
7020 print rvs$;"WORKING--PLEASE DON'T TOUCH!!"
7030 print ylw$
7040 :
7050 :
7060 rem *-get first info.-line-*
7070 for i = 1 to tk - 1
7080 if tlines$(i) = tlines$(1) then 7130
7090 if tlines$(i) = "!" then i = i + 1:goto 7130
7100 goto 7240:rem next i
7110 :
7120 :
7130 rem reverse order
7140 char = len(tlines$(i))
7150 for va = 1 to char:if asc(mid$(tlines$(i),va,1)) = 32 then vz = va
7160 next va
7170 if vz = 0 or vz > char then ad$(i) = tlines$(i):goto 7190
7180 ad$(i) = mid$(tlines$(i),vz + 1,char - vz) + ",  " +
     left$(tlines$(i),vz)
7190 ad$(i) = ad$(i) + "**" + tlines$(i + 1) + "**" + tlines$(i + 2)
7200 if tlines$(i + 3) <> "*" then ad$(i) = ad$(i) + "**" + tlines$(i
     + 3)
7210 if tlines$(i + 4) = "*" then 7230
7220 ad$(i) = ad$(i) + "**" + tlines$(i + 4):goto 7240
7230 ad$(i) = ad$(i) + "**" + tlines$(i + 5)
7240 next i
7250 :
```

```
7260 :
7270 rem renumber for sort
7280 j = 1
7290 for i + 1 to tk
7300 if len(ad$(i)) > 0 then nd$(j) = ad$(i):j = j + 1
7310 next i
7320 n = j - 1
7330 :
7340 :
```

As you can see, the routines get more complex. If you do not understand the left$, mid$, and right$ statements, the best thing to do is to get a clear definition of them from a book devoted to teaching BASIC and then practice their uses. Essentially, they perform the functions for which they are named. The left$ statement will retrieve a specified number of characters beginning at the left side of a string variable. Left$(a$,4) gets the first four characters of the string variable a$; *i.e.*, if a$ equals "COMMODORE-64", left$(a$,4) is "COMM". The right$ statement retrieves a specified number of characters from the right-most character of a string variable. Right$(b$,3) gets the last three characters in the string variable b$; *i.e.*, if b$ equals "COMMODORE-64", right$(b$,3) is "-64". The mid$ statement retrieves a specified number of characters from a specified position within a string variable. Mid$(c$,2,6) gets the next six characters beginning at the second character in the string variable c$; i.e. if c$ equals "COMMODORE-64", mid$(c$,2,6) is "OMMODO".

Therefore, the instructions in 7060 to 7100 identify the first information-line in each set of data. Lines 7130 through 7240 reverse the order of the first information-line and then combine all the other information-lines associated with it. Finally, 7270 to 7320 are the instructions that renumber the sets of information in such a way that the sort subroutine can function.

```
7350 rem ***--quicksort--***
7360 sa = 1
7370 print:print
7380 print rvs$;"STILL WORKING--PLEASE DON'T TOUCH!!"
7390 u(1) = 1
7400 r(1) = n
7410 ua   = u(sa)
7420 ra   = r(sa)
7430 sa   = sa - 1
7440 uz   = ua
7450 rz   = ra
7460 x$   = nd$(int((ua + ra)/2))
7470 c    = c + 1
```

```
7480 if nd$(uz) = x$ or nd$(uz) > x$ then 7510
7490 uz = uz + 1
7500 goto 7470
7510 c = ca
7520 if x$ = nd$(rz) or x$ > nd$(rz) then 7550
7530 rz = rz - 1
7540 goto 7510
7550 if uz > rz then 7620
7560 s = s + 1
7570 t$ = nd$(uz)
7580 nd$(uz) = nd$(rz)
7590 nd$(rz) = t$
7600 uz = uz + 1
7610 rz = rz - 1
7620 if uz = rz or uz < rz then 7470
7630 if uz = ra or uz > ra then 7670
7640 sa = sa + 1
7650 u(sa) = uz
7660 r(sa) = ra
7670 ra = rz
7680 if ua < ra then 7440
7690 if sa > 0 then 7410
7700 rem sort completed!
7710 :
7720 :
```

Now, you have access to a sorting method. The only code necessary outside this subroutine to transfer it to another program is to set:

1. The dim of u() and r() to the number of things to be sorted.
2. The numeric variable *n* = to the number of things to be sorted.

If you have a different sort method that you like or understand better and want to include it instead, the code for your sort should replace the code between lines 7350 and 7700.

We still need to display the results after sorting. I am going to present the code to display the results in an elementary way. This display routine may not work exactly right if your original file is not in the following format:

Information-line # 1: First Last (name)

Information-line # 2: Address

Information-line # 3: City State Zip

Information-line # 4: *

Information-line # 5: Phone number

Information-line # 6: !

The new, alphabetized display should have the following format:

Information-line # 1: Last, First (name)

Information-line # 2: Address

Information-line # 3: City State Zip

Information-line # 4: Phone number

I will leave to those of you who want to or are able to use the flexibility in string variables to format the display in any way you desire.

```
7730 rem **--display--**
7740 gosub 10000:rem display routine
7745 rem clr/home cursor down routine
7750 print home$:cd = 3:gosub 9000
7760 for i = 1 to n
7770 vz = 1:q = 1
7780 char = len(nd$(i))
7790 for va = 1 to char
7800 if mid$(nd$(i),va,2) = "**" then 7820
7810 goto 7850
7820 zi$(q) = mid$(nd$(i),vz,va - vz)
7830 vz = va + 2
7840 q = q + 1
7850 next va
7860 :
7870 zi$(q) = mid$(nd$(i),vz,char - (vz - 1))
7880 :
7890 for e = 1 to q
7900 print#file,zi$(e)
7910 next e
7920 :
7930 print#file,bnk$
7940 next i
7950 goto 20000:rem menu return routine
7960 :
7970 :
7980 :
```

We now have an opportunity to create a sequential access file in a way that may be more powerful than in our *mailing list system*. The usefulness of the new file-creation method depends on the programmer's knowledge of and willingness to work with string variables (*i.e.*, left$, mid$, right$, len, str$, val, and dim). All the associated information with tlines$(1), that is, the address, city, state, zip code, and phone number, are stored in the string variable nd$(1). Everything for the next name is stored in nd$(2), and so on. If you want to locate the zip code, all you need to do is use the mid$ function to determine where in the string the zip code is located. You could use the same mid$ function with our present file setup, but it might be more difficult to precisely locate the zip code. (For instance, some people might put the zip code on a separate line, while others would put it on the same line as the city and state. If everything is combined into one string variable, it might be easier to locate for all possible situations.) I have used a lot of conditional statements because there are many possibilities, and the correct choice often depends upon a number of factors: the programmer's experience and preference, the value of the file being established, the necessity of backup, the amount of use the file will get, and so forth. The code necessary to establish a separate file for our now-alphabetized information should be easy to develop.

Have you saved this new "mail.reader2" program? If not, be certain that the program is still in memory and type the following:

```
←mail.reader2
```

By using a different name from our original display program, the number 2 instead of the number 1, we have not written over that original program. Now, the list of files should show:

```
0 "form.10-20-84       " 84 2a
1     "hello"              prg
2     "example"            prg
1     "address file"       seq
12    "mail.create"        prg
1     "adrs-ptr"           seq
1     "adrs-data"          seq
4     "mail.reader1"       prg
15    "mail.adder1"        prg
19    "mail.adder2"        prg
17    "mail.menu"          prg
12    "shell"              prg
37    "mail.reader2"       prg
542 blocks free
```

The number of free blocks may be different, depending on the number of blocks used in the "adrs-data" sequential file. If you have already added a few names and addresses, then the number of blocks in that file will be larger than one and the number of free blocks will be less than 542. In the next chapter, we will examine ways of correcting, changing, or deleting information from our file.

QUESTIONS

1. *True or False:* Commodore-64 BASIC allows you to run a program from within another program.
2. What Commodore BASIC word allows you to horizontally position text on the screen?
3. Which BASIC word is used to instruct the computer to go to a subroutine?
4. Which BASIC word is used to instruct the computer to return from a subroutine?
5. *True or False:* In programming, it is a good idea to have just one main entrance and exit point in every routine.
6. Name three public domain sorting routines.
7. What are the three main BASIC words that provide a great deal of power in working with strings?
8. What BASIC word retrieves a specified number of characters from a specified position within a string variable?
9. Name four other BASIC words that can be used in some way with string variables.
10. *True or False:* When you save a file with the same name as a file already on the disk, the first file is replaced by the second file.

ANSWERS

1. False. Possible only after loading the DOS Wedge
2. TAB. Must be used in a print statement
3. GOSUB
4. RETURN
5. True
6. Bubble, Quicksort, Shell–Metzner
7. LEFT$, RIGHT$, MID$
8. MID$
9. LEN, STR$, VAL, DIM
10. False. Unless the replace character (@) is used

Program for MAIL.MENU

```
100 rem ***--mail.menu--***
110 :
120 :
130 rem **--initialization--**
140 home$ = chr$(147):rem clr/home
150 ::cd$ = chr$( 17):rem cursor down
160 ::cu$ = chr$(145):rem cursor up
170 ::cl$ = chr$(157):rem cursor left
180 ::cr$ = chr$( 29):rem cursor right
190 :blk$ = chr$(144):rem black
200 :ylw$ = chr$(158):rem yellow
210 :wht$ = chr$(  5):rem white
220 :rvs$ = chr$( 18):rem reverse video
230 :
240 poke 53280,14:rem border = lt.blue
250 poke 53272,23:rem upper/lower case
260 poke 53281, 6:rem set bkgrd to blue
270 :
280 :
500 rem **--menu--**
510 tb = 5:rem tab value--5 spaces rt.
520 print home$:rem clr/home
530 print wht$
540 print tab(tb + 3)
550 print rvs$;
560 print "MAIL PROGRAM MENU"
570 print
580 print ylw$
590 print tab(tb)
600 print "1. FILE CREATION PROGRAM"
610 print:print tab(tb)
620 print "2. FILE ADDITION PROGRAM"
630 print:print tab(tb)
640 print "3. FILE DISPLAY PROGRAM"
650 print:print tab(tb)
660 print "4. FILE CORRECTION PROGRAM"
670 print:print tab(tb)
680 print "5. LIST OF FILES"
690 print:print tab(tb)
700 print "6. END"
710 print:print tab(tb)
720 poke 19,32:rem disable input ?
730 input "Which Program Number? ";nu$
740 number = val(nu$)
750 :
760 if number = 1 then 1000
770 if number = 2 then 2000
780 if number = 3 then 3000
790 if number = 4 then 4000
800 if number = 5 then 5000
810 if number = 6 then 6000
820 :
```

```
830 rem *-incorrect choice message-*
840 print:print
850 print tab(tb)
860 print rvs$;"Incorrect Choice!"
870 print
880 print tab(tb)
890 print "Press ";wht$;"RETURN";ylw$;" to continue:";
900 gosub 19000:rem return key routine
910 goto 500:rem menu--check again
920 :
930 :
1000 rem **--file creation prog.--**
1010 print home$:rem clr/home
1020 cd = 2:rem 2 lines down
1030 gosub 9000:rem cursor down routine
1040 print tab(15)
1050 print rvs$;
1060 print "WARNING!"
1070 print:print
1080 print "If the 'adrs-data' file already exists"
1090 print
1100 print "do NOT run this program!"
1110 print
1120 print "Do you want the file creation program?"
1130 print
1140 gosub 8000:rem y/n input routine
1150 if yes$ = "n" then 500:rem menu
1160 print:print
1170 print "Are you sure? Type ";wht$;"YES";ylw$;" if you are:";
1180 input yes$
1190 if yes$ = "YES" or yes$ = "yes" then 1210
1200 goto 1000:rem check again
1210 file$ = "MAIL.CREATE"
1220 gosub 7100:rem new program routine after question
1230 ^"mail.create":rem load & run
1240 :
1250 :
2000 rem **--file addition prog.--**
2010 file$ = "MAIL.ADDER2"
2020 gosub 7000:rem new program routine
2030 ^"mail.adder2":rem load & run
2040 :
2050 :
3000 rem **--file display prog.--**
3010 file$ = "MAIL.READER2"
3020 gosub 7000:rem new program routine
3030 ^"mail.reader2":rem load & run
3040 :
3050 :
4000 rem **--file correction prog.--**
4010 file$ = "MAIL.CORRECTION"
4020 gosub 7000:rem new program routine
4030 ^"mail.correction":rem load & run
4040 :
4050 :
```

```
5000 rem **--list of files routine--**
5010 print home$:rem clr/home
5020 @"$":rem wedge/diskette directory
5030 print cu$;chr$(13):rem 13 = rtn
5040 print "Are you ready to return to the menu?"
5050 print
5060 gosub 8000:rem y/n input routine
5070 if yes$ = "y" then 500:rem menu
5080 goto 5000:rem check again
5090 :
5100 :
6000 rem **--end routine--**
6010 poke 19,0:rem restore input prompt
6020 print home$:rem clr/home
6030 cd = 5:rem 5 lines down
6040 gosub 9000:rem cursor down routine
6050 print tab(tb)
6060 print rvs$;
6070 print "That's all for this session!"
6080 print:print:print
6090 print tab(tb + 5)
6100 print rvs$;
6110 print "See you next time."
6120 print ylw$
6130 cd = 10:rem 10 lines down
6140 gosub 9000:rem cursor down routine
6150 end
6160 :
6170 :
7000 rem **--new program routine--**
7010 print home$:rem clr/home
7020 cd = 2:rem 2 lines down
7030 gosub 9000:rem cursor down routine
7040 print "You have selected the ";file$:print:print
     "program."
7050 print:print:print
7060 print "Is this the program you want?"
7070 print
7080 gosub 8000:rem y/n input routine
7090 if yes$ = "n" then 500:rem menu
7100 print home$:rem clr/home
7110 cd = 5:rem 5 lines down
7120 gosub 9000:rem cursor down routine
7130 print tab(tb)
7140 print rvs$;
7150 print "Please wait!"
7160 print:print:print
7170 print tab(tb + 5)
7180 print rvs$;
7190 print "I'm loading...."
7200 print:print:print
7210 print tab(tb + 10)
7220 print rvs$;
7230 print file$
7240 poke 19,0:rem restore input prompt
```

```
7250 return
7260 :
7270 :
8000 rem **--y/n input routine--**
8010 print "Type a ";wht$;"Y";ylw$;" or ";wht$;"N";ylw$;" :";
8020 poke 19,32:rem disable input ?
8030 input yes$
8040 print
8050 if yes$ = "y" or yes$ = "Y" then yes$ = "y":return
8060 if yes$ = "n" or yes$ = "N" then yes$ = "n":return
8070 print
8080 print rvs$;"Incorrect Choice!";ylw$
8090 print
8100 goto 8000:rem check again
8110 :
8120 :
9000 rem **--cursor down routine--**
9010 for i = 1 to cd
9020 print cd$;
9030 next i
9040 return
9050 :
9060 :
19000 rem **--return key routine--**
19010 poke 198,0:rem clr kbrd buffer
19020 for i = 631 to 640
19030 poke i,0:rem no value
19040 next i
19050 x = peek(197):rem store key press
19060 if x = 1 then 19080:rem 1 = rtn
19070 goto 19050:if not 1 go back
19080 poke 198,1:rem allow for cursor
19090 poke 631,0:rem clr kbrd
19100 nu$ = "":rem clr string variable
19110 return

ready.
```

■ Program for SHELL

```
100 rem ***--shell--***
110 :
120 :
130 rem **--initialization--**
140 home$ = chr$(147):rem clr/home
150 ::cd$ = chr$( 17):rem cursor down
160 ::cu$ = chr$(145):rem cursor up
170 ::cl$ = chr$(157):rem cursor left
180 ::cr$ = chr$( 29):rem cursor right
190 :blk$ = chr$(144):rem black
200 :ylw$ = chr$(158):rem yellow
210 :wht$ = chr$(  5):rem white
220 :rvs$ = chr$( 18):rem reverse video
225 :bnk$ = chr$( 10):rem blank line
230 :
240 poke 53280,14:rem border = lt.blue
250 poke 53272,23:rem upper/lower case
260 poke 53281, 2:rem set bkgrd to red
265 :
266 :
270 rem **--user message--**
271 print home$:rem clr/home
272 cd = 5:rem 5 lines down
273 gosub 9000:rem cursor down routine
274 print ylw$;"ONE MOMENT PLEASE!"
275 :
276 :
277 rem **--file input routine--**
278 :
279 rem *-pointer file-*
280 open 2,8,2,"0:adrs-ptr,seq,read"
281 input#2,rec
282 close 2
283 :
284 rem *-data file-*
285 dim tlines$(rec),nd$(rec),u(rec),r(rec),ad$(rec),zi$(rec)
286 open 3,8,3,"0:adrs-data,seq,read"
287 for i = 1 to rec
288 input#3,tlines$(i)
289 next i
290 close 3
291 :
292 tk = rec:rem total k = # of lines
293 :
294 :
8000 rem **--return to program menu--**
8010 poke 19,0:rem restore input prompt
8020 rem clr/home cursor down routine
8030 print home$:cd = 5:gosub 9000
8040 print tab(tb)
8050 print rvs$;
8060 print "LOADING THE MAIL MENU PROGRAM"
8070 ^"mail.menu"
```

```
8080 :
8090 :
9000 rem **--cursor down routine--**
9010 for i = 1 to cd
9020 print cd$;
9030 next i
9040 return
9050 :
9060 :
10000 rem **--display routine--**
10010 print home$:rem clr/home
10020 cd = 3:rem 3 lines down
10030 gosub 9000:rem cursor down routine
10040 print "Would you like a paper print out?"
10050 print
10080 gosub 18000:rem y/n input routine
10090 if yes$ = "y" then 10120:rem prnt
10100 if yes$ = "n" then 10300:rem scrn
10110 :
10120 print home$:rem clr/home
10130 cd = 3:rem 3 lines down
10140 gosub 9000:rem cursor down routine
10150 print "Please make sure the printer"
10160 print
10170 print "is on and ready to use."
10180 print
10190 print "Are you ready to begin printing?"
10200 print
10210 gosub 18000:rem y/n input routine
10220 if yes$ = "n" then 10000
10230 :
10240 rem *-printer display-*
10250 file = 4
10260 dvic = 4
10270 cmnd = 7
10280 goto 10500:rem open instruction
10290 :
10300 rem *-screen display-*
10310 file = 3
10320 dvic = 3
10330 cmnd = 1
10340 goto 10500:rem open instruction
10350 :
10360 :
10500 rem *-open instruction-*
10510 open file,dvic,cmnd
10520 return
10530 :
10540 :
10550 :
18000 rem **--y/n input routine--**
18010 print "Type a ";wht$;"Y";ylw$;" or ";wht$;"N";ylw$;" :";
18020 poke 19,32:rem disable input ?
18030 input yes$
18040 print
18050 if yes$ = "y" or yes$ = "Y" then yes$ = "y":return
```

```
18060 if yes$ = "n" or yes$ = "N" then yes$ = "n":return
18070 print
18080 print rvs$;"Incorrect Choice!";ylw$
18090 print
18100 goto 18000:rem begin again
18110 :
18120 :
18130 :
19000 rem **-return key routine--**
19010 poke 198,0:rem clr kbrd buffer
19020 for i = 631 to 640
19030 poke i,0:rem no value
19040 next i
19050 x = peek(197):rem store key press
19060 if x = 1 then 19080:rem 1 = rtn
19070 goto 19050:rem if not 1 go back
19080 poke 19,0:rem restore input prompt
19090 poke 198,1:rem allow for cursor
19100 poke 631,0:rem clr kbrd
19110 nu$ = "":rem clr string variable
19120 return
19130 :
19140 :
19150 :
20000 rem **--menu return routine--**
20010 print#file
20020 close file
20030 print
20040 poke 19,32:rem disable input ?
20050 print "Press ";wht$;"RETURN";ylw$;" to go to Display
      Menu:"
20060 gosub 19000:rem return key routine
20070 print
20080 goto 400:rem display menu routine

ready.
```

■ Program for MAIL.READER2

```
100 rem ***--mail.reader2--***
110 :
120 :
130 rem **--initialization--**
140 home$ = chr$(147):rem clr/home
150 ::cd$ = chr$( 17):rem cursor down
160 ::cu$ = chr$(145):rem cursor up
170 ::cl$ = chr$(157):rem cursor left
180 ::cr$ = chr$( 29):rem cursor right
190 :blk$ = chr$(144):rem black
200 :ylw$ = chr$(158):rem yellow
210 :wht$ = chr$(  5):rem white
220 :rvs$ = chr$( 18):rem reverse video
225 :bnk$ = chr$( 10):rem blank line
230 :
240 poke 53280,14:rem border = lt.blue
250 poke 53272,23:rem upper/lower case
260 poke 53281, 2:rem set bkgrd to red
265 :
266 :
270 rem **--user message--**
271 print home$:rem clr/home
272 cd = 5:rem 5 lines down
273 gosub 9000:rem cursor down routine
274 print ylw$;"ONE MOMENT PLEASE!"
275 :
276 :
277 rem **--file input routine--**
278 :
279 rem *-pointer file-*
280 open 2,8,2,"0:adrs-ptr,seq,read"
281 input#2,rec
282 close 2
283 :
284 rem *-data file-*
285 dim tlines$(rec),nd$(rec),u(rec),r(rec),ad$(rec),zi$(rec)
286 open 3,8,3,"0:adrs-data,seq,read"
287 for i = 1 to rec
288 input#3,tlines$(i)
289 next i
290 close 3
291 :
292 tk = rec:rem total k = # of lines
293 :
294 :
295 :
400 rem **--menu--**
410 tb = 5:rem tab value--5 spaces rt.
420 print home$:rem clr/home
430 print wht$
440 print tab(tb + 3)
450 print rvs$;
460 print "DISPLAY MENU"
```

```
470 print ylw$
480 print:print tab(tb)
490 print "1. INFORMATION--ORIG. ORDER"
500 print:print tab(tb)
510 print "2. NAMES ONLY"
520 print:print tab(tb)
530 print "3. INFORMATION--NO PHONE"
540 print:print tab(tb)
550 print "4. SPECIFIC NAME"
560 print:print tab(tb)
570 print "5. SPECIFIC NAME--NO PHONE"
580 print:print tab(tb)
590 print "6. INFORMATION--RANGE"
600 print:print tab(tb)
610 print "7. INFORMATION--ALPHABETICAL"
620 print:print tab(tb)
630 print "8. RETURN TO PROGRAM MENU"
640 print:print tab(tb)
650 input "Which Number Please ";nu$
660 number = val(nu$)
670 :
680 if number = 1 then 1000
690 if number = 2 then 2000
700 if number = 3 then 3000
710 if number = 4 then 4000
720 if number = 5 then 5000
730 if number = 6 then 6000
740 if number = 7 then 7000
750 if number = 8 then 8000
760 :
770 rem *-incorrect choice message-*
780 print:print tab(tb)
790 print rvs$;"Incorrect Choice!"
800 print:print tab(tb)
810 print "Press ";wht$;"RETURN";ylw$;" to continue:";
820 gosub 19000:rem return key routine
830 goto 400:rem menu--check again
840 :
850 :
860 :
1000 rem **--original order routine--**
1010 gosub 10000:rem display routine
1020 rem clr/home cursor down routine
1030 print home$:cd = 3:gosub 9000
1040 for i = 1 to tk
1050 if tlines$(i) = "*" then 1080
1060 if tlines$(i) = "!" then print#file,bnk$:goto 1080
1070 print#file,tlines$(i)
1080 next i
1090 goto 20000:rem menu return routine
1100 :
1110 :
1120 :
2000 rem **--name only routine--**
2010 gosub 10000:rem display routine
2020 print home$:rem clr/home
```

```
2030 for i = 1 to tk - 1
2040 if tlines$(i) = tlines$(1) then 2080
2050 if tlines$(i) = "!" then 2080
2060 goto 2150
2070 :
2080 rem *-line up numbers-*
2090 if i < 10 then print tab(3)
2100 if i > 9 and i < 100 then print tab(2)
2110 if i > 99 then print tab(1)
2120 :
2130 if tlines$(i) = tlines$(1) then print#file,i;tlines$(1)
2140 if tlines$(i) = "!" then print#file,i + 1;tlines$(i + 1)
2150 next i
2160 goto 20000:rem menu return routine
2170 :
2180 :
2190 :
3000 rem **--no phone routine--**
3010 gosub 10000:rem display routine
3020 print home$:rem clr/home
3030 for i = 1 to tk
3040 if tlines$(i) = "*" then i = i + 1:goto 3070
3050 if tlines$(i) = "!" then print#file,bnk$:goto 3070
3060 print#file,tlines$(i)
3070 next i
3080 goto 20000:rem menu return routine
3090 :
3100 :
3110 :
4000 rem **--search routine--**
4010 gosub 10000:rem display routine
4020 print home$:rem clr/home
4030 print "Type the word ";wht$;"END";ylw$;" when finished."
4040 poke 19,32:rem disable input ?
4050 print:input "Name to find: ";find$
4060 if find$ = "END" or find$ = "end" then 4240
4070 print
4080 for i = 1 to tk
4090 if tlines$(i) = find$ then 4110
4100 goto 4210
4110 if tlines$(i) = "*" then 4210
4120 if tlines$(i) = "!" then 4210
4130 print#file,bnk$
4140 print#file,tlines$(i)
4150 print#file,tlines$(i + 1)
4160 print#file,tlines$(i + 2)
4170 if tlines$(i + 3) <> "*" then print#file,tlines$(i + 3)
4180 if tlines$(i + 4) = "*" then 4200
4190 print#file,tlines$(i + 4):goto 4210
4200 print#file,tlines$(i + 5)
4210 next i
4220 print
4230 goto 4030:rem repeat until done
4240 goto 20000:rem menu return routine
4250 :
4260 :
```

```
4270 :
5000 rem **--search routine/no phone--**
5010 gosub 10000:rem display routine
5020 print home$:rem clr/home
5030 print "Type the word ";wht$;"END";ylw$;" when finished."
5040 poke 19,32:rem disable input ?
5050 print:input "Name to find: ";find$
5060 if find$ = "END" or find$ = "end" then 5250
5070 print
5080 for i = 1 to tk
5090 if tlines$(i) = find$ then 5110
5100 goto 5220:rem next i
5110 if tlines$(i) = "*" then i = i + 1:goto 5220
5120 if tlines$(i) = "!" then print#file,bnk$:goto 5220
5130 print#file,bnk$
5140 print#file,tlines$(i)
5150 print#file,tlines$(i + 1)
5160 print#file,tlines$(i + 2)
5170 if tlines$(i + 3) <> "*" then print#file,tlines$(i + 3)
5180 if tlines$(i + 3) = "*" then i = i + 1:goto 5220
5190 if tlines$(i + 4) = "*" then i = i + 1:goto 5220
5200 print#file,tlines$(i + 4):goto 5220
5210 print#file,tlines$(i + 5)
5220 next i
5230 print
5240 goto 5030:rem repeat until done
5250 goto 20000:rem menu return routine
5260 :
5270 :
5280 :
6000 rem **--range routine--**
6010 gosub 10000:rem display routine
6020 rem clr/home cursor down routine
6030 print home$:cd = 3:gosub 9000
6040 input "Type beginning line number please: ";bg
6050 print:print
6060 if bg < 1 then print "Number too small!":goto 6040
6070 input "Type ending line nuber please: ";ed
6080 print
6090 if ed > tk then print "Number too large!":goto 6070
6100 for i = bg to ed
6110 if tlines$(i) = "*" then i = i + 1:goto 6140
6120 if tlines$(i) = "!" then print#file,bnk$:goto 6140
6130 print#file,tlines$(i)
6140 next i
6150 goto 20000:rem menu return routine
6160 :
6170 :
6180 :
7000 rem **--alphabetical order--**
7005 rem clr/home cursor down routine
7010 print home$:cd = 5:gosub 9000
7020 print rvs$;"WORKING--PLEASE DON'T TOUCH!!"
7030 print ylw$
7040 :
7050 :
```

```
7060 rem *-get first info.-line-*
7070 for i = 1 to tk - 1
7080 if tlines$(i) = tlines$(1) then 7130
7090 if tlines$(i) = "!" then i = i + 1:goto 7130
7100 goto 7240:rem next i
7110 :
7120 :
7130 rem reverse order
7140 char = len(tlines$(i))
7150 for va = 1 to char:if asc(mid$(tlines$(i),va,1)) = 32
     then vz = va
7160 next va
7170 if vz = 0 or vz > char then ad$(i) = tlines$(i):goto 7190
7180 ad$(i) = mid$(tlines$(i),vz + 1,char - vz) + ", " +
     left$(tlines$(i),vz)
7190 ad$(i) = ad$(i) + "**" + tlines$(i + 1) + "**" +
     tlines$(i + 2)
7200 if tlines$(i + 3) <> "*" then ad$(i) = ad$(i) + "**" +
     tlines$(i + 3)
7210 if tlines$(i + 4) = "*" then 7230
7220 ad$(i) = ad$(i) + "**" + tlines$(i + 4):goto 7240
7230 ad$(i) = ad$(i) + "**" + tlines$(i + 5)
7240 next i
7250 :
7260 :
7270 rem renumber for sort
7280 j = 1
7290 for i = 1 to tk
7300 if len(ad$(i)) > 0 then nd$(j) = ad$(i): j = j + 1
7310 next i
7320 n = j - 1
7330 :
7340 :
7350 rem ***--quicksort--***
7360 sa = 1
7370 print:print
7380 print rvs$;"STILL WORKING--PLEASE DON'T TOUCH!!"
7390 u(1) = 1
7400 r(1) = n
7410 ua = u(sa)
7420 ra = r(sa)
7430 sa = sa - 1
7440 uz = ua
7450 rz = ra
7460 x$ = nd$(int((ua + ra)/2))
7470 c = c + 1
7480 if nd$(uz) = x$ or nd$(uz) > x$ then 7510
7490 uz = uz + 1
7500 goto 7470
7510 c = ca
7520 if x$ = nd$(rz) or x$ > nd$(rz) then 7550
7530 rz = rz - 1
7540 goto 7510
7550 if uz > rz then 7620
7560 s = s + 1
```

```
7570 t$ = nd$(uz)
7580 nd$(uz) = nd$(rz)
7590 nd$(rz) = t$
7600 uz = uz + 1
7610 rz = rz - 1
7620 if uz = rz or uz < rz then 7470
7630 if uz = ra or uz > ra then 7670
7640 sa = sa + 1
7650 u(sa) = uz
7660 r(sa) = ra
7670 ra = rz
7680 if ua < ra then 7440
7690 if sa > 0 then 7410
7700 rem sort completed!
7710 :
7720 :
7730 rem **--display--**
7740 gosub 10000:rem display routine
7745 rem clr/home cursor down routine
7750 print home$:cd = 3:gosub 9000
7760 for i = 1 to n
7770 vz = 1:q = 1
7780 char = len(nd$(i))
7790 for va = 1 to char
7800 if mid$(nd$(i),va,2) = "**" then 7820
7810 goto 7850
7820 zi$(q) = mid$(nd$(i),vz,va - vz)
7830 vz = va + 2
7840 q = q + 1
7850 next va
7860 :
7870 zi$(q) = mid$(nd$(i),vz,char - (vz - 1))
7880 :
7890 for e = 1 to q
7900 print#file,zi$(e)
7910 next e
7920 :
7930 print#file,bnk$
7940 next i
7950 goto 20000:rem menu return routine
7960 :
7970 :
7980 :
8000 rem **--return to program menu--**
8010 poke 19,0:rem restore input prompt
8020 rem clr/home cursor down routine
8030 print home$:cd = 5:gosub 9000
8040 print tab(tb)
8050 print rvs$;
8060 print "LOADING THE MAIL MENU PROGRAM"
8070 ^"mail.menu"
8080 :
8090 :
9000 rem **--cursor down routine--**
9010 for i = 1 to cd
```

```
9020 print cd$;
9030 next i
9040 return
9050 :
9060 :
10000 rem **--display routine--**
10010 print home$:rem clr/home
10020 cd = 3:rem 3 lines down
10030 gosub 9000:rem cursor down routine
10040 print "Would you like a paper print out?"
10050 print
10080 gosub 18000:rem y/n input routine
10090 if yes$ = "y" then 10120:rem prnt
10100 if yes$ = "n" then 10300:rem scrn
10110 :
10120 print home$:rem clr/home
10130 cd = 3:rem 3 lines down
10140 gosub 9000:rem cursor down routine
10150 print "Please make sure the printer"
10160 print
10170 print "is on and ready to use."
10180 print
10190 print "Are you ready to begin printing?"
10200 print
10210 gosub 18000:rem y/n input routine
10220 if yes$ = "n" then 10000
10230 :
10240 rem *-printer display-*
10250 file = 4
10260 dvic = 4
10270 cmnd = 7
10280 goto 10500:rem open instruction
10290 :
10300 rem *-screen display-*
10310 file = 3
10320 dvic = 3
10330 cmnd = 1
10340 goto 10500:rem open instruction
10350 :
10360 :
10500 rem *-open instruction-*
10510 open file,dvic,cmnd
10520 return
10530 :
10540 :
10550 :
18000 rem **--y/n input routine--**
18010 print "Type a ";wht$;"Y";ylw$;" or ";wht$;"N";ylw$;" :";
18020 poke 19,32:rem disable input ?
18030 input yes$
18040 print
18050 if yes$ = "y" or yes$ = "Y" then yes$ = "y":return
18060 if yes$ = "n" or yes$ = "N" then yes$ = "n":return
18070 print
18080 print rvs$;"Incorrect Choice!";ylw$
```

```
18090 print
18100 goto 18000:rem begin again
18110 :
18120 :
18130 :
19000 rem **--return key routine--**
19010 poke 198,0:rem clr kbrd buffer
19020 for i = 631 to 640
19030 poke i,0:rem no value
19040 next i
19050 x = peek(197):rem store key press
19060 if x = 1 then 19080:rem 1 = rtn
19070 goto 19050:if not 1 go back
19080 poke 19,0:rem restore input prompt
19090 poke 198,1:rem allow for cursor
19100 poke 631,0:rem clr kbrd
19110 nu$ = "":rem clr string variable
19120 return
19130 :
19140 :
19150 :
20000 rem **--menu return routine--**
20010 print#file
20020 close file
20030 print
20040 poke 19,32:rem disable input ?
20050 print "Press ";wht$;"RETURN";ylw$;" to go to the Display
      Menu:";
20060 gosub 19000:rem return key routine
20070 print
20080 goto 400:rem display menu routine

ready.
```

7 correcting sequential files

If you saved the "shell" program, you can load this file and use it as the basis for our "mail.correction" program. A few lines will need to be changed to reflect needs within this specific program, and the display routine may not be needed, but making use of the "shell" is much easier than retyping instruction-lines used by other programs.

The first change is with line 100, which should be changed to reflect the proper name for this program. Type:

```
100 rem ***--mail.correction--***
```

Then change the following lines to:

```
240 poke 53280, 5:rem border = green
260 poke 53281,11:rem set bkgrd = grey1
285 dim tlines$(rec)
20010 rem if printer used:print#file
20020 rem if printer used:close file
20030 print:print
20050 print "Press ";wht$;"RETURN";ylw$;" to go to the
      Correct.Menu:";
```

The "return to program menu" routine, lines 8000 to 8100, needs to be moved to lines 4000 to 4100 and then deleted from 8000 to 8100. The easiest way to do this is to:

```
list 8000–8100
```

Use the cursor up key (SHIFT and up/down arrow CRSR key) to go up to the 8 in 8000. Press the key with the number four (4) on it, changing the line number from 8000 to 4000. Then press the RETURN key. The cursor will drop to the next line number, 8010. You should repeat the procedure for each of the listed lines. When you have changed the line-numbers, the instructions still exist at lines 8000 to 8100. The last step is to delete these instruction-lines by typing the line-number and immediately pressing the RETURN key:

```
8000 {RETURN}
8010 {RETURN}
8020 {RETURN}
   .
   .
   .
8080 {RETURN}
8090 {RETURN}
8100 {RETURN}
```

The display routine is not necessary in this "mail.correction" program, but you can leave it as part of this program in case you ever want to print out information that has been changed or deleted. If you do not want to leave the display routine in the program, you will need to follow the procedure just described and delete the instructions in lines 10000 to 10550.

If you did not save the "shell" program, you will need to retype all the instructions included in it for the "mail.correction" program (see the listing at the end of Chapter 6). All that remains is to fill in the "shell" with instructions specific to our present program needs. Once again we need a menu, so our routine beginning at line 400 will be much the same also.

```
400 rem**--menu routine--**
410 tb = 5:rem tab value--5 sps.rt.
420 print home$:rem clr/home
430 print wht$
440 print tab(tb + 3)
450 print rvs$;
460 print "CORRECTION MENU"
470 print ylw$
```

```
480 print:print tab(tb)
490 print "1. CHANGE OR CORRECT INFO."
500 print:print tab(tb)
510 print "2. DELETE INFORMATION"
520 print:print tab(tb)
530 print "3. WRITE REVISED FILE"
540 print:print tab(tb)
550 print "4. RETURN TO PROGRAM MENU"
560 print:print tab(tb)
570 input "Which Number Please";nu$
580 number = val(nu$)
590 :
600 if number = 1 then 1000
610 if number = 2 then 2000
620 if number = 3 then 3000
630 if number = 4 then 4000
640 :
650 gosub 7000:rem incorrect choice
660 goto 400:rem menu routine
670:
680:
```

By now, these statements should be familiar enough that no further explanation need be given. We are going to simply display a menu of a number of choices on the screen. If the user has not typed a valid number, control is first transferred to the "incorrect choice routine" at line 7000 and then returned to the instruction (line 570), which again asks for a number. (The incorrect choice routine, 7000–7090, is listed at the end of the chapter within the mail.correction program. This routine does not contain any new code.)

The correction and deletion routines presented next are only one method out of many possible methods for accomplishing the same task. Some may object to rewriting the entire file for a single correction, but, for now, the method we will use is to bring the entire file into memory, make our necessary corrections or deletions, and then write the file back out to disk again.

CORRECTION ROUTINE

```
1000 rem**--correction routine--**
1010 print home$:rem clr/home
1020 cd = 3:rem 3 lines down
1030 gosub 9000:rem cursor down routine
1040 print tab(tb)
```

```
1050 print "Type a ";wht$;"0";ylw$;" when finished."
1060 print:print tab(tb)
1070 poke 19,32:rem disable input ?
1080 input "Display which line? ";nb$
1090 if nb$ = "0" then 20000:rem menu
1100 nb = val(nb$)
1110 rem incorrect choice/ask again
1120 if nb > tk then gosub 7000:goto 1000
1130 cd = 4:gosub 9000:rem crsr down 4
1140 print tab(tb - 1)
1150 print nb;" ";tlines$(nb)
1160 print:print tab(tb)
1170 print "Is this correct? "
1180 print:print tab(tb)
1190 gosub 18000:rem y/n input routine
1200 if yes$ = "y" then 1000
1210 print:print tab(tb)
1220 print "Type in the correct information:"
1230 print:print tab(tb - 1)
1240 print nb;" ";:input cinfo$
1250 print:tlines$(nb) = cinfo$
1260 rem clr/home--cursor down routine
1270 print home$:cd = 3:gosub 9000
1280 print:print tab(tb - 1)
1290 print nb;" ";tlines$(nb)
1300 print
1310 goto 1160:rem ask again
1320 :
1330 :
```

We ask for the line number the user believes to contain incorrect information. The line of information is displayed. If it is not correct, the individual is given an opportunity to type in the correct information. The amount of new information or corrected information is not limited except by the normal character string limitation. This feature is one big advantage over other correction methods, which may require that the corrected information be exactly the same number of characters as the original information. Finally, the corrected information is displayed and the correct information question is repeated. Line 1200 checks for a positive response to the question about correct information. If the information is correct, the user is taken back to the original request concerning the line number to be displayed. Line 1090 checks for a "0", which indicates that the user wishes to return to the menu. Line 1250 is the instruction that actually exchanges the corrected information for the old information. You will notice that nothing is written to disk at this time. This may cause problems for some individuals. Under this system, it is possible to make a number of changes before the file is rewritten to the disk. It is also possible, therefore, to forget to write the corrected file back to disk. Such a system may be impractical in certain situations, for example, when a somewhat forgetful person is making the changes. But, for our purposes, we want to make all corrections and deletions before rewriting the file.

DELETION ROUTINE

The deletion routine is more complicated than the correction routine.

```
2000 rem **--delete routine--**
2010 print homes$:rem clr/home
2020 cd = 3:gosub 9000:rem crsr down 3
2030 print tab(tb)
2040 print "Type a ";wht$;"0";ylw$;" when finished."
2050 print:print tab(tb)
2060 poke 19,32:rem disable input ?
2070 input "Delete which line? ";nb$
2080 if nb$ = "0" then 20000:rem menu
2090 nb = val(nb$)
2100 rem incorrect choice/ask again
2110 if nb > tk then gosub 7000:goto 2000
2120 cd = 4:gosub 9000:rem crsr down 4
2130 print tab(tb - 1)
2140 print nb;" ";tlines$(nb)
2150 print:print:print tab(tb)
2160 print "Are you sure?"
2170 print:print tab(tb)
2180 print "Type ";wht$;"YES";ylw$;" if you are sure!";
2190 input yes$
2200 if yes$ = "YES" or yes$ = "yes" then 2240
2210 goto 2000:rem begin again
2220 :
2230 :
2240 rem *-display deleted info.-*
2250 j = nb
2260 if tlines$(j) = "!" then 2290
2270 j = j + 1:goto 2260
2280 :
2290 rem *-format numbers & display-*
```

```
2300 rem clr/home--cursor down routine
2310 print home$:cd = 3:gosub 9000
2320 for i = nb to j
2330 if i < 10 then print tab(3)
2340 if i > 9 and i < 100 then print tab(2)
2350 if i > 99 then print tab(1)
2360 print i;" ";tlines$(i)
2370 tlines$(i) = "DELETED":d = d + 1
2380 next i
2390 print
2400 print "DELETING THIS INFORMATION"
2410 :
2420 :
2430 rem *-renumber w/out del.info.-*
2440 q = 1
2450 for i = 1 to tk
2460 if tlines$(i) = "DELETED" then 2490
2470 tlines$(q) = tlines$(i)
2480 q = q + 1
2490 next i
2500 :
2510 rem subtract # of lines deleted for new total
2520 tk = tk - d
2530 d = 0:j = 0
2540 print
2550 goto 20000:rem menu
2560 :
2570 :
2580 :
```

There are other ways of doing the same thing we did in this routine. Some of the other ways might be shorter, but this way is understandable. Several things need to be done in this deletion routine. First, the information to be deleted must be identified, displayed, and then deleted (lines 2000 to 2400). Second, the information following the deleted material must be renumbered (instruction-lines 2430 to 2490) so that there are no empty information-lines; otherwise, an ERROR will occur when these information-lines are encountered. Finally, the number of deleted information-lines must be subtracted (line 2520) from the original total number of lines.

Down to line 2160, there is nothing new. It is essentially the same beginning as the correction routine. At 2250, we set a counter (j) equal to the line number of the name to be deleted. Next, we increase the counter by one until we have found the information-line for the end of the information associated with the individual to be deleted (*i.e.*, the separator symbol "!"). We know which information-lines to delete: the lines beginning with nb and going through j, so now we can use a loop (2320–2380) to delete our information. We use another loop (2450–2490) to do the resequencing of the remaining information. We use two additional counters: to keep track of the new information line-numbers and d to keep track of the number of deleted lines. The q is set to 1 for the beginning of the file, but it could be set to nb, the start of the deleted material. Line 2460 is the key to the resequencing. If tlines$(i) equals the word "DELETED", then the counter q is not increased while the counter i is increased. Remember that q is keeping track of the new line numbers while i is the old line number. Line 2470 resequences the tlines$ string array. Line 2520 subtracts the number of deleted lines from the original number of lines (tk). Line 2550 is necessary in case more information is to be deleted during this session.

```
3000 rem **--file output routine--**
3010 :
3020 rem *-user message-*
3030 rem clr/home--cursor down routine
3040 print home$:cd = 3:gosub 9000
3050 print rvs$;
3060 print tab(tb)
3070 print "UPDATING FILES."
3080 print:print:print tab(tb + 10)
3090 print rvs$;:print "PLEASE WAIT!"
3100 :
3110 rem *-delete/rename backup-*
3120 open 3,8,3,"@0:adrs-backup,seq,write"
3130 close 3
3140 @"scratch:adrs-backup"
3150 @"rename:adrs-backup=adrs-data"
3160 :
3170 rem *-pointer file-*
3180 open 2,8,2,"@0:adrs-ptr,seq,write"
3190 print#2,tk
3200 close 2
3210 :
3220 rem *-data file-*
3230 open 3,8,3,"0:adrs-data,seq,write"
3240 for i = 1 to tk
3250 print#3,tlines$(i)
3260 next i
3270 close 3
3280 :
3290 rem *-user message/menu-*
3300 rem clr/home--cursor down routine
```

```
3310 print home$:cd = 5:gosub 9000
3320 print tab(tb)
3330 print rvs$;
3340 print "ALL FINISHED"
3350 cd = 10:gosub 9000
3360 goto 20000:rem menu routine
3370 :
3380 :
3390 :
```

There is something different with this file routine. Where did "adrs-backup" come from? The DOS command "open" will create a file by that name if the file does not already exist. Therefore, if the file "adrs-backup" does not already exist, the command open "adrs-backup" will create a file by that name. Next, we delete that file since it must either be an empty file or a now unnecessary backup copy. (The first time this program is used there will not be an "adrs-backup" file.) Line 3150 renames the file "adrs-data" (which now contains our uncorrected information) so that it becomes "adrs-backup". Finally, we open a new "adrs-data" file and write out our corrected information to it (lines 3220–3270). Line 3360 returns to the menu. At this point, if you have not already done so, you should save this program to the diskette that contains all the other Mailing List System programs.

```
←mail.correction
```

Typing @$ now should show:

```
0  "form.10-20-84       " 84 2a
1      "hello"              prg
2      "example"            prg
1      "address file"       seq
12     "mail.create"        prg
1      "adrs-ptr"           seq
1      "adrs-data"          seq
4      "mail.reader1"       prg
15     "mail.adder1"        prg
19     "mail.adder2"        prg
17     "mail.menu"          prg
12     "shell"              prg
37     "mail.reader2"       prg
27     "mail.correction"    prg
515 blocks free
```

It is not necessary to make changes in the "mail.menu" program in order to include this "mail.correction" program. Remember that additional code was added in anticipation of this program. The Mailing List System should now be complete. (A complete list of the final Mailing List System programs, in proper order, is provided at the end of this chapter.)

This general method of correcting or deleting information has the added benefit of providing us with a backup copy of our precorrected "adrs-data" file. The sequence of opening and deleting a backup file, renaming the uncorrected file as the new backup, and writing out the corrected information to a new file under the original file name is a very useful routine. If you have two disk drives, you can put the backup in one drive and the new master in the other drive and have the computer switch between the two drives. The more drives one has, the greater the flexibility in manipulating files in this manner.

Even without two drives, the "adrs-data" file and the "adrs-backup" file can be put on two different diskettes. Some method of making the computer pause after line 3150 would be necessary in order to allow the user to swap diskettes. Two possibilities would be (1) a loop of a certain duration, or (2) an input statement informing the user that it is time to switch diskettes.

Although the Mailing List System is complete, the system is by no means a commercial data-base program. Many additional routines, programs, and/or features can be added to accomplish specific needs. For example, it would be a good idea to have a program that would copy the "adrs-data" file onto a different diskette. A program that allowed the user to expand the information concerning a particular person would be handy in certain circumstances (*i.e.*, increase from six lines of information to seven or eight lines).

Perhaps the most useful additional program would be one that translated the "adrs-data" file into a format that a word processor could use to merge with a form letter to produce personalized form letters. This task is very easy to do since the format of the "adrs-data" file fits with the format many word processors use for just such *address files*. The advantage of using an existing file for the personalized form letter is the obvious lack of duplication of effort. In other words, if the names and addresses already exist, you do not need to retype them again in the format needed by the word processor.

The advantage of maintaining the names and addresses in a file external to the word-processing system are many. First, you are not limited to a single word processor if you happen to find a better one later. Second, the flexibility and versatility of an external file are far greater than the flexibility or versatility of a file created within the limitations of a specific word processor. Third, external files are more easily sorted and displayed in a variety of ways.

To conclude this chapter, I will present the structure for a program that transforms the "adrs-data" file into the format required for the *mail merge* portion of Commodore's Easy Script program. The process of using information created by one application program with another application program is often referred to as *integration* of data.

The first task is to read in the information from the "adrs-data" file. Second, format the information so that all sets of information have the same number of information-lines and that the separator symbols (* and !) are not part of the new file information. Third, access the first or last name and include it as the last line of each set of information. This first or last name is used for the greeting portion of the form letter. Fourth, if you require other variable information included in each letter, the program should allow for the addition of such variable information to each set of information. Finally, write the restructured file out to the diskette. The information is now in two separate files. It still exists in the "adrs-data" file, and it also now exists in a file that can be used by Easy Script's mail merge portion for the creation of personalized form letters.

In the next chapter, we will take a look at some more techniques for accessing sequential data files.

QUESTIONS

1. *True or False:* Under the correction method presented in this chapter, corrected information is immediately written to the disk.
2. What happens to the original "adrs.data" file once information in it has been changed?
3. What is the BASIC command used to remove unwanted files?
4. What is the BASIC command used to change the name of files?
5. *True or False:* Two disk drives are necessary in order to back up a data file.

ANSWERS

1. False
2. It becomes "adrs.backup".
3. Scratch
4. Rename
5. False

Program for MAIL.CORRECTION

```
100 rem ***--mail.correction--***
110 :
120 :
130 rem **--initialization--**
140 home$ = chr$(147):rem clr/home
150 ::cd$ = chr$( 17):rem cursor down
160 ::cu$ = chr$(145):rem cursor up
170 ::cl$ = chr$(157):rem cursor left
180 ::cr$ = chr$( 29):rem cursor right
190 :blk$ = chr$(144):rem black
200 :ylw$ = chr$(158):rem yellow
210 :wht$ = chr$(  5):rem white
220 :rvs$ = chr$( 18):rem reverse video
225 :bnk$ = chr$( 10):rem blank line
230 :
240 poke 53280, 5:rem border = green
250 poke 53272,23:rem upper/lower case
260 poke 53281,11:rem set bkgrd = grey1
265 :
266 :
270 rem **--user message--**
271 print home$:rem clr/home
272 cd = 5:rem 5 lines down
273 gosub 9000:rem cursor down routine
274 print ylw$;"ONE MOMENT PLEASE!"
275 :
276 :
277 rem **--file input routine--**
278 :
279 rem *-pointer file-*
280 open 2,8,2,"0:adrs-ptr,seq,read"
281 input#2,rec
282 close 2
283 :
284 rem *-data file-*
285 dim tlines$(rec)
286 open 3,8,3,"0:adrs-data,seq,read"
287 for i = 1 to rec
288 input#3,tlines$(i)
289 next i
290 close 3
291 :
292 tk = rec:rem total k = # of lines
293 :
294 :
295 :
400 rem **--menu routine--**
410 tb = 5:rem tab value--5 sps.rt.
420 print home$:rem clr/home
430 print wht$
440 print tab(tb + 3)
450 print rvs$;
460 print "CORRECTION MENU"
```

```
470 print ylw$
480 print:print tab(tb)
490 print "1. CHANGE OR CORRECT INFO."
500 print:print tab(tb)
510 print "2. DELETE INFORMATION"
520 print:print tab(tb)
530 print "3. WRITE REVISED FILE"
540 print:print tab(tb)
550 print "4. RETURN TO PROGRAM MENU"
560 print:print tab(tb)
570 input "Which Number Please";nu$
580 number = val(nu$)
590 :
600 if number = 1 then 1000
610 if number = 2 then 2000
620 if number = 3 then 3000
630 if number = 4 then 4000
640 :
650 gosub 7000:rem incorrect choice
660 goto 400:rem menu routine
670 :
680 :
1000 rem **--correction routine--**
1010 print home$:rem clr/home
1020 cd = 3:rem 3 lines down
1030 gosub 9000:rem cursor down routine
1040 print tab(tb)
1050 print "Type a ";wht$;"0";ylw$;" when finished."
1060 print:print tab(tb)
1070 poke 19,32:rem disable input ?
1080 input "Display which line? ";nb$
1090 if nb$ = "0" then 20000:rem menu
1100 nb = val(nb$)
1110 rem incorrect choice/ask again
1120 if nb > tk then gosub 7000:goto 1000
1130 cd = 4:gosub 9000:rem crsr down 4
1140 print tab(tb - 1)
1150 print nb;" ";tlines$(nb)
1160 print:print tab(tb)
1170 print "Is this correct? "
1180 print:print tab(tb)
1190 gosub 18000:rem y/n input routine
1200 if yes$ = "y" then 1000
1210 print:print tab(tb)
1220 print "Type in the correct information:"
1230 print:print tab(tb - 1)
1240 print nb;" ";:input cinfo$
1250 print:tlines$(nb) = cinfo$
1260 rem clr/home--cursor down routine
1270 print home$:cd = 3:gosub 9000
1280 print:print tab(tb - 1)
1290 print nb;" ";tlines$(nb)
1300 print
1310 goto 1160:rem ask again
1320 :
1330 :
```

```
1340 :
2000 rem **--delete routine--**
2010 print home$:rem clr/home
2020 cd = 3:gosub 9000:rem crsr down 3
2030 print tab(tb)
2040 print "Type a ";wht$;"0";ylw$;" when finished."
2050 print:print tab(tb)
2060 poke 19,32:rem disable input ?
2070 input "Delete which line? ";nb$
2080 if nb$ = "0" then 20000:rem menu
2090 nb = val(nb$)
2100 rem incorrect choice/ask again
2110 if nb > tk then gosub 7000:goto 2000
2120 cd = 4:gosub 9000:rem crsr down 4
2130 print tab(tb - 1)
2140 print nb;" ";tlines$(nb)
2150 print:print:print tab(tb)
2160 print "Are you sure?"
2170 print:print tab(tb)
2180 print "Type ";wht$;"YES";ylw$;" if you are sure!";
2190 input yes$
2200 if yes$ = "YES" or yes$ = "yes" then 2240
2210 goto 2000:rem begin again
2220 :
2230 :
2240 rem *-display deleted info.-*
2250 j = nb
2260 if tlines$(j) = "!" then 2290
2270 j = j + 1:goto 2260
2280 :
2290 rem *-format numbers & display-*
2300 rem clr/home--cursor down routine
2310 print home$:cd = 3:gosub 9000
2320 for i = nb to j
2330 if i < 10 then print tab(3)
2340 if i > 9 and i < 100 then print tab(2)
2350 if i > 99 then print tab(1)
2360 print i;" ";tlines$(i)
2370 tlines$(i) = "DELETED":d = d + 1
2380 next i
2390 print
2400 print "DELETING THIS INFORMATION"
2410 :
2420 :
2430 rem *-renumber w/out del.info.-*
2440 q = 1
2450 for i = 1 to tk
2460 if tlines$(i) = "DELETED" then 2490
2470 tlines$(q) = tlines$(i)
2480 q = q + 1
2490 next i
2500 :
2510 rem subtract # of lines deleted for new total
2520 tk = tk - d
2530 d = 0:j = 0
2540 print
```

```
2550 goto 20000:rem menu
2560 :
2570 :
2580 :
3000 rem **--file output routine--**
3010 :
3020 rem *-user message-*
3030 rem clr/home--cursor down routine
3040 print home$:cd = 3:gosub 9000
3050 print rvs$;
3060 print tab(tb)
3070 print "UPDATING FILES."
3080 print:print:print tab(tb + 10)
3090 print rvs$;:print "PLEASE WAIT!"
3100 :
3110 rem *-delete/rename backup-*
3120 open 3,8,3,"@0:adrs-backup,seq,write"
3130 close 3
3140 @"scratch:adrs-backup"
3150 @"rename:adrs-backup=adrs-data"
3160 :
3170 rem *-pointer file-*
3180 open 2,8,2,"@0:adrs-ptr,seq,write"
3190 print#2,tk
3200 close 2
3210 :
3220 rem *-data file-*
3230 open 3,8,3,"0:adrs-data,seq,write"
3240 for i = 1 to tk
3250 print#3,tlines$(i)
3260 next i
3270 close 3
3280 :
3290 rem *-user message/menu-*
3300 rem clr/home--cursor down routine
3310 print home$:cd = 5:gosub 9000
3320 print tab(tb)
3330 print rvs$;
3340 print "ALL FINISHED"
3350 cd = 10:gosub 9000
3360 goto 20000:rem menu routine
3370 :
3380 :
3390 :
4000 rem **--return to program menu--**
4010 poke 19,0:rem restore input prompt
4020 rem clr/home--cursor down routine
4030 print home$:cd = 5:gosub 9000
4040 print tab(tb)
4050 print rvs$;
4060 print "LOADING THE MAIL MENU PROGRAM"
4070 ^"mail.menu"
4080 :
4090 :
7000 rem **-incorrect choice message-**
7010 print:print:print tab(tb)
```

```
7020 print rvs$;"Incorrect Choice!"
7030 print:print tab(tb)
7040 print "Press ";wht$;"RETURN";ylw$;" to continue:";
7050 gosub 19000:rem return key routine
7060 return
7070 :
7080 :
7090 :
9000 rem **--cursor down routine--**
9010 for i = 1 to cd
9020 print cd$;
9030 next i
9040 return
9050 :
9060 :
10000 rem **--display routine--**
10010 print home$:rem clr/home
10020 cd = 3:rem 3 lines down
10030 gosub 9000:rem cursor down routine
10040 print "Would you like a paper print out?"
10050 print
10080 gosub 18000:rem y/n input routine
10090 if yes$ = "y" then 10120:rem prnt
10100 if yes$ = "n" then 10300:rem scrn
10110 :
10120 print home$:rem clr/home
10130 cd = 3:rem 3 lines down
10140 gosub 9000:rem cursor down routine
10150 print "Please make sure the printer"
10160 print
10170 print "is on and ready to use."
10180 print
10190 print "Are you ready to begin printing?"
10200 print
10210 gosub 18000:rem y/n input routine
10220 if yes$ = "n" then 10000
10230 :
10240 rem *-printer display-*
10250 file = 4
10260 dvic = 4
10270 cmnd = 7
10280 goto 10500:rem open instruction
10290 :
10300 rem *-screen display-*
10310 file = 3
10320 dvic = 3
10330 cmnd = 1
10340 goto 10500:rem open instruction
10350 :
10360 :
10500 rem *-open instruction-*
10510 open file,dvic,cmnd
10520 return
10530 :
10540 :
10550 :
```

```
18000 rem **--y/n input routine--**
18010 print "Type a ";wht$;"Y";ylw$;" or ";wht$;"N";ylw$;" :";
18020 poke 19,32:rem disable input ?
18030 input yes$
18040 print
18050 if yes$ = "y" or yes$ = "Y" then yes$ = "y":return
18060 if yes$ = "n" or yes$ = "N" then yes$ = "n":return
18070 print
18080 print rvs$;"Incorrect Choice!";ylw$
18090 print
18100 goto 18000:rem begin again
18110 :
18120 :
18130 :
19000 rem **--return key routine--**
19010 poke 198,0:rem clr kbrd buffer
19020 for i = 631 to 640
19030 poke i,0:rem no value
19040 next i
19050 x = peek(197):rem store key press
19060 if x = 1 then 19080:rem 1 = rtn.
19070 goto 19050:if not 1 go back
19080 poke 19,0:rem restore input prompt
19090 poke 198,1:rem allow for cursor
19100 poke 631,0:rem clr kbrd
19110 nu$ = "":rem clr string variable
19120 return
19130 :
19140 :
19150 :
20000 rem **--menu return routine--**
20010 rem if printer used:print#file
20020 rem if printer used:close file
20030 print:print
20040 poke 19,32:rem disable input ?
20050 print "Press ";wht$;"RETURN";ylw$;" to go to the
      Correct.Menu:";
20060 gosub 19000:rem return key routine
20070 print
20080 goto 400:rem display menu routine

ready.
```

```
0 "form.10-20-84    " 84 2a
1     "hello"              prg
2     "example"            prg
1     "address file"       seq
12    "mail.create"        prg
1     "adrs-ptr"           seq
1     "adrs-data"          seq
4     "mail.reader1"       prg
15    "mail.adder1"        prg
19    "mail.adder2"        prg
17    "mail.menu"          prg
12    "shell"              prg
37    "mail.reader2"       prg
27    "mail.correction"    prg
515 blocks free.

ready.
```

Program for MAIL.MENU

```
100 rem ***--mail.menu--***
110 :
120 :
130 rem **--initialization--**
140 home$ = chr$(147):rem clr/home
150 ::cd$ = chr$( 17):rem cursor down
160 ::cu$ = chr$(145):rem cursor up
170 ::cl$ = chr$(157):rem cursor left
180 ::cr$ = chr$( 29):rem cursor right
190 :blk$ = chr$(144):rem black
200 :ylw$ = chr$(158):rem yellow
210 :wht$ = chr$(  5):rem white
220 :rvs$ = chr$( 18):rem reverse video
230 :
240 poke 53280,14:rem border = lt.blue
250 poke 53272,23:rem upper/lower case
260 poke 53281, 6:rem set bkgrd to blue
270 :
280 :
500 rem **--menu--**
510 tb = 5:rem tab value--5 spaces rt.
520 print home$:rem clr/home
530 print wht$
540 print tab(tb + 3)
550 print rvs$;
560 print "MAIL PROGRAM MENU"
570 print
```

```
580 print ylw$
590 print tab(tb)
600 print "1. FILE CREATION PROGRAM"
610 print:print tab(tb)
620 print "2. FILE ADDITION PROGRAM"
630 print:print tab(tb)
640 print "3. FILE DISPLAY PROGRAM"
650 print:print tab(tb)
660 print "4. FILE CORRECTION PROGRAM"
670 print:print tab(tb)
680 print "5. LIST OF FILES"
690 print:print tab(tb)
700 print "6. END"
710 print:print tab(tb)
720 poke 19,32:rem disable input ?
730 input "Which Program Number? ";nu$
740 number = val(nu$)
750 :
760 if number = 1 then 1000
770 if number = 2 then 2000
780 if number = 3 then 3000
790 if number = 4 then 4000
800 if number = 5 then 5000
810 if number = 6 then 6000
820 :
830 rem *-incorrect choice message-*
840 print:print
850 print tab(tb)
860 print rvs$;"Incorrect Choice!"
870 print
880 print tab(tb)
890 print "Press ";wht$;"RETURN";ylw$;" to continue:";
900 gosub 19000:rem return key routine
910 goto 500:rem menu--check again
920 :
930 :
1000 rem **--file creation prog.--**
1010 print home$:rem clr/home
1020 cd = 2:rem 2 lines down
1030 gosub 9000:rem cursor down routine
1040 print tab(15)
1050 print rvs$;
1060 print "WARNING!"
1070 print:print
1080 print "If the 'adrs-data' file already exists"
1090 print
1100 print "do NOT run this program!"
1110 print
1120 print "Do you want the file creation program?"
1130 print
1140 gosub 8000:rem y/n input routine
1150 if yes$ = "n" then 500:rem menu
1160 print:print
1170 print "Are you sure? Type ";wht$;"YES";ylw$;" if you are:";
1180 input yes$
1190 if yes$ = "YES" or yes$ = "yes" then 1210
```

```
1200 goto 1000:rem check again
1210 file$ = "MAIL.CREATE"
1220 gosub 7100:rem new program routine after question
1230 ^"mail.create":rem load & run
1240 :
1250 :
2000 rem **--file addition prog.--**
2010 file$ = "MAIL.ADDER2"
2020 gosub 7000:rem new program routine
2030 ^"mail.adder2":rem load & run
2040 :
2050 :
3000 rem **--file display prog.--**
3010 file$ = "MAIL.READER2"
3020 gosub 7000:rem new program routine
3030 ^"mail.reader2":rem load & run
3040 :
3050 :
4000 rem **--file correction prog.--**
4010 file$ = "MAIL.CORRECTION"
4020 gosub 7000:rem new program routine
4030 ^"mail.correction":rem load & run
4040 :
4050 :
5000 rem **--list of files routine--**
5010 print home$:rem clr/home
5020 @"$":rem wedge/diskette directory
5030 print cu$;chr$(13):rem 13 = rtn
5040 print "Are you ready to return to the menu?"
5050 print
5060 gosub 8000:rem y/n input routine
5070 if yes$ = "y" then 500:rem menu
5080 goto 5000:rem check again
5090 :
5100 :
6000 rem **--end routine--**
6010 poke 19,0:rem restore input prompt
6020 print home$:rem clr/home
6030 cd = 5:rem 5 lines down
6040 gosub 9000:rem cursor down routine
6050 print tab(tb)
6060 print rvs$;
6070 print "That's all for this session!"
6080 print:print:print
6090 print tab(tb + 5)
6100 print rvs$;
6110 print "See you next time."
6120 print ylw$
6130 cd = 10:rem 10 lines down
6140 gosub 9000:rem cursor down routine
6150 end
6160 :
6170 :
7000 rem **--new program routine--**
7010 print home$:rem clr/home
```

```
7020 cd = 2:rem 2 lines down
7030 gosub 9000:rem cursor down routine
7040 print "You have selected the ";file$:print:print "program."
7050 print:print:print
7060 print "Is this the program you want?"
7070 print
7080 gosub 8000:rem y/n input routine
7090 if yes$ = "n" then 500:rem menu
7100 print home$:rem clr/home
7110 cd = 5:rem 5 lines down
7120 gosub 9000:rem cursor down routine
7130 print tab(tb)
7140 print rvs$;
7150 print "Please wait!"
7160 print:print:print
7170 print tab(tb + 5)
7180 print rvs$;
7190 print "I'm loading...."
7200 print:print:print
7210 print tab(tb + 10)
7220 print rvs$;
7230 print file$
7240 poke 19,0:rem restore input prompt
7250 return
7260 :
7270 :
8000 rem **--y/n input routine--**
8010 print "Type a ";wht$;"Y";ylw$;" or ";wht$;"N";ylw$;" :";
8020 poke 19,32:rem disable input ?
8030 input yes$
8040 print
8050 if yes$ = "y" or yes$ = "Y" then yes$ = "y":return
8060 if yes$ = "n" or yes$ = "N" then yes$ = "n":return
8070 print
8080 print rvs$;"Incorrect Choice!";ylw$
8090 print
8100 goto 8000:rem check again
8110 :
8120 :
9000 rem **--cursor down routine--**
9010 for i = 1 to cd
9020 print cd$;
9030 next i
9040 return
9050 :
9060 :
19000 rem **--return key routine--**
19010 poke 198,0:rem clr kbrd buffer
19020 for i = 631 to 640
19030 poke i,0:rem no value
19040 next i
19050 x = peek(197):rem store key press
19060 if x = 1 then 19080:rem 1 = rtn
19070 goto 19050:if not 1 go back
19080 poke 198,1:rem allow for cursor
```

```
19090 poke 631,0:rem clr kbrd
19100 nu$ = "":rem clr string variable
19110 return

ready.
```

Program for MAIL.CREATE

```
100 rem ***--mail.create--***
110 :
120 :
130 rem **--initialization--**
140 home$ = chr$(147):rem clr/home
150 ::cd$ = chr$( 17):rem cursor down
160 ::cu$ = chr$(145):rem cursor up
170 ::cl$ = chr$(157):rem cursor left
180 ::cr$ = chr$( 29):rem cursor right
190 :blk$ = chr$(144):rem black
200 :ylw$ = chr$(158):rem yellow
210 :wht$ = chr$(  5):rem white
220 :rvs$ = chr$( 18):rem reverse video
230 :
240 dim line$(20)
250 poke 53272,23:rem upper/lower case
260 poke 53281,0:rem set bkgrd to black
270 :
280 :
300 rem **--keyboard input routine--**
310 k = 1:rem line counter
320 print home$:rem clr/home
330 print tab(5)
340 print rvs$;:rem reverse
350 print "INSTRUCTIONS"
360 print ylw$:rem yellow
370 print "Type name and address as if"
380 print "addressing an envelope."
390 print "Do not use a comma or colon!"
400 print "Press ";wht$;"RETURN";ylw$;
410 print " after each line."
420 print
430 print "Type the word ";wht$;"END";ylw$;" when finished."
440 print
450 print "Type in line ";k;":"
460 poke 19,32:rem disable input ?
470 input line$(k)
480 print
490 if line$(k) = "end" or line$(k) = "END" then 540
500 if line$(k) = "" then print "We need some information.":
    goto 440
510 k = k + 1
520 goto 440:rem go back for more
530 :
```

```
540 line$(k) = "*":rem separator for phone number
550 k = k + 1
560 print home$:rem clr/home
570 cd = 3:rem 3 lines down
580 gosub 9000:rem cursor down routine
590 print "PHONE: ";:print "Press ";wht$;"RETURN";ylw$;" if
    none."
600 input line$(k)
610 if line$(k) = "" then line$(k) = "NONE"
620 k = k + 1
630 line$(k) = "!":rem separator between sets of information
640 :
650 :
660 rem **--correction routine--**
670 print home$:rem clr/home
680 cd = 3:rem 3 lines down
690 gosub 9000:rem cursor down routine
700 print "Do not change the line with the ";wht$;"*";ylw$;"."
710 print "This symbol is used as a separator."
720 print
730 for i = 1 to k - 1
740 print i;" ";line$(i)
750 next i
760 print
770 print "Change any line? ";
780 gosub 8000:rem y/n input routine
790 print
800 if yes$ = "y" then 850
810 if yes$ = "n" then 830
820 :
830 goto 3000:rem file creation routine
840 :
850 print:input "Change which line? ";ln
860 print
870 if ln > k - 1 then print "Number too large!":goto 850
880 if line$(ln) = "*" then print "Line";ln;"is the *":goto 850
890 print "Line";ln;"now is:"
900 print line$(ln)
910 print
920 print "Line";ln;"should be:"
930 input line$(ln)
940 goto 660:rem correction routine
950 :
960 :
3000 rem **--file creation routine--**
3010 :
3020 rem *-pointer file-*
3030 open 2,8,2,"0:adrs-ptr,seq,write"
3040 print#2,k
3050 close 2
3060 :
3070 rem *-data file-*
3080 open 3,8,3,"0:adrs-data,seq,write"
3090 for i = 1 to k
3100 print#3,line$(i)
3110 next i
```

```
3120 close 3
3130 :
3140 :
5000 rem **--return to program menu--**
5010 poke 19,0:rem restore input prompt
5020 rem clr/home cursor down routine
5030 print home$:cd = 5:gosub 9000
5040 print tab(tb)
5050 print rvs$;
5060 print "LOADING THE MAIL MENU PROGRAM"
5070 ^"mail.menu"
5080 :
5090 :
8000 rem **--y/n input routine--**
8010 print "Type a ";wht$;"Y";ylw$;" or ";wht$;"N";ylw$;" :";
8020 poke 19,32:rem disable input ?
8030 input yes$
8040 print
8050 if yes$ = "y" or yes$ = "Y" then yes$ = "y":return
8060 if yes$ = "n" or yes$ = "N" then yes$ = "n":return
8070 print
8080 print rvs$;"Incorrect Choice!";ylw$
8090 print
8100 goto 8000:rem ask again
8110 :
8120 :
9000 rem **--cursor down routine--**
9010 for i = 1 to cd
9020 print cd$;
9030 next i
9040 return

ready.
```

■ Program for MAIL.ADDER2

```
100 rem ***--mail.adder2--***
110 :
120 :
130 rem **--initialization--**
140 home$ = chr$(147):rem clr/home
150 : cd$ = chr$( 17):rem cursor down
160 : cu$ = chr$(145):rem cursor up
170 : cl$ = chr$(157):rem cursor left
180 : cr$ = chr$( 29):rem cursor right
190 :blk$ = chr$(144):rem black
200 :ylw$ = chr$(158):rem yellow
210 :wht$ = chr$(  5):rem white
220 :rvs$ = chr$( 18):rem reverse video
230 :
240 dim line$(20)
250 poke 53272,23:rem upper/lower case
260 poke 53281,0:rem set bkgrd to black
265 :
266 :
270 rem **--new lines for adder--**
271 print home$:rem clr/home
272 cd = 5:rem 5 lines down
273 gosub 9000:rem cursor down routine
274 print ylw$;"ONE MOMENT PLEASE!"
275 :
276 :
277 rem **--file input routine--**
278 :
279 rem *-pointer file-*
280 open 2,8,2,"0:adrs-ptr,seq,read"
281 input#2,rec
282 close 2
283 :
284 rem *-data file-*
285 dim tlines$(rec + 100):rem add up to 100 new lines
286 open 3,8,3,"0:adrs-data,seq,read"
287 for i = 1 to rec
288 input#3,tlines$(i)
289 next i
290 close 3
291 :
292 tk = rec:rem total k = # of lines
293 :
294 :
300 rem **--keyboard input routine--**
310 k = 1:rem line counter
320 print home$:rem clr/home
330 print tab(5)
340 print rvs$;:rem reverse
350 print "INSTRUCTIONS"
360 print ylw$:rem yellow
370 print "Type name and address as if"
380 print "addressing an envelope."
```

```
390 print "Do not use a comma or colon!"
400 print "Press ";wht$;"RETURN";ylw$;
410 print " after each line."
420 print
430 print "Type the word ";wht$;"END";ylw$;" when finished."
440 print
450 print "Type in line ";k;":"
460 poke 19,32:rem disable input ?
470 input line$(k)
480 print
490 if line$(k) = "end" or line$(k) = "END" then 540
500 if line$(k) = "" then print "We need some information.":
    goto 440
510 k = k + 1
520 goto 440:rem go back for more
530 :
540 line$(k) = "*":rem separator for phone number
550 k = k + 1
560 print home$:rem clr/home
570 cd = 3:rem 3 lines down
580 gosub 9000:rem cursor down routine
590 print "PHONE: ";:print "Press ";wht$;"RETURN";ylw$;" if
    none."
600 input line$(k)
610 if line$(k) = "" then line$(k) = "NONE"
620 k = k + 1
630 line$(k) = "!":rem separator between sets of information
640 :
650 :
660 rem **--correction routine--**
670 print home$:rem clr/home
680 cd = 3:rem 3 lines down
690 gosub 9000:rem cursor down routine
700 print "Do not change the line with the ";wht$;"*";ylw$;"."
710 print "This symbol is used as a separator."
720 print
730 for i = 1 to k - 1
740 print i;" ";line$(i)
750 next i
760 print
770 print "Change any line? ";
780 gosub 8000:rem y/n input routine
790 print
800 if yes$ = "y" then 850
810 if yes$ = "n" then 830
820 :
830 goto 1000:rem print label routine
840 :
850 print:input "Change which line? ";ln
860 print
870 if ln > k - 1 then print "Number too large!":goto 850
880 if line$(ln) = "*" then print "Line";ln;"is the *":goto 850
890 print "Line";ln;"now is:"
900 print line$(ln)
910 print
```

```
920 print "Line";ln;"should be:"
930 input line$(ln)
940 goto 660:rem correction routine
950 :
960 :
1000 rem **--print label routine--**
1010 print home$:rem clr/home
1020 cd = 3:rem 3 lines down
1030 gosub 9000:rem cursor down routine
1040 print "Would you like to print a"
1050 print
1060 print "mailing label now?"
1070 print
1080 gosub 8000:rem y/n input routine
1090 if yes$ = "y" then 1120
1100 if yes$ = "n" then 2000
1110 :
1120 print home$:rem clr/home
1130 cd = 3:rem 3 lines down
1140 gosub 9000:rem cursor down routine
1150 print "Please make sure the printer"
1160 print
1170 print "is on and ready to use."
1180 print
1190 print "Are you ready to begin printing?"
1200 print
1210 gosub 8000:rem y/n input routine
1220 if yes$ = "n" then 1000
1230 :
1240 rem **--printer channel--**
1250 open 4,4,7
1251 :
1252 rem first 4 = file #
1253 rem second 4 = printer device #
1254 rem 7 = command for upper/lower case
1255 :
1260 for i = 1 to k
1270 if line$(i) = "*" then i = i + 1:goto 1300
1280 if line$(i) = "!" then 1300
1290 print#4,line$(i)
1300 next i
1310 close 4
1320 :
1330 :
2000 rem **--repeat routine--**
2010 :
2020 rem *-add new lines to exist. file lines-*
2030 for i = 1 to k
2040 tlines$(tk + i) = line$(i):rem tk + i, not tk + 1
2050 next i
2060 tk = tk + k
2070 :
2080 print home$:rem clr/home
2090 cd = 3:rem 3 lines down
2100 gosub 9000:rem cursor down routine
2110 print "Do you want to add more information?"
```

```
2120 gosub 8000:rem y/n input routine
2130 if yes$ = "y" then 300
2140 if yes$ = "n" then 3000
2150 :
2160 :
3000 rem **--file addition routine--**
3010 :
3020 rem *-pointer file-*
3030 open 2,8,2,"@0:adrs-ptr,seq,write"
3040 print#2,tk
3050 close 2
3060 :
3070 rem *-data file-*
3080 open 3,8,3,"@0:adrs-data,seq,write"
3090 for i = 1 to tk
3100 print#3,tlines$(i)
3110 next i
3120 close 3
3130 :
3140 :
5000 rem **--end routine--**
5010 end
5020 :
5030 :
8000 rem **--y/n input routine--**
8010 print "Type a ";wht$;"Y";ylw$;" or ";wht$;"N";ylw$;" :";
8020 poke 19,32:rem disable input ?
8030 input yes$
8040 print
8050 if yes$ = "y" or yes$ = "Y" then yes$ = "y":return
8060 if yes$ = "n" or yes$ = "N" then yes$ = "n":return
8070 print
8080 print rvs$;"Incorrect Choice!";ylw$
8090 print
8100 goto 8000:rem ask again
8110 :
8120 :
9000 rem **--cursor down routine--**
9010 for i = 1 to cd
9020 print cd$;
9030 next i
9040 return

ready.
```

Program for MAIL.READER2

```
100 rem ***--mail.reader2--***
110 :
120 :
130 rem **--initialization--**
140 home$ = chr$(147):rem clr/home
150 :  cd$ = chr$( 17):rem cursor down
160 :  cu$ = chr$(145):rem cursor up
170 :  cl$ = chr$(157):rem cursor left
180 :  cr$ = chr$( 29):rem cursor right
190 : blk$ = chr$(144):rem black
200 : ylw$ = chr$(158):rem yellow
210 : wht$ = chr$(  5):rem white
220 : rvs$ = chr$( 18):rem reverse video
225 : bnk$ = chr$( 10):rem blank line
230 :
240 poke 53280,14:rem border = lt.blue
250 poke 53272,23:rem upper/lower case
260 poke 53281, 2:rem set bkgrd to red
265 :
266 :
270 rem **--user message--**
271 print home$:rem clr/home
272 cd = 5:rem 5 lines down
273 gosub 9000:rem cursor down routine
274 print ylw$;"ONE MOMENT PLEASE!"
275 :
276 :
277 rem **--file input routine--**
278 :
279 rem *-pointer file-*
280 open 2,8,2,"0:adrs-ptr,seq,read"
281 input#2,rec
282 close 2
283 :
284 rem *-data file-*
285 dim tlines$(rec),nd$(rec),u(rec),r(rec),ad$(rec),zi$(rec)
286 open 3,8,3,"0:adrs-data,seq,read"
287 for i = 1 to rec
288 input#3,tlines$(i)
289 next i
290 close 3
291 :
292 tk = rec:rem total k = # of lines
293 :
294 :
295 :
400 rem **--menu--**
410 tb = 5:rem tab value--5 spaces rt.
420 print home$:rem clr/home
430 print wht$
440 print tab(tb + 3)
450 print rvs$;
460 print "DISPLAY MENU"
```

```
470 print ylw$
480 print:print tab(tb)
490 print "1. INFORMATION--ORIG. ORDER"
500 print:print tab(tb)
510 print "2. NAMES ONLY"
520 print:print tab(tb)
530 print "3. INFORMATION--NO PHONE"
540 print:print tab(tb)
550 print "4. SPECIFIC NAME"
560 print:print tab(tb)
570 print "5. SPECIFIC NAME--NO PHONE"
580 print:print tab(tb)
590 print "6. INFORMATION--RANGE"
600 print:print tab(tb)
610 print "7. INFORMATION--ALPHABETICAL"
620 print:print tab(tb)
630 print "8. RETURN TO PROGRAM MENU"
640 print:print tab(tb)
650 input "Which Number Please ";nu$
660 number = val(nu$)
670 :
680 if number = 1 then 1000
690 if number = 2 then 2000
700 if number = 3 then 3000
710 if number = 4 then 4000
720 if number = 5 then 5000
730 if number = 6 then 6000
740 if number = 7 then 7000
750 if number = 8 then 8000
760 :
770 rem *-incorrect choice message-*
780 print:print tab(tb)
790 print rvs$;"Incorrect Choice!"
800 print:print tab(tb)
810 print "Press ";wht$;"RETURN";ylw$;" to continue:";
820 gosub 19000:rem return key routine
830 goto 400:rem menu--check again
840 :
850 :
860 :
1000 rem **--original order routine--**
1010 gosub 10000:rem display routine
1020 rem clr/home cursor down routine
1030 print home$:cd = 3:gosub 9000
1040 for i = 1 to tk
1050 if tlines$(i) = "*" then 1080
1060 if tlines$(i) = "!" then print#file,bnk$:goto 1080
1070 print#file,tlines$(i)
1080 next i
1090 goto 20000:rem menu return routine
1100 :
1110 :
1120 :
2000 rem **--name only routine--**
2010 gosub 10000:rem display routine
```

```
2020 print home$:rem clr/home
2030 for i = 1 to tk - 1
2040 if tlines$(i) = tlines$(1) then 2080
2050 if tlines$(i) = "!" then 2080
2060 goto 2150
2070 :
2080 rem *-line up numbers-*
2090 if i < 10 then print tab(3)
2100 if i > 9 and i < 100 then print tab(2)
2110 if i > 99 then print tab(1)
2120 :
2130 if tlines$(i) = tlines$(1) then print#file,i;tlines$(1)
2140 if tlines$(i) = "!" then print#file,i + 1;tlines$(i + 1)
2150 next i
2160 goto 20000:rem menu return routine
2170 :
2180 :
2190 :
3000 rem **--no phone routine--**
3010 gosub 10000:rem display routine
3020 print home$:rem clr/home
3030 for i = 1 to tk
3040 if tlines$(i) = "*" then i = i + 1:goto 3070
3050 if tlines$(i) = "!" then print#file,bnk$:goto 3070
3060 print#file,tlines$(i)
3070 next i
3080 goto 20000:rem menu return routine
3090 :
3100 :
3110 :
4000 rem **--search routine--**
4010 gosub 10000:rem display routine
4020 print home$:rem clr/home
4030 print "Type the word ";wht$;"END";ylw$;" when finished."
4040 poke 19,32:rem disable input ?
4050 print:input "Name to find: ";find$
4060 if find$ = "END" or find$ = "end" then 4240
4070 print
4080 for i = 1 to tk
4090 if tlines$(i) = find$ then 4110
4100 goto 4210
4110 if tlines$(i) = "*" then 4210
4120 if tlines$(i) = "!" then 4210
4130 print#file,bnk$
4140 print#file,tlines$(i)
4150 print#file,tlines$(i + 1)
4160 print#file,tlines$(i + 2)
4170 if tlines$(i + 3) <> "*" then print#file,tlines$(i + 3)
4180 if tlines$(i + 4) = "*" then 4200
4190 print#file,tlines$(i + 4):goto 4210
4200 print#file,tlines$(i + 5)
4210 next i
4220 print
4230 goto 4030:rem repeat until done
4240 goto 20000:rem menu return routine
```

```
4250 :
4260 :
4270 :
5000 rem **--search routine/no phone--**
5010 gosub 10000:rem display routine
5020 print home$:rem clr/home
5030 print "Type the word ";wht$;"END";ylw$;" when finished."
5040 poke 19,32:rem disable input ?
5050 print:input "Name to find: ";find$
5060 if find$ = "END" or find$ = "end" then 5250
5070 print
5080 for i = 1 to tk
5090 if tlines$(i) = find$ then 5110
5100 goto 5220:rem next i
5110 if tlines$(i) = "*" then i = i + 1:goto 5220
5120 if tlines$(i) = "!" then print#file,bnk$:goto 5220
5130 print#file,bnk$
5140 print#file,tlines$(i)
5150 print#file,tlines$(i + 1)
5160 print#file,tlines$(i + 2)
5170 if tlines$(i + 3) <> "*" then print#file,tlines$(i + 3)
5180 if tlines$(i + 3) = "*" then i = i + 1:goto 5220
5190 if tlines$(i + 4) = "*" then i = i + 1:goto 5220
5200 print#file,tlines$(i + 4):goto 5220
5210 print#file,tlines$(i + 5)
5220 next i
5230 print
5240 goto 5030:rem repeat until done
5250 goto 20000:rem menu return routine
5260 :
5270 :
5280 :
6000 rem **--range routine--**
6010 gosub 10000:rem display routine
6020 rem clr/home cursor down routine
6030 print home$:cd = 3:gosub 9000
6040 input "Type beginning line number please: ";bg
6050 print:print
6060 if bg < 1 then print "Number too small!":goto 6040
6070 input "Type ending line nuber please: ";ed
6080 print
6090 if ed > tk then print "Number too large!":goto 6070
6100 for i = bg to ed
6110 if tlines$(i) = "*" then i = i + 1:goto 6140
6120 if tlines$(i) = "!" then print#file,bnk$:goto 6140
6130 print#file,tlines$(i)
6140 next i
6150 goto 20000:rem menu return routine
6160 :
6170 :
6180 :
7000 rem **--alphabetical order--**
7005 rem clr/home cursor down routine
7010 print home$:cd = 5:gosub 9000
7020 print rvs$;"WORKING--PLEASE DON'T TOUCH!!"
7030 print ylw$
```

```
7040
7050
7060 rem *-get first info.-line-*
7070 for i = 1 to tk - 1
7080 if tlines$(i) = tlines$(1) then 7130
7090 if tlines$(i) = "!" then i = i + 1:goto 7130
7100 goto 7240:rem next i
7110 :
7120 :
7130 rem reverse order
7140 char = len(tlines$(i))
7150 for va = 1 to char:if asc(mid$(tlines$(i),va,1)) = 32
     then vz = va
7160 next va
7170 if vz = 0 or vz > char then ad$(i) = tlines$(i):goto 7190
7180 ad$(i) = mid$(tlines$(i),vz + 1,char - vz) + ", " +
     left$(tlines$(i),vz)
7190 ad$(i) = ad$(i) + "**" + tlines$(i + 1) + "**" +
     tlines$(i + 2)
7200 if tlines$(i + 3) <> "*" then ad$(i) = ad$(i) + "**" +
     tlines$(i + 3)
7210 if tlines$(i + 4) = "*" then 7230
7220 ad$(i) = ad$(i) + "**" + tlines$(i + 4):goto 7240
7230 ad$(i) = ad$(i) + "**" + tlines$(i + 5)
7240 next i
7250 :
7260 :
7270 rem renumber for sort
7280 j = 1
7290 for i = 1 to tk
7300 if len(ad$(i)) > 0 then nd$(j) = ad$(i): j = j + 1
7310 next i
7320 n = j - 1
7330 :
7340 :
7350 rem ***--quicksort--***
7360 sa = 1
7370 print:print
7380 print rvs$;"STILL WORKING--PLEASE DON'T TOUCH!!"
7390 u(1) = 1
7400 r(1) = n
7410 ua = u(sa)
7420 ra = r(sa)
7430 sa = sa - 1
7440 uz = ua
7450 rz = ra
7460 x$ = nd$(int((ua + ra)/2))
7470 c = c + 1
7480 if nd$(uz) = x$ or nd$(uz) > x$ then 7510
7490 uz = uz + 1
7500 goto 7470
7510 c = ca
7520 if x$ = nd$(rz) or x$ > nd$(rz) then 7550
7530 rz = rz - 1
7540 goto 7510
7550 if uz > rz then 7620
```

```
7560 s = s + 1
7570 t$ = nd$(uz)
7580 nd$(uz) = nd$(rz)
7590 nd$(rz) = t$
7600 uz = uz + 1
7610 rz = rz - 1
7620 if uz = rz or uz < rz then 7470
7630 if uz = ra or uz > ra then 7670
7640 sa = sa + 1
7650 u(sa) = uz
7660 r(sa) = ra
7670 ra = rz
7680 if ua < ra then 7440
7690 if sa > 0 then 7410
7700 rem sort completed!
7710 :
7720 :
7730 rem **--display--**
7740 gosub 10000:rem display routine
7745 rem clr/home cursor down routine
7750 print home$:cd = 3:gosub 9000
7760 for i = 1 to n
7770 vz = 1:q = 1
7780 char = len(nd$(i))
7790 for va = 1 to char
7800 if mid$(nd$(i),va,2) = "**" then 7820
7810 goto 7850
7820 zi$(q) = mid$(nd$(i),vz,va - vz)
7830 vz = va + 2
7840 q = q + 1
7850 next va
7860 :
7870 zi$(q) = mid$(nd$(i),vz,char - (vz - 1))
7880 :
7890 for e = 1 to q
7900 print#file,zi$(e)
7910 next e
7920 :
7930 print#file,bnk$
7940 next i
7950 goto 20000:rem menu return routine
7960 :
7970 :
7980 :
8000 rem **--return to program menu--**
8010 poke 19,0:rem restore input prompt
8020 rem clr/home cursor down routine
8030 print home$:cd = 5:gosub 9000
8040 print tab(tb)
8050 print rvs$;
8060 print "LOADING THE MAIL MENU PROGRAM"
8070 ^"mail.menu"
8080 :
8090 :
9000 rem **--cursor down routine--**
```

```
9010 for i = 1 to cd
9020 print cd$;
9030 next i
9040 return
9050 :
9060 :
10000 rem **--display routine--**
10010 print home$:rem clr/home
10020 cd = 3:rem 3 lines down
10030 gosub 9000:rem cursor down routine
10040 print "Would you like a paper print out?"
10050 print
10080 gosub 18000:rem y/n input routine
10090 if yes$ = "y" then 10120:rem prnt
10100 if yes$ = "n" then 10300:rem scrn
10110 :
10120 print home$:rem clr/home
10130 cd = 3:rem 3 lines down
10140 gosub 9000:rem cursor down routine
10150 print "Please make sure the printer"
10160 print
10170 print "is on and ready to use."
10180 print
10190 print "Are you ready to begin printing?"
10200 print
10210 gosub 18000:rem y/n input routine
10220 if yes$ = "n" then 10000
10230 :
10240 rem *-printer display-*
10250 file = 4
10260 dvic = 4
10270 cmnd = 7
10280 goto 10500:rem open instruction
10290 :
10300 rem *-screen display-*
10310 file = 3
10320 dvic = 3
10330 cmnd = 1
10340 goto 10500:rem open instruction
10350 :
10360 :
10500 rem *-open instruction-*
10510 open file,dvic,cmnd
10520 return
10530 :
10540 :
10550 :
18000 rem **--y/n input routine--**
18010 print "Type a ";wht$;"Y";ylw$;" or ";wht$;"N";ylw$;" :";
18020 poke 19,32:rem disable input ?
18030 input yes$
18040 print
18050 if yes$ = "y" or yes$ = "Y" then yes$ = "y":return
18060 if yes$ = "n" or yes$ = "N" then yes$ = "n":return
18070 print
18080 print rvs$;"Incorrect Choice!";ylw$
```

```
18090 print
18100 goto 18000:rem begin again
18110 :
18120 :
18130 :
19000 rem **--return key routine--**
19010 poke 198,0:rem clr kbrd buffer
19020 for i = 631 to 640
19030 poke i,0:rem no value
19040 next i
19050 x = peek(197):rem store key press
19060 if x = 1 then 19080:rem 1 = rtn
19070 goto 19050:if not 1 go back
19080 poke 19,0:rem restore input prompt
19090 poke 198,1:rem allow for cursor
19100 poke 631,0:rem clr kbrd
19110 nu$ = "":rem clr string variable
19120 return
19130 :
19140 :
19150 :
20000 rem **--menu return routine--**
20010 print#file
20020 close file
20030 print
20040 poke 19,32:rem disable input ?
20050 print "Press ";wht$;"RETURN";ylw$;" to go to the Display
      Menu:";
20060 gosub 19000:rem return key routine
20070 print
20080 goto 400:rem display menu routine

ready.
```

■ Program for MAIL.CORRECTION

```
100 rem ***--mail.correction--***
110 :
120 :
130 rem **--initialization--**
140 home$ = chr$(147):rem clr/home
150 ::cd$ = chr$( 17):rem cursor down
160 ::cu$ = chr$(145):rem cursor up
170 ::cl$ = chr$(157):rem cursor left
180 ::cr$ = chr$( 29):rem cursor right
190 :blk$ = chr$(144):rem black
200 :ylw$ = chr$(158):rem yellow
210 :wht$ = chr$(  5):rem white
220 :rvs$ = chr$( 18):rem reverse video
225 :bnk$ = chr$( 10):rem blank line
230 :
240 poke 53280, 5:rem border = green
250 poke 53272,23:rem upper/lower case
260 poke 53281,11:rem set bkgrd = greyl
265 :
266 :
270 rem **--user message--**
271 print home$:rem clr/home
272 cd = 5:rem 5 lines down
273 gosub 9000:rem cursor down routine
274 print ylw$;"ONE MOMENT PLEASE!"
275 :
276 :
277 rem **--file input routine--**
278 :
279 rem *-pointer file-*
280 open 2,8,2,"0:adrs-ptr,seq,read"
281 input#2,rec
282 close 2
283 :
284 rem *-data file-*
285 dim tlines$(rec)
286 open 3,8,3,"0:adrs-data,seq,read"
287 for i = 1 to rec
288 input#3,tlines$(i)
289 next i
290 close 3
291 :
292 tk = rec:rem total k = # of lines
293 :
294 :
295 :
400 rem **--menu routine--**
410 tb = 5:rem tab value--5 sps.rt.
420 print home$:rem clr/home
430 print wht$
440 print tab(tb + 3)
450 print rvs$;
460 print "CORRECTION MENU"
```

```
470 print ylw$
480 print:print tab(tb)
490 print "1. CHANGE OR CORRECT INFO."
500 print:print tab(tb)
510 print "2. DELETE INFORMATION"
520 print:print tab(tb)
530 print "3. WRITE REVISED FILE"
540 print:print tab(tb)
550 print "4. RETURN TO PROGRAM MENU"
560 print:print tab(tb)
570 input "Which Number Please";nu$
580 number = val(nu$)
590 :
600 if number = 1 then 1000
610 if number = 2 then 2000
620 if number = 3 then 3000
630 if number = 4 then 4000
640 :
650 gosub 7000:rem incorrect choice
660 goto 400:rem menu routine
670 :
680 :
1000 rem **--correction routine--**
1010 print home$:rem clr/home
1020 cd = 3:rem 3 lines down
1030 gosub 9000:rem cursor down routine
1040 print tab(tb)
1050 print "Type a ";wht$;"0";ylw$;" when finished."
1060 print:print tab(tb)
1070 poke 19,32:rem disable input ?
1080 input "Display which line? ";nb$
1090 if nb$ = "0" then 20000:rem menu
1100 nb = val(nb$)
1110 rem incorrect choice/ask again
1120 if nb > tk then gosub 7000:goto 1000
1130 cd = 4:gosub 9000:rem crsr down 4
1140 print tab(tb - 1)
1150 print nb;" ";tlines$(nb)
1160 print:print tab(tb)
1170 print "Is this correct? "
1180 print:print tab(tb)
1190 gosub 18000:rem y/n input routine
1200 if yes$ = "y" then 1000
1210 print:print tab(tb)
1220 print "Type in the correct information:"
1230 print:print tab(tb - 1)
1240 print nb;" ";:input cinfo$
1250 print:tlines$(nb) = cinfo$
1260 rem clr/home--cursor down routine
1270 print home$:cd = 3:gosub 9000
1280 print:print tab(tb - 1)
1290 print nb;" ";tlines$(nb)
1300 print
1310 goto 1160:rem ask again
1320 :
1330 :
```

```
1340 :
2000 rem **--delete routine--**
2010 print home$:rem clr/home
2020 cd = 3:gosub 9000:rem crsr down 3
2030 print tab(tb)
2040 print "Type a ";wht$;"0";ylw$;" when finished."
2050 print:print tab(tb)
2060 poke 19,32:rem disable input ?
2070 input "Delete which line? ";nb$
2080 if nb$ = "0" then 20000:rem menu
2090 nb = val(nb$)
2100 rem incorrect choice/ask again
2110 if nb > tk then gosub 7000:goto 2000
2120 cd = 4:gosub 9000:rem crsr down 4
2130 print tab(tb - 1)
2140 print nb;" ";tlines$(nb)
2150 print:print:print tab(tb)
2160 print "Are you sure?"
2170 print:print tab(tb)
2180 print "Type ";wht$;"YES";ylw$;" if you are sure!";
2190 input yes$
2200 if yes$ = "YES" or yes$ = "yes" then 2240
2210 goto 2000:rem begin again
2220 :
2230 :
2240 rem *-display deleted info.-*
2250 j = nb
2260 if tlines$(j) = "!" then 2290
2270 j = j + 1:goto 2260
2280 :
2290 rem *-format numbers & display-*
2300 rem clr/home--cursor down routine
2310 print home$:cd = 3:gosub 9000
2320 for i = nb to j
2330 if i < 10 then print tab(3)
2340 if i > 9 and i < 100 then print tab(2)
2350 if i > 99 then print tab(1)
2360 print i;" ";tlines$(i)
2370 tlines$(i) = "DELETED":d = d + 1
2380 next i
2390 print
2400 print "DELETING THIS INFORMATION"
2410 :
2420 :
2430 rem *-renumber w/out del.info.-*
2440 q = 1
2450 for i = 1 to tk
2460 if tlines$(i) = "DELETED" then 2490
2470 tlines$(q) = tlines$(i)
2480 q = q + 1
2490 next i
2500 :
2510 rem subtract # of lines deleted for new total
2520 tk = tk - d
2530 d = 0:j = 0
2540 print
```

```
2550 goto 20000:rem menu
2560 :
2570 :
2580 :
3000 rem **--file output routine--**
3010 :
3020 rem *-user message-*
3030 rem clr/home--cursor down routine
3040 print home$:cd = 3:gosub 9000
3050 print rvs$;
3060 print tab(tb)
3070 print "UPDATING FILES."
3080 print:print:print tab(tb + 10)
3090 print rvs$;:print "PLEASE WAIT!"
3100 :
3110 rem *-delete/rename backup-*
3120 open 3,8,3,"@0:adrs-backup,seq,write"
3130 close 3
3140 @"scratch:adrs-backup"
3150 @"rename:adrs-backup=adrs-data"
3160 :
3170 rem *-pointer file-*
3180 open 2,8,2,"@0:adrs-ptr,seq,write"
3190 print#2,tk
3200 close 2
3210 :
3220 rem *-data file-*
3230 open 3,8,3,"0:adrs-data,seq,write"
3240 for i = 1 to tk
3250 print#3,tlines$(i)
3260 next i
3270 close 3
3280 :
3290 rem *-user message/menu-*
3300 rem clr/home--cursor down routine
3310 print home$:cd = 5:gosub 9000
3320 print tab(tb)
3330 print rvs$;
3340 print "ALL FINISHED"
3350 cd = 10:gosub 9000
3360 goto 20000:rem menu routine
3370 :
3380 :
3390 :
4000 rem **--return to program menu--**
4010 poke 19,0:rem restore input prompt
4020 rem clr/home--cursor down routine
4030 print home$:cd = 5:gosub 9000
4040 print tab(tb)
4050 print rvs$;
4060 print "LOADING THE MAIL MENU PROGRAM"
4070 ^"mail.menu"
4080 :
4090 :
7000 rem **-incorrect choice message-**
7010 print:print:print tab(tb)
```

```
7020 print rvs$;"Incorrect Choice!"
7030 print:print tab(tb)
7040 print "Press ";wht$;"RETURN";ylw$;" to continue:";
7050 gosub 19000:rem return key routine
7060 return
7070 :
7080 :
7090 :
9000 rem **--cursor down routine--**
9010 for i = 1 to cd
9020 print cd$;
9030 next i
9040 return
9050 :
9060 :
10000 rem **--display routine--**
10010 print home$:rem clr/home
10020 cd = 3:rem 3 lines down
10030 gosub 9000:rem cursor down routine
10040 print "Would you like a paper print out?"
10050 print
10080 gosub 18000:rem y/n input routine
10090 if yes$ = "y" then 10120:rem prnt
10100 if yes$ = "n" then 10300:rem scrn
10110 :
10120 print home$:rem clr/home
10130 cd = 3:rem 3 lines down
10140 gosub 9000:rem cursor down routine
10150 print "Please make sure the printer"
10160 print
10170 print "is on and ready to use."
10180 print
10190 print "Are you ready to begin printing?"
10200 print
10210 gosub 18000:rem y/n input routine
10220 if yes$ = "n" then 10000
10230 :
10240 rem *-printer display-*
10250 file = 4
10260 dvic = 4
10270 cmnd = 7
10280 goto 10500:rem open instruction
10290 :
10300 rem *-screen display-*
10310 file = 3
10320 dvic = 3
10330 cmnd = 1
10340 goto 10500:rem open instruction
10350 :
10360 :
10500 rem *-open instruction-*
10510 open file,dvic,cmnd
10520 return
10530 :
10540 :
10550 :
```

```
18000 rem **--y/n input routine--**
18010 print "Type a ";wht$;"Y";ylw$;" or ";wht$;"N";ylw$;" :";
18020 poke 19,32:rem disable input ?
18030 input yes$
18040 print
18050 if yes$ = "y" or yes$ = "Y" then yes$ = "y":return
18060 if yes$ = "n" or yes$ = "N" then yes$ = "n":return
18070 print
18080 print rvs$;"Incorrect Choice!";ylw$
18090 print
18100 goto 18000:rem begin again
18110 :
18120 :
18130 :
19000 rem **--return key routine--**
19010 poke 198,0:rem clr kbrd buffer
19020 for i = 631 to 640
19030 poke i,0:rem no value
19040 next i
19050 x = peek(197):rem store key press
19060 if x = 1 then 19080:rem 1 = rtn.
19070 goto 19050:if not 1 go back
19080 poke 19,0:rem restore input prompt
19090 poke 198,1:rem allow for cursor
19100 poke 631,0:rem clr kbrd
19110 nu$ = "":rem clr string variable
19120 return
19130 :
19140 :
19150 :
20000 rem **--menu return routine--**
20010 rem if printer used:print#file
20020 rem if printer used:close file
20030 print:print
20040 poke 19,32:rem disable input ?
20050 print "Press ";wht$;"RETURN";ylw$;" to go to the
      Correct.Menu:";
20060 gosub 19000:rem return key routine
20070 print
20080 goto 400:rem display menu routine

ready.
```

8 additional sequential file techniques

We are going to explore some other ways to work with sequential files and look at additional techniques for file handling. In this chapter, I am going to concentrate on the file routines of the various programs presented and not discuss the rest of the programming. The listings for the complete programs are included at the end of this chapter along with an explanation of the new commands used in these programs.

We will begin with a series of programs that allows an individual to practice math and keep a record of the scores achieved. These programs are essentially drill and practice and may not be the best educational use of the computer. But for the purpose of demonstrating how files can be used in a variety of ways, these drill and practice programs will be sufficient.

We again start with careful thought and preparation. We need a separate program for each mathematical operation, along with a program for the scores. This means that another program menu would be convenient. The essential difference between the operation programs is the sign of the operation: "+" for addition, "×" for multiplication, etc. With the exception of division, the numbers can be displayed in basically the same way. Therefore, the program presented for addition can also be used for subtraction and multiplication with changes made to only seven lines: 100, 480, 510, 830, 840, 850, and 1170. In all those lines, the references to addition should be changed to the desired operation. After the "addition" program has been typed in, the procedure to make the necessary changes should be:

1. Load the "add" program:
   /add
2. List the first line to be changed:
   list 100
   100 rem ***--addition--***
3. Make the necessary change for the specific program:
   100 rem ***--subtraction--***
   or
   100 rem ***--multiplication--***
4. List the next line and make the changes.
5. Repeat for each of the seven lines.

The seven lines with their changes follow:

```
add     : 100 rem--addition--***
subtract: 100 rem--subtraction--***
multiply: 100 rem--multiplication--***

add     : 480 input "number you are adding by? ";max$
subtract: 480 input "number you are subtracting by? ";max$
multiply: 480 input "number you are multiplying by? ";max$

add     : 510 {same as 480}
subtract: 510 {same as 480}
multiply: 510 {same as 480}

add     : 830 c    = a + b
subtract: 830 c    = a - b
multiply: 830 c    = a * b

add     : 840 s$   = "+"
subtract: 840 s$   = "-"
multiply: 840 s$   = "x"

add     : 850 sn$  = "addition"
subtract: 850 sn$  = "subtraction"
multiply: 850 sn$  = "multiplication"

add     : 1170 print tab(tb + 2) rvs$;nc$;" 's ";sn$;" practice."
subtract: 1170 print tab(tb + 1) rvs$;nc$;" 's ";sn$;" practice."
multiply: 1170 print tab(tb - 1) rvs$;nc$;" 's ";sn$;" practice."
```

Once all the changes have been made, save the new program:

←SUBTRACT or ←MULTIPLY

The program for division has additional code because the numbers must be formatted differently, and provision has been made so that all problems come out even.

All these programs can be included in one large program, but the flow of logic in the program would not be as easy to follow as it is with separate programs. Little would be gained by forcing everything into one program since BASIC allows us to switch from one program to another if you are using a disk drive.

We must carefully consider what we want to save in our scores data file. There are several pieces of information that might be important to save, but a good rule is to save only what is absolutely necessary—what it would be hard or impossible to calculate from existing information. For example, we could save the total number of problems, the number correct, the number wrong, the percentage, the name of the individual, the kind of mathematical operation, the number of digits chosen, and so on. If the programs were slightly altered, we could also save the actual problems missed, the number of tries on a particular problem, and the last question the person tried. Obviously, all this information is not necessary, although certain individuals might value and save information that others would not want.

So the first step is to decide what information to save. In this example, we will save four things: the type of operation, the number of digits in the operation, the number of correct answers, and the number of wrong answers. Once we decide what to save, we need only save the assigned variables for these pieces of information. The code to do this is given below.

```
3000 rem **--file input/output--**
3010 :
3020 rem *-user message-*
3030 poke 19,0:rem reset input prompt
3040 cd = 5:gosub 9000:rem crsr down 5
3050 print tab(8)
3060 print rvs$;
3070 print "UPDATING FILES."
3080 print:print:print tab(8)
3090 print rvs$;"PLEASE WAIT!"
3100 :
3110 rem **--file input routine--**
3120 k = 1
3130 open 3,8,3,cv$ + ",seq,read"
3140 input#3,s$(k):rem sign
3150 input#3,dt(k):rem # of digits
```

```
3160 input#3,cr(k):rem # of correct
3170 input#3,wr(k):rem # of wrong
3180 if status = 0 then k = k + 1:goto 3140
3190 if status = 64 then k = k + 1
3200 :
3210 rem status = 0--all ok
3220 rem status = 64--eof
3230 rem status not 0 or 64--1st use
3240 :
3250 s$(k) = s$:dt(k) = dt:cr(k) = cr:wr(k) = wr
3260 close 3
3270 :
3280 :
3300 rem **--file output routine--**
3310 open 4,8,4,"@0:" + cv$ + ",seq,write"
3320 for i = 1 to k
3330 print#4,s$(i):rem sign
3340 print#4,dt(i):rem # of digits
3350 print #4,cr(i):rem # of correct
3360 print#4,wr(i):rem # of wrong
3370 next i
3380 :
3390 close 4
3400 :
3410 :
```

Some of this should be familiar. But the sequence and a few commands may appear different.

Remember that in our Mailing List System programs, we used one program to create the "adrs-data" file and another program to add to it. Such a sequence is usually necessary when creating a file that will later be added to. The use of the "status" command eliminates the need for two separate programs. Now, we have the following sequence: The first time the program is run, the computer will attempt to read information from a file that does not yet exist. When it finds that no such file exists, it creates the file and then writes the first set of information into the file. Thus, the file is created and the first set of information is written into the file. The second time (and succeeding times) the program is run, the computer reads the information from the file because it finds that such a file does exist. We have accomplished in one routine what would normally have taken two routines to do.

The status command provides us with the current "status" of the system following an input/output (I/O) operation. The first time this program is used, the status will indicate that no information has been read into the computer, because no such file yet exists. Since nothing has been read into the arrays, the counter (k) retains the value of one (1). Control passes to line 3250, which stores the value of the current session's information in the appropriate array. Since the array now contains some information, we can proceed to write that information out to the diskette. The file output routine accomplishes the task of writing the information to the diskette in pretty much the same manner we have used before.

But you should notice that we are using a variable for the file name. In our Mailing List System programs, we always used the constant "adrs-data" for our file name. But in this situation, and many file routines, it is more convenient to assign a variable as the file name. Anytime an individual uses any of these programs, the information is kept in a file under that person's name. By using a variable for the file name, we eliminate the need for separate programs for each person that uses any of the math operation programs.

You must be careful to type your name the same way every time you use the programs. For example, if I answer that my name is DAVID the first time I use these programs, the file will be created under the name of DAVID. If I come back later and answer that my name is DAVE, a new and separate file will be created for DAVE. This need for consistency is the reason the entered name (line 560) is converted to lower case characters (7000–7180). It is also the reason the variable cv$ (instead of name$) is used for the file name. It is possible to have at least three different logical forms of the same name: DAVID, David, or david. Without the conversion routine, each of these forms would create a new file. With this conversion routine, the name is always changed into lower case letters and, therefore, one file is created and updated with the file name appearing in lower case characters. As with most things, there are advantages to the use of a variable for the file name, but there are also disadvantages. The user may get tired of being required to type his or her name. But the use of a variable for the file name remains a popular programming technique. The variable must be a string variable since no file name can begin with a number. (The file name can contain a number but just cannot begin with a number.)

The file routine used in the program "math.scores" is very similar to the one just discussed, but instead of writing information to the disk, this routine reads information from the disk.

```
380 rem **--file input routine--**
390 dim s$(100),dt(100),cr(100),wr(100)
400 open 2,8,2,cv$ + ",seq,read"
410 k = 1
420 input#2,s$(k):rem sign of operation
430 input#2,dt(k):rem # of digits
440 input#2,cr(k):rem # of correct
450 input#2,wr(k):rem # of wrong
460 k = k + 1
470 if status = 0 then 420
```

```
480 close 2
490 :
```

This time the status function is used to test for the end of file number 2, or the end of the data. If the status function is not included, we have no way of telling how much information or how many records exist in the file. We did not keep track of that information by writing out a counter to the file as we did in the Mailing List System. Without the status function, we would experience an "end of data error" and the program would halt—the RUN/STOP key would need to be pressed to bring the computer back. But with the status function, the computer is instructed to get information only so long as an error condition does not exist. Then, when the end of the file or "end of data error" occurs, the computer is informed to go to the next instruction (line 480) and proceed from there. At this point, we close the file, since we are now certain that we have all the information the file contains. The use of the status function saves both programming and disk space.

You should notice one other major difference in this routine. In most of our programs, we have used FOR . . . NEXT loops. But this time, we do not know how many items the file contains and, therefore, we do not know how large the counter needs to eventually become. It is true that we could pick an arbitrary number, but a better method is the one used in this routine. This method is still a loop, since the computer is instructed to follow the instructions down to line 470 and then go back to the instruction at line 420 and do everything over again. What gets us out of this loop? The status function does when it executes as the end of the file is encountered. When this loop is finished, we should have the values we want from the file and can proceed to the display routine.

These math programs provide additional file handling techniques, as well as a set of useful drill and practice programs. The menu program uses the same method we have been using to display a set of choices and then run the appropriate program. Apart from file handling, the math programs also have some programming techniques that might prove interesting.

To conclude this chapter, I have added two other programs that make use of file handling and fit our purpose of demonstrating filing techniques. The programs are presented in a rough form. Individuals may wish (and, in fact, are encouraged) to add parts to these programs or modify the format. The final programs present an elementary method of drill and practice on any subject.

With the exception of the menu program and its associated lines in the various math programs, these math programs can be adapted to tape use by changing all lines that open a disk file. The programs are of moderate size and will require some time to load from tape. In fact, because the Commodore-64 uses a serial process for its disk access (where information is fed from the computer to the disk one piece at a time, similar to character by character) instead of the more common parallel process (where information is fed from the computer to the disk in groups, similar to word by word rather than character by character), the loading of these programs and the Mailing List System programs can take quite a bit of time. There is another significant difference between disk use and tape use. Disk use allows us to reduce the time in certain applications even more. The random-access section of this book will demonstrate that it is not necessary to read in all the data in order to display, add to, or change that information. In fact, some might find that the applications presented in this sequential access section might better be implemented by random access programs. If that is the case for you, I would encourage you to make the necessary changes in the Mailing List System and Math System programs after reading the random-access section so that you have random-access files instead of sequential access files.

By now, some of you have no doubt found out that certain of these commands can be abbreviated and that there are "shortcuts." I have intentionally avoided using these abbreviations and shortcuts because my purpose is to make the code as self-explanatory as possible. I encourage you to follow the example set in this book, but it is not necessary to spell out some of these commands or include the rem statements in order for these programs to work. One argument against including this expanded code format is that the program will operate faster since each line and each character in the line must be interpreted by the command processor. I personally have not found a significant difference in speed of operation for file application programs once the program has been loaded into the computer. But, the inclusion of all the rem statements and unabbreviated code does greatly expand the size of the file and, therefore, requires more time to load into the computer. If the slowness of the loading process seems to bother you, you might want to redo the programs without the rem statements and the unabbreviated code. I would suggest that you maintain a copy of the original program becuase I have found that a fully documented program is worth a little extra load time.

In the final chapter on sequential access files, we will take a brief look at the possibility of a standard method for storing data so that the data can be used by a variety of commercial programs.

NEW COMMANDS OR TERMS IN THE FOLLOWING PROGRAMS

1. **^** Raise to the power of the number following this symbol (when used as a math function).
2. **RND** Generate a random number.
3. **INT** Take only the integer portion of the number in parentheses.
4. **LEN** Find the length of the string in terms of the number of characters in the string.
5. **STR$** Convert the specified number into a string value.

6. **VAL** Give the numeric value of a string.
7. **SGN** Returns the signum function.
8. **DEF FN** Define a function. This useful command allows a programmer to set a single variable equal to a complete equation.

QUESTIONS

1. A good rule to follow in deciding what information to save is to save (A) everything possible, (B) as little as possible, (C) only what is absolutely necessary.
2. *True or False*: It is possible to delete and rename files from within a program.
3. *True or False*: It is never possible to use a variable as a file name.
4. What type of variable can be used as a file name?
5. Which BASIC statement retrieves only the integer portion of a number?
6. Which BASIC statement converts a number into a string?
7. Which BASIC statement converts a string into a number?
8. Which BASIC statement can be used to test for the end of a sequential access file?

ANSWERS

1. C
2. True
3. False
4. String
5. INT
6. STR$
7. VAL
8. STATUS

■ Program for MATH.MENU

```
100 rem ***--math.menu--***
110 :
120 :
130 rem **--initialization--**
140 home$ = chr$(147):rem clr/home
150 ::cd$ = chr$( 17):rem cursor down
160 ::cu$ = chr$(145):rem cursor up
170 ::cl$ = chr$(157):rem cursor left
180 ::cr$ = chr$( 29):rem cursor right
190 :blk$ = chr$(144):rem black
200 :ylw$ = chr$(158):rem yellow
210 :wht$ = chr$(  5):rem white
220 :rvs$ = chr$( 18):rem reverse video
230 :
240 poke 53280,14:rem border = lt.blue
250 poke 53272,23:rem upper/lower case
260 poke 53281, 6:rem set bkgrd to blue
270 :
280 :
500 rem **--menu--**
510 tb = 10:rem tab value-10 spaces rt.
520 print home$:rem clr/home
530 print wht$;
540 print tab(tb)
550 print rvs$;
560 print "MATH PROGRAM MENU"
570 print
580 print ylw$
590 print tab(tb)
600 print "1. ADDITION"
610 print:print tab(tb)
620 print "2. SUBTRACTION"
630 print:print tab(tb)
640 print "3. MULTIPLICATION"
650 print:print tab(tb)
660 print "4. DIVISION"
670 print:print tab(tb)
680 print "5. SCORES"
690 print:print tab(tb)
700 print "6. INFORMATION"
710 print:print tab(tb)
720 print "7. LIST OF FILES"
730 print:print tab(tb)
740 print "8. END"
750 print:print tab(tb)
760 poke 19,32:rem disable input ?
770 input "Which Program Number? ";nu$
780 number = val(nu$)
790 :
800 if number = 1 then 1000
810 if number = 2 then 2000
820 if number = 3 then 3000
830 if number = 4 then 4000
```

```
840 if number = 5 then 5000
850 if number = 6 then 6000
860 if number = 7 then 7000
870 if number = 8 then 8000
880 :
890 rem *-incorrect choice message-*
900 print:print:print tab(tb)
910 print rvs$;"Incorrect Choice!"
920 print:print tab(tb)
930 print "Press ";wht$;"RETURN";ylw$;" to continue:";
940 gosub 19030:rem return key routine
950 goto 500:rem menu--check again
960 :
970 :
1000 rem **--math.add--**
1010 file$ = "MATH.ADD"
1020 gosub 17000:rem new program routine
1030 ^"math.add":rem load & run
1040 :
1050 :
2000 rem **--math.subtract--**
2010 file$ = "MATH.SUBTRACT"
2020 gosub 17000:rem new program routine
2030 ^"math.subtract":rem load & run
2040 :
2050 :
3000 rem **--math.multiply--**
3010 file$ = "MATH.MULTIPLY"
3020 gosub 17000:rem new program routine
3030 ^"math.multiply":rem load & run
3040 :
3050 :
4000 rem **--math.divide--**
4010 file$ = "MATH.DIVIDE"
4020 gosub 17000:rem new program routine
4030 ^"math.divide":rem load & run
4040 :
4050 :
5000 rem **--math.scores--**
5010 file$ = "MATH.SCORES"
5020 gosub 17000:rem new program routine
5030 ^"math.scores":rem load & run
5040 :
5050 :
6000 rem **--information--**
6010 print home$:rem clr/home
6020 print "This is a series of math drill and"
6030 print
6040 print "practice programs. It is designed to"
6050 print
6060 print "allow for as much flexibility as pos-"
6070 print
6080 print "sible. The question about the number of"
6090 print
6100 print "digits might, at first, seem confusing."
6110 print
```

```
6120 print "The question simply asks for the great-"
6130 print
6140 print "est number of digits possible in either"
6150 print
6160 print "figure. The next two questions further"
6170 print
6180 print "allow you to limit the possible prob-"
6190 print
6200 print "lems. For example, if you wanted to"
6210 print
6220 :
6230 gosub 19000:rem return key routine
6240 :
6250 print "practice multiplying by '5', you could"
6260 print
6270 print "choose three digit numbers and then"
6280 print
6290 print "answer with a '5' for each of the next"
6300 print
6310 print "two questions. You would then be given"
6320 print
6330 print "problems like: 345 x 5 or 823 x 5."
6340 print
6350 print "Another example would be to add two"
6360 print
6370 print "digit numbers by answering the ques-"
6380 print
6390 print "tions in this way:
6400 print
6410 print tab(tb):print "How many digits--2"
6420 print
6430 print tab(tb):print "Largest number--99"
6440 print
6450 print tab(tb):print "Smallest number--1"
6460 print
6470 :
6480 gosub 19000:rem return key routine
6490 :
6500 print "You could then get problems like:"
6510 print
6520 print tab(tb):print "58 + 34 or 87 + 9."
6530 print
6540 print "Trying the different possibilities will"
6550 print
6560 print "soon indicate the flexibility."
6570 print
6580 print "     The division section will only"
6590 print
6600 print "offer problems that come out even. You"
6610 print
6620 print "may have to wait a short time for the"
6630 print
6640 print "next problem. This is because the num-"
6650 print
6660 print "bers generated must meet certain spec-"
6670 print
```

```
6680 print "ifications. The process speeds up when"
6690 print
6700 :
6710 gosub 19000:rem return key routine
6720 :
6730 print "the number being divided contains at"
6740 print
6750 print "least two more digits than the divisor."
6760 print
6770 print "     This is not a professional program"
6780 print
6790 print "and, therefore, does not do a lot of"
6800 print
6810 print "error checking. You can crash the pro-"
6820 print
6830 print "grams with confusing answers or mis-"
6840 print
6850 print "takes in typing. These programs were"
6860 print
6870 print "done mainly to demonstrate, in a useful"
6880 print
6890 print "manner, certain file handling capabil-"
6900 print
6910 print "ities and techniques."
6920 print
6930 :
6940 gosub 19000:rem return key routine
6950 :
6960 goto 500
6970 :
6980 :
7000 rem **--list of files routine--**
7010 print home$:rem clr/home
7020 @"$"
7030 print cu$;chr$(13):rem 13 = rtn
7040 print "Are you ready to return to the menu?"
7050 print
7060 gosub 18000:rem y/n input routine
7070 if yes$ = "y" then 500:rem menu
7080 goto 7000:rem check again
7090 :
7100 :
8000 rem **--end routine--**
8010 poke 19,0:rem restore input prompt
8020 print home$:rem clr/home
8030 cd = 5:rem 5 lines down
8040 gosub 9000:rem crsr down routine
8050 print tab(tb - 5)
8060 print rvs$;
8070 print "That's all for this session!"
8080 print:print:print
8090 print tab(tb)
8100 print rvs$;
8110 print "See you next time."
8120 print ylw$
8130 cd = 10:rem 10 lines down
```

```
8140 gosub 9000:rem crsr down routine
8150 end
8160 :
8170 :
9000 rem **--cursor down routine--**
9010 for i = 1 to cd
9020 print cd$;
9030 next i
9040 return
9050 :
9060 :
17000 rem **--new program routine--**
17010 print home$:rem clr/home
17020 cd = 2:rem 2 lines down
17030 gosub 9000:rem crsr down routine
17040 print "You have selected the ";file$:print:print "program."
17050 print:print:print
17060 print "Is this the program you want?"
17070 print
17080 gosub 18000:rem y/n input routine
17090 if yes$ = "n" then 500:rem menu
17100 print home$:rem clr/home
17110 cd = 5:rem 5 lines down
17120 gosub 9000:rem crsr down routine
17130 print tab(tb - 5)
17140 print rvs$;
17150 print "Please wait!"
17160 print:print:print
17170 print tab(tb)
17180 print rvs$;
17190 print "I'm loading...."
17200 print:print:print
17210 print tab(tb + 8)
17220 print rvs$;
17230 print file$
17240 poke 19,0:rem restore input prompt
17250 return
17260 :
17270 :
18000 rem **--y/n input routine--**
18010 print "Type a ";wht$;"Y";ylw$;" or ";wht$;"N";ylw$;" :";
18020 poke 19,32:rem disable input ?
18030 input yes$
18040 print
18050 if yes$ = "y" or yes$ = "Y" then yes$ = "y":return
18060 if yes$ = "n" or yes$ = "N" then yes$ = "n":return
18070 print
18080 print rvs$;"Incorrect Choice!";ylw$
18090 print
18100 goto 18000:rem check again
18110 :
18120 :
19000 rem **--return key routine--**
19010 print
19020 print "Press ";wht$;"RETURN";ylw$;" to continue:";
```

```
19030 poke 198,0:rem clr kbrd buffer
19040 for i = 631 to 640
19050 poke i,0:rem no value
19060 next i
19070 x = peek(197):rem store key press
19080 if x = 1 then 19100
19090 goto 19070:if not 1 go back
19100 poke 198,1:rem allow 1 for cursor
19110 poke 631,0:rem clr kbrd
19120 nu$ = "":rem clr string variable
19130 print home$:rem clr/home
19140 return

ready.
```

■ Program for MATH.ADD

```
100 rem ***--addition--***
110 :
120 :
130 rem **--initialization--**
140 home$ = chr$(147):rem clr/home
150 ::cd$ = chr$( 17):rem cursor down
160 ::cu$ = chr$(145):rem cursor up
170 ::cl$ = chr$(157):rem cursor left
180 ::cr$ = chr$( 29):rem cursor right
190 :blk$ = chr$(144):rem black
200 :ylw$ = chr$(158):rem yellow
210 :wht$ = chr$(  5):rem white
220 :rvs$ = chr$( 18):rem reverse video
225 :bnk$ = chr$( 10):rem blank line
226 :brn$ = chr$(149):rem brown
227 :bue$ = chr$( 31):rem blue
230 :
240 poke 53280,14:rem border = lt.blue
250 poke 53272,23:rem upper/lower case
260 poke 53281, 7:rem set bkgrd to ylw
262 dim s$(100),dt(100),cr(100),wr(100)
263 tb = 5:rem tab value
265 :
266 :
270 rem **--variable list--**
280 rem a  = top number
281 rem b  = bottom number
282 rem c  = correct answer
283 rem d  = student's answer
284 rem q  = counter
285 rem w  = previous answer
286 rem z  = number of tries
287 rem cr = # of correct answers
288 rem wr = # of wrong answers
289 rem dt = # of digits
290 rem da = # of digits in a
291 rem db = # of digits in b
292 rem dc = # of digits in c
293 rem dm = # of digits in max amnt
294 rem other variables are descriptive
295 :
296 :
297 :
400 rem **--request user info.--**
410 print brn$:rem brown text/ylw bkgrd
420 poke 19,32:rem disable input ?
430 rem clr/home--cursor down 3
440 print home$:cd = 3:gosub 9000
450 input "How many digits? ";digit$
460 print:print:print
470 print "What is the largest figure for the"
480 input "number you are adding by? ";max$
490 print:print:print
```

```
500 print "What is the smallest figure for the"
510 input "number you are adding by? ";mn$
520 dt = val(digit$):max = val(max$):mn = val(mn$)
530 digit = val(digit$)
540 digit = 10 ^ digit
550 print:print:print
560 input "What is your name? ";name$
570 :
580 rem convert to lowercase
590 cv$ = name$
600 gosub 7000:rem lowercase subroutine
610 :
620 :
630 rem **--create problem--**
640 :
650 dm = len(max$)
660 :
670 rem when b's digits < dt
680 if dt = dm + 1 or dt < dm + 1 then 750
690 dm = 10 ^ dm
700 b = int(rnd(0) * dm)
710 if b < mn then 700
720 if b > max then 700
730 goto 800:rem get # for a
740 :
750 z = 1
760 b = int(rnd(0) * digit)
770 if b < mn then 760
780 if b > max then 760
790 :
800 a = int(rnd(0) * digit)
810 :
820 rem *-answer-*
830 c = a + b
840 s$ = "+":rem determine operation
850 sn$ = "addition"
860 if c < 0 then 760:rem for subtract.
870 if c = w then 760:rem previous ans.
880 w = c
890 :
900 :
1000 rem **--display problem--**
1010 rem determine lengths
1020 a$ = str$(a)
1030 da = len(a$)
1040 a$ = right$(a$,da - 1):rem no sign
1050 da = len(a$)
1060 b$ = str$(b)
1070 db = len(b$)
1080 b$ = right$(b$,db - 1):rem no sign
1090 db = len(b$)
1100 c$ = str$(c)
1110 dc = len(c$)
1120 c$ = right$(c$,dc - 1):rem no sign
1130 dc = len(c$)
1140 :
```

```
1150 rem format
1160 print home$:rem clr/home
1170 print tab(tb + 2) rvs$;nc$;"'s ";sn$;" practice."
1180 cd = 3:gosub 9000:rem crsr down 3
1190 print tab(4)
1200 print "Type the word ";blk$;"END";brn$;" when finished!"
1210 cd = 5:gosub 9000:rem crsr down 5
1220 print tab(22 - da):print a$
1230 print tab(22 - (db + 1)):print s$;b$
1240 :
1250 rem draw line
1260 q = 1
1270 if da > db then q = 0
1280 print tab(22 - (dt + q))
1290 for i = 1 to (dt + q)
1300 print "-";
1310 next i
1320 :
1330 :
1500 rem **--get answer--**
1510 print
1520 print tab(22 - dc)
1530 input answer$
1540 :
1550 if answer$ = "END" or answer$ = "end" then 2000
1560 d = val(answer$)
1570 if d = c then 5000:rem correct
1580 if z < 3 then 6000:rem wrong
1590 :
1600 rem give answer after 3 tries
1610 print:print:print:print tab(8)
1620 print "No, the answer is ";bue$;c;brn$
1630 print:print:print tab(8)
1640 print a;" ";s$;" ";b;" = ";c
1650 print:print:z = 1:wr = wr + 1
1660 print tab(8)
1670 print "Press ";blk$;"RETURN";brn$;" to continue: ";
1680 gosub 19000:rem return key routine
1690 goto 630:rem another problem
1700 :
1710 :
1720 :
2000 rem **--total routine--**
2010 rem clr/home--cursor down 5
2020 print home$:cd = 5:gosub 9000
2030 print tab(8)
2040 print "You got";bue$;cr;brn$;"right!"
2050 print:print tab(8)
2060 print "You missed";bue$;wr;brn$;"."
2070 :
2080 :
3000 rem **--file input/output--**
3010 :
3020 rem *-user message-*
3030 poke 19,0:rem reset input prompt
3040 cd = 5:gosub 9000:rem crsr down 5
```

```
3050 print tab(8)
3060 print rvs$;
3070 print "UPDATING FILES."
3080 print:print:print tab(8)
3090 print rvs$;"PLEASE WAIT!"
3100 :
3110 rem **--file input routine--**
3120 k = 1
3130 open 3,8,3,cv$ + ",seq,read"
3140 input#3,s$(k):rem sign
3150 input#3,dt(k):rem # of digits
3160 input#3,cr(k):rem # of correct
3170 input#3,wr(k):rem # of wrong
3180 if status = 0 then k = k + 1:goto 3140
3190 if status = 64 then k = k + 1
3200 :
3210 rem status =  0--all ok
3220 rem status = 64--eof
3230 rem status not 0 or 64--1st use
3240 :
3250 s$(k) = s$:dt(k) = dt: cr(k) = cr:wr(k) = wr
3260 close 3
3270 :
3280 :
3300 rem **--file output routine--**
3310 open 4,8,4,"@0:" + cv$ + ",seq,write"
3320 for i = 1 to k
3330 print#4,s$(i):rem sign
3340 print#4,dt(i):rem # of digits
3350 print#4,cr(i):rem # of correct
3360 print#4,wr(i):rem # of wrong
3370 next i
3380 :
3390 close 4
3400 :
3410 :
4000 rem **--return to program menu--**
4010 poke 19,0:rem restore input prompt
4020 rem clr/home cursor down routine
4030 print home$:cd = 5:gosub 9000
4040 print tab(tb)
4050 print rvs$;
4060 print "LOADING THE MATH MENU PROGRAM"
4070 ^"math.menu"
4080 :
4090 :
4100 :
5000 rem **--correct answer routine--**
5010 cd = 5:gosub 9000:rem crsr down 5
5020 print:print tab(18)
5030 print "GOOD!"
5040 for i = 1 to 1000:next i
5050 cr = cr + 1
5060 goto 630:rem another problem
5070 :
5080 :
```

```
6000 rem **--wrong answer routine--**
6010 cd = 5:gosub 9000:rem crsr down 5
6020 print:print tab(8)
6030 print "No, Please try again."
6040 z = z + 1
6050 print
6060 for i = 1 to 1000:next i
6070 goto 1150:rem ask again
6080 :
6090 :
7000 rem **--convert to lowercase--**
7010 for cv = 1 to len(cv$)
7020 x = asc(mid$(cv$,cv,1))
7030 if x > 192 then x = x - 128
7040 nc$ = nc$ + chr$(x)
7050 next cv
7060 :
7070 cv$ = nc$
7080 f = asc(left$(cv$,1))
7090 f = f + 128
7100 nc$ = chr$(f) + right$(cv$,len(cv$)- 1)
7110 return
7120 :
7130 rem na$ = originally typed name
7140 rem cv$ = converted to lowercase
7150 rem nc$ = 1st letter/uppercase
7160 :
7170 :
7180 :
9000 rem **--cursor down routine--**
9010 for i = 1 to cd
9020 print cd$;
9030 next i
9040 return
9050 :
9060 :
9070 :
19000 rem **--return key routine--**
19010 poke 198,0:rem clr kbrd buffer
19020 for i = 631 to 640
19030 poke i,0:rem no value
19040 next i
19050 x = peek(197):rem store key press
19060 if x = 1 then 19080:rem 1 = rtn.
19070 goto 19050:if not 1 go back
19080 poke 198,1:rem allow for cursor
19090 poke 631,0:rem clr kbrd
19100 nu$ = "":rem clr string variable
19110 return

ready.
```

■ Program for MATH.SUBTRACT

```
100 rem ***--subtraction--***
110 :
120 :
130 rem **--initialization--**
140 home$ = chr$(147):rem clr/home
150 ::cd$ = chr$( 17):rem cursor down
160 ::cu$ = chr$(145):rem cursor up
170 ::cl$ = chr$(157):rem cursor left
180 ::cr$ = chr$( 29):rem cursor right
190 :blk$ = chr$(144):rem black
200 :ylw$ = chr$(158):rem yellow
210 :wht$ = chr$(  5):rem white
220 :rvs$ = chr$( 18):rem reverse video
225 :bnk$ = chr$( 10):rem blank line
226 :brn$ = chr$(149):rem brown
227 :bue$ = chr$( 31):rem blue
230 :
240 poke 53280,14:rem border = lt.blue
250 poke 53272,23:rem upper/lower case
260 poke 53281, 7:rem set bkgrd to ylw
262 dim s$(100),dt(100),cr(100),wr(100)
263 tb = 5:rem tab value
265 :
266 :
270 rem **--variable list--**
280 rem a  = top number
281 rem b  = bottom number
282 rem c  = correct answer
283 rem d  = student's answer
284 rem q  = counter
285 rem w  = previous answer
286 rem z  = number of tries
287 rem cr = # of correct answers
288 rem wr = # of wrong answers
289 rem dt = # of digits
290 rem da = # of digits in a
291 rem db = # of digits in b
292 rem dc = # of digits in c
293 rem dm = # of digits in max amnt
294 rem other variables are descriptive
295 :
296 :
297 :
400 rem **--request user info.--**
410 print brn$:rem brown text/ylw bkgrd
420 poke 19,32:rem disable input ?
430 rem clr/home--cursor down 3
440 print home$:cd = 3:gosub 9000
450 input "How many digits? ";digit$
460 print:print:print
470 print "What is the largest figure for the"
480 input "number you are subtracting by? ";max$
490 print:print:print
```

```
500 print "What is the smallest figure for the"
510 input "number you are subtracting by? ";mn$
520 dt = val(digit$):max = val(max$):mn = val(mn$)
530 digit = val(digit$)
540 digit = 10 ^ digit
550 print:print:print
560 input "What is your name? ";name$
570 :
580 rem convert to lowercase
590 cv$ = name$
600 gosub 7000:rem lowercase subroutine
610 :
620 :
630 rem **--create problem--**
640 :
650 dm = len(max$)
660 :
670 rem when b's digits < dt
680 if dt = dm + 1 or dt < dm + 1 then 750
690 dm = 10 ^ dm
700 b = int(rnd(0) * dm)
710 if b < mn then 700
720 if b > max then 700
730 goto 800:rem get # for a
740 :
750 z = 1
760 b = int(rnd(0) * digit)
770 if b < mn then 760
780 if b > max then 760
790 :
800 a = int(rnd(0) * digit)
810 :
820 rem *-answer-*
830 c = a - b
840 s$ = "-":rem determine operation
850 sn$ = "subtraction"
860 if c < 0 then 760:rem for subtract.
870 if c = w then 760:rem previous ans.
880 w = c
890 :
900 :
1000 rem **--display problem--**
1010 rem determine lengths
1020 a$ = str$(a)
1030 da = len(a$)
1040 a$ = right$(a$,da - 1):rem no sign
1050 da = len(a$)
1060 b$ = str$(b)
1070 db = len(b$)
1080 b$ = right$(b$,db - 1):rem no sign
1090 db = len(b$)
1100 c$ = str$(c)
1110 dc = len(c$)
1120 c$ = right$(c$,dc - 1):rem no sign
1130 dc = len(c$)
1140 :
```

```
1150 rem format
1160 print home$:rem clr/home
1170 print tab(tb + 1) rvs$;nc$;"'s ";sn$;" practice."
1180 cd = 3:gosub 9000:rem crsr down 3
1190 print tab(4)
1200 print "Type the word ";blk$;"END";brn$;" when finished!"
1210 cd = 5:gosub 9000:rem crsr down 5
1220 print tab(22 - da):print a$
1230 print tab(22 - (db + 1)):print s$;b$
1240 :
1250 rem draw line
1260 q = 1
1270 if da > db then q = 0
1280 print tab(22 - (dt + q))
1290 for i = 1 to (dt + q)
1300 print "-";
1310 next i
1320 :
1330 :
1500 rem **--get answer--**
1510 print
1520 print tab(22 - dc)
1530 input answer$
1540 :
1550 if answer$ = "END" or answer$ = "end" then 2000
1560 d = val(answer$)
1570 if d = c then 5000:rem correct
1580 if z < 3 then 6000:rem wrong
1590 :
1600 rem give answer after 3 tries
1610 print:print:print:print tab(8)
1620 print "No, the answer is ";bue$;c;brn$
1630 print:print:print tab(8)
1640 print a;" ";s$;" ";b;" = ";c
1650 print:print:z = 1:wr = wr + 1
1660 print tab(8)
1670 print "Press ";blk$;"RETURN";brn$;" to continue: ";
1680 gosub 19000:rem return key routine
1690 goto 630:rem another problem
1700 :
1710 :
1720 :
2000 rem **--total routine--**
2010 rem clr/home--cursor down 5
2020 print home$:cd = 5:gosub 9000
2030 print tab(8)
2040 print "You got";bue$;cr;brn$;"right!"
2050 print:print tab(8)
2060 print "You missed";bue$;wr;brn$;"."
2070 :
2080 :
3000 rem **--file input/output--**
3010 :
3020 rem *-user message-*
3030 poke 19,0:rem reset input prompt
3040 cd = 5:gosub 9000:rem crsr down 5
```

```
3050 print tab(8)
3060 print rvs$;
3070 print "UPDATING FILES."
3080 print:print:print tab(8)
3090 print rvs$;"PLEASE WAIT!"
3100 :
3110 rem **--file input routine--**
3120 k = 1
3130 open 3,8,3,cv$ + ",seq,read"
3140 input#3,s$(k):rem sign
3150 input#3,dt(k):rem # of digits
3160 input#3,cr(k):rem # of correct
3170 input#3,wr(k):rem # of wrong
3180 if status = 0 then k = k + 1:goto 3140
3190 if status = 64 then k = k + 1
3200 :
3210 rem status =  0--all ok
3220 rem status = 64--eof
3230 rem status not 0 or 64--1st use
3240 :
3250 s$(k) = s$:dt(k) = dt: cr(k) = cr:wr(k) = wr
3260 close 3
3270 :
3280 :
3300 rem **--file output routine--**
3310 open 4,8,4,"@0:" + cv$ + ",seq,write"
3320 for i = 1 to k
3330 print#4,s$(i):rem sign
3340 print#4,dt(i):rem # of digits
3350 print#4,cr(i):rem # of correct
3360 print#4,wr(i):rem # of wrong
3370 next i
3380 :
3390 close 4
3400 :
3410 :
4000 rem **--return to program menu--**
4010 poke 19,0:rem restore input prompt
4020 rem clr/home cursor down routine
4030 print home$:cd = 5:gosub 9000
4040 print tab(tb)
4050 print rvs$;
4060 print "LOADING THE MATH MENU PROGRAM"
4070 ^"math.menu"
4080 :
4090 :
4100 :
5000 rem **--correct answer routine--**
5010 cd = 5:gosub 9000:rem crsr down 5
5020 print:print tab(18)
5030 print "GOOD!"
5040 for i = 1 to 1000:next i
5050 cr = cr + 1
5060 goto 630:rem another problem
5070 :
5080 :
```

```
6000 rem **--wrong answer routine--**
6010 cd = 5:gosub 9000:rem crsr down 5
6020 print:print tab(8)
6030 print "No, Please try again."
6040 z = z + 1
6050 print
6060 for i = 1 to 1000:next i
6070 goto 1150:rem ask again
6080 :
6090 :
7000 rem **--convert to lowercase--**
7010 for cv = 1 to len(cv$)
7020 x = asc(mid$(cv$,cv,1))
7030 if x > 192 then x = x - 128
7040 nc$ = nc$ + chr$(x)
7050 next cv
7060 :
7070 cv$ = nc$
7080 f = asc(left$(cv$,1))
7090 f = f + 128
7100 nc$ = chr$(f) + right$(cv$,len(cv$)- 1)
7110 return
7120 :
7130 rem na$ = originally typed name
7140 rem cv$ = converted to lowercase
7150 rem nc$ = 1st letter/uppercase
7160 :
7170 :
7180 :
9000 rem **--cursor down routine--**
9010 for i = 1 to cd
9020 print cd$;
9030 next i
9040 return
9050 :
9060 :
9070 :
19000 rem **--return key routine--**
19010 poke 198,0:rem clr kbrd buffer
19020 for i = 631 to 640
19030 poke i,0:rem no value
19040 next i
19050 x = peek(197):rem store key press
19060 if x = 1 then 19080:rem 1 = rtn.
19070 goto 19050:if not 1 go back
19080 poke 198,1:rem allow for cursor
19090 poke 631,0:rem clr kbrd
19100 nu$ = "":rem clr string variable
19110 return

ready.
```

Program for MATH.MULTIPLY

```
100 rem ***--multiplication--***
110 :
120 :
130 rem **--initialization--**
140 home$ = chr$(147):rem clr/home
150 ::cd$ = chr$( 17):rem cursor down
160 ::cu$ = chr$(145):rem cursor up
170 ::cl$ = chr$(157):rem cursor left
180 ::cr$ = chr$( 29):rem cursor right
190 :blk$ = chr$(144):rem black
200 :ylw$ = chr$(158):rem yellow
210 :wht$ = chr$(  5):rem white
220 :rvs$ = chr$( 18):rem reverse video
225 :bnk$ = chr$( 10):rem blank line
226 :brn$ = chr$(149):rem brown
227 :bue$ = chr$( 31):rem blue
230 :
240 poke 53280,14:rem border = lt.blue
250 poke 53272,23:rem upper/lower case
260 poke 53281, 7:rem set bkgrd to ylw
262 dim s$(100),dt(100),cr(100),wr(100)
263 tb = 5:rem tab value
265 :
266 :
270 rem **--variable list--**
280 rem a  = top number
281 rem b  = bottom number
282 rem c  = correct answer
283 rem d  = student's answer
284 rem q  = counter
285 rem w  = previous answer
286 rem z  = number of tries
287 rem cr = # of correct answers
288 rem wr = # of wrong answers
289 rem dt = # of digits
290 rem da = # of digits in a
291 rem db = # of digits in b
292 rem dc = # of digits in c
293 rem dm = # of digits in max amnt
294 rem other variables are descriptive
295 :
296 :
297 :
400 rem **--request user info.--**
410 print brn$:rem brown text/ylw bkgrd
420 poke 19,32:rem disable input ?
430 rem clr/home--cursor down 3
440 print home$:cd = 3:gosub 9000
450 input "How many digits? ";digit$
460 print:print:print
470 print "What is the largest figure for the"
480 input "number you are multiplying by? ";max$
490 print:print:print
```

```
500 print "What is the smallest figure for the"
510 input "number you are multiplying by? ";mn$
520 dt = val(digit$):max = val(max$):mn = val(mn$)
530 digit = val(digit$)
540 digit = 10 ^ digit
550 print:print:print
560 input "What is your name? ";name$
570 :
580 rem convert to lowercase
590 cv$ = name$
600 gosub 7000:rem lowercase subroutine
610 :
620 :
630 rem **--create problem--**
640 :
650 dm = len(max$)
660 :
670 rem when b's digits < dt
680 if dt = dm + 1 or dt < dm + 1 then 750
690 dm = 10 ^ dm
700 b = int(rnd(0) * dm)
710 if b < mn then 700
720 if b > max then 700
730 goto 800:rem get # for a
740 :
750 z = 1
760 b = int(rnd(0) * digit)
770 if b < mn then 760
780 if b > max then 760
790 :
800 a = int(rnd(0) * digit)
810 :
820 rem *-answer-*
830 c = a * b
840 s$ = "x":rem determine operation
850 sn$ = "multiplication"
860 if c < 0 then 760:rem for subtract.
870 if c = w then 760:rem previous ans.
880 w = c
890 :
900 :
1000 rem **--display problem--**
1010 rem determine lengths
1020 a$ = str$(a)
1030 da = len(a$)
1040 a$ = right$(a$,da - 1):rem no sign
1050 da = len(a$)
1060 b$ = str$(b)
1070 db = len(b$)
1080 b$ = right$(b$,db - 1):rem no sign
1090 db = len(b$)
1100 c$ = str$(c)
1110 dc = len(c$)
1120 c$ = right$(c$,dc - 1):rem no sign
1130 dc = len(c$)
1140 :
```

```
1150 rem format
1160 print home$:rem clr/home
1170 print tab(tb - 1) rvs$;nc$;"'s ";sn$;" practice."
1180 cd = 3:gosub 9000:rem crsr down 3
1190 print tab(4)
1200 print "Type the word ";blk$;"END";brn$;" when finished!"
1210 cd = 5:gosub 9000:rem crsr down 5
1220 print tab(22 - da):print a$
1230 print tab(22 - (db + 1)):print s$;b$
1240 :
1250 rem draw line
1260 q = 1
1270 if da > db then q = 0
1280 print tab(22 - (dt + q))
1290 for i = 1 to (dt + q)
1300 print "-";
1310 next i
1320 :
1330 :
1500 rem **--get answer--**
1510 print
1520 print tab(22 - dc)
1530 input answer$
1540 :
1550 if answer$ = "END" or answer$ = "end" then 2000
1560 d = val(answer$)
1570 if d = c then 5000:rem correct
1580 if z < 3 then 6000:rem wrong
1590 :
1600 rem give answer after 3 tries
1610 print:print:print:print tab(8)
1620 print "No, the answer is ";bue$;c;brn$
1630 print:print:print tab(8)
1640 print a;" ";s$;" ";b;" = ";c
1650 print:print:z = 1:wr = wr + 1
1660 print tab(8)
1670 print "Press ";blk$;"RETURN";brn$;" to continue: ";
1680 gosub 19000:rem return key routine
1690 goto 630:rem another problem
1700 :
1710 :
1720 :
2000 rem **--total routine--**
2010 rem clr/home--cursor down 5
2020 print home$:cd = 5:gosub 9000
2030 print tab(8)
2040 print "You got";bue$;cr;brn$;"right!"
2050 print:print tab(8)
2060 print "You missed";bue$;wr;brn$;"."
2070 :
2080 :
3000 rem **--file input/output--**
3010 :
3020 rem *-user message-*
3030 poke 19,0:rem reset input prompt
```

```
3040 cd = 5:gosub 9000:rem crsr down 5
3050 print tab(8)
3060 print rvs$;
3070 print "UPDATING FILES."
3080 print:print:print tab(8)
3090 print rvs$;"PLEASE WAIT!"
3100 :
3110 rem **--file input routine--**
3120 k = 1
3130 open 3,8,3,cv$ + ",seq,read"
3140 input#3,s$(k):rem sign
3150 input#3,dt(k):rem # of digits
3160 input#3,cr(k):rem # of correct
3170 input#3,wr(k):rem # of wrong
3180 if status = 0 then k = k + 1:goto 3140
3190 if status = 64 then k = k + 1
3200 :
3210 rem status =  0--all ok
3220 rem status = 64--eof
3230 rem status not 0 or 64--1st use
3240 :
3250 s$(k) = s$:dt(k) = dt: cr(k) = cr:wr(k) = wr
3260 close 3
3270 :
3280 :
3300 rem **--file output routine--**
3310 open 4,8,4,"@0:" + cv$ + ",seq,write"
3320 for i = 1 to k
3330 print#4,s$(i):rem sign
3340 print#4,dt(i):rem # of digits
3350 print#4,cr(i):rem # of correct
3360 print#4,wr(i):rem # of wrong
3370 next i
3380 :
3390 close 4
3400 :
3410 :
4000 rem **--return to program menu--**
4010 poke 19,0:rem restore input prompt
4020 rem clr/home cursor down routine
4030 print home$:cd = 5:gosub 9000
4040 print tab(tb)
4050 print rvs$;
4060 print "LOADING THE MATH MENU PROGRAM"
4070 ^"math.menu"
4080 :
4090 :
4100 :
5000 rem **--correct answer routine--**
5010 cd = 5:gosub 9000:rem crsr down 5
5020 print:print tab(18)
5030 print "GOOD!"
5040 for i = 1 to 1000:next i
5050 cr = cr + 1
5060 goto 630:rem another problem
5070 :
```

```
5080 :
6000 rem **--wrong answer routine--**
6010 cd = 5:gosub 9000:rem crsr down 5
6020 print:print tab(8)
6030 print "No, Please try again."
6040 z = z + 1
6050 print
6060 for i = 1 to 1000:next i
6070 goto 1150:rem ask again
6080 :
6090 :
7000 rem **--convert to lowercase--**
7010 for cv = 1 to len(cv$)
7020 x = asc(mid$(cv$,cv,1))
7030 if x > 192 then x = x - 128
7040 nc$ = nc$ + chr$(x)
7050 next cv
7060 :
7070 cv$ = nc$
7080 f = asc(left$(cv$,1))
7090 f = f + 128
7100 nc$ = chr$(f) + right$(cv$,len(cv$)- 1)
7110 return
7120 :
7130 rem na$ = originally typed name
7140 rem cv$ = converted to lowercase
7150 rem nc$ = 1st letter/uppercase
7160 :
7170 :
7180 :
9000 rem **--cursor down routine--**
9010 for i = 1 to cd
9020 print cd$;
9030 next i
9040 return
9050 :
9060 :
9070 :
19000 rem **--return key routine--**
19010 poke 198,0:rem clr kbrd buffer
19020 for i = 631 to 640
19030 poke i,0:rem no value
19040 next i
19050 x = peek(197):rem store key press
19060 if x = 1 then 19080:rem 1 = rtn.
19070 goto 19050:if not 1 go back
19080 poke 198,1:rem allow for cursor
19090 poke 631,0:rem clr kbrd
19100 nu$ = "":rem clr string variable
19110 return

ready.
```

■ Program for MATH.DIVIDE

```
100 rem ***--division--***
110 :
120 :
130 rem **--initialization--**
140 home$ = chr$(147):rem clr/home
150 ::cd$ = chr$( 17):rem cursor down
160 ::cu$ = chr$(145):rem cursor up
170 ::cl$ = chr$(157):rem cursor left
180 ::cr$ = chr$( 29):rem cursor right
190 :blk$ = chr$(144):rem black
200 :ylw$ = chr$(158):rem yellow
210 :wht$ = chr$(  5):rem white
220 :rvs$ = chr$( 18):rem reverse video
225 :bnk$ = chr$( 10):rem blank line
226 :brn$ = chr$(149):rem brown
227 :bue$ = chr$( 31):rem blue
230 :
240 poke 53280,14:rem border = lt.blue
250 poke 53272,23:rem upper/lower case
260 poke 53281, 7:rem set bkgrd to ylw
262 dim s$(100),dt(100),cr(100),wr(100)
263 tb = 5:rem tab value
265 :
266 :
270 rem **--variable list--**
280 rem a  = divisor
281 rem b  = dividend
282 rem c  = correct answer
283 rem d  = student's answer
284 rem q  = counter
285 rem w  = previous answer
286 rem z  = number of tries
287 rem cr = # of correct answers
288 rem wr = # of wrong answers
289 rem dt = # of digits
290 rem da = # of digits in a
291 rem db = # of digits in b
292 rem dc = # of digits in c
293 rem dm = # of digits in max amnt
294 rem other variables are descriptive
295
296
297
400 rem **--request user info.--**
410 print brn$:rem brown text/ylw bkgrd
420 poke 19,32:rem disable input ?
430 rem clr/home--cursor down 3
440 print home$:cd = 3:gosub 9000
450 input "How many digits? ";digit$
460 print:print:print
470 print "What is the largest figure for the"
480 input "number you are dividing by? ";max$
490 print:print:print
```

```
500 print "What is the smallest figure for the"
510 input "number you are dividing by? ";mn$
520 dt = val(digit$):max = val(max$):mn = val(mn$)
530 digit = val(digit$)
540 digit = 10 ^ digit
550 print:print:print
560 input "What is your name? ";name$
570 :
580 rem convert to lowercase
590 cv$ = name$
600 gosub 7000:rem lowercase subroutine
610 :
620 :
630 rem **--create problem--**
640 :
650 dm = len(max$)
660 :
670 rem when b's digits < dt
680 if dt = dm + 1 or dt < dm + 1 then 750
690 dm = 10 ^ dm
700 b = int(rnd(0) * dm)
710 if b < mn then 700
720 if b > max then 700
730 goto 800:rem get # for a
740 :
750 z = 1
760 b = int(rnd(0) * digit)
770 if b < mn then 760
780 if b > max then 760
790 :
800 a = int(rnd(0) * digit)
810 if a = 0 or a < b then 800
820 :
830 rem *-answer-*
840 def fn mod(c) = int((a/b - int(a/b))* b + .05) * sgn(a/b)
850 c = int(a)/(b)
860 c = int(c)
870 s$ = "/":rem determine operation
880 sn$ = "division"
890 if c < 0 then 760:rem for subtract.
900 if c = w then 760:rem previous ans.
910 if fn mod(rm) <> 0 then 800
920 w = c
930 :
940 :
1000 rem **--display problem--**
1010 rem determine lengths
1020 a$ = str$(a)
1030 da = len(a$)
1040 a$ = right$(a$,da - 1):rem no sign
1050 da = len(a$)
1060 b$ = str$(b)
1070 db = len(b$)
1080 b$ = right$(b$,db - 1):rem no sign
1090 db = len(b$)
1100 c$ = str$(c)
```

```
1110 dc = len(c$)
1120 c$ = right$(c$,dc - 1):rem no sign
1130 dc = len(c$)
1140 :
1150 rem format
1160 print home$:rem clr/home
1170 print tab(tb + 2) rvs$;nc$;"'s ";sn$;" practice."
1180 cd = 3:gosub 9000:rem crsr down 3
1190 print tab(4)
1200 print "Type the word ";blk$;"END";brn$;" when finished!"
1210 cd = 5:gosub 9000:rem crsr down 5
1220 print tab(18)
1230 for i = 1 to dt + 1
1240 print "-";
1250 next i
1260 print
1270 print tab(18 - db) b$;")";a$
1280 :
1290 :
1500 rem **--get answer--**
1510 print:print cu$;cu$;cu$;cu$;
1520 print tab((18 + da) - (dc - 1))
1530 input answer$
1540 :
1550 if answer$ = "END" or answer$ = "end" then 2000
1560 d = val(answer$)
1570 if d = c then 5000:rem correct
1580 if z < 3 then 6000:rem wrong
1590 :
1600 rem give answer after 3 tries
1610 print:print:print:print tab(8)
1620 print "No, the answer is ";bue$;c;brn$
1630 print:print:print tab(8)
1640 print a;" ";s$;" ";b;" = ";c
1650 print:print:z = 1:wr = wr + 1
1660 print tab(8)
1670 print "Press ";blk$;"RETURN";brn$;" to continue: ";
1680 gosub 19000:rem return key routine
1690 goto 630:rem another problem
1700 :
1710 :
1720 :
2000 rem **--total routine--**
2010 rem clr/home--cursor down 5
2020 print home$:cd = 5:gosub 9000
2030 print tab(8)
2040 print "You got";bue$;cr;brn$;"right!"
2050 print:print tab(8)
2060 print "You missed";bue$;wr;brn$;"."
2070 :
2080 :
3000 rem **--file input/output--**
3010 :
3020 rem *-user message-*
3030 poke 19,0:rem reset input prompt
3040 cd = 5:gosub 9000:rem crsr down 5
```

```
3050 print tab(8)
3060 print rvs$;
3070 print "UPDATING FILES."
3080 print:print:print tab(8)
3090 print rvs$;"PLEASE WAIT!"
3100 :
3110 rem **--file input routine--**
3120 k = 1
3130 open 3,8,3,cv$ + ",seq,read"
3140 input#3,s$(k):rem sign
3150 input#3,dt(k):rem # of digits
3160 input#3,cr(k):rem # of correct
3170 input#3,wr(k):rem # of wrong
3180 if status = 0 then k = k + 1:goto 3140
3190 if status = 64 then k = k + 1
3200 :
3210 rem status =  0--all ok
3220 rem status = 64--eof
3230 rem status not 0 or 64--1st use
3240 :
3250 s$(k) = s$:dt(k) = dt: cr(k) = cr:wr(k) = wr
3260 close 3
3270 :
3280 :
3300 rem **--file output routine--**
3310 open 4,8,4,"@0:" + cv$ + ",seq,write"
3320 for i = 1 to k
3330 print#4,s$(i):rem sign
3340 print#4,dt(i):rem # of digits
3350 print#4,cr(i):rem # of correct
3360 print#4,wr(i):rem # of wrong
3370 next i
3380 :
3390 close 4
3400 :
3410 :
4000 rem **--return to program menu--**
4010 poke 19,0:rem restore input prompt
4020 rem clr/home cursor down routine
4030 print home$:cd = 5:gosub 9000
4040 print tab(tb)
4050 print rvs$;
4060 print "LOADING THE MATH MENU PROGRAM"
4070 ^"math.menu"
4080 :
4090 :
4100 :
5000 rem **--correct answer routine--**
5010 cd = 5:gosub 9000:rem crsr down 5
5020 print:print tab(18)
5030 print "GOOD!"
5040 for i = 1 to 1000:next i
5050 cr = cr + 1
5060 goto 630:rem another problem
5070 :
```

```
5080 :
6000 rem **--wrong answer routine--**
6010 cd = 5:gosub 9000:rem crsr down 5
6020 print:print tab(8)
6030 print "No, Please try again."
6040 z = z + 1
6050 print
6060 for i = 1 to 1000:next i
6070 goto 1150:rem ask again
6080 :
6090 :
7000 rem **--convert to lowercase--**
7010 for cv = 1 to len(cv$)
7020 x = asc(mid$(cv$,cv,1))
7030 if x > 192 then x = x - 128
7040 nc$ = nc$ + chr$(x)
7050 next cv
7060
7070 cv$ = nc$
7080 f = asc(left$(cv$,1))
7090 f = f + 128
7100 nc$ = chr$(f) + right$(cv$,len(cv$)- 1)
7110 return
7120 :
7130 rem na$ = originally typed name
7140 rem cv$ = converted to lowercase
7150 rem nc$ = 1st letter/uppercase
7160 :
7170 :
7180 :
9000 rem **--cursor down routine--**
9010 for i = 1 to cd
9020 print cd$;
9030 next i
9040 return
9050 :
9060 :
9070 :
19000 rem **--return key routine--**
19010 poke 198,0:rem clr kbrd buffer
19020 for i = 631 to 640
19030 poke i,0:rem no value
19040 next i
19050 x = peek(197):rem store key press
19060 if x = 1 then 19080:rem 1 = rtn.
19070 goto 19050:if not 1 go back
19080 poke 198,1:rem allow for cursor
19090 poke 631,0:rem clr kbrd
19100 nu$ = "":rem clr string variable
19110 return

ready.
```

Program for MATH.SCORES

```
100 rem ***--math.scores--***
110 :
120 :
130 rem **--initialization--**
140 home$ = chr$(147):rem clr/home
150 ::cd$ = chr$( 17):rem cursor down
160 ::cu$ = chr$(145):rem cursor up
170 ::cl$ = chr$(157):rem cursor left
180 ::cr$ = chr$( 29):rem cursor right
190 :blk$ = chr$(144):rem black
200 :ylw$ = chr$(158):rem yellow
210 :wht$ = chr$(  5):rem white
220 :rvs$ = chr$( 18):rem reverse video
225 :bnk$ = chr$( 10):rem blank line
230 :
240 poke 53280,14:rem border = lt.blue
250 poke 53272,23:rem upper/lower case
260 poke 53281, 2:rem set bkgrd to red
265 :
266 :
270 rem **--user message--**
280 print home$:rem clr/home
290 cd = 5:gosub 9000:rem crsr down 5
300 poke 19,32:rem disable input ?
310 input "Student's name please: ";na$
320 rem convert to lowercase
330 cv$ = na$:gosub 7000
340 gosub 10000:rem display routine
350 print home$:cd = 5:gosub 9000
360 print ylw$;"ONE MOMENT PLEASE!"
370 :
380 rem **--file input routine--**
390 dim s$(100),dt(100),cr(100),wr(100)
400 open 2,8,2,cv$ + ",seq,read"
410 k = 1
420 input#2,s$(k):rem sign of operation
430 input#2,dt(k):rem # of digits
440 input#2,cr(k):rem # correct
450 input#2,wr(k):rem # wrong
460 k = k + 1
470 if status = 0 then 420
480 close 2
490 :
500 rem **--display scores--**
510 gosub 6000:rem titles routine
520 j = 1
530 for q = 1 to k - 1
540 if s$(q) = "+" then s$(q) = "ADD"
550 if s$(q) = "-" then s$(q) = "SUB"
560 if s$(q) = "x" then s$(q) = "MLT"
570 if s$(q) = "/" then s$(q) = "DIV"
580 if q < 10 then print#file,"";tab( 1) q;:goto 600
```

```
590 print#file,"";q;
600 print#file,"";tab(10) s$(q);
610 print#file,"";tab(19) dt(q);
620 if cr(q) > 9 then u = - 1
630 print#file,"";tab(28 + u) cr(q);
640 u = 0
650 if wr(q) > 9 then u = - 1
660 print#file,"";tab(35 + u) wr(q)
670 u = 0
680 j = j + 1
690 rem 19000 is rtn key routine
700 rem  6000 is titles routine        7
710 if j > 15 then gosub 19000:gosub 6000
720 next q
730 :
740 gosub 19000:rem rtn key routine
750 :
760 :
800 rem **--return to program menu--**
810 poke 19,0:rem restore input prompt
820 rem clr/home cursor down routine
830 print home$:cd = 5:gosub 9000
840 print tab(5)
850 print rvs$;
860 print "LOADING THE MATH MENU PROGRAM"
870 ^"math.menu"
880 :
890 :
900 :
6000 rem **--titles routine--**
6010 print home$:rem clr/home
6015 print tab(17) nc$:print:print
6020 print "SESS.";
6030 print tab( 7):print "OPERATION";
6040 print tab(18):print "DIGITS";
6050 print tab(26):print "CORRECT";
6060 print tab(34):print "WRONG"
6070 return
6080 :
6090 :
6100 :
7000 rem **--convert to lowercase--**
7010 for cv = 1 to len(cv$)
7020 x = asc(mid$(cv$,cv,1))
7030 if x > 192 then x = x - 128
7040 nc$ = nc$ + chr$(x)
7050 next cv
7060 :
7070 cv$ = nc$
7080 f = asc(left$(cv$,1))
7090 f = f + 128
7100 nc$ = chr$(f) + right$(cv$,len(cv$)- 1)
7110 return
7120 :
7130 rem na$ = originally typed name
7140 rem cv$ = converted to lowercase
```

```
7150 rem nc$ = 1st letter/uppercase
7160 :
7170 :
7180 :
9000 rem **--cursor down routine--**
9010 for i = 1 to cd
9020 print cd$;
9030 next i
9040 return
9050 :
9060 :
9070 :
10000 rem **--display routine--**
10010 print home$:rem clr/home
10020 cd = 3:rem 3 lines down
10030 gosub 9000:rem cursor down routine
10040 print "Would you like a paper print out?"
10050 print
10080 gosub 18000:rem y/n input routine
10090 if yes$ = "y" then 10240:rem prnt
10100 if yes$ = "n" then 10300:rem scrn
10110 :
10120 print home$:rem clr/home
10130 cd = 3:rem 3 lines down
10140 gosub 9000:rem cursor down routine
10150 print "Please make sure the printer"
10160 print
10170 print "is on and ready to use."
10180 print
10190 print "Are you ready to begin printing?"
10200 print
10210 gosub 18000:rem y/n input routine
10220 if yes$ = "n" then 10000
10230 :
10240 rem *-printer display-*
10250 file = 4
10260 dvic = 4
10270 cmnd = 7
10280 goto 10500:rem open instruction
10290 :
10300 rem *-screen display-*
10310 file = 3
10320 dvic = 3
10330 cmnd = 1
10340 goto 10500:rem open instruction
10350 :
10360 :
10500 rem *-open instruction-*
10510 open file,dvic,cmnd
10520 return
10530 :
10540 :
10550 :
18000 rem **--y/n input routine--**
18010 print "Type a ";wht$;"Y";ylw$;" or ";wht$;"N";ylw$;" :";
```

```
18020 poke 19,32:rem disable input ?
18030 input yes$
18040 print
18050 if yes$ = "y" or yes$ = "Y" then yes$ = "y":return
18060 if yes$ = "n" or yes$ = "N" then yes$ = "n":return
18070 print
18080 print rvs$;"Incorrect Choice!";ylw$
18090 print
18100 goto 18000:rem begin again
18110 :
18120 :
18130 :
19000 rem **--return key routine--**
19010 print
19020 print "Press ";wht$;"RETURN";ylw$;" to continue: ";
19030 poke 198,0:rem clr kbrd buffer
19040 for i = 631 to 640
19050 poke i,0:rem no value
19060 next i
19070 x = peek(197):rem store key press
19080 if x = 1 then 19100:rem 1 = rtn.
19090 goto 19070:if not 1 go back
19100 poke 19,0:rem restore input prompt
19110 poke 198,1:rem allow for cursor
19120 poke 631,0:rem clr kbrd
19130 nu$ = "":rem clr string variable
19140 j = 1
19150 return

ready.
```

■ Program for CREATE Q & A

```
100 rem ***--create q & a--***
110 :
120 :
130 rem **--initialization--**
140 home$ = chr$(147):rem clr/home
150 ::cd$ = chr$( 17):rem cursor down
160 ::cu$ = chr$(145):rem cursor up
170 ::cl$ = chr$(157):rem cursor left
180 ::cr$ = chr$( 29):rem cursor right
190 :blk$ = chr$(144):rem black
200 :ylw$ = chr$(158):rem yellow
210 :wht$ = chr$(  5):rem white
220 :rvs$ = chr$( 18):rem reverse video
225 :bnk$ = chr$( 10):rem blank line
230 :
240 poke 53280,14:rem border = lt.blue
250 poke 53272,23:rem upper/lower case
260 poke 53281, 0:rem set bkgrd to red
262 dim q$(50),a$(50)
263 k = 1
264 poke 19,32:rem disable input ?
265 :
266 :
500 rem **--input routine--**
505 print ylw$
510 print home$:cd = 5:gosub 9000
520 input "Subject name? ";sub$
530 sub$ = sub$ + ".quest"
540 print home$:cd = 5:gosub 9000
550 print "Type ";wht$;"END";ylw$;" when finished."
560 print:print
570 print "QUESTION #";k;":"
580 print
590 input q$(k)
600 if q$(k) = "END" or q$(k) = "end" then 1000
610 print:print
620 print "ANSWER:"
630 print
640 input a$(k)
650 print home$:cd = 5:gosub 9000
660 print q$(k)
670 print
680 print a$(k)
690 print
700 print "Is this correct? ";
710 gosub 18000:rem y/n input routine
720 if yes$ = "n" then 540
730 k = k + 1
740 goto 540
750 :
760 :
1000 rem **--file output routine--**
1010 open 2,8,2,sub$ + ",seq,write"
```

```
1020 print#2,k-1
1030 for j = 1 to k-1
1040 print#2,q$(j)
1050 print#2,a$(j)
1060 next j
1070 close 2
1080 poke 19,0:rem restore input prompt
1090 end
1100 :
1110 :
1120 :
9000 rem **--cursor down routine--**
9010 for i = 1 to cd
9020 print cd$;
9030 next i
9040 return
9050 :
9060 :
9070 :
18000 rem **--y/n input routine--**
18010 print "Type a ";wht$;"Y";ylw$;" or ";wht$;"N";ylw$;" :";
18020 poke 19,32:rem disable input ?
18030 input yes$
18040 print
18050 if yes$ = "y" or yes$ = "Y" then yes$ = "y":return
18060 if yes$ = "n" or yes$ = "N" then yes$ = "n":return
18070 print
18080 print rvs$;"Incorrect Choice!";ylw$
18090 print
18100 goto 18000:rem begin again

ready.
```

■ Program for DRILL & PRACTICE

```
100 rem ***--drill & practice--***
110 :
120 :
130 rem **--initialization--**
140 home$ = chr$(147):rem clr/home
150 ::cd$ = chr$( 17):rem cursor down
160 ::cu$ = chr$(145):rem cursor up
170 ::cl$ = chr$(157):rem cursor left
180 ::cr$ = chr$( 29):rem cursor right
190 :blk$ = chr$(144):rem black
200 :ylw$ = chr$(158):rem yellow
210 :wht$ = chr$(  5):rem white
220 :rvs$ = chr$( 18):rem reverse video
225 :bnk$ = chr$( 10):rem blank line
230 :
240 poke 53280,14:rem border = lt.blue
250 poke 53272,23:rem upper/lower case
260 poke 53281, 2:rem set bkgrd to red
265 :
266 :
270 rem **--user message--**
280 print home$:rem clr/home
290 cd = 5:gosub 9000:rem crsr down 5
300 poke 19,32:rem disable input ?
310 input "Subject's name please: ";sb$
320 rem convert to lowercase
330 cv$ = sb$:gosub 7000
340 sb$ = cv$ + ".quest"
350 gosub 10000:rem display routine
360 print home$:cd = 5:gosub 9000
370 print ylw$;"ONE MOMENT PLEASE!"
380 :
390 :
400 rem **--file input routine--**
410 dim q$(50),a$(50)
420 open 2,8,2,sb$ + ",seq,read"
430 input#2,j
440 for i = 1 to j
450 input#2,q$(i):rem questions
460 input#2,a$(i):rem answers
470 next i
480 close 2
490 :
500 rem **--display questions--**
510 i = rnd(0) * 10:za = i:i = int(i)
520 if i > j or i < 1 then 510
530 print home$:cd = 5:gosub 9000
540 print "Answer with ";wht$;"END";ylw$;" when finished."
550 print:print
560 print q$(i)
570 print:print
580 input "Your answer is: ";ans$
585 nc$ = ""
```

```
590 cv$ = ans$:gosub 7000:ans$ = cv$
595 nc$ = ""
600 cv$ = a$(i):gosub 7000:a$(i) = cv$
610 print
620 if ans$ = "end" then 1000
630 if ans$ = a$(i) then print "CORRECT":a = a + 1:goto 800
640 if z > 0 then 700
650 print "No, try once more."
660 print
670 z = 1
680 a2 = a2 + 1
690 goto 570
700 print "No, the answer is: ";a$(i)
710 m = m + 1
800 z = 0
810 print
820 for k = 1 to 1000:next k
830 goto 500
880 :
890 :
900 :
1000 rem **--display score--**
1010 a2 = a2 - m
1020 a = a - a2
1030 print home$:cd = 3:gosub 9000
1040 print "You got";a;"right on the first try."
1050 print:print
1060 print "You got";a2;"right on the second try."
1070 print:print
1080 print "You missed";m;"answers."
1090 end
1100 :
1110 :
6000 rem **--titles routine--**
6010 print home$:rem clr/home
6015 print tab(17) nc$:print:print
6020 print "SESS.";
6030 print tab( 7):print "OPERATION";
6040 print tab(18):print "DIGITS";
6050 print tab(26):print "CORRECT";
6060 print tab(34):print "WRONG"
6070 return
6080 :
6090 :
6100 :
7000 rem **--convert to lowercase--**
7010 for cv = 1 to len(cv$)
7020 x = asc(mid$(cv$,cv,1))
7030 if x > 192 then x = x - 128
7040 nc$ = nc$ + chr$(x)
7050 next cv
7060 :
7070 cv$ = nc$
7080 f = asc(left$(cv$,1))
7090 f = f + 128
7100 nc$ = chr$(f) + right$(cv$,len(cv$)- 1)
```

```
7110 return
7120 :
7130 rem na$ = originally typed name
7140 rem cv$ = converted to lowercase
7150 rem nc$ = 1st letter/uppercase
7160 :
7170 :
7180 :
9000 rem **--cursor down routine--**
9010 for d = 1 to cd
9020 print cd$;
9030 next d
9040 return
9050 :
9060 :
9070 :
10000 rem **--display routine--**
10010 print home$:rem clr/home
10020 cd = 3:rem 3 lines down
10030 gosub 9000:rem cursor down routine
10040 print "Would you like a paper print out?"
10050 print
10080 gosub 18000:rem y/n input routine
10090 if yes$ = "y" then 10240:rem prnt
10100 if yes$ = "n" then 10300:rem scrn
10110 :
10120 print home$:rem clr/home
10130 cd = 3:rem 3 lines down
10140 gosub 9000:rem cursor down routinerun
10150 print "Please make sure the printer"
10160 print
10170 print "is on and ready to use."
10180 print
10190 print "Are you ready to begin printing?"
10200 print
10210 gosub 18000:rem y/n input routine
10220 if yes$ = "n" then 10000
10230 :
10240 rem *-printer display-*
10250 file = 4
10260 dvic = 4
10270 cmnd = 7
10280 goto 10500:rem open instruction
10290 :
10300 rem *-screen display-*
10310 file = 3
10320 dvic = 3
10330 cmnd = 1
10340 goto 10500:rem open instruction
10350 :
10360 :
10500 rem *-open instruction-*
10510 open file,dvic,cmnd
10520 return
10530 :
10540 :
```

```
10550 :
18000 rem **--y/n input routine--**
18010 print "Type a ";wht$;"Y";ylw$;" or ";wht$;"N";ylw$;" :";
18020 poke 19,32:rem disable input ?
18030 input yes$
18040 print
18050 if yes$ = "y" or yes$ = "Y" then yes$ = "y":return
18060 if yes$ = "n" or yes$ = "N" then yes$ = "n":return
18070 print
18080 print rvs$;"Incorrect Choice!";ylw$
18090 print
18100 goto 18000:rem begin again
18110 :
18120 :
18130 :
19000 rem **--return key routine--**
19010 print
19020 print "Press ";wht$;"RETURN";ylw$;" to continue: ";
19030 poke 198,0:rem clr kbrd buffer
19040 for i = 631 to 640
19050 poke i,0:rem no value
19060 next i
19070 x = peek(197):rem store key press
19080 if x = 1 then 19100:rem 1 = rtn.
19090 goto 19070:if not 1 go back
19100 poke 19,0:rem restore input prompt
19110 poke 198,1:rem allow for cursor
19120 poke 631,0:rem clr kbrd
19130 nu$ = "":rem clr string variable
19140 j = 1
19150 return

ready.
```

9 DIF files

One of the more exciting possibilities in file handling is the prospect of a standard format for transferring file information. At least one such standard is now being supported by a number of major pieces of application software. The DIF file format was developed by Software Arts, writers of VisiCalc. It is important to keep in mind the intent of this standard. The standard does not suggest that all files be stored according to the DIF format. Such a requirement would place an impossible burden on too many applications to make the standard truly acceptable. Instead, the standard suggests a specific format for file transfer.

If you never expect to transfer your file information from one program to another, you have no real need to use DIF. But if you wish to have different programs share the same data, then a standard such as DIF is very valuable. For example, if you never expect to use another program with your Mailing List System names and addresses, then there is no reason to store those names and addresses according to the DIF format. On the other hand, if you want to use Calc Result (or some other DIF-supporting spreadsheet program) with the scores obtained from the math system, then the DIF format becomes important. Without the standard, it would be necessary to type all the scores into the Calc Result program. With DIF, Calc Result can read the scores directly from the disk. On a small file, retyping is not a big consideration, but as the file grows, it becomes a major problem.

Regardless of the file size, rekeying the information for every application program that makes use of the same data is annoying, inconvenient, and unnecessary. If an application program such as Calc Result makes use of, or supports, the DIF file format, any information stored according to that standard can be used by that application program.

Most application programs supporting DIF actually offer you two methods of saving your information or data. The first or standard method is the most efficient and effective way to store information for the specific program. The second method is the DIF format. In other words, the file is saved twice, once in the normal manner according to the program needs, and the second time in a format that allows other programs to access and use the information. This two-method system is necessary because the DIF format (or any standard format) is not a very efficient way of storing and retrieving information. Let's look at the DIF format and use it to store the scores from the Math System so that Calc Result can directly access those scores.

Before getting into the exact way DIF files are stored, it is necessary to understand that, in order to make a standard method of saving information, the file must contain information about itself: where it starts and ends, whether the information is numeric or alphabetic, label information, or actual data. The creators of DIF decided that all DIF files must be divided into two basic parts. The first part contains information about the file itself, and the second contains the actual data. The first part is called the *Header Section* and the second part the *Data Section*. Next, since there are many ways of displaying information, they decided to group all information into two categories: *Vectors* and *Tuples*. Basically, Vectors and Tuples are just columns and rows. Finally, each piece of information must carry with it the type of information it is: numeric, alphabetic (alphanumeric), or special (descriptive). To distinguish between these types of information, they assigned the following codes: a "0" indicates numeric information, a "1" indicates alphanumeric information, and a "– 1" indicates special or descriptive file information.

The only other major decision to be made is the exact organization of the file. This organizational decision is indeed more complex, but it does follow a logical pattern and can be learned with practice. The Header Section (the part of the file that carries information about itself) comes first. Obviously, then, the Data Section comes after the Header Section. The beginning and ending of each of these sections must then be indicated in some way.

If you remember, in the Mailing List System we used two symbols as separators, the "!" and the "*" (see Chapter 4). In much the same way, the creators of DIF have used symbols to set off the beginning and ending points of the two file sections. The word "TABLE" is used to begin the file and is the first entry in the Header Section. The characters "EOD" (End Of Data) are used as the last entry of the file and the end of the Data Section.

Finally, something must divide the two sections. The DIF creators decided that the division should occur in the Header Section and had to be the last entry in that section. That last entry, then, has to follow the pattern for the Header Section. This means that the division between the Header Section and the Data Section needs to be in the following format:

```
DATA
0,0
""
```

We now have the beginning and ending of the file and the division between the two sections.

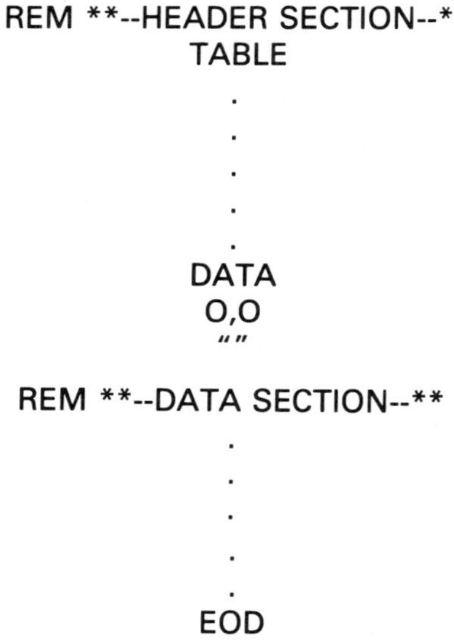

The two sections are organized in slightly different ways. The Header Section requires three lines of information for each entry, while the Data Section uses two lines of information for each entry.

HEADER SECTION

The first line in each entry of the Header Section gives the topic of the entry. TABLE, VECTORS, TUPLES, and DATA are the usual topic lines. The second line in each entry gives numeric information about each topic, such as the number of VECTORS and the number of TUPLES. The third line allows for a name for each topic if a name is necessary. A typical Header Section might look like the following:

```
TABLE
0,1
"SCORES"
:
VECTORS
0,5
""
:
TUPLES
0,4
""
:
LABEL
1,0
"SESSION #"
:
LABEL
2,0
"OPERATION"
:
LABEL
3,0
"DIGITS"
:
LABEL
4,0
"# CORRECT"
:
LABEL
5,0
"# WRONG"
:
DATA
0,0
""
```

(I have added the colons to separate the individual entries.)

Remember that this is the way the information would look in the file and that this section contains information about the file itself. Since VECTORS and TUPLES are basically columns and rows, it is not too difficult to understand the numeric information required in the second line of information in each entry of the Header Section. The first number is the VECTOR number or column number. The second number is a specific value related to the topic of the entry.

	Math scores			
Session #	*Operation*	*Digits*	*Correct*	*Wrong*
1	*ADD*	*2*	*8*	*2*
2	*MUL*	*3*	*12*	*8*
3	*DIV*	*3*	*7*	*13*
4	*SUB*	*5*	*24*	*1*

For example, in a table of five columns, the second line of information under the topic of VECTORS would be "0,5". Since the topic "VECTORS" is not actually in the table, it does not have a column number (Vector name), so the "0" is first. The "5" indicates the value relating to the topic, VECTORS or five columns. Under the topic of LABEL, you can list the actual names of the columns, their relative positions, and any specific value. With a LABEL, the value is usually "0" in a simple table. TUPLES, or rows, might have a second line of "0,4" indicating that the topic TUPLES was not actually in the table but had a value of 4 (*i.e.*, 4 rows).The value for the topic TABLE is the version number and must be a "1". So we see that the Header Section describes a file of information that, in our example, consists of 5 columns and 4 rows (5 VECTORS and 4 TUPLES).

DATA SECTION

Each entry of the Data Section consists of two lines of information. The first line is numeric and gives two pieces of information: the type of information and the value associated with that information. The second line provides alphabetic information associated with the entry. For instance, if the information being stored was the number "62.5", the Data Section Entry would be:

```
0,62.5
V
```

If the information being stored was the word "PERCENT", the entry would be:

```
1,0
"PERCENT"
```

In the first example, the information or data is numeric, so the first number in the first line of this entry is a "0". The value associated with this entry is the information itself, "62.5". The second line of a numeric piece of information can have one of five possibilities:

1. V for a numeric value.
2. NA for not available; the numeric value is 0.
3. ERROR when an invalid calculation has resulted in an error; the numeric value is 0.
4. TRUE for the logical value; the numeric value is 1.
5. FALSE for the logical value; the numeric value is 0.

These five possibilities lend greater flexibility to those who may have need for complex data manipulation. In simpler files, numeric information will usually have a second line of "V".

In the second example, the information being stored is alphabetic, so the first number in the first line of this entry is a "1". The value associated with alphabetic information is usually "0" so that the first line is "1,0". The second line provides alphabetic information about the entry, and since the information is alphabetic, this second line is the information itself. In other words, if the information is alphanumeric (a "1" is indicated in the first line of the entry), the second line contains that alphanumeric information.

The other possibility for an entry in the Data Section is that of a *special value*. There are two special values: one for the beginning of each Tuple and one for the end of the Data Section. Information is grouped within the Data Section by TUPLES (rows) with a special entry marking the beginning of each TUPLE. The entry for this beginning is:

```
-1,0
BOT
```

And the entry for the end of the Data Section is:

```
-1,0
EOD
```

The first number in the first line is the type of information (a "−1" indicating a special entry), and the second is the value associated with that entry (a "0" for special entries). The second line contains either a BOT for Beginning Of Tuple or EOD for End Of Data.

We should now be able to write out a sample TUPLE for the file using the scores from the Math System.

```
-1,0          (beginning of tuple)
BOT
:
```

(Continued on following page)

```
0,1            (math session number)
V
:
1,0            (type of operation)
"ADD"
:
0,2            (number of digits)
V
:
0,15           (number correct)
V
:
0,2            (number wrong)
V
:
-1,0           (beginning of next tuple)
BOT
```

The words in parentheses would not be included in the file. They are there to help explain each entry. Again, I have added the colons to separate each entry.

The organization of the Header Section and the Data Section allows for a large variety in file manipulation, far more variety than I have gone into with this explanation. Further information on the structure and flexibility of DIF files can be obtained from: (1) the DIF Clearinghouse, POB 527, Cambridge, MA 02139, or (2) by reading the information contained in the VisiCalc program, or (3) by reading "DIF: A Format for Data Exchange between Applications Programs," *BYTE MAGAZINE*, November, 1981, p. 174, or (4) in the comprehensive new book *The DIF File* by Donald H. Beil, Reston Publishing Company, Reston, VA 22090.

Now, we should be able to write a simple program that will reformat our math scores file in such a way that it conforms to the DIF standard. The first part of this program reads the scores into memory. The second part does the reformatting. Again, I will only present the code that relates to file handling. The entire program is included at the end of the chapter.

```
370 rem **--file input routine--**
380 dim s$(100),dt(100),cr(100),wr(100)
390 open 2,8,2, cv$ + ",seq,read"
400 k = 1
410 input#2,s $(k):rem sign of operation
420 input#2,d t(k):rem # digits
430 input#2,c r(k):rem # correct
```

```
440 input#2,wr(k):rem # wrong
450 if s$(k)    = "+" then s$(k) = "ADD"
460 if s$(k)    = "-" then s$(k) = "SUB"
470 if s$(k)    = "x" then s$(k) = "MLT"
480 if s$(k)    = "/" then s$(k) = "DIV"
490 k = k       + 1
500 if status = 0 then 410
510 close 2
520 :
530 :
```

This is virtually the same routine we used for the "math.scores" program. The next part of the program is designed by following the necessary organization of either the Header Section or the Data Section.

```
1000 rem **--dif routine--**
1010 print home$:cd = 5:gosub 9000
1020 print rvs$;"WRITING DIF FILE"
1030 print
1040 j = k - 1:nv = 5:nt = k - 1
1050 q$ = chr$(34):rem quote mark
1060 rem j  = counter
1070 rem nv = number of vectors
1080 rem nt = number of tuples
1090 file$    = cv$ + ".dif"
1100 open 3,8,3,"@0:" + file$ + ",seq,write"
1110 :
1120 :
2000 rem **--header section--**
2010 :
2020 print#3, "TABLE"
2030 print#3,"0,1"
2040 print#3,q$nc$q$
2050 :
2060 print#3,"VECTORS"
2070 print#3,"0, ";nv
2080 print#3,q$q$
2090 :
2100 print#3, "TUPLES"
2110 print#3,"0,";nt
2120 print#3,q$q$
2130 :
```

```
2140 print#3, "DATA"
2150 print#3, "0,0"
2160 print#3,q$q$
2170 :
2180 :
```

These lines create the Header Section. They follow the rules of the Header Section in that each entry has three lines: the topic line, the numeric line, and the title or string line. The instructions at line 1040 could be handled with input variable statements instead of constants. Line 1090 combines the name of the file with the suffix ".DIF" to distinguish between the two files. This suffix may be required for some application programs.

The next section of code creates the Data Section.

```
3000 rem **--data section--**
3010 :
3020 print#3," -1,0"
3030 print#3,"BOT"
3040 :
3050 print#3,"1,0"
3060 print#3,q$"Session #"q$
3070 :
3080 print#3,"1,0"
3090 print#3,q$"Operation"q$
3100 :
3110 print#3,"1,0"
3120 print#3,q$"Digits"q$
3130 :
3140 print#3,"1,0"
3150 print#3,q$"Correct"q$
3160 :
3170 print#3,"1,0"
3180 print#3,q$"Wrong"q$
3190 :
3200 for i = 1 to j
3210 :
3220 print#3," -1,0"
3230 print#3,"BOT"
3240 :
3250 print#3,"0,";i:rem math session #
3260 print#3,"V"
3270 :
3280 print#3,"1,0":rem operation
```

```
3290 print#3,s$(i)
3300 :
3310 print#3,"0,";dt(i):rem # of digits
3320 print#3,"V"
3330 :
3340 print#3,"0,";cr(i):rem # correct
3350 print#3,"V"
3360 :
3370 print#3,"0,";wr(i):rem # wrong
3380 print#3,"V"
3390 :
3400 next i
3410 print#3,"-1,0"
3420 print#3,"EOD"
3430 :
3440 close 3
3450 :
3460 :
3470 :
```

We include the labels with the Data Section so that Calc Result will view them as data and include them in the display. (Calc Result does not support the "LABEL" topic in the Header Section.) Once the label information has been included, we write out the actual data by printing the contents of the various arrays. We use a loop to accomplish this. When the loop is finished, the special entry EOD is written and the file closed. Now, we should have a program that will create a duplicate file of an individual's math scores in the DIF file format.

We are able to create a DIF file that can be accessed by DIF supporting application programs. One other step remains. We may need to use data obtained with an application program. This requires that we create a program that reads DIF files. Reading a DIF file is simply reading a sequential file that has its information stored in a specific order. The following program will read a Calc Result DIF file. The display portion of the program is left in its original form since each file may require a different display format.

```
370 rem **--file input routine--**
380 dim a$(200),s(200),n(200)
390 open 2,8,2,cv$ + ".dif,seq,read"
400 k = 1
410 input#2,t$:rem read the topic name
420 input#2,s,n:rem vector #, value
430 input#2,s$:rem string value
440 if t$ = "VECTORS" then nv = n
```

```
450 if t$ = "TUPLES"   then nt = n
460 if t$ <> "DATA"    then 410
470 :
480 input#2,s(k),n(k):rem data 1st line
490 input#2,a$(k):rem data 2nd line
500 if a$(k) = "EOD" then 540
510 k = k + 1
520 goto 480
530 :
540 close 2
550 :
560 :
1000 rem **--display routine--**
1010 print home$:cd = 5:gosub 9000
1020 for j = 1 to k
1030 print s(j);",";n(j)
1040 print a$(j)
1050 next j
1060 :
1070 :
```

The display routine is left in its elementary form since the point of the program is to show how to access files from DIF supporting application programs. All these lines should be familiar. Line 460 tells the computer to go back to line 410 until T$ equals "DATA". At that time, the computer is to drop down to the loop used to read and store the Data Section information (lines 480 through 520). When a$(k) reads the value "EOD", we know that the file is finished, and we need to close the file and proceed to the display routine.

As with all programs, there are other ways of writing a DIF reader program and obtaining essentially the same results. We could have read and saved all the information contained in the Header Section. We could have used a number of GOSUBS (especially in the DIF creator program). But most of these differences are stylistic differences and not substantive differences.

You now have the ability to read and write DIF files. That ability may not prove immediately useful, but I think you will find that this may eventually be the most valuable thing you have learned in this book. If you are not completely sure you understand the format, a second look through this chapter and additional work with DIF creator or reader programs should make you comfortable with DIF.

I have not tried to explain all the possibilities or variations of DIF. This chapter is intended only as an introduction to this file transfer standard. I firmly believe that some such standard is essential if micros are to be taken seriously.

I will conclude this chapter with a tutorial on the specific procedure necessary to transfer the information stored in the scores files to the Calc Result program

(CBM 64 Advanced Version). This section will be useful to you only if you have Calc Result and have actually typed in and run the math system programs. You will need to have typed in the "scores.dif" program discussed in this chapter also. (Diskettes containing all the programs in this book are available for those who do not want to type in every program. See the Bookware page in the front of the book for ordering information.)

STEP 1: Type: /scores.dif

STEP 2: Type RUN and press the RETURN key.

STEP 3: Answer the question with your name if you have used the Math System, or with the name of someone who has used the Math System.

STEP 4: The disk comes on. Soon the READY prompt returns. ***--VERY IMPORTANT--*** *Turn off the Commodore-64 at this point.*

STEP 5: With the Commodore-64 off, put the Calc Result cartridge in the Commodore-64 cartridge slot. Place the Calc Result diskette in the 1541 disk drive.

STEP 6: Turn on the Commodore-64. Read the screen and press any key, if necessary.

STEP 7: After the Calc Result display appears, *remove the Calc Result diskette*. Replace the Calc Result diskette with the diskette used to create the new DIF file. Press the F7 key. *Do not press the RETURN key!* Do not press the RETURN key from this point on unless given specific instructions to do so.

STEP 8: Next press the D key.

STEP 9: Now type the D key once more.

STEP 10: Press the L key. The disk drive will come on and a list of the files on the diskette will be displayed.

STEP 11: Press the CRSR down key to move the cursor rectangle over the name of the newly created DIF file (the file with the ".dif" extension). When the correct file is under the cursor (the file name is highlighted), press the RETURN key. Then immediately, press the RETURN key a second time.

STEP 12: Near the top of the screen the computer asks the question: FROM A1. Press the RETURN key to indicate acceptance of this location as the starting point for the DIF file.

STEP 13: Once again, near the top of the screen, the computer displays the question: BY ROWS OR BY COLUMNS.

STEP 14: Press the C key.

STEP 15: The disk drive comes back on and soon the screen displays information that originally came from the Math System programs.

STEP 16: Press the F7 key again.

STEP 17: Press the G key.

STEP 18: Press the F key.

STEP 19: Finally, press the L key. The numbers should now be lined up under the proper column titles. Further adjustment can be made to the column widths and so on.

At this point, the scores obtained under the Math System can be manipulated in any fashion desired within the bounds of the Calc Result program.

No attempt is made to explain the reason for each step. If you want to understand why various keys are pressed while in Calc Result, obtain a copy of the Calc Result manual or purchase one or more of the books that are being published on the use of spreadsheet programs.

QUESTIONS

1. *True or False:* DIF suggests a standard way of saving all files.
2. Name the two parts of a DIF file.
3. Which part contains information about the file itself?
4. Which part contains the actual file information?
5. How many lines are associated with each entry in the Header Section?
6. How many lines are associated with each entry in the Data Section?
7. What value is used to indicate numeric information in the Data Section?
8. What value is used to indicate alphanumeric information in the Data Section?
9. What characters are used as the last entry in a DIF file?

ANSWERS

1. False
2. Header Section and Data Section
3. Header Section
4. Data Section
5. 3
6. 2
7. 0
8. 1
9. EOD

Program for SCORES.DIF

```
100 rem ***--scores.dif--***
110 :
120 :
130 rem **--initialization--**
140 home$ = chr$(147):rem clr/home
150 ::cd$ = chr$( 17):rem cursor down
160 ::cu$ = chr$(145):rem cursor up
170 ::cl$ = chr$(157):rem cursor left
180 ::cr$ = chr$( 29):rem cursor right
190 :blk$ = chr$(144):rem black
200 :ylw$ = chr$(158):rem yellow
210 :wht$ = chr$(  5):rem white
220 :rvs$ = chr$( 18):rem reverse video
225 :bnk$ = chr$( 10):rem blank line
226 :brn$ = chr$(149):rem brown
227 :bue$ = chr$( 31):rem blue
230 :
240 poke 53280,14:rem border = lt.blue
250 poke 53272,23:rem upper/lower case
260 poke 53281, 1:rem set bkgrd to wht
265 :
266 :
270 rem **--user message--**
280 print blk$;home$:rem clr/home
285 print tab(10) "DIF TRANSLATION"
290 cd = 5:gosub 9000:rem crsr down 5
300 poke 19,32:rem disable input ?
310 input "Student's name please: ";na$
320 rem convert to lowercase
330 cv$ = na$:gosub 7000
340 print home$:cd = 5:gosub 9000
350 print blk$;"ONE MOMENT PLEASE!"
360 :
370 rem **--file input routine--**
380 dim s$(100),dt(100),cr(100),wr(100)
390 open 2,8,2,cv$ + ",seq,read"
400 k = 1
410 input#2,s$(k):rem sign of operation
420 input#2,dt(k):rem # of digits
430 input#2,cr(k):rem # correct
440 input#2,wr(k):rem # wrong
450 if s$(k) = "+" then s$(k) = "ADD"
460 if s$(k) = "-" then s$(k) = "SUB"
470 if s$(k) = "x" then s$(k) = "MLT"
480 if s$(k) = "/" then s$(k) = "DIV"
490 k = k + 1
500 if status = 0 then 410
510 close 2
520 :
530 :
1000 rem **--dif routine--**
1010 print home$:cd = 5:gosub 9000
1020 print rvs$;"WRITING DIF FILE"
```

```
1030 print
1040 j = k - 1:nv = 5:nt = k - 1
1050 q$ = chr$(34):rem quote mark
1060 rem j  = counter
1070 rem nv = number of vectors
1080 rem nt = number of tuples
1090 file$  = cv$ + ".dif"
1100 open 3,8,3,"@0:" + file$ + ",seq,write"
1110 :
1120 :
2000 rem **--header section--**
2010 :
2020 print#3,"TABLE"
2030 print#3,"0,1"
2040 print#3,q$nc$q$
2050 :
2060 print#3,"VECTORS"
2070 print#3,"0,";nv
2080 print#3,q$q$
2090 :
2100 print#3,"TUPLES"
2110 print#3,"0,";nt
2120 print#3,,q$q$
2130 :
2140 print#3,"DATA"
2150 print#3,"0,0"
2160 print#3,q$q$
2170 :
2180 :
3000 rem **--data section--**
3010 :
3020 print#3,"-1,0"
3030 print#3,"BOT"
3040 :
3050 print#3,"1,0"
3060 print#3,q$"Session #"q$
3070 :
3080 print#3,"1,0"
3090 print#3,q$"Operation"q$
3100 :
3110 print#3,"1,0"
3120 print#3,q$"Digits"q$
3130 :
3140 print#3,"1,0"
3150 print#3,q$"Correct"q$
3160 :
3170 print#3,"1,0"
3180 print#3,q$"Wrong"q$
3190 :
3200 for i = 1 to j
3210 :
3220 print#3,"-1,0"
3230 print#3,"BOT"
3240 :
3250 print#3,"0,";i:rem math session #
3260 print#3,"V"
```

```
3270 :
3280 print#3,"1,0":rem operation
3290 print#3,s$(i)
3300 :
3310 print#3,"0,";dt(i):rem # digits
3320 print#3,"V"
3330 :
3340 print#3,"0,";cr(i):rem # correct
3350 print#3,"V"
3360 :
3370 print#3,"0,";wr(i):rem # wrong
3380 print#3,"V"
3390 :
3400 next i
3410 print#3,"-1,0"
3420 print#3,"EOD"
3430 :
3440 close 3
3450 :
3460 :
3470 :
5000 rem--end routine--**
5010 poke 19,0:rem restore input prompt
5020 poke 53281, 6:rem set bkgrd to blu
5030 print wht$
5040 print home$:cd = 5:gosub 9000
5050 print rvs$;"ALL FINISHED"
5060 end
5070 :
5080 :
7000 rem **--convert to lowercase--**
7010 for cv = 1 to len(cv$)
7020 x = asc(mid$(cv$,cv,1))
7030 if x > 192 then x = x - 128
7040 nc$ = nc$ + chr$(x)
7050 next cv
7060 :
7070 cv$ = nc$
7080 f = asc(left$(cv$,1))
7090 f = f + 128
7100 nc$ = chr$(f) + right$(cv$,len(cv$)- 1)
7110 return
7120 :
7130 rem na$ = originally typed name
7140 rem cv$ = converted to lowercase
7150 rem nc$ = 1st letter/uppercase
7160 :
7170 :
7180 :
9000 rem **--cursor down routine--**
9010 for i = 1 to cd
9020 print cd$;
9030 next i
9040 return

ready.
```

Program for READ.DIF

```
100 rem ***--read dif--***
110 :
120 :
130 rem **--initialization--**
140 home$ = chr$(147):rem clr/home
150 ::cd$ = chr$( 17):rem cursor down
160 ::cu$ = chr$(145):rem cursor up
170 ::cl$ = chr$(157):rem cursor left
180 ::cr$ = chr$( 29):rem cursor right
190 :blk$ = chr$(144):rem black
200 :ylw$ = chr$(158):rem yellow
210 :wht$ = chr$(  5):rem white
220 :rvs$ = chr$( 18):rem reverse video
225 :bnk$ = chr$( 10):rem blank line
226 :brn$ = chr$(149):rem brown
227 :bue$ = chr$( 31):rem blue
230 :
240 poke 53280,14:rem border = lt.blue
250 poke 53272,23:rem upper/lower case
260 poke 53281, 1:rem set bkgrd to wht
265 :
265 :
270 rem **--user message--**
280 print blk$;home$:rem clr/home
285 print tab(15) "DIF FILE"
290 cd = 5:gosub 9000:rem crsr down 5
300 poke 19,32:rem disable input ?
310 input "File name please: ";na$
320 rem convert to lowercase
330 cv$ = na$:gosub 7000
340 print home$:cd = 5:gosub 9000
350 print blk$;"ONE MOMENT PLEASE!"
360 :
370 rem **--file input routine--**
380 dim a$(200),s(200),n(200)
390 open 2,8,2,cv$ + ".dif,seq,read"
400 k = 1
410 input#2,t$:rem read the topic name
420 input#2,s,n:rem vector #, value
430 input#2,s$:rem string value
440 if t$ = "VECTORS" then nv = n
450 if t$ = "TUPLES"  then nt = n
460 if t$ <> "DATA"   then 410
470 :
480 input#2,s(k),n(k):rem data 1st line
490 input#2,a$(k):rem data 2nd line
500 if a$(k) = "EOD" then 540
510 k = k + 1
520 goto 480
530 :
540 close 2
550 :
560 :
```

```
1000 rem **--display routine--**
1010 print home$:cd = 5:gosub 9000
1020 for j = 1 to k
1030 print s(j);",";n(j)
1040 print a$(j)
1050 next j
1060 :
1070 :
5000 rem--end routine--**
5010 poke 19,0:rem restore input prompt
5020 poke 53281, 6:rem set bkgrd to blu
5030 print wht$
5050 print rvs$;"ALL FINISHED"
5060 end
5070 :
5080 :
7000 rem **--convert to lowercase--**
7010 for cv = 1 to len(cv$)
7020 x = asc(mid$(cv$,cv,1))
7030 if x > 192 then x = x - 128
7040 nc$ = nc$ + chr$(x)
7050 next cv
7060 :
7070 cv$ = nc$
7080 f = asc(left$(cv$,1))
7090 f = f + 128
7100 nc$ = chr$(f) + right$(cv$,len(cv$)- 1)
7110 return
7120 :
7130 rem na$ = originally typed name
7140 rem cv$ = converted to lowercase
7150 rem nc$ = 1st letter/uppercase
7160 :
7170 :
7180 :
9000 rem **--cursor down routine--**
9010 for i = 1 to cd
9020 print cd$;
9030 next i
9040 return

ready.
```

```
0 "form.10-20-84   " 84 2a
1    "hello"            prg
2    "example"          prg
1    "address file"     seq
12   "mail.create"      prg
1    "adrs-ptr"         seq
1    "adrs-data"        seq
4    "mail.reader1"     prg
15   "mail.adder1"      prg
19   "mail.adder2"      prg
17   "mail.menu"        prg
12   "shell"            prg
37   "mail.reader2"     prg
27   "mail.correction"  prg
25   "math.menu"        prg
23   "math.add"         prg
23   "math.subtract"    prg
23   "math.multiply"    prg
23   "math.divide"      prg
17   "math.scores"      prg
7    "create q & a"     prg
16   "drill & practice" prg
12   "scores.dif"       prg
8    "read.dif"         prg
338 blocks free.

ready.
```

10 random (relative) file introduction

The biggest barrier I have found in explaining random-access files is fear. People are afraid that random access is too hard for them to learn. Actually, once you understand the principles behind sequential access, learning to work with random access is not that difficult. I believe that if you have followed all the examples in the previous chapters, you will be able to learn to work with random files. Don't become intimidated by the different approach random access requires.

If you have skipped the sequential-access chapters and are just starting this book, there are a few points that must be understood. For those who have read all the previous chapters, the following information is repeated from Chapter 3.

Data files have two ways of storing and retrieving information. (Remember that the information really stays on the diskette and we are just getting a copy of the information!) These two ways of storing and retrieving information are sequential access and direct (random) access. Sequential access data files mean that the information stored in the file is kept in sequential order. Direct access data files usually mean that each part of the file is divided equally and can be reached directly and at random instead of going through all previous records. The process of looking at each record in order (sequence) to decide if it is the record you want is a characteristic of sequential files and can require more time than the direct method of random access files.

Commodore refers to random access files as *relative* files. But the term "relative" in the computer world often means "in relation to" and can be misleading when used as the name of the method for *directly* accessing records within a file. To further confuse matters, Commodore also provides a subset of their relative files which they call *random* files. Since Commodore's random files are basically an elementary version of their relative files, we will not cover them in a direct way. Anything that can be done with Commodore's random files in the BASIC language can be accomplished with relative files and in a much easier way. Therefore, any mention in this book of random files is meant to refer to Commodore's relative files, not Commodore's random files. In other words, whenever I use the term *random access,* I am talking about the same thing that Commodore is when they refer to relative files. And, after checking with individuals at Commodore, I have decided to use the term "random" rather than use Commodore's term "relative" because, in the long run, readers of this book will be less confused by a correct application of the appropriate term.

The basic difference between sequential data files and random data files is somewhat like the difference between a cassette tape and a phonograph record. If I want to find a specific song on a cassette tape, even using the best available tape deck, I must begin at the current location of the tape and proceed either forward or backward, passing over all intervening songs until I have found the song I want. The process proceeds in sequence, one song after another. For example, if I want to play only the fourth song on the tape, I would have to advance the tape through the first, second, and third songs until I get to the fourth one. On the other hand, if the songs are on a phonograph record, all I would have to do to play the fourth song would be to place the phono cartridge containing the needle at the start of the fourth division instead of at the start of the first song. I can do that because I am able to clearly see the divisions between songs and because those individual songs are directly accessible. I do not have to go through the grooves of the first three songs to get to the fourth. And moving the needle by hand takes only seconds. So imagine that the data drawer (in a file cabinet) contains two basic divisions: the first division contains files that operate in a way similar to cassette tapes, while the second division contains files that operate like phonograph records in the way described.

But these two kinds of data files do have things in common, just as tapes have things in common with phono records. The most obvious common characteristic is that they both usually contain information that is not in the form of instructions for the computer. In other words, they contain information like lists of things, addresses, receipts, and inventories. Second, both files make use of some of the same BASIC file commands, but with different parameters. Both sequential and random-access data files primarily use four types of commands: (1) OPEN, (2) CLOSE, (3) some way of reading the file (INPUT# or GET#), and (4) some method of writing to the file (PRINT#). With this minimum background, we are ready to begin the study of random access files.

There are usually two kinds of random access files: (1) random files that consist of undivided equal-length records, and (2) random files that consist of divided equal-length records. Notice the only difference is that in one kind the records are divided into parts, while in the other kind the records remain as a whole. This latter kind will be discussed first.

UNDIVIDED RANDOM FILES

Normally, undivided random files are easy to create and use. In fact, they are usually very similar to sequential files in that the contents of a keyboard line equal the contents of the complete record. It should, therefore, be easy to access individual records. Unfortunately, the use of undivided random access (Commodore's "relative") files is unreliable on the Commodore 64. Page 35 of the 1541 *User's Manual* indicates that the position parameter is "optional" and implies that undivided random (relative) files are possible. Without going into great detail at this point (the appendix contains a full description detailing the problems that exist with files created without a position parameter), I found these undivided random-access files to be unusable. Without the position parameter, every fifth record beginning with record 6 would "hang" the computer (cause the computer to completely stop, requiring a full reset—the STOP and RESTORE keys) when that particular record was accessed. Then, beginning at record 66, the problem advanced one record. Record 67 and every following fifth record would cause the computer to hang. The explanation for the cause of this problem is quite strange. Without the position parameter, the 64 begins storing information 13 spaces into each record. That means that if I were trying to store my name in record one, the first available space in that record would not contain the *D* in David. The *D* would not be stored until space 13. The *a* would then be in space 14, the *v* in space 15, and so on. This pattern exists for every record except those records that cause the computer to hang. When the computer stores information in those records, it does begin with the first space. The INPUT# command apparently looks for information to begin 13 spaces into each record and hangs the computer when it comes to these records that have information stored beginning with the first space.

If you have not followed this explanation, it is not that important. The point is that without the position parameter (the main distinguishing difference between undivided and divided random access files), undivided random access files on the Commodore 64 do not function reliably. If the position parameter is included and set to one, undivided records can be used without a problem. For practical purposes, the position parameter is not optional and, therefore, technically undivided random access is not available on the Commodore-64. This distinction is mainly technical and semantic and should not hinder anyone from doing what he or she desires on the 64 provided he or she includes the position parameter.

DIVIDED RANDOM FILES

Both kinds of random files must consist of equal-length records. This means that you must decide on the length of the longest record you will ever have. For instance, in our Mailing List System, each line had a maximum length of 80 characters because that is the maximum number of characters allowed in a single Commodore keyboard line. Probably none of your lines (or records) actually had the maximum length, but that was the length possible for each record. You did not need to specify this number, because in sequential files, the next record begins immediately after the end of the last character and the record delimiter, no matter what the actual length of the record. But you must specify the maximum length in random files because the next record does not begin immediately after the last character in the previous record. It actually begins the specified record length after the beginning of the previous record, regardless of the number of characters in that record.

For example, if the length is given as 50, it means that each record has a maximum of fifty characters possible and that each record begins fifty characters (*i.e.,* spaces, or bytes) from the start of the previous record. If the first record begins at byte 0, the second begins at 50, the third record at 100, and so on. You do not need to be concerned with the actual location on the disk. It is important to understand that, since each record must be of equal length, it is very easy for the computer to calculate the starting position of each record and possible for you to specify any record in any order. You must provide the computer with that maximum length by assigning a value after the L parameter (for length) that follows the file name in random files. The number given after the L in an OPEN statement indicates the maximum number of characters or bytes you expect in any record in that file. It also indicates that each record will be that number of characters or bytes long.

If you have a record that is not as long as the number given after the L, you will have a certain amount of disk space that is unused. So it is important to figure carefully and keep the number after L as low as possible. If the number is very large but most of your records are rather small, you will be wasting a lot of disk space. A certain amount of wasted disk space is inevitable in using random files, since few files will contain information of exactly equal length. But in using random files, you are willing to waste a little disk space in order to gain the advantage of much faster disk access.

The divided random file consists of records that are broken into varying-length parts or fields. Each record is the same length, but within each record the fields or parts of the record can be of varying lengths. In other words, a random access file that consists of records with a length of 100 characters or bytes can have each record divided into parts of equal or unequal lengths. The first field might be 25 bytes (spaces) long, the second field 10 bytes, the third field 15 bytes and the last field 50 bytes. The total number of bytes or characters equals 100, but no two fields need be the same length.

In our Mailing List System example, with random files that contained divided records, we could specify a certain length for the first name and other lengths for the last name, city, zip code, and so on. Each record, therefore, could contain a complete set of the information needed for the Mailing List System. Under sequential access, the complete set of information usually required six or seven records (lines). For instance, if we decide that each line of information or each record would have no more than 150 characters in it, we could further decide that the first field of each record would exist from byte 0 to byte 10, the second from byte 11 to byte 15, the third field from byte 16 to byte 30, and so on. Each record could contain the first name in the first field, the middle initial in the second field, the last name in the third field, the numerical address in the fourth field, the street address in the fifth field, any apartment number etc. in the sixth field, the city in the seventh field, the state in the eighth field, and the zip code in the ninth field. Under this setup, it would be easy to access any part of any record in any order we desire. For example, if we just want the zip code and first name in that order, we would have no trouble accessing just that information.

I have been using the term *byte* in connection with the word *character* so that you might get used to the idea that the length of a record is measured in bytes. Each character or number is one byte. If a file has equal-length records of 50, that is 50 bytes. If the second field begins 27 characters from the first character, that is the 27th byte of the record. To access that byte, we set the position parameter to the desired location.

At this point, a short tutorial may best explain the exact syntax and operation of random-access files. Take a formatted diskette that has plenty of room on it or format a new one (refer to Chapter 2 if necessary). Load the DOS Wedge from the TEST/DEMO diskette (refer to Chapter 3). Enter the following program (in lower case mode):

```
100 rem ***--random file example--***
110 :
120 :
130 rem **--file output routine--**
140 open 2,8,15:rem open command chnl
150 open 3,8,4,"random example,l," + chr$(50)
160 for i = 1 to 25
170 gosub 1000:rem figure rec.# routine
180 print#2,"p";chr$(4);chr$(rlow);chr$(rhigh);chr$( 1)
190 print#3,"record";i
200 print#2,"p";chr$(4);chr$(rlow);chr$(rhigh);chr$(20)
210 print#3,"abcdef";i
220 next i
230 close 3: close 2
240 input "Press 'RETURN' to continue: ";r$
```

```
250 :
260 :
1000 rem **--figure rec.# routine--**
1010 rlow = i
1020 rhigh = 0
1030 if rlow > 255 then 1050
1040 return
1050 rhigh = int(rlow/256)
1060 rlow  = rlow - 256 * rhigh
1070 return
```

There are a lot of different numbers in these routines, but if you have gone through the sequential access portion of this book, the numbers in the "open" statements should be familiar. For those who may have skipped over the sequential-access portion, I will briefly explain each value. The first number after the word "open" is the file number: 2 in line 140 and 3 in line 150. The 8 in both lines refers to the disk drive device number (random access is not available to tape users). The third number after the "open" command is the channel number. For disk use, channel numbers should normally be between 2 and 14. The number 15 in line 140 is reserved for the operating system's command channel. Quite often the file number and the channel number are arbitrarily assigned the same number to avoid the need to remember additional numbers. In this case, I intentionally assigned different numbers in order to more clearly distinguish which values should be used at specific times.

Line 150 contains additional differences. First, there is no longer the need to indicate the type of file or the access mode. Second, the "L" or "l" parameter must be included with separating commas. Third, the actual length of each record must be specified within the chr$ parentheses. As stated previously, random access files must consist of equal-length records. This means that you must decide on the length of the longest record you will ever have. In this example, the length is specified as 50. In other words, each record in this file called "random example" will have 50 spaces available to it. Again, this does not mean that each record must actually contain 50 characters, but that no record may contain more than 50 characters.

Line 160 defines the dimensions of our loop used to quickly and easily write information to this file. We are going to have 25 records, so the value of the numeric variable *i* will vary from 1 up to 25. Line 170 sends control to a subroutine located at line 1000. All the code in this subroutine could have been included in the program at this point, but I chose to put this code into a subroutine because other portions of our example program will eventually need to make use of the exact same instructions. The purpose of this subroutine is stated in the title. The routine is designed to separate the decimal value of the record number into its low-byte and high-byte values.

It is at this point that confusion usually begins. All the numbers specified in chr$ statements are decimal numbers (base 10) except the number used to determine which record we are accessing. That number, in Commodore's operating system, must be expressed in something like a base 256 format. This means that the number 20, for example, would equal a 0 for the high-byte value (the number 20 is less than 256) and a 20 for the low-byte value. In other words, if I wanted to see what was in record 20, I would tell the computer to show me what was in the record specified by: chr$(20) + chr$(0) (low-byte is specified first). If I wanted to see what was in record 258, I would tell the computer to show me what was in the record specified by: chr$(2) + chr$(1), or the value of the first number 2 added to the value of the second number. The value of that second number is not 1. Instead its value is 256. The high-byte value is multiplied by 256. If the high-byte value were 2, the first number (2) would be added to 512 (256 times 2). If the high-byte value is 3, the first number is added to 768 (256 times 3), *etc*. The routine at 1000 is used to convert decimal value record numbers into their low-byte (rlow) and high-byte (rhigh) values. If you have not followed the explanation for this routine, you only need to know that the routine, or some similar set of instructions, is necessary in order to access the desired record number. Once the computer has a value for the numeric variables "rlow" and "rhigh", control can be returned to the file output routine.

The following two paragraphs should be read very carefully!

Line 180 is an example of what Commodore calls the "POSITION COMMAND". This instruction is used to position the computer: (1) to the desired channel number, (2) to the desired record number, and (3) to the desired position within the specific record. The position of each of these values, relative to each other, is fixed and not arbitrary (*i.e.*, channel number, low-byte record number, high-byte record number, position within the record). Since a string of numbers inside chr$ parentheses is not very descriptive, I prefer to assign the desired values to descriptive variables and use the variables in place of the actual numbers. Later, this method of using descriptive variables will be expanded; but for now the variables rlow and rhigh, as explained above, indicate the actual record number.

```
180 print#2,"p";chr$(4);chr$(rlow);chr$(rhigh);chr$( 1)
```

The number immediately following the # symbol must be the file number used in the open statement for the specific file. In line 180, this number is a 2, which was the file number used with the operating system's command channel. The "p" is used to tell the computer that this is a "position command" instruction. The first number used inside chr$ parentheses in line 180 must be the channel number chosen for use with the random access file (*i.e.*, the third number in the open statement for that file). This point has caused a great deal of confusion and probably is one reason some people have felt that similar programs act in different ways at different times. In this example, the 4 is the channel number and is the number to be used in the first chr$ parameter. If the file number (3) is used instead, unpredictable results can occur. If both file number and channel number are the same, no problem should occur. Future programs will follow the convention of using the same number for both the file number and the channel number. The only reason it is not done in this example is to provide a clear distinction between the two numbers.

The second and third chr$ () values are the low-byte and high-byte values for the record number. The last number in line 180 is the number Commodore indicates is optional. For all practical purposes this value is not optional and should be set to one even if the record will not be further divided. You should also notice that this number is the only value that is different in line 200. The last value used with chr$ in the "position command" instruction is the specific position within the record for the current information (in either read or write mode). Therefore, chr$(1) in line 180 indicates that the first piece of information is to begin in the first space of the record. The chr$(20) in line 200 indicates that the second piece of information is to begin at the twentieth space of the record. The information that is to be written in those two locations is given in the line that follows each (190 and 210). The number after the # symbol in line 190 is the file number of the random access file specified in the open command (line 150). The information (in either constant or variable form) that follows the comma is the information that is written to the diskette. In line 190, that information consists of the word "record" and the value of the variable *i*. In line 210, the information consists of the characters "abcdef" and the value of the variable *i*. Line 230 closes both files once the value of *i* has exceeded the number specified in line 160. Line 240 is our method of pausing before the next routine.

```
300 rem **--file input routine--**
310 open 2,8,15:rem open command chnl
320 open 3,8,4,"random example,l," + chr$(50)
330 for i = 1 to 25
340 gosub 1000:rem figure rec.# routine
350 print#2,"p";chr$(4);chr$(rlow);chr$(rhigh);chr$( 1)
360 input#3,a$
370 print a$;
380 print#2,"p";chr$(4);chr$(rlow);chr$(rhigh);chr$(20)
390 input#3,b$
400 print tab(15) b$
410 next i
420 close 3:close 2
430 input "Press 'RETURN' to continue: ";r$
440
450
```

This routine is essentially the same as the file output routine, with the only real difference occurring in lines 360, 370, 390, and 400. In those lines, information is obtained from the diskette and then displayed on the screen instead of written to the diskette. Notice the semicolon at the end of line 370. It is there for screen formatting purposes only. In all other aspects, the parameters within the routines are the same with the same meaning. The parameters do not need to be the same as those used in the file output routine (*i.e.*, when information is written to the diskette), but it is often easier to keep track of which number goes where if the same numbers are used. The one exception to this rule is the position parameter. If these numbers are not kept the same, unintended results will occur. In other words, the last numbers in lines 350 and 380 should be the same as those used in lines 180 and 200. Otherwise, file numbers and channel numbers (except channel 15) can be changed as long as the previously accessed file output routine has closed the files.

The files need to be closed in a specific order also. Regardless of the number of files used, the command channel file must be the last file closed. If it is closed before the random access file is closed, file errors might occur. The display lines, lines 370 and 400, do not need to be located where they are. They can be placed anywhere before the "next i" instruction. The last routine provides an example of the ability to access any of these records at random.

```
500 rem **--random access routine--**
510 input "Which record number ";nb$
520 nb = val(nb$)
530 if nb = 0 then 900:rem end
540 if nb > 25 then 510:rem ask again
550 i = nb:gosub 1000:rem figure rec.#
560 open 2,8,15:rem open command chnl
570 open 3,8,4,"random example,l," + chr$(50)
580 print#2,"p";chr$(4);chr$(rlow);chr$(rhigh);chr$(20)
590 input#3,b$
600 print b$;
610 print#2,"p";chr$(4);chr$(rlow);chr$(rhigh);chr$( 1)
620 input#3,a$
630 print tab(15) a$
640 close 3: close 2
650 goto 510
660 :
670 :
900 rem **--end routine--**
910 end
920 :
930 :
```

This routine provides the first real example of what random access is all about. The user can indicate any record number between 1 and 25 in line 510, and the computer will go to that record number and obtain the information in whatever order the programmer has specified. Notice that I turned the position statements around. The first information obtained and displayed is the information stored beginning at the twentieth byte or space in the record. The second piece of information obtained is the information stored at the first byte or space of the record. And the record numbers do not have to be given in order. We can ask for record 21 and then ask for record 2. Or, ask for record 9 and then record 19. The order does not matter, because the computer has been instructed to go *directly* to the specified record and the specified location within that record. Once again, the same values were used for all parameters, but with the exceptions noted in the description of the file input routine, these parameters could have different values.

When you have finished entering the program instructions, save them to the diskette as "random test 1".

```
←random test 1
```

Then, run the program:

```
run
```

For a short time, the disk drive red light should come on and the cursor should disappear. Eventually, the statement from line 240 will be displayed on the screen and the red disk light will go out. When you are ready, press the RETURN key and watch the screen carefully. Two columns should appear. If you do not get two columns on the same line, check line 370 for the semicolon. The left-most column should contain the word "record" (or RECORD if you are in upper case mode) and an increasing number, up to the number 25. The right-most column should contain the characters "abcdef" (or "ABCDEF") and the same increasing number, up to 25. When the number 25 has been reached, the statement from line 430 should be displayed.

Again, when you are ready, press the RETURN key. Now, you will be asked to indicate which record number you wish to see. Indicate record number 11. This time you should see two columns but in reverse order. The characters "abcdef 11" should be in the left-most column and the word "record 11" should be in the right hand column. At this point, you can try out additional record numbers. I would also encourage you to experiment with different combinations of these instructions and parameters just to see what happens. You can also substitute the word "GET#" for the word "INPUT#".

MEDICAL RECORDS SYSTEM

With this background, we are going to go over what I hope is a useful program. The example is a file used to store personal family medical records. In these random file examples, I will not go over all the routines as I did in the sequential file examples. Instead, I will concentrate on the file routines. The complete listing for the program will be found at the end of the chapter.

If you take a look at the complete listing, you will see that we begin with a menu routine. The first thing that needs to be done the first time the program is used is to set the value of the record pointer to zero and write that value out to a sequential file. After setting the pointer value that first time, the program instructions automatically update the pointer value. The record pointer file is used to keep track of the total number of records in the random file.

■ *File Output Routine*

Next comes a keyboard input routine in order to obtain our original information. We are asking the user to supply: (1) the name of the individual (name$), (2) the date (dte$), (3) the type of record, that is, whether it is a record of a Dr. Visit, Medication, Illness, Accident or Injury, Shot or Immunization, or X-ray (type$), and (4) any miscellaneous information such as the name of the medication and frequency of use, the kind of illness, location of injury, and so on (misc$). Once we have all our information and have verified that it is correct, we are ready to write that information out to the disk file.

```
1700 rem **--file output routine--**
1705 :
1710 rem *-pointer file-*
1715 rem must set ptr. before first use
1720 open 2,8,2,"med-records.ptr,seq,read"
1725 input#2,ptr
1730 close 2
1735 ptr = ptr + 1
1740 :
1745 rem *-data file-*
1750 open 15,8,15:rem open command chnl
1755 open 3,8,3,"med-records,l," + chr$(50)
1760 rem l in line 1755 is letter not #
1765 rem 50 in line 1755 is rec.length--not # of records
1770 chnl$ = chr(3):rem channel #
1775 rlow  = ptr:rem low byte of rec.#
1780 rhigh = 0:rem high byte of rec.#
```

```
1785 if rlow > 255 then gosub 15000
1790 rec$ = chr$(rlow) + chr$(rhigh)
1795 :
1800 pztn$ = chr$( 1):rem position
1805 print#15,"p";chnl$;rec$;pztn$
1810 print#3,name$
1815 :
1820 pztn$ = chr$(15):rem position
1825 print#15,"p",chnl$;rec$;pztn$
1830 print#3,dte$
1835 :
1840 pztn$ = chr$(26):rem position
1845 print#15,"p";chnl$;rec$;pztn$
1850 print#3,type$
1855 :
1860 pztn$ = chr$(28):rem position
1865 print#15,"p";chnl$;rec$;pztn$
1870 print#3,misc$
1875 close 3:close 2
1880 :
1885 :
1890 rem *-update ptr file-*
1895 open 2,8,2,"@0:med-records.ptr,seq,write"
1900 print#2,ptr
1905 close 2
1910 goto 500:rem menu
1915 :
1920 :
1925 :
```

There are three parts to this output routine. The first part (lines 1710–1735) accesses the pointer file and updates the pointer value. The second part (lines 1745–1875) defines the data file and writes the information to it. Finally, the last part (lines 1890–1905) again accesses the pointer file, this time to write out the new value of the pointer. We are concerned with the second part since that is the part that deals with a random access file.

Line 1750 opens the operating system's command channel as file number 15. Line 1755 opens the random access file "med-records" as file number 3 on channel number 3 with a length of 50 bytes available for each record. The two rem lines, 1760 and 1765, clarify two points in line 1755. The lower case l on some printers looks the same as the number 1. It is very important to understand that the character l in line 1755 is the lower case letter l and not the number 1. In addition, you should clearly understand that the number inside the parentheses specifies the length of each record rather than the total number of records.

Line 1770 is the first line used to help make the parameters, in the "position command" instruction, descriptive. The string variable chnl$ is used to store the value of the channel number. Since that value is used with the chr$ instruction, a string variable can be used to describe the complete instruction with its value. Line 1775 defines the numeric variable "rlow" as equaling the current value of the pointer (ptr) or the total number of records so far plus one (line 1735). Line 1780 establishes the value of the high-byte part of the record number as zero. This value should only change if the number of records goes above 255 (line 1785). If the number of records does get above 255, the routine at 15000 converts the record number to its appropriate low-byte and high-byte values. Line 1790 combines the chr$ values of both rlow and rhigh into the single string variable rec$. Once again, this is possible because the values were expressed as chr$ values. At this point, we have the channel number in the chnl$ variable and the record number in the rec$ variable. Line 1800 defines the current position within the record that we want to write our first information to. The pztn$ variable (for position) can also be used, because the value of the position within the record is defined with a chr$ statement. (The variable cannot be pstn$ due to the embedded reserved word "st" used to indicate the status of an input/output operation.) The "position command" instruction now becomes (line 1805): print#15,"p";chnl$;rec$;pztn$. This is more descriptive and understandable than the format suggested in the 1541 *User's Manual:* print#15,"p"chr$(3)chr$(1)chr$(0)chr$(1).

The same sequence is followed for the rest of the information that is to be written to the file. The position variable needs to be set before every "position command" instruction or the next information will write over the information just written in that location. As soon as the last piece of information for this record has been written, the random access file is closed and then the operating system command channel is closed.

One point should be emphasized before moving on. Notice that it is not necessary to use string arrays: name$(). We do not have to use string arrays because of the versatility of random files. In this program, the information for a complete record is written to the disk before additional information is obtained from the user. The idea that we can use the disk without extensive use of string arrays will become more apparent with the section on reading and displaying our medical information.

File Input Routine

We move now to the section of our program that allows us to see the information we have stored in the "med-records" file. In this first section, we read the file and immediately display the information.

```
2000 rem **--read file routine--**
2010 gosub 10000:rem display routine
2020 :
2030 rem *-pointer file-*
2040 open 2,8,2,"med-records.ptr,seq,read"
2050 input#2,ptr
2060 close 2
2070 :
2080 rem *-data file-*
2090 open 15,8,15:rem command channel
2100 open 5,8,5,"med-records,l," + chr$(50)
2110 rem l in line 2100 is letter not #
2120 chnl$ = chr$(5):rem channel #
2130 for rec = 1 to ptr
2140 rlow = rec:rhigh = 0
2150 if rlow > 255 then 15000
2160 rec$ = chr$(rlow) + chr$(rhigh)
2170 print
2180 :
2190 :
2200 pztn$ = chr$( 1):rem position
2210 print#15,"p";chnl$;rec$;pztn$
2220 input#5,name$
2230 :
2240 :
2250 pznt$ = chr$(15):rem position
2260 print#15,"p";chnl$;rec$;pztn$
2270 input#5,dte$
2280 :
2290 :
2300 pztn$ = chr$(26):rem position
2310 print#15,"p";chnl$;rec$;pztn$
2320 input#5,type$
2330 :
2340 :
2350 pztn$ = chr$(28):rem position
2360 print#15,"p";chnl$;rec$;pztn$
2370 input#5,misc$
2380 :
2390 :
2400 rem *-display information-*
2410 gosub 16000:rem get full type msg.
```

```
2420 :
2430 rem clear screen/crsr down 5
2440 print home$:cd = 5:gosub 9000
2450 :
2460 print:print#file,""tab(tb) "1. NAME: ";name$
2470 print:print#file,""tab(tb) "2. DATE: ";dte$
2480 print:print#file,""tab(tb) "3. TYPE: ";tp$
2490 print:print#file,""tab(tb) "4. MISC: ";misc$
2500 print:print#file,""tab(tb)
2510 print "Press ";wht$;"RETURN";brn$;" to continue:";
2520 gosub 19000:rem return key routine
2530 next rec:rem dsp next set of info.
2540 :
2550 :
2560 close 5:close 15
2570 print home$:cd = 5:gosub 9000
2580 print tab(tb + 3):print rvs$;"ALL FINISHED"
2590 cd = 10:gosub 9000:rem crsr down 10
2600 gosub 20000:rem menu return routine
2610 goto 500:rem menu
2620 :
2630 :
2640 :
```

The first thing that is done is to name the routine (line 2000) and ask if the user wants a paper printout (line 2010). Next, the pointer file is accessed and the value of the pointer (the number of records currently in the data file) is stored in the numeric variable "ptr". It is not necessary to immediately close the pointer file (med-records.ptr), but it is a good programming habit. In line 2090, the operating system command channel is opened with the data file, "med-records", opened in line 2100 as our third accessed file. It is defined as having records of 50 bytes or characters in length. Line 2120 sets the channel number to five because the number three channel might already be opened by the display routine. Lines 2140 to 2160 establish the necessary values for the record indicator with lines 2200 to 2370 nearly duplicating lines 1800 to 1870 of the file output routine. The only difference comes in the third line of each set. This time we are bringing information in (input#) instead of writing information out (print#). Again, the middle line of each set is the "position command" instruction and clearly indicates that we are providing the computer with the channel number, the record number, and a position within the specified record. Once we have values for all the desired variables, we proceed to the display portion of the routine—lines 2400 to 2500. Lines 2510 and 2520 wait until the user presses the RETURN key. When the RETURN key is pressed, the process begins again with the next set of information obtained by reading the next record in the data file. The entire routine is repeated until the complete file has been read and displayed.

The subroutine at 16000 has a very specialized purpose. The purpose of this subroutine is to match the single character symbol with its complete corresponding "type" name: for example, exchange "d" for "Dr. Visit". Once the exchange has been made, control is returned to the statement immediately following the GOSUB statement. Then, instead of displaying the value of the variable we brought in from the diskette, we display the value of the variable "tp$" obtained from the subroutine.

The only section of the program left to examine is the search routine. Lines 3000 to 3250 establish exactly what we will be searching for, and lines 3280 through 3750 conduct the actual search and display the results.

```
3280 rem **--file input routine--**
3290 :
3300 rem *-pointer file-*
3310 open 2,8,2,"med-records.ptr,seq,read"
3320 input#2,ptr
3330 close 2
3340 :
3350 rem *-data file-*
3360 open 15,8,15:rem open cmnd chnl
3370 open 5,8,5,"med-records,l," + chr$(50)
3380 rem l in line 3370 is letter not #
3390 ln = len(srch$):chnl$ = chr$(5)
3400 for rec = 1 to ptr
3410 rlow = rec:rhigh = 0
3420 if rlow > 255 then 15000
3430 rec$ = chr$(rlow) + chr$(rhigh)
3440 :
3450 print#15,"p";chnl$;rec$;pztn$
3460 input#5,find$
3470 :
3480 cvt$ = left$(find$,ln)
3490 gosub 17000:rem convert to l.c.
3500 if srch$ <> cvt$ then 3750
3510 :
3520 for k = 1 to 4
3530 if k = 1 then pt$ = chr$( 1)
3540 if k = 2 then pt$ = chr$(15)
3550 if k = 3 then pt$ = chr$(26)
3560 if k = 4 then pt$ = chr$(28)
3570 print#15,"p";chnl$;rec$;pt$
3580 input#5,info$(k)
```

```
3590 if k = 3 then type$ = info$(k):gosub 16000:info$(k)= tp$
3600 next k
3610 :
3620 :
3630 rem *-display information-*
                    .
                    .
                    .
3750 next rec
3760 :
3770 :
3780 close 5:close 15
```

This is an elementary search and display routine. Lines 3300 to 3330 open the pointer file and obtain the value of the pointer. The data file is then opened (line 3370) and defined.

Next comes a technique that allows the user to search for just the beginning portion of a field in case the user does not know the complete spelling of the entire field. The search is limited to just the number of characters the user has supplied in answer to the question in line 3200 (see the program listing at the end of this chapter). We determine this number (line 3390) and then use the number in 3480 to limit the number of characters that will go through the process of conversion to lower case. Once those characters have been converted to lower case, we can compare then to the characters supplied by the user (srch$). If they are not equal, the computer is instructed to increment the value of "rec" and proceed.

Line 3400 establishes the boundaries for a loop. Within that loop, we look for just the desired part of each record. When that part is located, the rest of the information associated with that part is read in (3520 to 3600) and displayed (lines 3630 to 3710). Those instruction-lines are skipped for information that does not match or equal the string variable for which we are searching (line 3500). When the entire file has been searched, the file is closed, and control is transferred back to the beginning of the search routine to see if the user wishes to search for more information.

This program provides a reasonable example of the techniques involved with creating, adding to, and reading from a random access file. It does not get too fancy, yet it is a useful program. You may want to supply additional routines.

At this point, you should find yourself capable of "reading" a program listing. As we progress through the book, the amount of text decreases while the amount of program instructions that you should "read" increases. In Chapter 11, we will use random files in a more elaborate manner.

One additional comment needs to be made in concluding this chapter. There are a variety of ways of using random-access files of either the divided or undivided kind. The method presented in this chapter is not meant to suggest itself as the only method or even the best method. It is a method that does work and is understandable. In working with files, I have found that comprehension is of more value than program efficiency or speed. And one cautionary note: things don't always function as they seem they logically should, especially when working with random files of the undivided kind. For this reason, I would not encourage extensive use of the undivided type of random files until you are very comfortable with the way they operate.

QUESTIONS

1. Name the two kinds of random files.
2. *True or False:* Random files can contain records of different lengths.
3. What are the two BASIC words used to obtain information from a diskette and place information on a diskette?
4. *True or False:* In random files, the next record begins immediately after the last character in the previous record.
5. What parameter must an OPEN command have in a random file?
6. *True or False:* Random files waste disk space but have much faster disk access than do sequential files.
7. *True or False:* The relationship that exists between the various parts of a divided random-access file can be defined in the following way: A random-access file consists of equal-length records. Each record may consist of equal and/or unequal length fields. The number following the L parameter in an OPEN statement indicates the length of each record.
8. What is the length of each record measured in?
9. *True or False:* Random files require greater use of string arrays than do sequential files.

ANSWERS

1. Divided and undivided random files
2. False
3. INPUT#, PRINT#
4. False
5. L
6. True
7. True
8. Bytes
9. False

Program for RANDOM FILE EXAMPLE

```
100 rem ***--random file example--***
110 :
120 :
130 rem **--file output routine--**
140 open 2,8,15:rem open command chnl
150 open 3,8,4,"random example,l," + chr$(50)
160 for i = 1 to 25
170 gosub 1000:rem figure rec.# routine
180 print#2,"p";chr$(4);chr$(rlow);chr$(rhigh);chr$( 1)
190 print#3,"record";i
200 print#2,"p";chr$(4);chr$(rlow);chr$(rhigh);chr$(20)
210 print#3,"abcdef";i
220 next i
230 close 3:close 2
240 input "Press 'RETURN' to continue: ";r$
250 :
260 :
300 rem **--file input routine--**
310 open 2,8,15:rem open command chnl
320 open 3,8,4,"random example,l," + chr$(50)
330 for i = 1 to 25
340 gosub 1000:rem figure rec.# routine
350 print#2,"p";chr$(4);chr$(rlow);chr$(rhigh);chr$( 1)
360 input#3,a$
370 print a$;
380 print#2,"p";chr$(4);chr$(rlow);chr$(rhigh);chr$(20)
390 input#3,b$
400 print tab(15) b$
410 next i
420 close 3:close 2
430 input "Press 'RETURN' to continue: ";r$
440 :
450 :
500 rem **--random access routine--**
510 input "Which record number";nb$
520 nb = val(nb$)
530 if nb = 0 then 900:rem end
540 if nb > 25 then 510:rem ask again
550 i = nb:gosub 1000:rem figure rec.#
560 open 2,8,15:rem open command chnl
570 open 3,8,4,"random example,l," + chr$(50)
580 print#2,"p";chr$(4);chr$(rlow);chr$(rhigh);chr$(20)
590 input#3,b$
600 print b$;
610 print#2,"p";chr$(4);chr$(rlow);chr$(rhigh);chr$( 1)
620 input#3,a$
630 print tab(15) a$
640 close 3:close 2
650 goto 510
660 :
670 :
900 rem **--end routine--**
```

```
910 end
920 :
930 :
1000 rem **--figure rec.# routine--**
1010 rlow  = i
1020 rhigh = 0
1030 if rlow > 255 then 1050
1040 return
1050 rhigh = int(rlow/256)
1060 rlow  = rlow - 256 * rhigh
1070 return
```

■ Program for MEDICAL REC.SYS.

```
100 rem ***--medical records syst.--***
110 :
120 :
130 rem **--initialization--**
140 home$ = chr$(147):rem clr/home
150 ::cd$ = chr$( 17):rem cursor down
160 ::cu$ = chr$(145):rem cursor up
170 ::cl$ = chr$(157):rem cursor left
180 ::cr$ = chr$( 29):rem cursor right
190 :blk$ = chr$(144):rem black
200 :ylw$ = chr$(158):rem yellow
210 :wht$ = chr$(  5):rem white
220 :rvs$ = chr$( 18):rem reverse video
230 :bnk$ = chr$( 10):rem blank line
240 :brn$ = chr$(149):rem brown
250 :bue$ = chr$( 31):rem blue
260 :
270 poke 53280, 6:rem border = blue
280 poke 53272,23:rem upper/lower case
290 poke 53281, 7:rem set bkgrd to ylw.
300 :
310 :
320 rem **--variables list--**
330 rem  rlow = low  byte of rec.#
340 rem rhigh = high byte of rec.#
350 rem  file = file # in open cmnd
360 rem  dvic = device # in open cmnd
370 rem  cmnd = command # in open cmnd
380 rem   ptr = pointer for # of recd's
390 rem chnl$ = channel # in open cmnd
400 rem  rec$ = rec.# from rlow & rhigh
410 rem pztn$ = position within record
420 rem name$ = name associated w/info.
430 rem  dte$ = date of medical info.
440 rem type$ = type of medical info.
450 rem misc$ = misc. medical info.
460 rem  cvt$ = convert to lower case
470 rem srch$ = search for info.
480 rem find$ = info. in data file
490 rem info$ = associated srch$ info.
495 :
496 :
500 rem **--menu--**
510 tb = 8:rem tab value--8 spaces rt.
520 print home$:rem clr/home
530 print wht$
540 print tab(tb)
550 print rvs$;
560 print "MEDICAL RECORDS MENU"
570 print brn$
580 print:print tab(tb)
590 print "1. WRITE RECORD"
600 print:print tab(tb)
```

```
610 print "2. READ RECORD"
620 print:print tab(tb)
630 print "3. SEARCH RECORD"
640 print:print tab(tb)
650 print "4. SET POINTER"
660 print:print tab(tb)
670 print "5. LIST OF FILES"
680 print:print tab(tb)
690 print "6. END SESSION"
700 print:print tab(tb)
710 poke 19,32:rem disable input ?
720 input "Which Number Please? ";nu$
730 number = val(nu$)
740 :
750 if number = 1 then 1000
760 if number = 2 then 2000
770 if number = 3 then 3000
780 if number = 4 then 4000
790 if number = 5 then 5000
800 if number = 6 then 6000
810 :
820 gosub 14000:rem incorrect choice
830 goto 500:rem display menu again
840 :
850 :
1000 rem **--write record routine--**
1005 rem clear screen/crsr down 5
1010 print home$:cd = 5:gosub 9000
1015 :
1020 :
1025 rem *-name information-*
1030 print "Type in individual's name please: "
1035 print:input name$
1040 if len(name$) > 13 then name$ = left$(name$,13)
1045 print:print
1050 :
1055 :
1060 rem *-date information-*
1065 print "Type in the date in the form: 2-9-86."
1070 print:input dte$
1075 if len(dte$) > 10 then dte$ = left$(dte$,10)
1080 :
1085 :
1090 rem *-type of information-*
1095 gosub 11000:rem dsp info. types
1100 print tab(tb):input type$
1105 cvt$ = type$
1110 gosub 17000:rem convert to l.c.
1115 type$ = cvt$
1120 :
1125 :
1130 rem *-misc.information-*
1135 rem clear screen/crsr down 5
1140 print home$:cd = 5:gosub 9000
1145 print "Type in any misc. information: "
1150 print:print
```

```
1155 for i = 1 to 21
1160 print chr$(175);:rem underline
1165 next i
1170 print:print:print
1175 print "Do not go beyond the end of the line!"
1180 rem crsr up 5
1185 print cu$;cu$;cu$;cu$;cu$
1190 input misc$
1195 if len(misc$) > 21 then misc$ = left$(misc$,21)
1200 rem strip excess underline char
1205 sp = 21:s$ = misc$:gosub 12000:misc$ = s$
1210 :
1215 :
1400 rem *-display for correction-*
1405 gosub 16000:rem get full type msg.
1410 :
1415 rem clear screen/crsr down 5
1420 print home$:cd = 5:gosub 9000
1425 :
1430 print:print tab(tb) "1. NAME: ";name$
1435 print:print tab(tb) "2. DATE: ";dte$
1440 print:print tab(tb) "3. TYPE: ";tp$
1445 print:print tab(tb) "4. MISC: ";misc$
1450 print:print tab(tb)
1455 print "Is this correct? "
1460 print:print tab(tb)
1465 gosub 18000:rem y/n input routine
1470 if yes$ = "y" then 1700
1475 :
1480 print:print tab(tb)
1485 input "Which number is wrong? ";nb$
1490 nb = val(nb$)
1495 if nb < 1 or nb > 4 then gosub 14000:goto 1480
1500 if nb = 3 then gosub 11000:rem dsp info. types
1505 print:print:print tab(tb) "Type in correct information: "
1510 print:print tab(tb):input cinfo$
1515 if nb = 1 then name$ = left$(cinfo$,13):goto 1415:rem ask again
1520 if nb = 2 then  dte$ = left$(cinfo$,10):goto 1415:rem ask again
1525 if nb = 3 then type$ = left$(cinfo$,1) :goto 1400:rem ask again
1530 if nb = 4 then misc$ = left$(cinfo$,21):goto 1415:rem ask again
1535 :
1540 :
1700 rem **--file output routine--**
1705 :
1710 rem *-pointer file-*
1715 rem must set ptr. before first use
1720 open 2,8,2,"med-records.ptr,seq,read"
1725 input#2,ptr
1730 close 2
1735 ptr = ptr + 1
1740 :
1745 rem *-data file-*
1750 open 15,8,15:rem open command chnl
1755 open  3,8,3,"med-records,l," + chr$(50)
1760 rem l in line 1755 is letter not #
1765 rem 50 in line 1755 is rec.length--not # of records
```

```
1770 chnl$ = chr$(3):rem channel #
1775 rlow  = ptr:rem low byte of rec.#
1780 rhigh = 0:rem  high byte of rec.#
1785 if rlow > 255 then 15000
1790 rec$  = chr$(rlow) + chr$(rhigh)
1795 :
1800 pztn$ = chr$( 1):rem position
1805 print#15,"p";chnl$;rec$;pztn$
1810 print#3,name$
1815 :
1820 pztn$ = chr$(15):rem position
1825 print#15,"p";chnl$;rec$;pztn$
1830 print#3,dte$
1835 :
1840 pztn$ = chr$(26):rem position
1845 print#15,"p";chnl$;rec$;pztn$
1850 print#3,type$
1855 :
1860 pztn$ = chr$(28):rem position
1865 print#15,"p";chnl$;rec$;pztn$
1870 print#3,misc$
1875 close 3:close 15
1880 :
1885 :
1890 rem *-update ptr file-*
1895 open 2,8,2,"@0:med-records.ptr,seq,write"
1900 print#2,ptr
1905 close 2
1910 goto 500:rem menu
1915 :
1920 :
1925 :
2000 rem **--read file routine--**
2010 gosub 10000:rem display routine
2020 :
2030 rem *-pointer file-*
2040 open 2,8,2,"med-records.ptr,seq,read"
2050 input#2,ptr
2060 close 2
2070 :
2080 rem *-data file-*
2090 open 15,8,15:rem open command chnl
2100 open  5,8,5,"med-records,l," + chr$(50)
2110 rem l in line 2100 is letter not #
2120 chnl$ = chr$(5):rem channel #
2130 for rec = 1 to ptr
2140 rlow = rec:rhigh = 0
2150 if rlow > 255 then 15000
2160 rec$ = chr$(rlow) + chr$(rhigh)
2170 print
2180 :
2190 :
2200 pztn$ = chr$( 1):rem position
2210 print#15,"p";chnl$;rec$;pztn$
2220 input#5,name$
2230 :
```

```
2240 :
2250 pztn$ = chr$(15):rem position
2260 print#15,"p";chnl$;rec$;pztn$
2270 input#5,dte$
2280 :
2290 :
2300 pztn$ = chr$(26):rem position
2310 print#15,"p";chnl$;rec$;pztn$
2320 input#5,type$
2330 :
2340 :
2350 pztn$ = chr$(28):rem position
2360 print#15,"p";chnl$;rec$;pztn$
2370 input#5,misc$
2380 :
2390 :
2400 rem *-display information-*
2410 gosub 16000:rem get full type msg.
2420 :
2430 rem clear screen/crsr down 5
2440 print home$:cd = 5:gosub 9000
2450 :
2460 print:print#file,""tab(tb) "1. NAME: ";name$
2470 print:print#file,""tab(tb) "2. DATE: ";dte$
2480 print:print#file,""tab(tb) "5. TYPE: ";tp$
2490 print:print#file,""tab(tb) "4. MISC: ";misc$
2500 print:print#file,""tab(tb)
2510 print "Press ";wht$;"RETURN";brn$;" to continue:";
2520 gosub 19000:rem return key routine
2530 next rec:rem dsp next set of info.
2540 :
2550 :
2560 close 5:close 15
2570 print home$:cd = 5:gosub 9000
2580 print tab(tb + 3):print rvs$;"ALL FINISHED"
2590 cd = 10:gosub 9000:rem crsr down 10
2600 gosub 20000:rem menu return routine
2610 goto 500:rem menu
2620 :
2630 :
2640 :
3000 rem **--search routine--**
3010 rem clear screen/crsr down 3
3020 print home$:cd = 3:gosub 9000
3030 print tab(tb) "SEARCH FOR...."
3040 print:print
3050 print:print tab(tb) "1. NAME"
3060 print:print tab(tb) "2. DATE"
3070 print:print tab(tb) "3. TYPE"
3080 print:print tab(tb) "4. MISC"
3090 print:print tab(tb) "5. END SEARCH"
3100 print:print tab(tb) "Which number? ";:input nb$
3110 nb = val(nb$)
3120 :
3130 if nb = 1 then pztn$ = chr$( 1):b$ = "NAME"
3140 if nb = 2 then pztn$ = chr$(15):b$ = "DATE"
```

```
3150 if nb = 3 then pztn$ = chr$(26):b$ = "TYPE"
3160 if nb = 4 then pztn$ = chr$(28):b$ = "MISC"
3170 if nb = 5 then 500:rem menu
3180 if nb < 1 or nb > 5 then gosub 14000:goto 3000
3190 :
3200 print:print:print tab(tb) "Which ";b$;:input "?";srch$
3210 gosub 10000:rem display routine
3220 :
3230 cvt$ = srch$
3240 gosub 17000:rem convert to l.c.
3250 srch$ = cvt$
3260 :
3270 :
3280 rem **--file input routine--**
3290 :
3300 rem *-pointer file-*
3310 open 2,8,2,"med-records.ptr,seq,read"
3320 input#2,ptr
3330 close 2
3340 :
3350 rem *-data file-*
3360 open 15,8,15:rem open command chnl
3370 open  5,8,5,"med-records,l," + chr$(50)
3380 rem l in line 3370 is letter not #
3390 ln = len(srch$):chnl$ = chr$(5)
3400 for rec = 1 to ptr
3410 rlow = rec:rhigh = 0
3420 if rlow > 255 then 15000
3430 rec$ = chr$(rlow) + chr$(rhigh)
3440 :
3450 print#15,"p";chnl$;rec$;pztn$
3460 input#5,find$
3470 :
3480 cvt$ = left$(find$,ln)
3490 gosub 17000:rem convert to l.c.
3500 if srch$ <> cvt$ then 3750
3510 :
3520 for k = 1 to 4
3530 if  k = 1 then pt$ = chr$( 1)
3540 if  k = 2 then pt$ = chr$(15)
3550 if  k = 3 then pt$ = chr$(26)
3560 if  k = 4 then pt$ = chr$(28)
3570 print#15,"p";chnl$;rec$;pt$
3580 input#5,info$(k)
3590 if  k = 3 then type$ = info$(k):gosub 16000:info$(k) = tp$
3600 next k
3610 :
3620 :
3630 rem *-display information-*
3640 rem clear screen/crsr down 5
3650 print home$:cd = 5:gosub 9000
3660 :
3670 print:print#file,""tab(tb) "1. NAME: ";info$(1)
3680 print:print#file,""tab(tb) "2. DATE: ";info$(2)
3690 print:print#file,""tab(tb) "5. TYPE: ";info$(3)
3700 print:print#file,""tab(tb) "4. MISC: ";info$(4)
```

```
3710 print:print#file,""tab(tb)
3720 print "Press ";wht$;"RETURN";brn$;" to continue:";
3730 print:print:print
3740 gosub 19000:rem return key routine
3750 next rec
3760 :
3770 :
3780 close 5:close 15
3790 rem clear screen/crsr down 5
3800 print home$:cd = 5:gosub 9000
3810 print tab(tb + 3) "Search Completed!"
3820 cd = 10:gosub 9000
3830 print tab(tb)
3840 print "Press ";wht$;"RETURN";brn$;" to continue:";
3850 gosub 19000:rem return key routine
3860 close file
3870 goto 3000:rem search again
3880 :
3890 :
3900 :
4000 rem **--set pointer--**
4010 print home$:rem clr/home
4020 print tab(tb + 5) "SET POINTER"
4030 print:print
4040 print "You should only need to set the pointer"
4050 print
4060 print "the first time the program is used."
4070 print
4080 print "That first time, the value should be"
4090 print
4100 print "set to a '0'. After that, if the ptr."
4110 print
4120 print "file MED-RECORDS.PTR is not erased, "
4130 print
4140 print "this routine should not be needed. If"
4150 print
4160 print "the pointer file is erased, use this"
4170 print
4180 print "routine to reset the value of the ptr."
4190 print
4200 print "to the correct number of records."
4210 print:print
4220 print "Press ";wht$;"RETURN";brn$;" to continue:";
4230 gosub 19000:rem return key routine
4240 print home$:cd = 3:gosub 9000
4250 print "Do you want to set a value for the "
4260 print
4270 print "pointer? ";
4280 gosub 18000:rem y/n routine
4290 if yes$ = "y" then 4310
4300 goto 500:rem menu
4310 print
4320 print "Type in a value for the pointer: ";
4330 input ptr$
4340 print:print
4350 print "Is this the correct value: ";ptr$
```

```
4360 print
4370 print "Type ";wht$;"YES";brn$;" if it is: ";:input yes$
4380 print
4390 if yes$ = "YES" or yes$ = "yes" then 4410
4400 goto 4000:rem begin again
4410 :
4420 rem *-pointer file-*
4430 print:print "ONE MOMENT PLEASE!"
4440 ptr = val(ptr$)
4450 open 2,8,2,"@0:med-records.ptr,seq,write"
4460 print#2,ptr
4470 close 2
4480 print
4490 print "The pointer has now been set to: ";ptr
4500 cd = 5:gosub 9000:rem crsr down 5
4510 print "Press ";wht$;"RETURN";brn$;" to continue:";
4520 gosub 19000:rem return key routine
4530 goto 500:rem menu
4540 :
4550 :
4560 :
5000 rem **--list of files routine--**
5010 print home$:rem clr/home
5020 @"$":rem wedge/diskette directory
5030 print cu$;chr$(13):rem 13 = rtn
5040 print "Are you ready to return to the menu?"
5050 print
5060 gosub 18000:rem y/n input routine
5070 if yes$ = "y" then 500:rem menu
5080 goto 5000:rem check again
5090 :
5100 :
6000 rem **--end routine--**
6010 poke 19,0:rem restore input prompt
6020 print home$:rem clr/home
6030 cd = 5:rem 5 lines down
6040 gosub 9000:rem crsr down routine
6050 print tab(tb - 5)
6060 print rvs$;
6070 print "That's all for this session!"
6080 print:print:print
6090 print tab(tb)
6100 print rvs$;
6110 print "See you next time."
6120 print brn$
6130 cd = 10:rem 10 lines down
6140 gosub 9000:rem crsr down routine
6150 end
6160 :
6170 :
9000 rem **--cursor down routine--**
9010 for i = 1 to cd
9020 print cd$;
9030 next i
9040 return
9050 :
```

```
9060 :
10000 rem **--display routine--**
10010 print home$:rem clr/home
10020 cd = 3:rem 3 lines down
10030 gosub 9000:rem cursor down routine
10040 print "Would you like a paper print out?"
10050 print
10080 gosub 18000:rem y/n input routine
10090 if yes$ = "y" then 10120:rem prnt
10100 if yes$ = "n" then 10300:rem scrn
10110 :
10120 print home$:rem clr/home
10130 cd = 3:rem 3 lines down
10140 gosub 9000:rem cursor down routine
10150 print "Please make sure the printer"
10160 print
10170 print "is on and ready to use."
10180 print
10190 print "Are you ready to begin printing?"
10200 print
10210 gosub 18000:rem y/n input routine
10220 if yes$ = "n" then 10000
10230 :
10240 rem *-printer display-*
10250 file = 4
10260 dvic = 4
10270 cmnd = 7
10280 goto 10500:rem open instruction
10290 :
10300 rem *-screen display-*
10310 file = 3
10320 dvic = 3
10330 cmnd = 1
10340 goto 10500:rem open instruction
10350 :
10360 :
10500 rem *-open instruction-*
10510 open file,dvic,cmnd
10520 return
10530 :
10540 :
10550 :
11000 rem **--display type info--**
11010 rem clear screen/crsr down 2
11020 print home$:cd = 2:gosub 9000
11030 print tab(tb)
11040 print rvs$;"TYPE OF RECORD"
11050 print:print
11060 print tab(tb) "D--Dr. visit"
11070 print
11080 print tab(tb) "M--Medication"
11090 print
11100 print tab(tb) "I--Illness"
11110 print
11120 print tab(tb) "A--Accident/injury"
11130 print
```

```
11140 print tab(tb) "S--Shot/immunization"
11150 print
11160 print tab(tb) "X--X-Ray"
11170 print
11180 print tab(tb) "Which type of record?"
11190 print tab(tb) "(Type: D,M,I,A,S, or X.)"
11200 print
11210 return
11220 :
11230 :
11240 :
12000 rem **--strip excess underline character--**
12010 s2$ = s$
12020 i = 1
12030 if mid$(s2$,i,1) = chr$(175) then 12070
12040 i = i + 1
12050 if i > sp then 12070
12060 goto 12030
12070 s$ = left$(s2$,i - 1)
12080 return
12090 :
12100 :
12110 :
14000 rem *-incorrect choice message-*
14010 print:print tab(tb)
14020 print rvs$;"Incorrect Choice!"
14030 print:print tab(tb)
14040 print "Press ";wht$;"RETURN";brn$;" to continue:";
14050 gosub 19000:rem return key routine
14060 return
14070 :
14080 :
14090 :
15000 rem **--figure rec.# routine--**
15010 rhigh = int(rlow/256)
15020 rlow  = rlow - 256 * rhigh
15030 return
15040 :
15050 :
15060 :
16000 rem **--full type message--**
16010 if type$ = "d" then tp$ = "Dr. visit"
16020 if type$ = "m" then tp$ = "Medication"
16030 if type$ = "i" then tp$ = "Illness"
16040 if type$ = "a" then tp$ = "Accident/injury"
16050 if type$ = "s" then tp$ = "Shot/immunization"
16060 if type$ = "x" then tp$ = "X-Rays"
16070 return
16080 :
16090 :
16100 :
17000 rem **--convert to lowercase--**
17010 nc$ = ""
17020 for cv = 1 to len(cvt$)
17030 x = asc(mid$(cvt$,cv,1))
17040 if x > 192 then x = x - 128
```

```
17050 nc$ = nc$ + chr$(x)
17060 next cv
17070 :
17080 cvt$ = nc$
17090 f = asc(left$(cvt$,1))
17100 f = f + 128
17110 nc$ = chr$(f) + right$(cvt$,len(cvt$)- 1)
17120 return
17130 :
17140 rem cvt$ = converted to lowercase
17150 rem  nc$ = 1st letter/uppercase
17160 :
17170 :
17180 :
18000 rem **--y/n input routine--**
18010 print "Type a ";wht$;"Y";brn$;" or ";wht$;"N";brn$;" :";
18020 poke 19,32:rem disable input ?
18030 input yes$
18040 print
18050 if yes$ = "y" or yes$ = "Y" then yes$ = "y":return
18060 if yes$ = "n" or yes$ = "N" then yes$ = "n":return
18070 print
18080 print rvs$;"Incorrect Choice!";brn$
18090 print
18100 goto 18000:rem begin again
18110 :
18120 :
18130 :
19000 rem **-return key routine--**
19010 poke 198,0:rem clr kbrd buffer
19020 for i = 631 to 640
19030 poke i,0:rem no value
19040 next i
19050 x = peek(197):rem store key press
19060 if x = 1 then 19080:rem 1 = rtn
19070 goto 19050:rem if not 1 go back
19080 poke 198,1:rem allow for cursor
19090 poke 631,0:rem clr kbrd
19100 nu$ = "":rem clr string variable
19110 poke 19,32:rem disable input ?
19120 return
19130 :
19140 :
19150 :
20000 rem **--menu return routine--**
20010 print#file
20020 close file
20030 print
20040 poke 19,32:rem disable input ?
20050 print "Press ";wht$;"RETURN";brn$;" to go to Medical
      Menu:"
20060 gosub 19000:rem return key routine
20070 print
20080 return

ready.
```

11 home inventory system: advanced random access file manipulation

We are going to look at a simple, yet fairly complete, random access system for home inventory. We will examine the file handling portions of the various programs in detail with the expectation of modifying them for use with other applications. The purpose of such modification is to suggest the possibility of the development of a general purpose data base system.

There are seven programs in this *home inventory system:* "homeinv.menu", "homeinv.write", "homeinv.read", "homeinv.search", "homeinv.correct", "homeinv.trans", and "homeinv.copy". Each program name attempts to describe the main function of the particular program. Homeinv.menu is the general menu that allows the user to easily switch among the other programs. Homeinv.write is used to create and add to the inventory file. Homeinv.read displays the entire inventory file in the order the information was entered. Homeinv.search is really the heart of the system. This program has a menu of its own with seven options. Six of these options relate to pulling specific information from the file and displaying it. The next program, "homeinv.correct", allows the user to change or delete information in the inventory file. Homeinv.trans provides a translation of the inventory file into the DIF format. The final program, "homeinv.copy", produces a backup copy of the file on any diskette the user chooses.

CREATE HOME INVENTORY

The "homeinv.menu", "homeinv.trans", and "homeinv.copy" programs do not contain any new programming code or code not contained in another program, so they will not be discussed. The first program we will look at is the "homeinv.write" program. The complete listing for this program is given at the end of this chapter. You will probably find it helpful to first look over the program before reading this description.

There is one piece of code that needs explaining. Each of the input sections includes an "sp" value. This "sp" value is the number of spaces that the various inputs are allowed in the file. This value is checked to see that the user does not exceed the allotted amount. The "gosub" routine is used to print the varying number of underline spaces.

Lines 1000 to 2000 are the instructions used to check the information and allow the user to change anything before the information is written to the disk.

Lines 2000 to 3000 are the file-handling lines and will be discussed in detail.

```
2000 rem **--file output routine--**
2010 :
2020 rem *-pointer file-*
2030 open 2,8,2,"inventory.ptr,seq,read"
2040 input#2,ptr
2050 close 2
2060 if status = 16 then 3000
2070 ptr = ptr + 1
2080 :
```

Line 2060 is our method of checking whether or not the file has already been created. If the file exists, then the status variable will not equal 16 and no error should occur in bringing in the value of the pointer. But, if this is the first time the program has been used, an error will occur. The error will occur when line 2040 tries to bring in a value for ptr, since no such value has yet been written to the disk. When the error occurs, the status variable will register a value of 16 (unrecoverable read error). We do not wish the program to halt when this error happens; rather, we want the problem fixed. So we use the routine located between lines 3000 and 4000 to write out a value for ptr and then return to the beginning of the file output routine to start the process over. After use of this error routine, a value does exist on the disk, and line 2040 can input a value for ptr without an error occurring. Once we have a value for the pointer, we add one to that value.

```
2090 rem *-data file-*
2100 open 15,8,15:rem open command chnl
```

```
2110 open 3,8,3,"inventory.rec,l," + chr$(100)
2120 rem l in line 2110 is letter not #
2130 chnl$  = chr$(3):rem channel #
2140 rlow   = ptr:rem low byte of rec.#
2150 rhigh  = 0:rem high byte of rec.#
2160 if rlow > 255 then gosub 15000
2170 rec$   = chr$(rlow) + chr$(rhigh)
2180 :
2190 pztn$ = chr$( 1):rem position
2200 print#15,"p";chnl$;rec$;pztn$
2210 print#3,item$
2220 :
2230 pztn$ = chr$(25):rem position
2240 print#15,"p";chnl$;rec$;pztn$
2250 print#3,serl$
2260 :
2270 pztn$ = chr$(40):rem position
2280 print#15,"p";chnl$;rec$;pztn$
2290 print#3,cst$
2300 :
2310 pztn$ =  chr$(50):rem position
2320 print#15,"p";chnl$;rec$;pztn$
2330 print#3,room$
2340 :
2350 pztn$ = chr$(70):rem position
2360 print#15,"p";chnl$;rec$;pztn$
2370 print#3,desc$
2380 close 3:close 15
2390 :
2400 :
2410 rem *-update ptr file-*
2420 open 2,8,2,"@0:inventory.ptr,seq,write"
2430 print#2,ptr
2440 close 2
2450 :
2460 :
2470 goto 4000:rem repeat routine
2480 :
2490 :
```

Lines 2190 to 2370 instruct the computer to write out the information collected from the user to the inventory file. Each piece of information is given a certain maximum number of spaces. Most information will not take up the maximum, so some space in each field will be left blank. Item$ information can contain up to 24 characters or bytes of information (23 characters of information and 1 byte for the delimiter). Serial$ information can have up to 15 bytes of information. Cst$ information has a maximum of 10 bytes, room$ information 20 bytes, and Desc$ can have up to 30 bytes of information.

When all the information has been transferred to the disk, the pointer value is written out to its sequential file. The user is queried about adding more information to the file and the appropriate action taken upon obtaining a response.

DISPLAY HOME INVENTORY

The "homeinv.read" program is really the reverse of the routine just covered. The word input# is substituted for the word print#, and the values of the variables are formatted for display on the screen rather than being written to the disk. Otherwise, the routines are very similar. Each field of each record is read into the computer from the disk and displayed. When all records have been read in and displayed, the user is transferred to the "homeinv.menu" program.

SEARCH/SORT HOME INVENTORY

The main program of this Home Inventory System is the "homeinv.search" program. There are six sort or search routines and an option to return to the main home inventory menu.

1. Search For Item

2. Search For Serial #

3. Search For Cost

4. Search For Room Items

5. Sort Items--Alpha. Order

6. Sort Items--Serial #

7. Return to Home Inv.Menu

Numbers 1, 2, and 4 use a common search subroutine. The two sort options (numbers 5 and 6) use a common sort subroutine, the Shell–Metzner sort. Option number 3 uses its own search routines for both parts of this selection. We will cover the common search subroutine first.

```
16000 rem **--common search routine--**
16010 :
16020 :
```

```
16030 rem *-data file-*
16040 open 15,8,15:rem open command chnl
16050 open 5,8,5,"inventory.rec,l," + chr$(100)
16060 chnl$ = chr$(5):rem channel #
16070 :
16080 rec = rec + 1
16090 rlow = rec:rhigh = 0
16100 if rlow > 255 then gosub 15000
16110 rec$ = chr$(rlow) + chr$(rhigh)
16120 :
16130 print#15,"p";chnl$;rec$;pztn$
16140 input#5,find$
16150 :
16160 rem convert to lower case
16170 ln = len(srch$)
16180 cvt$ = left$(find$,ln)
16190 gosub 17000:find$ = cvt$
16200 :
16210 if srch$ = find$ then 16330
16220 if rec < ptr then 16080
16230 scf = 1:rem set search comp.flag
16240 rem clear screen/crsr down 5
16250 print home$:cd = 5:gosub 9000
16260 print tab(tb + 3)
16270 print "Search Completed!"
16280 for k = 1 to 1000:next k
16290 cd = 10:gosub 9000:rem crsr 10
16300 close 5:close 15
16310 return
        .
        .
        .Same code as file input routine
        .
        .
16590 return
```

This subroutine is common to the first two options and to the room search option. Each option routine that uses this subroutine establishes the necessary conditions prior to entering the subroutine. The values of srch$ and pztn$ are determined prior to the "gosub" statement in each of the option routines. Once these values are known, the specified part of the file can be searched for any match (line 16210). If a match occurs, control passes to the instructions at lines 16330 to 16590. These instructions read in from the diskette the information associated with the item searched for. The "return" statement in line 16590 returns control to the instruction following the "gosub" statement in the original option routine—1, 2, or 4. When a match does not occur, the record counter (rec) is first checked to see that its value does not exceed the value of the total number of records (ptr); then the record counter is incremented by one and the process is repeated.

The next section of code discussed is part one of the Search For Cost option. In lines 3000 to 3200, a decision is made by the user: whether to search for items above a certain cost or items below a certain cost. The appropriate part of this option routine is then given control. The following code is for items above a specific value.

```
3200 rem **--items above $ amount--**
3205 rem clear screen/crsr down 5
3210 print home$:cd = 5:gosub 9000
3215 input "Above which amount? ";amt
3220 gosub 10000:rem display routine
3225 rem clear screen/crsr down 2
3230 print home$:cd = 2:gosub 9000
3235 print#file,""tab(10) "ITEMS ABOVE $";amt
3240 print#file,bnk$:print#file,bnk$
3245 gosub 22000:rem open file
3250 for w = 1 to ptr
3255 gosub 23000:rem figure rec.#
3260 :
3265 pztn$ = chr$( 1):rem position
3270 print#15,"p";chnl$;rec$;pztn$
3275 input#5,item$
3280 :
3285 pztn$ = chr$(40):rem position
3290 print#15,"p";chnl$;rec$;pztn$
3295 input#5,cst$
3300 :
3305 c$ = cst$
3310 if left$(c$,7) = "DELETED" then 3345:rem next w
3315 if left$(c$,1) = "$" then gosub 11000:rem strip $
3320 if val(c$) > amt then 3330
3325 goto 3345:rem next w
3330 ttlamt = ttlamt + val(c$)
3335 print#file,item$;
3340 print#file,""tab(18) cst$
3345 next w
3350 :
3355 print
```

```
3360 print#file,"TOTAL VALUE = ";ttlamt
3365 gosub 24000:rem close files
3370 gosub 21000:rem clear variables
3375 gosub 20000:rem menu return
3380 goto 600:rem menu
3385 :
3390 :
```

The items that are valued above a certain amount are searched for in line 3320. The amount is previously determined in line 3215 and displayed in 3235. Line 3250 begins a loop that extends through 3345. Each record is searched for costs that exceed the specified amount. Line 3320 says that, if the cost of the record being examined exceeds the amount specified, then control is passed to line 3330. When such an item has been found, (1) a running total is kept of the cumulative value of these items (line 3330), and (2) the item and its value are displayed (lines 3335 and 3340). After all the records have been examined, the total value of all items above the specific amount is given (3360), and control is transferred to the file closing (3365) and housekeeping subroutines (3370 and 3375). Finally, control is shifted back to the menu for further instructions (3380).

The routine to find items below a certain value is virtually the same as that just given. The only significant difference occurs in line 3740 where the sign is reversed. We are looking for items whose value is less than the specified amount. Those items whose value is greater than the specified amount are passed over.

We have looked briefly at the first four options, the search options. The next two options are sort options and use a common sort subroutine, the Shell–Metzner sort. I will explain only the procedures involved in setting up and using a sort subroutine with Commodore disk files. We will look first at the alphabetizing routine.

```
5000 rem **--sort items alpha.order--**
5010 q = 1:rem valid record counter
5020 rem clear screen/crsr down 5
5030 print home$:cd = 5:gosub 9000
5040 print tab(5) "WORKING--PLEASE DON'T TOUCH!"
5050 gosub 22000:rem open file
5060 pztn$ = chr$( 1):rem position
5070 for w = 1 to ptr
5080 gosub 23000:rem figure rec.#
5090 :
5100 print#15,"p";chnl$;rec$;pztn$
5110 input#5,item$
5115 if item$ = "DELETED" then 5170:rem next w
5120 :
```

```
5130 rem convert to upper case
5140 cvt$ = item$:gosub 17500:item$ = cvt$
5150 a$(q) = item$:rem store in array for internal sort
5160 q = q + 1
5170 next w
5180 :
5190 :
5200 gosub 24000:rem close files
5210 n = q - 1
5220 print:print:print
5230 print tab(5) "STILL WORKING--PLEASE WAIT!"
5240 gosub 25000:rem sort routine
5250 :
5260 :
5270 rem display results
5280 gosub 10000:rem display routine
5290 rem clear screen/crsr down 5
5300 print home$:cd = 5:gosub 9000
5310 for i = 1 to q - 1
5320 print#file,i,a$(i)
5330 next i
5340 :
5350 gosub 21000:rem clear variables
5360 gosub 20000:rem menu return
5370 goto 600:rem menu
5380 :
5390 :
```

The keys to this routine are (1) reading in only the item names, (2) storing them in a string array, (3) sorting them with the sort subroutine located between 25000 and 25150, and (4) displaying them in their now-alphabetized order.

A separate record counter is used (line 5010) to keep track of the valid records since there may be some records that have been deleted and now contain the value "DELETED". If there are such records, they are skipped and the loop (w) is increased by one. But the valid record counter (q) is not increased. If the record is not valid (it contains "DELETED"), it is also not included in the string array of valid records to be sorted. Once the loop is completed, the string array a$() should contain all the valid item names. A new warning message is displayed (line 5230), and control is transferred to the sort subroutine. When the sorting has been completed, the results are displayed through another loop (lines 5310 to 5330).

The last two lines in this routine (5360 and 5370) are common to all the routines and simply "clean up" various conditions that may have been "set" during execution of the routine.

The last of the options, sort by serial number, again makes use of the left$ and mid$ string array commands. It is also the longest of the routines. The routine sorts by serial number and then displays the resulting list in serial number order, along with the associated item name. It is conceivable that an individual or insurance company would need all the associated information instead of just the item name. Therefore, if you are interested in developing a completely useful Home Inventory System, you might wish to add the code necessary to display all related information in both serial number order and alphabetical order.

```
6000 rem **--sort items serial#--**
6010 q = 1:rem valid record counter
6020 rem clear screen/crsr down 5
6030 print home$:cd = 5:gosub 9000
6040 print tab(5) "WORKING--PLEASE DON'T TOUCH!"
6050 gosub 22000:rem open file
6060 :
6070 for w = 1 to ptr
6080 gosub 23000:rem figure rec.#
6090 :
6100 pztn$ = chr$( 1):rem position
6110 print#15,"p";chnl$;rec$;pztn$
6120 input#5,item$
6125 if item$ = "DELETED" then 6230:rem next w
6130 :
6140 pztn$ = chr$(25):rem position
6150 print#15,"p";chnl$;rec$;pztn$
6160 input#5,serl$
6170 :
6180 rem convert to upper case
6190 cvt$ = serl$:gosub 17500:serl$ = cvt$
6200 :
6205 rem combine for internal sort
6210 a$(q) = serl$ + "*" + item$
6220 q = q + 1
6230 next w
6240 :
6250 gosub 24000:rem close files
6260 n = q - 1
6270 print:print:print
6280 print tab(5) "STILL WORKING--PLEASE WAIT!"
6290 gosub 25000:rem sort routine
6300 :
6310 rem display results
```

```
6320 gosub 10000:rem display routine
6330 rem clear screen/crsr down 5
6340 print home$:cd = 5:gosub 9000
6350 for i = 1 to q - 1
6360 rem separate and display
6370 la = len(a$(i))
6380 print#file,i;
6390 if mid$(a$(i),j,l) = "*" then 6410
6400 j = j + 1:goto 6390
6410 print#file,left$(a$(i),j - 1);
6420 print#file, ""tab(18) mid$(a$(i),j + 1,la)
6430 j = 1
6440 next i
6450 :
6460 gosub 21000:rem clear variables
6470 gosub 20000:rem menu return
6480 goto 600:rem menu
6490 :
6500 :
```

Lines 6140 to 6160 bring in the serial number of each item. If the serial number has been deleted (contains the word "DELETED"), the record is skipped as in the previous routine. In fact, the two sort routines have nearly identical beginnings. The main difference occurs in lines 6180 to 6190 when the serial number, instead of the item name, goes through the conversion to upper case. The only other major difference occurs when the item name is concatenated (joined) to the serial number. Line 6210 combines: (1) the existing value of the serial number (serl$), (2) the current value of the item name (item$), and (3) a separator (the asterisk) into one new string array value, a$(q).

Once the entire file is read and the correct number of valid records determined, control is passed to the sort subroutine (line 6290). Lines 6310 to 6440 are used to display the results of the sort. Here again, we need to make use of the power of the left$, mid$, and len functions. The numeric variable la is set to equal the length of each of the string arrays (line 6370). The mid$ function is used to determine where in the string the asterisk is located (6390). The left$ and mid$ functions are used to print out the desired parts of the string in a acceptable format (6380 to 6420). This sequence is repeated until all valid records have been displayed in serial number order. The end of this routine is the same as the end of the other five routines.

This concludes the discussion of the Search/Sort Home Inventory (home-inv.search) program. There are a number of other points that could be discussed, but those points relate mainly to different techniques of programming in BASIC rather than techniques for working with Commodore BASIC files. By now, if you have worked through all the programs, you should be able to "read" a program and recognize some of the different techniques used.

CORRECT HOME INVENTORY

The next program in this Home Inventory System provides the ability to change or delete information in the "inventory.rec" file. Both parts of this program make use of two routines: a "file output routine", and a "file input routine". These two routines have been used in our other programs in this system. The "correct record routine" (lines 1000 to 2000) is essentially the same as the correction routine in the "homeinv.write" program (lines 1000 to 2000). The difference is, in the "homeinv.write" program, the information being checked for accuracy comes from the keyboard. In the "homeinv.correct" program, the information comes from the disk. That is the reason for line 1110. This line transfers control to the file input routine, which inputs from the specified record on the disk the values for item$, serl$, cst$, room$, and desc$. These values are then displayed, and a check is made to see if they are correct.

At this point, one other new line of code is encountered (line 1040). Lines 1040, 1280, 1290, and 1450 are all related. All deal with a string variable called flag$. Line 1040 sets the original value of flag$ equal to the word "NO". This indicates that no information has yet been changed. Lines 1280 and 1290 check the value of flag$ and direct the computer accordingly. If the information is correct and no change has been made, the value of flag$ is still "NO", and the computer is directed to start this routine over again. If the information has been changed, the value of flag$ will have been changed by line 1450 to "YES", indicating altered information. If the information is correct and has been changed, we are now ready to write that information back out to the file on the disk (the file output routine). This technique allows the user to scan through the records if he or she is not sure of the record number of the incorrect information.

The deletion routine is a relatively uncomplicated routine. The suspected record is brought in from disk (line 2100) and displayed (lines 2180 to 2220). A request is made of the user to see if this is the information to be deleted. If it is not, the deletion routine starts again. If the information is to be deleted, the user is required to type the word "YES" rather than just the "Y". If "YES" is typed, all string variables are given the value "DELETED", and control is passed to the file output routine where "DELETED" replaces the now deleted information. Notice that the entire file does not need to be resequenced and rewritten to the disk. Instead, only the information requiring change is affected.

The change and delete routines for random access files are considerably easier than similar routines for sequential access files. This ease is one of the major strengths of random files. Access is direct to any part of the file desired. In fact, in a very large inventory system, it is possible to read from disk and check only the desired part of the record, rather than the entire record. Programming can often be simpler and easier to read. There is less need for string arrays and, therefore, less need for large amounts of internal computer memory. The disk can be used as an extension of the internal memory with random files since the same principles are involved. The major difference is in the time involved, disk access being much slower than internal memory access.

At the end of the chapter, I have included the first two programs of another system, a Magazine Article System, created by modifying this current Home Inventory System. (The full Magazine Article System is included on the diskettes mentioned in the front of the book.) The modification is not extensive. The main reason for including the first portion of the Magazine Article System is to suggest the possibility of a general purpose data base program. All our systems have included some method for: (1) creating and adding to a file, (2) displaying information from that file in various ways, and (3) editing the file. These are the essential characteristics in any data base system. It should be possible to create a general purpose data base system that would request certain necessary information from the user. Based on the supplied information, this general data base system would create a file and set up the procedures to display and edit information in that file.

The better commercial data base programs have expanded on these essential characteristics. They have added features that some users may need but others will never use. One feature that I feel is essential is transportability of file information. If a data base system does not allow some method of universal access to the files created under its system, I believe that system is severely limited in its usefulness to anyone other than the casual user. *Files created under a general data-base system must be able to be accessed by other commercial application programs!* Without such access, the user must reenter data in each application program used with the file information. This is the reason DIF is so important (see Chapter 9). Some general purpose data base systems do support DIF, while others at least make their files available through normal Commodore DOS file structure.

In the Preface, I said that "Reading this book will not make you capable of creating complete data base programs . . .", but at this point, you should have an appreciation of the effort that goes into creating a good general purpose data base system. For your individual use, you may find that you can create a semi-general purpose data base system, a system that can serve your needs but would not be universal in meeting the needs of everyone. This is the reason for including the beginning of the Magazine Article System as a modification of the Home Inventory System. Structured carefully, with enough user-supplied variables, this series of programs can form the basis for such a personal data-base system.

The next chapter will deal with the planning necessary in creating the programs for any file system. The example will be a Stock Market System for keeping track of the price and volume changes of certain issues.

QUESTIONS

1. What BASIC reserved phrase is only used the first time the "homeinv.write" program is run?
2. Give the name of the string variable that allows us to use one search routine for three different program modules.
3. What sort routine is used in both systems in this chapter?
4. What word means "joining string variables together"?
5. *True or False:* It is more difficult to change information in a random-access file than in a sequential file.

ANSWERS

1. Status = 16
2. Find$
3. Shell–Metzner
4. Concatenate
5. False

Program for HOMEINV.MENU

```
100 rem ***--homeinv.menu--***
110 :
120 :
130 rem **--initialization--**
140 home$ = chr$(147):rem clr/home
150 ::cd$ = chr$( 17):rem cursor down
160 ::cu$ = chr$(145):rem cursor up
170 ::cl$ = chr$(157):rem cursor left
180 ::cr$ = chr$( 29):rem cursor right
190 :blk$ = chr$(144):rem black
200 :ylw$ = chr$(158):rem yellow
210 :wht$ = chr$(  5):rem white
220 :rvs$ = chr$( 18):rem reverse video
230 :
240 poke 53280,14:rem border = lt.blue
250 poke 53272,23:rem upper/lower case
260 poke 53281, 9:rem set bkgrd to brn
270 :
280 :
500 rem **--menu--**
510 tb = 10:rem tab value-10 spaces rt.
520 print home$:rem clr/home
530 print wht$;
540 print tab(tb)
550 print rvs$;
560 print "HOME INVENTORY SYSTEM"
570 print
580 print ylw$
590 print tab(tb)
600 print "1. WRITE RECORD"
610 print:print tab(tb)
620 print "2. READ RECORD"
630 print:print tab(tb)
640 print "3. SEARCH RECORD"
650 print:print tab(tb)
660 print "4. CORRECT RECORD"
670 print:print tab(tb)
680 print "5. TRANSLATE RECORD"
690 print:print tab(tb)
700 print "6. COPY FILE"
710 print:print tab(tb)
720 print "7. LIST OF FILES"
730 print:print tab(tb)
740 print "8. END"
750 print:print tab(tb)
760 poke 19,32:rem disable input ?
770 input "Which Program Number? ";nu$
780 number = val(nu$)
790 :
800 if number = 1 then 1000
810 if number = 2 then 2000
820 if number = 3 then 3000
830 if number = 4 then 4000
```

```
840 if number = 5 then 5000
850 if number = 6 then 6000
860 if number = 7 then 7000
870 if number = 8 then 8000
880 :
890 rem *-incorrect choice message-*
900 print:print:print tab(tb)
910 print rvs$;"Incorrect Choice!"
920 print:print tab(tb)
930 print "Press ";wht$;"RETURN";ylw$;" to continue:";
940 gosub 19030:rem return key routine
950 goto 500:rem menu--check again
960 :
970 :
1000 rem **--write record program--**
1010 file$ = "HOMEINV.WRITE"
1020 gosub 17000:rem new program routine
1030 ^"homeinv.write":rem load & run
1040 :
1050 :
2000 rem **--read record program--**
2010 file$ = "HOMEINV.READ"
2020 gosub 17000:rem new program routine
2030 ^"homeinv.read":rem load & run
2040 :
2050 :
3000 rem **--search record program--**
3010 file$ = "HOMEINV.SEARCH"
3020 gosub 17000:rem new program routine
3030 ^"homeinv.search":rem load & run
3040 :
3050 :
4000 rem **--correct record program--**
4010 file$ = "HOMEINV.CORRECT"
4020 gosub 17000:rem new program routine
4030 ^"homeinv.correct":rem load & run
4040 :
4050 :
5000 rem **--trans. record program--**
5010 file$ = "HOMEINV.TRANSLATE"
5020 gosub 17000:rem new program routine
5030 ^"homeinv.trans":rem load & run
5040 :
5050 :
6000 rem **--copy file--**
6010 file$ = "HOMEINV.COPY"
6020 gosub 17000:rem new program routine
6030 ^"homeinv.copy":rem load & run
6040 :
6050 :
7000 rem **--list of files routine--**
7010 print home$:rem clr/home
7020 @"$"
7030 print cu$;chr$(13):rem 13 = rtn
7040 print "Are you ready to return to the menu?"
7050 print
```

```
7060 gosub 18000:rem y/n input routine
7070 if yes$ = "y" then 500:rem menu
7080 goto 7000:rem check again
7090 :
7100 :
8000 rem **--end routine--**
8010 poke 19,0:rem restore input prompt
8020 print home$:rem clr/home
8030 cd = 5:rem 5 lines down
8040 gosub 9000:rem crsr down routine
8050 print tab(tb - 5)
8060 print rvs$;
8070 print "That's all for this session!"
8080 print:print:print
8090 print tab(tb)
8100 print rvs$;
8110 print "See you next time."
8120 print ylw$
8130 cd = 10:rem 10 lines down
8140 gosub 9000:rem crsr down routine
8150 end
8160 :
8170 :
9000 rem **--cursor down routine--**
9010 for i = 1 to cd
9020 print cd$;
9030 next i
9040 return
9050 :
9060 :
17000 rem **--new program routine--**
17010 print home$:rem clr/home
17020 cd = 2:rem 2 lines down
17030 gosub 9000:rem crsr down routine
17040 print "You have selected the ";file$:print:print
      "program."
17050 print:print:print
17060 print "Is this the program you want?"
17070 print
17080 gosub 18000:rem y/n input routine
17090 if yes$ = "n" then 500:rem menu
17100 print home$:rem clr/home
17110 cd = 5:rem 5 lines down
17120 gosub 9000:rem crsr down routine
17130 print tab(tb - 5)
17140 print rvs$;
17150 print "Please wait!"
17160 print:print:print
17170 print tab(tb)
17180 print rvs$;
17190 print "I'm loading...."
17200 print:print:print
17210 print tab(tb + 8)
17220 print rvs$;
17230 print file$
```

```
17240 poke 19,0:rem restore input prompt
17250 return
17260 :
17270 :
18000 rem **--y/n input routine--**
18010 print "Type a ";wht$;"Y";ylw$;" or ";wht$;"N";ylw$;" :";
18020 poke 19,32:rem disable input ?
18030 input yes$
18040 print
18050 if yes$ = "y" or yes$ = "Y" then yes$ = "y":return
18060 if yes$ = "n" or yes$ = "N" then yes$ = "n":return
18070 print
18080 print rvs$;"Incorrect Choice!";ylw$
18090 print
18100 goto 18000:rem check again
18110 :
18120 :
19000 rem **--return key routine--**
19010 print
19020 print "Press ";wht$;"RETURN";ylw$;" to continue:";
19030 poke 198,0:rem clr kbrd buffer
19040 for i = 631 to 640
19050 poke i,0:rem no value
19060 next i
19070 x = peek(197):rem store key press
19080 if x = 1 then 19100
19090 goto 19070:if not 1 go back
19100 poke 198,1:rem allow 1 for cursor
19110 poke 631,0:rem clr kbrd
19120 nu$ = "":rem clr string variable
19130 print home$:rem clr/home
19140 return

ready.
```

■ Program for HOMEINV.WRITE

```
100 rem ***--write inventory rec.--***
110 :
120 :
130 rem **--initialization--**
140 home$ = chr$(147):rem clr/home
150 ::cd$ = chr$( 17):rem cursor down
160 ::cu$ = chr$(145):rem cursor up
170 ::cl$ = chr$(157):rem cursor left
180 ::cr$ = chr$( 29):rem cursor right
190 :blk$ = chr$(144):rem black
200 :ylw$ = chr$(158):rem yellow
210 :wht$ = chr$(  5):rem white
220 :rvs$ = chr$( 18):rem reverse video
230 :bnk$ = chr$( 10):rem blank line
240 :brn$ = chr$(149):rem brown
250 :bue$ = chr$( 31):rem blue
260 :
270 poke 53280,14:rem border = lt.blue
280 poke 53272,23:rem upper/lower case
290 poke 53281, 9:rem set bkgrd to ylw.
300 :
310 :
320 rem **--variables list--**
330 rem  rlow = low  byte of rec.#
340 rem rhigh = high byte of rec.#
350 rem  file = file # in open cmnd
360 rem  dvic = device # in open cmnd
370 rem  cmnd = command # in open cmnd
380 rem   ptr = pointer for # of recd's
390 rem chnl$ = channel # in open cmnd
400 rem  rec$ = rec.# from rlow & rhigh
410 rem pztn$ = position within record
420 rem item$ = name of item
430 rem serl$ = serial # of item
440 rem  cst$ = cost of item
450 rem room$ = location of item
460 rem desc$ = description of item
470 rem    sp = # of spaces for input
480 :
490 :
1000 rem **--keyboard input routine--**
1005 print ylw$
1010 tb = 8:rem tab value
1015 poke 19,32:rem disable input ?
1020 :
1025 :
1030 :
1100 rem **--name of item--**
1105 print home$:rem clr/home
1110 print tab(10) rvs$; "ADD TO HOME INVENTORY"
1115 cd = 7:gosub 9000:rem crsr down 7
1120 print "1. Type in item's name please: "
1125 print:print
```

```
1130 sp = 23
1135 gosub 5000:rem input subroutine
1140 input item$
1145 if len(item$) > 23 then item$ = left$(item$,23)
1150 s$ = item$:gosub 12000:item$ = s$
1155 :
1160 :
1200 rem **--serial # of item--**
1205 print home$:rem clr/home
1210 print tab(10) rvs$; "ADD TO HOME INVENTORY"
1215 cd = 7:gosub 9000:rem crsr down 7
1220 print "2. Type in item's serial # please: "
1225 print:print
1230 sp = 14
1235 gosub 5000:rem input subroutine
1240 input serl$
1245 if len(serl$) > 14 then serl$ = left$(serl$,14)
1250 s$ = serl$:gosub 12000:serl$ = s$
1255 :
1260 :
1300 rem **--cost of item--**
1305 print home$:rem clr/home
1310 print tab(10) rvs$; "ADD TO HOME INVENTORY"
1315 cd = 7:gosub 9000:rem crsr down 7
1320 print "3. Type in item's cost please: "
1325 print:print
1330 sp = 9
1335 gosub 5000:rem input subroutine
1340 input cst$
1345 if len(cst$) > 9 then cst$ = left$(cst$,9)
1350 s$ = cst$:gosub 12000:cst$ = s$
1355 :
1360 :
1400 rem **--room of item--**
1405 print home$:rem clr/home
1410 print tab(10) rvs$; "ADD TO HOME INVENTORY"
1415 cd = 7:gosub 9000:rem crsr down 7
1420 print "4. Type in item's room please: "
1425 print:print
1430 sp = 19
1435 gosub 5000:rem input subroutine
1440 input room$
1445 if len(room$) > 19 then room$ = left$(room$,19)
1450 s$ = room$:gosub 12000:room$ = s$
1455 :
1460 :
1500 rem **--desc.of item--**
1505 print home$:rem clr/home
1510 print tab(10) rvs$; "ADD TO HOME INVENTORY"
1515 cd = 7:gosub 9000:rem crsr down 7
1520 print "5. Type in item's description please: "
1525 print:print
1530 sp = 29
1535 gosub 5000:rem input subroutine
1540 input desc$
1545 if len(desc$) > 29 then desc$ = left$(desc$,29)
```

```
1550 s$ = desc$:gosub 12000:desc$ = s$
1555 :
1560 :
1600 rem **-display for correction--**
1610 :
1620 rem clear screen/crsr down 3
1630 print home$:cd = 3:gosub 9000
1640 :
1650 print:print tab(tb) "1. ITEM: ";item$
1660 print:print tab(tb) "2. SER#: ";serl$
1670 print:print tab(tb) "3. COST: ";cst$
1680 print:print tab(tb) "4. ROOM: ";room$
1690 print:print tab(tb) "5. DESC: ";desc$
1700 print:print tab(tb)
1710 print "Is this correct? "
1720 print:print tab(tb)
1730 gosub 18000:rem y/n input routine
1740 if yes$ = "y" then 2000
1750 print:print tab(tb)
1760 input "Which number is wrong? ";nb$
1770 nb = val(nb$)
1780 if nb = 1 then sp = 23
1790 if nb = 2 then sp = 14
1800 if nb = 3 then sp =  9
1810 if nb = 4 then sp = 19
1820 if nb = 5 then sp = 29
1830 if nb < 1 or nb > 5 then gosub 14000:goto 1750
1840 print home$:cd = 8:gosub 9000
1850 print "Type in correct information: "
1860 print
1870 gosub 5000:rem input routine
1880 input cinfo$
1890 s$ = cinfo$:gosub 12000:cinfo$ = s$
1900 if nb = 1 then item$ = left$(cinfo$,23):goto 1600:rem
     ask again
1910 if nb = 2 then serl$ = left$(cinfo$,14):goto 1600:rem
     ask again
1920 if nb = 3 then cst$  = left$(cinfo$, 9):goto 1600:rem
     ask again
1930 if nb = 4 then room$ = left$(cinfo$,19):goto 1600:rem
     ask again
1940 if nb = 5 then desc$ = left$(cinfo$,29):goto 1600:rem
     ask again
1950 :
1960 :
2000 rem **--file output routine--**
2010 :
2020 rem *-pointer file-*
2030 open 2,8,2,"inventory.ptr,seq,read"
2040 input#2,ptr
2050 close 2
2060 if status = 16 then 3000
2070 ptr = ptr + 1
2080 :
2090 rem *-data file-*
2100 open 15,8,15:rem open command chnl
```

```
2110 open  3,8,3,"inventory.rec,l," + chr$(100)
2120 rem l in line 2110 is letter not #
2130 chnl$ = chr$(3):rem channel #
2140 rlow  = ptr:rem low byte of rec.#
2150 rhigh = 0:rem  high byte of rec.#
2160 if rlow > 255 then gosub 15000
2170 rec$  = chr$(rlow) + chr$(rhigh)
2180 :
2190 pztn$ = chr$( 1):rem position
2200 print#15,"p";chnl$;rec$;pztn$
2210 print#3,item$
2220 :
2230 pztn$ = chr$(25):rem position
2240 print#15,"p";chnl$;rec$;pztn$
2250 print#3,serl$
2260 :
2270 pztn$ = chr$(40):rem position
2280 print#15,"p";chnl$;rec$;pztn$
2290 print#3,cst$
2300 :
2310 pztn$ = chr$(50):rem position
2320 print#15,"p";chnl$;rec$;pztn$
2330 print#3,room$
2340 :
2350 pztn$ = chr$(70):rem position
2360 print#15,"p";chnl$;rec$;pztn$
2370 print#3,desc$
2380 close 3:close 15
2390 :
2400 :
2410 rem *-update ptr file-*
2420 open 2,8,2,"@0:inventory.ptr,seq,write"
2430 print#2,ptr
2440 close 2
2450 :
2460 :
2470 goto 4000:rem repeat routine
2480 :
2490 :
3000 rem **--first time use only--**
3010 close 2
3020 open 2,8,2,"inventory.ptr,seq,write"
3030 print#2,"0"
3040 close 2
3050 :
3060 goto 2000:rem begin file routine
3070 :
3080 :
4000 rem **--repeat routine--**
4010 print home$:rem clr/home
4020 cd = 3:rem 3 lines down
4030 gosub 9000:rem crsr down routine
4040 print "Do you want to add more items?"
4050 print
4060 gosub 18000:rem y/n input routine
4070 if yes$ = "y" then 1000
```

```
4080 if yes$ = "n" then 6000
4090 :
4100 :
5000 rem **--input subroutine--**
5010 for i = 1 to sp
5020 print chr$(175);:rem underline
5030 next i
5040 print:print:print
5050 print "Do not go beyond the end of the line!"
5060 rem crsr up 5
5070 print cu$;cu$;cu$;cu$;cu$
5080 return
5090 :
5100 :
6000 rem **--return to inv.menu--**
6010 poke 19,0:rem restore input prompt
6020 print home$:rem clr/home
6030 cd = 5:rem 5 lines down
6040 gosub 9000:rem crsr down routine
6050 print tab(tb)
6060 print rvs$;
6070 print "LOADING THE INVENTORY MENU"
6080 ^"homeinv.menu"
6090 :
6100 :
9000 rem **--cursor down routine--**
9010 for i = 1 to cd
9020 print cd$;
9030 next i
9040 return
9050 :
9060 :
12000 rem **--strip excess underline character--**
12010 s2$ = s$
12020 i = 1
12030 if mid$(s2$,i,1) = chr$(175) then 12070
12040 i = i + 1
12050 if i > sp then 12070
12060 goto 12030
12070 s$ = left$(s2$,i - 1)
12080 return
12090 :
12100 :
12110 :
14000 rem *-incorrect choice message-*
14010 print:print tab(tb)
14020 print rvs$;"Incorrect Choice!"
14030 print:print tab(tb)
14040 print "Press ";wht$;"RETURN";ylw$;" to continue:";
14050 gosub 19000:rem return key routine
14060 return
14070 :
14080 :
14090 :
15000 rem **--figure rec.# routine--**
15010 rhigh = int(rlow/256)
```

```
15020 rlow  = rlow - 256 * rhigh
15030 return
15040 :
15050 :
15060 :
18000 rem **--y/n input routine--**
18010 print "Type a ";wht$;"Y";ylw$;" or ";wht$;"N";ylw$;" :"
18020 poke 19,32:rem disable input ?
18030 input yes$
18040 print
18050 if yes$ = "y" or yes$ = "Y" then yes$ = "y":return
18060 if yes$ = "n" or yes$ = "N" then yes$ = "n":return
18070 print
18080 print rvs$;"Incorrect Choice!";ylw$
18090 print
18100 goto 18000:rem begin again
18110 :
18120 :
18130 :
19000 rem **-return key routine--**
19010 poke 198,0:rem clr kbrd buffer
19020 for i = 631 to 640
19030 poke i,0:rem no value
19040 next i
19050 x = peek(197):rem store key press
19060 if x = 1 then 19080:rem 1 = rtn
19070 goto 19050:rem if not 1 go back
19080 poke 198,1:rem allow for cursor
19090 poke 631,0:rem clr kbrd
19100 nu$ = "":rem clr string variable
19110 poke 19,32:rem disable input ?
19120 return

ready.
```

■ Program for HOMEINV.READ

```
100 rem ***--read inventory rec.--***
110 :
120 :
130 rem **--initialization--**
140 home$ = chr$(147):rem clr/home
150 ::cd$ = chr$( 17):rem cursor down
160 ::cu$ = chr$(145):rem cursor up
170 ::cl$ = chr$(157):rem cursor left
180 ::cr$ = chr$( 29):rem cursor right
190 :blk$ = chr$(144):rem black
200 :ylw$ = chr$(158):rem yellow
210 :wht$ = chr$(  5):rem white
220 :rvs$ = chr$( 18):rem reverse video
230 :bnk$ = chr$( 10):rem blank line
240 :brn$ = chr$(149):rem brown
250 :bue$ = chr$( 31):rem blue
260 :
270 poke 53280,14:rem border = lt.blue
280 poke 53272,23:rem upper/lower case
290 poke 53281, 9:rem set bkgrd to brn.
300 :
310 :
320 rem **--variables list--**
330 rem  rlow = low  byte of rec.#
340 rem rhigh = high byte of rec.#
350 rem  file = file # in open cmnd
360 rem  dvic = device # in open cmnd
370 rem  cmnd = command # in open cmnd
380 rem   ptr = pointer for # of recd's
390 rem chnl$ = channel # in open cmnd
400 rem  rec$ = rec.# from rlow & rhigh
410 rem pztn$ = position within record
420 rem item$ = name of item
430 rem serl$ = serial # of item
440 rem  cst$ = cost of item
450 rem room$ = location of item
460 rem desc$ = description of item
470 rem    sp = # of spaces for input
480 :
490 :
1000 rem **--read file routine--**
1010 print ylw$
1020 tb = 8:rem tab value
1030 gosub 10000:rem display routine
1040 :
1050 rem *-pointer file-*
1060 open 2,8,2,"inventory.ptr,seq,read"
1070 input#2,ptr
1080 close 2
1090 :
1100 rem *-data file-*
1110 open 15,8,15:rem open command chnl
1120 open  5,8,5,"inventory.rec,1," + chr$(100)
```

```
1130 rem l in line 1120 is letter not #
1140 chnl$ = chr$(5):rem channel #
1150 for rec = 1 to ptr
1160 rlow = rec:rhigh = 0
1170 if rlow > 255 then 15000
1180 rec$ = chr$(rlow) + chr$(rhigh)
1190 print
1200
1210 :
1220 pztn$ = chr$( 1):rem position
1230 print#15,"p";chnl$;rec$;pztn$
1240 input#5,item$
1245 if item$ = "deleted" then 1600
1250 :
1260 :
1270 pztn$ = chr$(25):rem position
1280 print#15,"p";chnl$;rec$;pztn$
1290 input#5,serl$
1300 :
1310 :
1320 pztn$ = chr$(40):rem position
1330 print#15,"p";chnl$;rec$;pztn$
1340 input#5,cst$
1350 :
1360 :
1370 pztn$ = chr$(50):rem position
1380 print#15,"p";chnl$;rec$;pztn$
1390 input#5,room$
1400 :
1410 :
1420 pztn$ = chr$(70):rem position
1430 print#15,"p";chnl$;rec$;pztn$
1440 input#5,desc$
1450 :
1460 :
1470 rem *-display information-*
1480 :
1490 rem clear screen/crsr down 5
1500 print home$:cd = 5:gosub 9000
1510 :
1520 print:print#file,""tab(tb) "1. ITEM: ";item$
1530 print:print#file,""tab(tb) "2. SER#: ";serl$
1540 print:print#file,""tab(tb) "3. COST: ";cst$
1550 print:print#file,""tab(tb) "4. ROOM: ";room$
1560 print:print#file,""tab(tb) "5. DESC: ";desc$
1570 print:print#file,""tab(tb)
1580 print "Press ";wht$;"RETURN";ylw$;" to continue:";
1590 gosub 19000:rem return key routine
1600 next rec:rem dsp next set of info.
1610 :
1620 :
1630 close 5:close 15:print#file:close file
1640 print home$:cd = 5:gosub 9000
1650 print tab(tb + 3):print rvs$;"ALL FINISHED"
1660 cd = 10:gosub 9000:rem crsr down 10
1670 print tab(tb) "Press ";wht$;"RETURN";ylw$;" to continue:";
```

```
1680 gosub 19000:rem return key routine
1690 :
1700 :
1710 :
6000 rem **--return to inv.menu--**
6010 poke 19,0:rem restore input prompt
6020 print home$:rem clr/home
6030 cd = 5:rem 5 lines down
6040 gosub 9000:rem crsr down routine
6050 print tab(tb)
6060 print rvs$;
6070 print "LOADING THE INVENTORY MENU"
6080 ^"homeinv.menu"
6090 :
6100 :
9000 rem **--cursor down routine--**
9010 for i = 1 to cd
9020 print cd$;
9030 next i
9040 return
9050 :
9060 :
10000 rem **--display routine--**
10010 print home$:rem clr/home
10020 cd = 3:rem 3 lines down
10030 gosub 9000:rem cursor down routine
10040 print "Would you like a paper print out?"
10050 print
10080 gosub 18000:rem y/n input routine
10090 if yes$ = "y" then 10120:rem prnt
10100 if yes$ = "n" then 10300:rem scrn
10110 :
10120 print home$:rem clr/home
10130 cd = 3:rem 3 lines down
10140 gosub 9000:rem cursor down routine
10150 print "Please make sure the printer"
10160 print
10170 print "is on and ready to use."
10180 print
10190 print "Are you ready to begin printing?"
10200 print
10210 gosub 18000:rem y/n input routine
10220 if yes$ = "n" then 10000
10230 :
10240 rem *-printer display-*
10250 file = 4
10260 dvic = 4
10270 cmnd = 7
10280 goto 10500:rem open instruction
10290 :
10300 rem *-screen display-*
10310 file = 3
10320 dvic = 3
10330 cmnd = 1
10340 goto 10500:rem open instruction
10350 :
```

```
10360 :
10500 rem *-open instruction-*
10510 open file,dvic,cmnd
10520 return
10530 :
10540 :
10550 :
15000 rem **--figure rec.# routine--**
15010 rhigh = int(rlow/256)
15020 rlow  = rlow - 256 * rhigh
15030 return
15040 :
15050 :
15060 :
18000 rem **--y/n input routine--**
18010 print "Type a ";wht$;"Y";ylw$;" or ";wht$;"N";ylw$;" :";
18020 poke 19,32:rem disable input ?
18030 input yes$
18040 print
18050 if yes$ = "y" or yes$ = "Y" then yes$ = "y":return
18060 if yes$ = "n" or yes$ = "N" then yes$ = "n":return
18070 print
18080 print rvs$;"Incorrect Choice!";ylw$
18090 print
18100 goto 18000:rem begin again
18110 :
18120 :
18130 :
19000 rem **-return key routine--**
19010 poke 198,0:rem clr kbrd buffer
19020 for i = 631 to 640
19030 poke i,0:rem no value
19040 next i
19050 x = peek(197):rem store key press
19060 if x = 1 then 19080:rem 1 = rtn
19070 goto 19050:rem if not 1 go back
19080 poke 198,1:rem allow for cursor
19090 poke 631,0:rem clr kbrd
19100 nu$ = "":rem clr string variable
19110 poke 19,32:rem disable input ?
19120 return

ready.
```

■ Program for HOMEINV.SEARCH

```
100 rem ***--search/sort homeinv.--***
110 :
120 :
130 rem **--initialization--**
140 home$ = chr$(147):rem clr/home
150 ::cd$ = chr$( 17):rem cursor down
160 ::cu$ = chr$(145):rem cursor up
170 ::cl$ = chr$(157):rem cursor left
180 ::cr$ = chr$( 29):rem cursor right
190 :blk$ = chr$(144):rem black
200 :ylw$ = chr$(158):rem yellow
210 :wht$ = chr$(  5):rem white
220 :rvs$ = chr$( 18):rem reverse video
230 :bnk$ = chr$( 10):rem blank line
240 :brn$ = chr$(149):rem brown
250 :bue$ = chr$( 31):rem blue
260 :
270 poke 53280,14:rem border = lt.blue
280 poke 53272,23:rem upper/lower case
290 poke 53281, 9:rem set bkgrd to brn.
300 :
310 :
320 rem **--variables list--**
330 rem  rlow = low  byte of rec.#
340 rem rhigh = high byte of rec.#
350 rem  file = file # in open cmnd
360 rem  dvic = device # in open cmnd
370 rem  cmnd = command # in open cmnd
380 rem   ptr = pointer for # of recd's
390 rem chnl$ = channel # in open cmnd
400 rem  rec$ = rec.# from rlow & rhigh
410 rem pztn$ = position within record
420 rem item$ = name of item
430 rem serl$ = serial # of item
440 rem  cst$ = cost of item
450 rem room$ = location of item
460 rem desc$ = description of item
470 rem    sp = # of spaces for input
480 :
490 :
500 rem *-pointer file-*
510 open 2,8,2,"inventory.ptr,seq,read"
520 input#2,ptr
530 close 2
540 dim a$(ptr)
550 :
560 :
600 rem **--menu routine--**
610 print ylw$
620 tb = 8:rem tab value
630 poke 19,32:rem disable input ?
640 rem clear screen/crsr down 1
```

```
650 print home$:cd = 1:gosub 9000
660 print tab(tb + 3) "SEARCH/SORT MENU"
670 print
680 print:print tab(tb)
690 print "1. Search For Item"
700 print:print tab(tb)
710 print "2. Search For Serial #"
720 print:print tab(tb)
730 print "3. Search For Cost"
740 print:print tab(tb)
750 print "4. Search For Room Items"
760 print:print tab(tb)
770 print "5. Sort Items--Alpha. Order"
780 print:print tab(tb)
790 print "6. Sort Items--Serial #"
800 print:print tab(tb)
810 print "7. Return to Home Inv. Menu"
820 print:print tab(tb)
830 print tab(tb):input "Which number please? ";nb$
840 nb = val(nb$)
850 :
860 if nb = 1 then 1000
870 if nb = 2 then 2000
880 if nb = 3 then 3000
890 if nb = 4 then 4000
900 if nb = 5 then 5000
910 if nb = 6 then 6000
920 if nb = 7 then 7000
930 print
940 gosub 14000:rem incorrect choice
950 goto 600:rem menu
960 :
970 :
980 :
1000 rem **--search for item--**
1010 gosub 10000:rem display routine
1020 rem clear screen/crsr down 5
1030 print home$:cd = 5:gosub 9000
1040 input "Which item? ";srch$
1050 rem convert to lower case
1060 cvt$ = srch$:gosub 17000:srch$ = cvt$
1070 rec = 0
1080 pztn$ = chr$( 1):rem position
1090 gosub 16000:rem common search
1100 if scf = 1 then 1120:rem srch comp
1110 gosub 13000:rem common display
1120 gosub 21000:rem clear variables
1130 if rec = ptr or rec > ptr then 1150
1140 goto 1080:rem continue search
1150 gosub 20000:rem menu return
1160 goto 600:rem menu
1170 :
1180 :
2000 rem **--search for serial #--**
2010 gosub 10000:rem display routine
2015 rem clear screen/crsr down 5
```

```
2020 print home$:cd = 5:gosub 9000
2030 input "What serial number? ";srch$
2040 rem convert to lower case
2050 cvt$ = srch$:gosub 17000:srch$ = cvt$
2060 rec = 0
2070 pztn$ = chr$(25):rem position
2080 gosub 16000:rem common search
2090 if scf = 1 then 2110:rem srch comp
2100 gosub 13000:rem common display
2110 gosub 21000:rem clear variables
2120 if rec = ptr or rec > ptr then 2140
2130 goto 2070:rem continue search
2140 gosub 20000:rem menu return
2150 goto 600:rem menu
2160 :
2170 :
3000 rem **--search for cost--**
3010 ttlamt = 0:rem zero out total amt
3020 rem clear screen/crsr down 5
3030 print home$:cd = 5:gosub 9000
3040 print tab(tb) "SEARCH FOR ITEMS..."
3050 print:print:print
3060 print tab(tb) "A....Above a certain amount"
3070 print
3080 print tab(tb) "B....Below a certain amount"
3090 print:print
3100 print tab(tb) "Which letter ";wht$;"A";ylw$;" or ";wht$;
     "B";ylw$;" :";
3110 input lt$
3120 if lt$ = "A" or lt$ = "a" then 3200
3130 if lt$ = "B" or lt$ = "b" then 3500
3140 gosub 14000:rem incorrect choice
3150 goto 3000:rem ask again
3160 :
3170 :
3200 rem **--items above $ amount--**
3205 rem clear screen/crsr down 5
3210 print home$:cd = 5:gosub 9000
3215 input "Above which amount? ";amt
3220 gosub 10000:rem display routine
3225 rem clear screen/crsr down 2
3230 print home$:cd = 2:gosub 9000
3235 print#file,""tab(10) "ITEMS ABOVE $";amt
3240 print#file,bnk$:print#file,bnk$
3245 gosub 22000:rem open file
3250 for w = 1 to ptr
3255 gosub 23000:rem figure rec.#
3260 :
3265 pztn$ = chr$( 1):rem position
3270 print#15,"p";chnl$;rec$;pztn$
3275 input#5,item$
3280 :
3285 pztn$ = chr$(40):rem position
3290 print#15,"p";chnl$;rec$;pztn$
3295 input#5,cst$
3300 :
```

```
3305 c$ = cst$
3310 if left$(c$,7) = "DELETED" then 3345:rem next w
3315 if left$(c$,1) = "$" then gosub 11000:rem strip $
3320 if val(c$) > amt then 3330
3325 goto 3345:rem next w
3330 ttlamt = ttlamt + val(c$)
3335 print#file,item$;
3340 print#file,""tab(18) cst$
3345 next w
3350 :
3355 print
3360 print#file,"TOTAL VALUE = ";ttlamt
3365 gosub 24000:rem close files
3370 gosub 21000:rem clear variables
3375 gosub 20000:rem menu return
3380 goto 600:rem menu
3385 :
3390 :
3500 rem **--items below $ amount--**
3510 rem clear screen/crsr down 5
3520 print home$:cd = 5:gosub 9000
3530 input "Below which amount? ";amt
3540 gosub 10000:rem display routine
3550 rem clear screen/crsr down 2
3560 print home$:cd = 2:gosub 9000
3570 print#file,""tab(10) "ITEMS BELOW $";amt
3580 print:print
3590 gosub 22000:rem open file
3600 for w = 1 to ptr
3610 gosub 23000:rem figure rec.#
3620 :
3630 pztn$ = chr$( 1):rem position
3640 print#15,"p";chnl$;rec$;pztn$
3650 input#5,item$
3660 :
3670 pztn$ = chr$(40):rem position
3680 print#15,"p";chnl$;rec$;pztn$
3690 input#5,cst$
3700 :
3710 c$ = cst$
3720 if left$(c$,7) = "DELETED" then 3790:rem next w
3730 if left$(c$,1) = "$" then gosub 11000:rem strip $
3740 if val(c$) < amt then 3760
3750 goto 3790:rem next w
3760 ttlamt = ttlamt + val(c$)
3770 print#file,item$;
3780 print#file,""tab(18) cst$
3790 next w
3800 :
3810 :
3820 print
3830 print#file,"TOTAL VALUE = ";ttlamt
3840 gosub 24000:rem close files
3850 gosub 21000:rem clear variables
3860 gosub 20000:rem menu return
3870 goto 600:rem menu
```

```
3880 :
3890 :
4000 rem **--search for room items--**
4010 gosub 10000:rem display routine
4020 rem clear screen/crsr down 5
4030 print home$:cd = 5:gosub 9000
4040 input "Which room? ";srch$
4050 rem convert to lower case
4060 cvt$ = srch$:gosub 17000:srch$ = cvt$
4070 rec = 0
4080 pztn$ = chr$(50):rem position
4090 gosub 16000:rem common search
4100 if scf = 1 then 4120:rem srch comp
4110 gosub 13000:rem common display
4120 gosub 21000:rem clear variables
4130 if rec = ptr or rec > ptr then 4150
4140 goto 4080:rem continue search
4150 gosub 20000:rem menu return
4160 goto 600:rem menu
4170 :
4180 :
5000 rem **--sort items alpha.order--**
5010 q = 1:rem valid record counter
5020 rem clear screen/crsr down 5
5030 print home$:cd = 5:gosub 9000
5040 print tab(5) "WORKING--PLEASE DON'T TOUCH!"
5050 gosub 22000:rem open file
5060 pztn$ = chr$( 1):rem position
5070 for w = 1 to ptr
5080 gosub 23000:rem figure rec.#
5090 :
5100 print#15,"p";chn1$;rec$;pztn$
5110 input#5,item$
5120 :
5125 if item$ = "DELETED" then 5170
5130 rem convert to upper case
5140 cvt$ = item$:gosub 17500:item$ = cvt$
5150 a$(q) = item$:rem store in array for internal sort
5160 q = q + 1
5170 next w
5180 :
5190 :
5200 gosub 24000:rem close files
5210 n = q - 1
5220 print:print:print
5230 print tab(5) "STILL WORKING--PLEASE WAIT!"
5240 gosub 25000:rem sort routine
5250 :
5260 :
5270 rem display results
5280 gosub 10000:rem display routine
5290 rem clear screen/crsr down 5
5300 print home$:cd = 5:gosub 9000
5310 for i = 1 to q - 1
5320 print#file,i;a$(i)
5330 next i
```

```
5340 :
5350 gosub 21000:rem clear variables
5360 gosub 20000:rem menu return
5370 goto 600:rem menu
5380 :
5390 :
6000 rem **--sort items serial #--**
6010 q = 1:rem valid record counter
6020 rem clear screen/crsr down 5
6030 print home$:cd = 5:gosub 9000
6040 print tab(5) "WORKING--PLEASE DON'T TOUCH!"
6050 gosub 22000:rem open file
6070 for w = 1 to ptr
6080 gosub 23000:rem figure rec.#
6090 :
6100 pztn$ = chr$( 1):rem position
6110 print#15,"p";chnl$;rec$;pztn$
6120 input#5,item$
6125 if item$ = "DELETED" then 6230
6130 :
6140 pztn$ = chr$(25):rem position
6150 print#15,"p";chnl$;rec$;pztn$
6160 input#5,serl$
6170 :
6180 rem convert to upper case
6190 cvt$ = serl$:gosub 17500:serl$ = cvt$
6200
6205 rem combine for internal sort
6210 a$(q) = serl$ + "*" + item$
6220 q = q + 1
6230 next w
6240 :
6250 gosub 24000:rem close files
6260 q = q - 1
6270 print:print:print
6280 print tab(5) "STILL WORKING--PLEASE WAIT!"
6290 gosub 25000:rem sort routine
6300 :
6310 rem display results
6320 gosub 10000:rem display routine
6330 rem clear screen/crsr down 5
6340 print home$:cd = 5:gosub 9000
6350 for i = 1 to q - 1
6360 rem separate and display
6370 la = len(a$(i))
6380 print#file,i;
6390 if mid$(a$(i),j,1) = "*" then 6410
6400 j = j + 1:goto 6390
6410 print#file,left$(a$(i),j - 1);
6420 print#file,""tab(18) mid$(a$(i),j + 1,la)
6430 j = 1
6440 next i
6450 :
6460 gosub 21000:rem clear variables
6470 gosub 20000:rem menu return
6480 goto 600:rem menu
```

```
6490 :
6500 :
7000 rem **--return to homeinv.menu--**
7010 poke 19,0:rem restore input prompt
7020 print home$:rem clr/home
7030 cd = 5:rem 5 lines down
7040 gosub 9000:rem crsr down routine
7050 print tab(tb)
7060 print rvs$;
7070 print "LOADING THE HOME INV. MENU"
7080 ^"homeinv.menu"
7090 :
7100 :
7110 :
9000 rem **--cursor down routine--**
9010 for i = 1 to cd
9020 print cd$;
9030 next i
9040 return
9050 :
9060 :
9070 :
10000 rem **--display routine--**
10010 print home$:rem clr/home
10020 cd = 3:rem 3 lines down
10030 gosub 9000:rem cursor down routine
10040 print "Would you like a paper print out?"
10050 print
10080 gosub 18000:rem y/n input routine
10090 if yes$ = "y" then 10120:rem prnt
10100 if yes$ = "n" then 10300:rem scrn
10110 :
10120 print home$:rem clr/home
10130 cd = 3:rem 3 lines down
10140 gosub 9000:rem cursor down routine
10150 print "Please make sure the printer"
10160 print
10170 print "is on and ready to use."
10180 print
10190 print "Are you ready to begin printing?"
10200 print
10210 gosub 18000:rem y/n input routine
10220 if yes$ = "n" then 10000
10230 :
10240 rem *-printer display-*
10250 file = 4
10260 dvic = 4
10270 cmnd = 7
10280 goto 10500:rem open instruction
10290 :
10300 rem *-screen display-*
10310 file = 3
10320 dvic = 3
10330 cmnd = 1
10340 goto 10500:rem open instruction
10350 :
```

```
10360 :
10500 rem *-open instruction-*
10510 open file,dvic,cmnd
10520 return
10530 :
10540 :
10550 :
11000 rem **--strip $ sign--**
11010 lc = len(c$)
11020 a$ = right(c$,lc - 1)
11030 c$ = a$
11040 return
11050 :
11060 :
11070 :
13000 rem *-display information-*
13010 :
13020 rem clear screen/crsr down 5
13030 print home$:cd = 5:gosub 9000
13040 :
13050 print:print#file,""tab(tb) "1. ITEM: ";item$
13060 print:print#file,""tab(tb) "2. SER#: ";serl$
13070 print:print#file,""tab(tb) "3. COST: ";cst$
13080 print:print#file,""tab(tb) "4. ROOM: ";room$
13090 print:print#file,""tab(tb) "5. DESC: ";desc$
13100 print:print#file,""tab(tb)
13110 print "Press ";wht$;"RETURN";ylw$;" to continue:";
13120 gosub 19000:rem return key routine
13130 return
13140 :
13150 :
13160 :
14000 rem *-incorrect choice message-*
14010 print:print tab(tb)
14020 print rvs$;"Incorrect Choice!"
14030 print:print tab(tb)
14040 print "Press ";wht$;"RETURN";ylw$;" to continue:";
14050 gosub 19000:rem return key routine
14060 return
14070 :
14080 :
14090 :
15000 rem **--figure rec.# > 255--**
15010 rhigh = int(rlow/256)
15020 rlow  = rlow - 256 * rhigh
15030 return
15040 :
15050 :
15060 :
16000 rem **--common search routine--**
16010 :
16020 :
16030 rem *-data file-*
16040 open 15,8,15:rem open command chnl
16050 open  5,8,5,"inventory.rec,l," + chr$(100)
16060 chnl$ = chr$(5):rem channel #
```

```
16070 :
16080 rec = rec + 1
16090 rlow = rec:rhigh = 0
16100 if rlow > 255 then gosub 15000
16110 rec$ = chr$(rlow) + chr$(rhigh)
16120 :
16130 print#15,"p";chnl$;rec$;pztn$
16140 input#5,find$
16150 :
16160 rem convert to lower case
16170 ln = len(srch$)
16180 cvt$ = left$(find$,ln)
16190 gosub 17000:find$ = cvt$
16200 :
16210 if srch$ = find$ then 16330
16220 if rec < ptr then 16080
16230 scf = 1:rem set search comp.flag
16240 rem clear screen/crsr down 5
16250 print home$:cd = 5:gosub 9000
16260 print tab(tb + 3)
16270 print "Search Completed!"
16280 for k = 1 to 1000:next k
16290 cd = 10:gosub 9000:rem crsr 10
16300 close 5:close 15
16310 return
16320 :
16330 pztn$ = chr$( 1):rem position
16340 print#15,"p";chnl$;rec$;pztn$
16350 input#5,item$
16360 :
16370 :
16380 pztn$ = chr$(25):rem position
16390 print#15,"p";chnl$;rec$;pztn$
16400 input#5,serl$
16410 :
16420 :
16430 pztn$ = chr$(40):rem position
16440 print#15,"p";chnl$;rec$;pztn$
16450 input#5,cst$
16460 :
16470 :
16480 pztn$ = chr$(50):rem position
16490 print#15,"p";chnl$;rec$;pztn$
16500 input#5,room$
16510 :
16520 :
16530 pztn$ = chr$(70):rem position
16540 print#15,"p";chnl$;rec$;pztn$
16550 input#5,desc$
16560 :
16570 :
16580 close 5:close 15
16590 return
16600 :
16610 :
16620 :
```

```
17000 rem **--convert to lowercase--**
17010 nc$ = ""
17020 for cv = 1 to len(cvt$)
17030 x = asc(mid$(cvt$,cv,1))
17040 if x > 192 then x = x - 128
17050 nc$ = nc$ + chr$(x)
17060 next cv
17070 :
17080 cvt$ = nc$
17090 f = asc(left$(cvt$,1))
17100 f = f + 128
17110 nc$ = chr$(f) + right$(cvt$,len(cvt$)- 1)
17120 return
17130 :
17140 rem cvt$ = converted to lowercase
17150 rem  nc$ = 1st letter/uppercase
17160 :
17170 :
17180 :
17500 rem **--convert to uppercase--**
17510 nc$ = ""
17520 for cv = 1 to len(cvt$)
17530 x = asc(mid$(cvt$,cv,1))
17540 if x > 64 and x < 91 then x = x + 128
17550 nc$ = nc$ + chr$(x)
17560 next cv
17570 :
17580 cvt$ = nc$
17590 return
17600 :
17610 :
17620 :
18000 rem **--y/n input routine--**
18010 print "Type a ";wht$;"Y";ylw$;" or ";wht$;"N";ylw$;" :";
18020 poke 19,32:rem disable input ?
18030 input yes$
18040 print
18050 if yes$ = "y" or yes$ = "Y" then yes$ = "y":return
18060 if yes$ = "n" or yes$ = "N" then yes$ = "n":return
18070 print
18080 print rvs$;"Incorrect Choice!";ylw$
18090 print
18100 goto 18000:rem begin again
18110 :
18120 :
18130 :
19000 rem **-return key routine--**
19010 poke 198,0:rem clr kbrd buffer
19020 for i = 631 to 640
19030 poke i,0:rem no value
19040 next i
19050 x = peek(197):rem store key press
19060 if x = 1 then 19080:rem 1 = rtn
19070 goto 19050:rem if not 1 go back
19080 poke 198,1:rem allow for cursor
19090 poke 631,0:rem clr kbrd
```

```
19100 nu$ = "":rem clr string variable
19110 poke 19,32:rem disable input ?
19120 return
19130 :
19140 :
19150 :
20000 rem **--menu return routine--**
20010 print#file
20020 close file
20030 print
20040 poke 19,32:rem disable input ?
20050 print tab(3) "Press ";wht$;"RETURN";ylw$;" to go to
      Search Menu:"
20060 gosub 19000:rem return key routine
20070 print
20080 return
20090 :
20100 :
20110 :
21000 rem **--clear variables--**
21010 item$ = ""
21020 serl$ = ""
21030  cst$ = ""
21040 room$ = ""
21050 desc$ = ""
21055   scf = 0
21060 return
21070 :
21080 :
21090 :
22000 rem **--open data file--**
22010 open 15,8,15:rem open command chnl
22020 open  5,8,5,"inventory.rec,l," + chr$(100)
22030 chnl$ = chr$(5):rem channel #
22040 return
22050 :
22060 :
22070 :
23000 rem **--figure record number--**
23010 rlow = w:rhigh = 0
23020 if rlow > 255 then gosub 15000
23030 rec$ = chr$(rlow) + chr$(rhigh)
23040 return
23050 :
23060 :
23070 :

24000 rem **--close files--**
24010 close 5
24020 close 15
24030 return
24040 :
24050 :
24060 :
25000 rem **--shell-metzner sort--**
25010 m = n
```

```
25020 m = int (m / 2)
25030 if m = 0 then 25150
25040 j = 1:k = n - m
25050 i = j
25060 z = i + m
25070 if a$(i) < a$(z) then 25120
25080 t$ = a$(i):a$(i) = a$(z):a$(z) = t$
25090 i = i - m
25100 if i < 1 then 25120
25110 goto 25060
25120 j = j + 1
25130 if j > k then 25020
25140 goto 25050
25150 return

ready.
```

Program for HOMEINV.CORRECT

```
100 rem ***--correct/delete inv.--***
110 :
120 :
130 rem **--initialization--**
140 home$ = chr$(147):rem clr/home
150 ::cd$ = chr$( 17):rem cursor down
160 ::cu$ = chr$(145):rem cursor up
170 ::cl$ = chr$(157):rem cursor left
180 ::cr$ = chr$( 29):rem cursor right
190 :blk$ = chr$(144):rem black
200 :ylw$ = chr$(158):rem yellow
210 :wht$ = chr$(  5):rem white
220 :rvs$ = chr$( 18):rem reverse video
230 :bnk$ = chr$( 10):rem blank line
240 :brn$ = chr$(149):rem brown
250 :bue$ = chr$( 31):rem blue
260 :
270 poke 53280,14:rem border = lt.blue
280 poke 53272,23:rem upper/lower case
290 poke 53281, 9:rem set bkgrd to brn.
300 :
310 :
320 rem **--variables list--**
330 rem  rlow = low  byte of rec.#
340 rem rhigh = high byte of rec.#
350 rem  file = file # in open cmnd
360 rem  dvic = device # in open cmnd
370 rem  cmnd = command # in open cmnd
380 rem   ptr = pointer for # of recd's
390 rem chnl$ = channel # in open cmnd
400 rem  rec$ = rec.# from rlow & rhigh
410 rem pztn$ = position within record
420 rem item$ = name of item
430 rem serl$ = serial # of item
440 rem  cst$ = cost of item
450 rem room$ = location of item
460 rem desc$ = description of item
470 rem    sp = # of spaces for input
480 :
490 :
500 rem *-pointer file-*
510 open 2,8,2,"inventory.ptr,seq,read"
520 input#2,ptr
530 close 2
540 :
550 :
560 :
600 rem **--menu routine--**
610 print ylw$
620 tb = 3:rem tab value
630 poke 19,32:rem disable input ?
640 rem clear screen/crsr down 3
650 print home$:cd = 3:gosub 9000
```

```
660 print tab(8) "CORRECT/DELETE MENU"
670 print:print:print
680 print:print tab(tb)
690 print "C....Correct Inventory Record"
700 print:print tab(tb)
710 print "D....Delete  Inventory Record"
720 print:print tab(tb)
730 print "R....Return to Inventory Menu"
740 print:print tab(tb)
750 print tab(tb):input "Which letter please? ";lt$
760 if lt$ = "C" or lt$ = "c" then 1000
770 if lt$ = "D" or lt$ = "d" then 2000
780 if lt$ = "R" or lt$ = "r" then 3000
790 goto 14000:rem incorrect choice
800 goto 750
810 :
820 :
830 :
1000 rem **--correct record routine--**
1010 tb = 8:rem tab value
1020 rem clear screen/crsr down 5
1030 print home$:cd = 5:gosub 9000
1040 flag$ = "no":rem info not yet chgd
1050 print "Type a '0' to return to the menu."
1060 print:print
1070 input "Correct which record? ";rec
1080 if rec = 0 then 600:rem menu
1090 if rec > ptr then 14000
1100 :
1110 gosub 5000:rem file input routine
1120 :
1130 :
1140 rem **-display for correction--**
1150 :
1160 rem clear screen/crsr down 3
1170 print home$:cd = 3:gosub 9000
1180 :
1190 print:print tab(tb) "1. ITEM: ";item$
1200 print:print tab(tb) "2. SER#: ";serl$
1210 print:print tab(tb) "3. COST: ";cst$
1220 print:print tab(tb) "4. ROOM: ";room$
1230 print:print tab(tb) "5. DESC: ";desc$
1240 print:print tab(tb)
1250 print "Is this correct? "
1260 print:print tab(tb)
1270 gosub 18000:rem y/n input routine
1280 if yes$ = "y" and flag$ = "yes" then 6000:rem info has
     been changed
1290 if yes$ = "y" and flag$ = "no" then 1000:rem info has
     not been changed
1300 print:print tab(tb)
1310 input "Which number is wrong? ";nb$
1320 nb = val(nb$)
1330 if nb = 1 then sp = 23
1340 if nb = 2 then sp = 14
1350 if nb = 3 then sp =  9
```

```
1360 if nb = 4 then sp = 19
1370 if nb = 5 then sp = 29
1380 if nb < 1 or nb > 5 then gosub 14000:goto 1300
1390 rem clear screen/crsr down 8
1400 print home$:cd = 8:gosub 9000
1410 print "Type in correct information: "
1420 print
1430 gosub 7000:rem input routine
1440 input cinfo$
1450 flag$ = "yes"
1460 s$ = cinfo$:gosub 12000:cinfo$ = s$
1470 if nb = 1 then item$ = left$(cinfo$,23):goto 1140:rem
     ask again
1480 if nb = 2 then serl$ = left$(cinfo$,14):goto 1140:rem
     ask again
1490 if nb = 3 then cst$  = left$(cinfo$, 9):goto 1140:rem
     ask again
1500 if nb = 4 then room$ = left$(cinfo$,19):goto 1140:rem
     ask again
1510 if nb = 5 then desc$ = left$(cinfo$,29):goto 1140:rem
     ask again
1520 :
1530 :
1540 :
2000 rem **--delete record routine--**
2010 tb = 8:rem tab value
2020 rem clear screen/crsr down 5
2030 print home$:cd = 5:gosub 9000
2040 print "Type a '0' to return to the menu."
2050 print:print
2060 input "Delete which record? ";rec
2070 if rec = 0 then 600
2080 if rec > ptr then 14000
2090 :
2100 gosub 5000:rem file input routine
2110 :
2120 :
2130 rem **-display for deletion--**
2140 :
2150 rem clear screen/crsr down 3
2160 print home$:cd = 3:gosub 9000
2170 :
2180 print:print tab(tb) "1. ITEM: ";item$
2190 print:print tab(tb) "2. SER#: ";serl$
2200 print:print tab(tb) "3. COST: ";cst$
2210 print:print tab(tb) "4. ROOM: ";room$
2220 print:print tab(tb) "5. DESC: ";desc$
2230 print:print tab(tb)
2240 print "Delete this record? "
2250 print:print tab(tb)
2260 gosub 18000:rem y/n input routine
2270 if yes$ = "y" then 2290
2280 goto 2000:rem ask again
2290 print:print tab(tb)
2300 print "Are you sure? Type ";wht$;"YES";ylw$
2310 print:print tab(tb)
2320 print "to delete this record. ";:input yes$
```

```
2330 if yes$ = "YES" or yes$ = "yes" then 2350
2340 goto 2000:rem ask again
2350 item$ = "DELETED"
2360 serl$ = "DELETED"
2370  cst$ = "DELETED"
2380 room$ = "DELETED"
2390 desc$ = "DELETED"
2400 goto 6000:rem file output routine
2410 :
2420 :
2430 :
3000 rem **--return to inv.menu--**
3010 poke 19,0:rem restore input prompt
3020 print home$:rem clr/home
3030 cd = 5:rem 5 lines down
3040 gosub 9000:rem crsr down routine
3050 print tab(tb)
3060 print rvs$;
3070 print "LOADING THE INVENTORY MENU"
3080 ^"homeinv.menu"
3090 :
3100 :
3110 :
5000 rem **--file input routine--**
5010 :
5020 :
5030 rem *-data file-*
5040 open 15,8,15:rem open command chnl
5050 open  5,8,5,"inventory.rec,l," + chr$(100)
5060 chnl$ = chr$(5):rem channel #
5070 rlow = rec:rhigh = 0
5080 if rlow > 255 then 15000
5090 rec$ = chr$(rlow) + chr$(rhigh)
5100 print
5110 :
5120 :
5130 pztn$ = chr$( 1):rem position
5140 print#15,"p";chnl$;rec$;pztn$
5150 input#5,item$
5160 :
5170 :
5180 pztn$ = chr$(25):rem position
5190 print#15,"p";chnl$;rec$;pztn$
5200 input#5,serl$
5210 :
5220 :
5230 pztn$ = chr$(40):rem position
5240 print#15,"p";chnl$;rec$;pztn$
5250 input#5,cst$
5260 :
5270 :
5280 pztn$ = chr$(50):rem position
5290 print#15,"p";chnl$;rec$;pztn$
5300 input#5,room$
5310 :
5320 :
```

```
5330 pztn$ = chr$(70):rem position
5340 print#15,"p";chnl$;rec$;pztn$
5350 input#5,desc$
5360 :
5370 :
5380 close 5:close 15
5390 return
5400 :
5410 :
5420 :
6000 rem **--file output routine--**
6010 :
6020 :
6030 rem *-data file-*
6040 open 15,8,15:rem open command chnl
6050 open  3,8,3,"inventory.rec,1," + chr$(100)
6060 chnl$ = chr$(3):rem channel #
6070 rlow  = rec:rem low byte of rec.#
6080 rhigh = 0:rem  high byte of rec.#
6090 if rlow > 255 then 15000
6100 rec$  = chr$(rlow) + chr$(rhigh)
6110 :
6120 :
6130 pztn$ = chr$( 1):rem position
6140 print#15,"p";chnl$;rec$;pztn$
6150 print#3,item$
6160 :
6170 :
6180 pztn$ = chr$(25):rem position
6190 print#15,"p";chnl$;rec$;pztn$
6200 print#3,serl$
6210 :
6220 :
6230 pztn$ = chr$(40):rem position
6240 print#15,"p";chnl$;rec$;pztn$
6250 print#3,cst$
6260 :
6270 :
6280 pztn$ = chr$(50):rem position
6290 print#15,"p";chnl$;rec$;pztn$
6300 print#3,room$
6310 :
6320 :
6330 pztn$ = chr$(70):rem position
6340 print#15,"p";chnl$;rec$;pztn$
6350 print#3,desc$
6360 :
6370 :
6380 close 3:close 15
6390 :
6400 :
6410 goto 600:rem menu
6420 :
6430 :
6440 :
7000 rem **--input subroutine--**
```

```
7010 for i = 1 to sp
7020 print chr$(175);:rem underline
7030 next i
7040 print:print:print
7050 print "Do not go beyond the end of the line!"
7060 rem crsr up 5
7070 print cu$;cu$;cu$;cu$;cu$
7080 return
7090 :
7100 :
7110 :
9000 rem **--cursor down routine--**
9010 for i = 1 to cd
9020 print cd$;
9030 next i
9040 return
9050 :
9060 :
9070 :
12000 rem **--strip excess underline character--**
12010 s2$ = s$
12020 i = 1
12030 if mid$(s2$,i,1) = chr$(175) then 12070
12040 i = i + 1
12050 if i > sp then 12070
12060 goto 12030
12070 s$ = left$(s2$,i - 1)
12080 return
12090 :
12100 :
12110 :
14000 rem *-incorrect choice message-*
14010 print:print tab(tb)
14020 print rvs$;"Incorrect Choice!"
14030 print:print tab(tb)
14040 print "Press ";wht$;"RETURN";ylw$;" to continue:";
14050 gosub 19000:rem return key routine
14060 return
14070 :
14080 :
14090 :
15000 rem **--figure rec.# routine--**
15010 rhigh = int(rlow/256)
15020 rlow  = rlow - 256 * rhigh
15030 return
15040 :
15050 :
15060 :
18000 rem **--y/n input routine--**
18010 print "Type a ";wht$;"Y";ylw$;" or ";wht$;"N";ylw$;" :";
18020 poke 19,32:rem disable input ?
18030 input yes$
18040 print
18050 if yes$ = "y" or yes$ = "Y" then yes$ = "y":return
18060 if yes$ = "n" or yes$ = "N" then yes$ = "n":return
18070 print
```

```
18080 print rvs$;"Incorrect Choice!";ylw$
18090 print
18100 goto 18000:rem begin again
18110 :
18120 :
18130 :
19000 rem **-return key routine--**
19010 poke 198,0:rem clr kbrd buffer
19020 for i = 631 to 640
19030 poke i,0:rem no value
19040 next i
19050 x = peek(197):rem store key press
19060 if x = 1 then 19080:rem 1 = rtn
19070 goto 19050:rem if not 1 go back
19080 poke 198,1:rem allow for cursor
19090 poke 631,0:rem clr kbrd
19100 nu$ = "":rem clr string variable
19110 poke 19,32:rem disable input ?
19120 return

ready.
```

■ Program for HOMEINV.TRANS

```
100 rem ***--homeinv.translate--***
110 :
120 :
130 rem **--initialization--**
140 home$ = chr$(147):rem clr/home
150 ::cd$ = chr$( 17):rem cursor down
160 ::cu$ = chr$(145):rem cursor up
170 ::cl$ = chr$(157):rem cursor left
180 ::cr$ = chr$( 29):rem cursor right
190 :blk$ = chr$(144):rem black
200 :ylw$ = chr$(158):rem yellow
210 :wht$ = chr$(  5):rem white
220 :rvs$ = chr$( 18):rem reverse video
230 :bnk$ = chr$( 10):rem blank line
240 :brn$ = chr$(149):rem brown
250 :bue$ = chr$( 31):rem blue
260 :
270 poke 53280,14:rem border = lt.blue
280 poke 53272,23:rem upper/lower case
290 poke 53281, 9:rem set bkgrd to brn.
300 :
310 :
320 rem **--variables list--**
330 rem  rlow = low  byte of rec.#
340 rem rhigh = high byte of rec.#
350 rem  file = file # in open cmnd
360 rem  dvic = device # in open cmnd
370 rem  cmnd = command # in open cmnd
380 rem   ptr = pointer for # of recd's
390 rem chnl$ = channel # in open cmnd
400 rem  rec$ = rec.# from rlow & rhigh
410 rem pztn$ = position within record
420 rem item$ = name of item
430 rem serl$ = serial # of item
440 rem  cst$ = cost of item
450 rem room$ = location of item
460 rem desc$ = description of item
470 rem    sp = # of spaces for input
480 :
490 :
500 rem *-pointer file-*
510 open 2,8,2,"inventory.ptr,seq,read"
520 input#2,ptr
530 close 2
540 :
550 dim item$(ptr),serl$(ptr),cst$(ptr),room$(ptr),desc$(ptr)
560 :
570 :
580 :
1000 rem **--file input routine--**
1010 :
1020 :
```

```
1030 print home$:cd = 5:gosub 9000
1040 print tab(8) rvs$; "READING FILE INFORMATION!"
1050 rem *-data file-*
1060 open 15,8,15:rem open command chnl
1070 open  5,8,5,"inventory.rec,1," + chr$(100)
1080 chnl$ = chr$(5):rem channel #
1090 :
1100 :
1110 for k = 1 to ptr
1120 rlow = k:rhigh = 0
1130 if rlow > 255 then 15000
1140 rec$ = chr$(rlow) + chr$(rhigh)
1150 print
1160 :
1170 :
1180 pztn$ = chr$( 1):rem position
1190 print#15,"p";chnl$;rec$;pztn$
1200 input#5,item$(k)
1210 :
1220 :
1230 pztn$ = chr$(25):rem position
1240 print#15,"p";chnl$;rec$;pztn$
1250 input#5,ser1$(k)
1260 :
1270 :
1280 pztn$ = chr$(40):rem position
1290 print#15,"p";chnl$;rec$;pztn$
1300 input#5,cst$(k)
1310 :
1320 :
1330 pztn$ = chr$(50):rem position
1340 print#15,"p";chnl$;rec$;pztn$
1350 input#5,room$(k)
1360 :
1370 :
1380 pztn$ = chr$(70):rem position
1390 print#15,"p";chnl$;rec$;pztn$
1400 input#5,desc$(k)
1410 next k
1420 :
1430 :
1440 close 5:close 15
1450 print home$:cd = 5:gosub 9000
1460 print tab(5) "Insert diskette for translation!"
1470 print:print
1480 print tab(8) "Press ";wht$;"RETURN";ylw$;" to continue: "
1490 gosub 19000:rem return routine
1500 :
1510 :
1520 :
2000 rem **--create dif file--**
2010 :
2020 rem clear screen/crsr down 5
2030 print home$:cd = 5:gosub 9000
2040 print tab(11) rvs$;"WRITING DIF FILE"
2050 rem nv = number of vectors
```

```
2060 rem nt = number of tuples
2070 nv = 5:nt = ptr + 1
2080 q$ = chr$(34):rem quote mark
2090 open 2,8,2,"homeinv.dif,seq,write"
2100
2110 rem *-header section-*
2120 :
2130 print#2,"TABLE"
2140 print#2,"0,1"
2150 print#2,q$q$
2160 :
2170 print#2,"VECTORS"
2180 print#2,"0,";nv
2190 print#2,q$q$
2200 :
2210 print#2,"TUPLES"
2220 print#2,"0,";nt
2230 print#2,q$q$
2240 :
2250 print#2,"DATA"
2260 print#2,"0,0"
2270 print#2,q$q$
2280 :
2290 :
2300 rem *-data section-*
2310 :
2320 print#2,"-1,0"
2330 print#2,"BOT"
2340 :
2350 print#2,"1,0"
2360 print#2,q$"ITEM"q$
2370 :
2380 print#2,"1,0"
2390 print#2,q$"SERIAL #"q$
2400 :
2410 print#2,"1,0"
2420 print#2,q$"COST"q$
2430 :
2440 print#2,"1,0"
2450 print#2,q$"ROOM"q$
2460 :
2470 print#2,"1,0"
2480 print#2,q$"DESC."q$
2490 :
2500 for i = 1 to ptr
2510 :
2520 i$ = item$(i)
2530 if left$(i$,7) = "DELETED" then 2790:rem next i
2540 c$ = cst$(i)
2550 if left$(c$,1) = "$" then 2570
2560 goto 2610
2570 lc = len(c$)
2580 a$ = right$(c$,lc - 1)
2590 c$ = a$
2600 :
2610 print#2,"-1,0"
```

```
2620 print#2,"BOT"
2630 :
2640 print#2,"1,0"
2650 print#2,item$(i)
2660 :
2670 print#2,"1,0"
2680 print#2,serl$(i)
2690 :
2700 print#2,"0,";val(c$)
2710 print#2,"V"
2720 :
2730 print#2,"1,0"
2740 print#2,room$(i)
2750 :
2760 print#2,"1,0"
2770 print#2,desc$(i)
2780 :
2790 next i
2800 print#2,"-1,0"
2810 print#2,"EOD"
2820 :
2830 close 2
2840 print home$:cd = 5:gosub 9000
2850 print tab(14) "ALL FINISHED"
2860 print:print
2870 print tab(8)
2880 print "Insert Program Diskette!"
2890 print:print:print
2900 print tab(8) "Press ";wht$;"RETURN";ylw$;" to continue: "
2910 gosub 19000:rem return routine
2920 :
2930 :
2940 :
3000 rem **--return to inv.menu--**
3010 poke 19,0:rem restore input prompt
3020 print home$:rem clr/home
3030 cd = 5:rem 5 lines down
3040 gosub 9000:rem crsr down routine
3050 print tab(8)
3060 print rvs$;
3070 print "LOADING THE INVENTORY MENU"
3080 ^"homeinv.menu"
3090 :
3100 :
3110 :
9000 rem **--cursor down routine--**
9010 for i = 1 to cd
9020 print cd$;
9030 next i
9040 return
9050 :
9060 :
9070 :
15000 rem **--figure rec.# routine--**
15010 rhigh = int(rlow/256)
15020 rlow  = rlow - 256 * rhigh
```

```
15030 return
15040 :
15050 :
15060 :
19000 rem **-return key routine--**
19010 poke 198,0:rem clr kbrd buffer
19020 for i = 631 to 640
19030 poke i,0:rem no value
19040 next i
19050 x = peek(197):rem store key press
19060 if x = 1 then 19080:rem 1 = rtn
19070 goto 19050:rem if not 1 go back
19080 poke 198,1:rem allow for cursor
19090 poke 631,0:rem clr kbrd
19100 nu$ = "":rem clr string variable
19110 poke 19,32:rem disable input ?
19120 return

ready.
```

Program for HOMEINV.COPY

```
100 rem ***--copy file info.--***
110 :
120 :
130 rem **--initialization--**
140 home$ = chr$(147):rem clr/home
150 ::cd$ = chr$( 17):rem cursor down
160 ::cu$ = chr$(145):rem cursor up
170 ::cl$ = chr$(157):rem cursor left
180 ::cr$ = chr$( 29):rem cursor right
190 :blk$ = chr$(144):rem black
200 :ylw$ = chr$(158):rem yellow
210 :wht$ = chr$(  5):rem white
220 :rvs$ = chr$( 18):rem reverse video
230 :bnk$ = chr$( 10):rem blank line
240 :brn$ = chr$(149):rem brown
250 :bue$ = chr$( 31):rem blue
260 :
270 poke 53280,14:rem border = lt.blue
280 poke 53272,23:rem upper/lower case
290 poke 53281, 9:rem set bkgrd to brn.
300 :
310 :
320 rem **--variables list--**
330 rem  rlow = low  byte of rec.#
340 rem rhigh = high byte of rec.#
350 rem  file = file # in open cmnd
360 rem  dvic = device # in open cmnd
370 rem  cmnd = command # in open cmnd
380 rem   ptr = pointer for # of recd's
390 rem chnl$ = channel # in open cmnd
400 rem  rec$ = rec.# from rlow & rhigh
410 rem pztn$ = position within record
420 rem item$ = name of item
430 rem serl$ = serial # of item
440 rem  cst$ = cost of item
450 rem room$ = location of item
460 rem desc$ = description of item
470 rem    sp = # of spaces for input
480 :
490 :
500 rem *-pointer file-*
510 open 2,8,2,"inventory.ptr,seq,read"
520 input#2,ptr
530 close 2
540 :
550 dim item$(ptr),serl$(ptr),cst$(ptr),room$(ptr),desc$(ptr)
560 :
570 :
580 :
1000 rem **--file input routine--**
1010 :
1020 :
```

```
1030 print home$:cd = 5:gosub 9000
1040 print tab(8) rvs$; "READING FILE INFORMATION!"
1050 rem *-data file-*
1060 open 15,8,15:rem open command chnl
1070 open  5,8,5,"inventory.rec,l," + chr$(100)
1080 chnl$ = chr$(5):rem channel #
1090 :
1100 :
1110 for k = 1 to ptr
1120 rlow = k:rhigh = 0
1130 if rlow > 255 then 15000
1140 rec$ = chr$(rlow) + chr$(rhigh)
1150 print
1160 :
1170 :
1180 pztn$ = chr$( 1):rem position
1190 print#15,"p";chnl$;rec$;pztn$
1200 input#5,item$(k)
1210 :
1220 :
1230 pztn$ = chr$(25):rem position
1240 print#15,"p";chnl$;rec$;pztn$
1250 input#5,serl$(k)
1260 :
1270 :
1280 pztn$ = chr$(40):rem position
1290 print#15,"p";chnl$;rec$;pztn$
1300 input#5,cst$(k)
1310 :
1320 :
1330 pztn$ = chr$(50):rem position
1340 print#15,"p";chnl$;rec$;pztn$
1350 input#5,room$(k)
1360 :
1370 :
1380 pztn$ = chr$(70):rem position
1390 print#15,"p";chnl$;rec$;pztn$
1400 input#5,desc$(k)
1410 next k
1420 :
1430 :
1440 close 5:close 15
1450 print home$:cd = 5:gosub 9000
1460 print tab(8) "Insert diskette for copy!"
1470 print:print
1480 print tab(8) "Press ";wht$;"RETURN";ylw$;" to continue: "
1490 gosub 19000:rem return routine
1500 :
1510 :
1520 :
2000 rem **--file output routine--**
2010 :
2020 :
2030 print home$:cd = 5:gosub 9000
2040 print tab(8) rvs$; "WRITING FILE INFORMATION!"
2050 rem *-data file-*
```

```
2060 open 15,8,15:rem open command chnl
2070 open  3,8,3,"inventory.bak,l," + chr$(100)
2080 chnl$ = chr$(3):rem channel #
2090 :
2100 :
2110 for k = 1 to ptr
2120 rlow  = k:rem low byte of rec.#
2130 rhigh = 0:rem  high byte of rec.#
2140 if rlow > 255 then 15000
2150 rec$  = chr$(rlow) + chr$(rhigh)
2160 :
2170 :
2180 pztn$ = chr$( 1):rem position
2190 print#15,"p";chnl$;rec$;pztn$
2200 print#3,item$(k)
2210 :
2220 :
2230 pztn$ = chr$(25):rem position
2240 print#15,"p";chnl$;rec$;pztn$
2250 print#3,serl$(k)
2260 :
2270 :
2280 pztn$ = chr$(40):rem position
2290 print#15,"p";chnl$;rec$;pztn$
2300 print#3,cst$(k)
2310 :
2320 :
2330 pztn$ = chr$(50):rem position
2340 print#15,"p";chnl$;rec$;pztn$
2350 print#3,room$(k)
2360 :
2370 :
2380 pztn$ = chr$(70):rem position
2390 print#15,"p";chnl$;rec$;pztn$
2400 print#3,desc$(k)
2410 next k
2420 :
2430 :
2440 close 3:close 15
2450 print home$:cd = 5:gosub 9000
2460 print tab(8) "ALL FINISHED"
2470 print:print
2480 print tab(8) "Press ";wht$;"RETURN";ylw$;" to continue: "
2490 gosub 19000:rem return routine
2500 :
2510 :
2520 :
3000 rem **--return to inv.menu--**
3010 poke 19,0:rem restore input prompt
3020 print home$:rem clr/home
3030 cd = 5:rem 5 lines down
3040 gosub 9000:rem crsr down routine
3050 print tab(8)
3060 print rvs$;
3070 print "LOADING THE INVENTORY MENU"
3080 ^"homeinv.menu"
```

```
3090 :
3100 :
3110 :
9000 rem **--cursor down routine--**
9010 for i = 1 to cd
9020 print cd$;
9030 next i
9040 return
9050 :
9060 :
9070 :
15000 rem **--figure rec.# routine--**
15010 rhigh = int(rlow/256)
15020 rlow  = rlow - 256 * rhigh
15030 return
15040 :
15050 :
15060 :
19000 rem **-return key routine--**
19010 poke 198,0:rem clr kbrd buffer
19020 for i = 631 to 640
19030 poke i,0:rem no value
19040 next i
19050 x = peek(197):rem store key press
19060 if x = 1 then 19080:rem 1 = rtn
19070 goto 19050:rem if not 1 go back
19080 poke 198,1:rem allow for cursor
19090 poke 631,0:rem clr kbrd
19100 nu$ = "":rem clr string variable
19110 poke 19,32:rem disable input ?
19120 return

ready.
```

■ Program for MAGAZINE.MENU

```
100 rem ***--magazine.menu--***
110 :
120 :
130 rem **--initialization--**
140 home$ = chr$(147):rem clr/home
150 ::cd$ = chr$( 17):rem cursor down
160 ::cu$ = chr$(145):rem cursor up
170 ::cl$ = chr$(157):rem cursor left
180 ::cr$ = chr$( 29):rem cursor right
190 :blk$ = chr$(144):rem black
200 :ylw$ = chr$(158):rem yellow
210 :wht$ = chr$(  5):rem white
220 :rvs$ = chr$( 18):rem reverse video
230 :
240 poke 53280,14:rem border = lt.blue
250 poke 53272,23:rem upper/lower case
260 poke 53281, 9:rem set bkgrd to brn
270 :
280 :
500 rem **--menu--**
510 tb = 10:rem tab value-10 spaces rt.
520 print home$:rem clr/home
530 print wht$;
540 print tab(tb)
550 print rvs$;
560 print "MAGAZINE ARTICLES SYSTEM"
570 print
580 print ylw$
590 print tab(tb)
600 print "1. WRITE RECORD"
610 print:print tab(tb)
620 print "2. READ RECORD"
630 print:print tab(tb)
640 print "3. SEARCH RECORD"
650 print:print tab(tb)
660 print "4. CORRECT RECORD"
670 print:print tab(tb)
680 print "5. TRANSLATE RECORD"
690 print:print tab(tb)
700 print "6. COPY FILE"
710 print:print tab(tb)
720 print "7. LIST OF FILES"
730 print:print tab(tb)
740 print "8. END"
750 print:print tab(tb)
760 poke 19,32:rem disable input ?
770 input "Which Program Number? ";nu$
780 number = val(nu$)
790 :
800 if number = 1 then 1000
810 if number = 2 then 2000
820 if number = 3 then 3000
830 if number = 4 then 4000
```

```
840 if number = 5 then 5000
850 if number = 6 then 6000
860 if number = 7 then 7000
870 if number = 8 then 8000
880 :
890 rem *-incorrect choice message-*
900 print:print:print tab(tb)
910 print rvs$;"Incorrect Choice!"
920 print:print tab(tb)
930 print "Press ";wht$;"RETURN";ylw$;" to continue:";
940 gosub 19030:rem return key routine
950 goto 500:rem menu--check again
960 :
970 :
1000 rem **--write record program--**
1010 file$ = "MAGAZINE.WRITE"
1020 gosub 17000:rem new program routine
1030 ^"magazine.write":rem load & run
1040 :
1050 :
2000 rem **--read record program--**
2010 file$ = "MAGAZINE.READ"
2020 gosub 17000:rem new program routine
2030 ^"magazine.read":rem load & run
2040 :
2050 :
3000 rem **--search record program--**
3010 file$ = "MAGAZINE.SEARCH"
3020 gosub 17000:rem new program routine
3030 ^"magazine.search":rem load & run
3040 :
3050 :
4000 rem **--correct record program--**
4010 file$ = "MAGAZINE.CORRECT"
4020 gosub 17000:rem new program routine
4030 ^"magazine.correct":rem load & run
4040 :
4050 :
5000 rem **--trans. record program--**
5010 file$ = "MAGAZINE.TRANSLATE"
5020 gosub 17000:rem new program routine
5030 ^"magazine.trans":rem load & run
5040 :
5050 :
6000 rem **--copy file--**
6010 file$ = "MAGAZINE.COPY"
6020 gosub 17000:rem new program routine
6030 ^"magazine.copy":rem load & run
6040 :
6050 :
7000 rem **--list of files routine--**
7010 print home$:rem clr/home
7020 @"$"
7030 print cu$;chr$(13):rem 13 = rtn
7040 print "Are you ready to return to the menu?"
7050 print
```

```
7060 gosub 18000:rem y/n input routine
7070 if yes$ = "y" then 500:rem menu
7080 goto 7000:rem check again
7090 :
7100 :
8000 rem **--end routine--**
8010 poke 19,0:rem restore input prompt
8020 print home$:rem clr/home
8030 cd = 5:rem 5 lines down
8040 gosub 9000:rem crsr down routine
8050 print tab(tb - 5)
8060 print rvs$;
8070 print "That's all for this session!"
8080 print:print:print
8090 print tab(tb)
8100 print rvs$;
8110 print "See you next time."
8120 print ylw$
8130 cd = 10:rem 10 lines down
8140 gosub 9000:rem crsr down routine
8150 end
8160 :
8170 :
9000 rem **--cursor down routine--**
9010 for i = 1 to cd
9020 print cd$;
9030 next i
9040 return
9050 :
9060 :
17000 rem **--new program routine--**
17010 print home$:rem clr/home
17020 cd = 2:rem 2 lines down
17030 gosub 9000:rem crsr down routine
17040 print "You have selected the ";file$:print:print
      "program."
17050 print:print:print
17060 print "Is this the program you want?"
17070 print
17080 gosub 18000:rem y/n input routine
17090 if yes$ = "n" then 500:rem menu
17100 print home$:rem clr/home
17110 cd = 5:rem 5 lines down
17120 gosub 9000:rem crsr down routine
17130 print tab(tb - 5)
17140 print rvs$;
17150 print "Please wait!"
17160 print:print:print
17170 print tab(tb)
17180 print rvs$;
17190 print "I'm loading...."
17200 print:print:print
17210 print tab(tb + 8)
17220 print rvs$;
17230 print file$
17240 poke 19,0:rem restore input prompt
```

```
17250 return
17260 :
17270 :
18000 rem **--y/n input routine--**
18010 print "Type a ";wht$;"Y";ylw$;" or ";wht$;"N";ylw$;" :";
18020 poke 19,32:rem disable input ?
18030 input yes$
18040 print
18050 if yes$ = "y" or yes$ = "Y" then yes$ = "y":return
18060 if yes$ = "n" or yes$ = "N" then yes$ = "n":return
18070 print
18080 print rvs$;"Incorrect Choice!";ylw$
18090 print
18100 goto 18000:rem check again
18110 :
18120 :
19000 rem **--return key routine--**
19010 print
19020 print "Press ";wht$;"RETURN";ylw$;" to continue:";
19030 poke 198,0:rem clr kbrd buffer
19040 for i = 631 to 640
19050 poke i,0:rem no value
19060 next i
19070 x = peek(197):rem store key press
19080 if x = 1 then 19100
19090 goto 19070:if not 1 go back
19100 poke 198,1:rem allow 1 for cursor
19110 poke 631,0:rem clr kbrd
19120 nu$ = "":rem clr string variable
19130 print home$:rem clr/home
19140 return

ready.
```

■ Program for MAGAZINE.WRITE

```
100 rem ***--write magazines rec.--***
110 :
120 :
130 rem **--initialization--**
140 home$ = chr$(147):rem clr/home
150 ::cd$ = chr$( 17):rem cursor down
160 ::cu$ = chr$(145):rem cursor up
170 ::cl$ = chr$(157):rem cursor left
180 ::cr$ = chr$( 29):rem cursor right
190 :blk$ = chr$(144):rem black
200 :ylw$ = chr$(158):rem yellow
210 :wht$ = chr$(  5):rem white
220 :rvs$ = chr$( 18):rem reverse video
230 :bnk$ = chr$( 10):rem blank line
240 :brn$ = chr$(149):rem brown
250 :bue$ = chr$( 31):rem blue
260 :
270 poke 53280,14:rem border = lt.blue
280 poke 53272,23:rem upper/lower case
290 poke 53281, 9:rem set bkgrd to ylw.
300 :
310 :
320 rem **--variables list--**
330 rem  rlow = low  byte of rec.#
340 rem rhigh = high byte of rec.#
350 rem  file = file # in open cmnd
360 rem  dvic = device # in open cmnd
370 rem  cmnd = command # in open cmnd
380 rem   ptr = pointer for # of recd's
390 rem chnl$ = channel # in open cmnd
400 rem  rec$ = rec.# from rlow & rhigh
410 rem pztn$ = position within record
420 rem titl$ = name of article
430 rem auth$ = author of article
440 rem magz$ = name of magazine
445 rem  dte$ = date of art/# of mag.
450 rem page$ = page # of article
460 rem code$ = description of article
470 rem    sp = # of spaces for input
480 :
490 :
1000 rem **--keyboard input routine--**
1005 print ylw$
1010 tb = 8:rem tab value
1015 poke 19,32:rem disable input ?
1020 :
1025 :
1030 :
1100 rem **--name of article--**
1105 print home$:rem clr/home
1110 print tab(10) rvs$; "ADD TO FILE OF ARTICLES"
1115 cd = 7:gosub 9000:rem crsr down 7
1120 print "1. Type in article's name please: "
```

```
1125 print:print
1130 sp = 23
1135 gosub 5000:rem input subroutine
1140 input titl$
1145 if len(titl$) > 23 then titl$ = left$(titl$,23)
1150 s$ = titl$:gosub 12000:titl$ = s$
1155 :
1160 :
1200 rem **--author of article--**
1205 print home$:rem clr/home
1210 print tab(10) rvs$; "ADD TO FILE OF ARTICLES"
1215 cd = 7:gosub 9000:rem crsr down 7
1220 print "2. Type in article's author please: "
1225 print:print
1230 sp = 14
1235 gosub 5000:rem input subroutine
1240 input auth$
1245 if len(auth$) > 14 then auth$ = left$(auth$,14)
1250 s$ = auth$:gosub 12000:auth$ = s$
1255 :
1260 :
1300 rem **--name of magazine--**
1305 print home$:rem clr/home
1310 print tab(10) rvs$; "ADD TO FILE OF ARTICLES"
1315 cd = 7:gosub 9000:rem crsr down 7
1320 print "3. Type in magazine's name please: "
1325 print:print
1330 sp = 19
1335 gosub 5000:rem input subroutine
1340 input magz$
1345 if len(magz$) > 19 then magz$ = left$(magz$,19)
1350 s$ = magz$:gosub 12000:magz$ = s$
1355 :
1360 :
1370 rem **--date of magazine--**
1372 print home$:rem clr/home
1374 print tab(10) rvs$; "ADD TO FILE OF ARTICLES"
1376 cd = 7:gosub 9000:rem crsr down 7
1378 print "3. Type in magazine's date please: "
1380 print:print
1382 sp = 9
1384 gosub 5000:rem input subroutine
1386 input dte$
1388 if len(dte$) > 9 then dte$ = left$(dte$,9)
1390 s$ = dte$:gosub 12000:dte$ = s$
1392 :
1394 :
1400 rem **--page# of article--**
1405 print home$:rem clr/home
1410 print tab(10) rvs$; "ADD TO FILE OF ARTICLES"
1415 cd = 7:gosub 9000:rem crsr down 7
1420 print "4. Type in article's page # please: "
1425 print:print
1430 sp = 4
1435 gosub 5000:rem input subroutine
1440 input page$
```

```
1445 if len(page$) > 4 then page$ = left$(page$,4)
1450 s$ = page$:gosub 12000:page$ = s$
1455 :
1460 :
1500 rem **--categeory of article--**
1505 print home$:rem clr/home
1510 print tab(10) rvs$; "ADD TO FILE OF ARTICLES"
1515 cd = 7:gosub 9000:rem crsr down 7
1520 print "5. Type in article's category/code please: "
1525 print:print
1530 sp = 9
1535 gosub 5000:rem input subroutine
1540 input code$
1545 if len(code$) > 9 then code$ = left$(code$,9)
1550 s$ = code$:gosub 12000:code$ = s$
1555 :
1560 :
1600 rem **-display for correction--**
1610 :
1620 rem clear screen/crsr down 3
1630 print home$:cd = 3:gosub 9000
1640 :                                       165
1650 print:print tab(tb) "1. TITLE: ";titl$
1660 print:print tab(tb) "2. AUTHR: ";auth$
1670 print:print tab(tb) "3. MAGZN: ";magz
1675 print:print tab(tb) "4.  DATE: ";dte$
1680 print:print tab(tb) "5.  PAGE: ";page$
1690 print:print tab(tb) "6.  CODE: ";code$
1700 print:print tab(tb)
1710 print "Is this correct? "
1720 print:print tab(tb)
1730 gosub 18000:rem y/n input routine
1740 if yes$ = "y" then 2000
1750 print:print tab(tb)
1760 input "Which number is wrong? ";nb$
1770 nb = val(nb$)
1780 if nb = 1 then sp = 23
1790 if nb = 2 then sp = 14
1800 if nb = 3 then sp = 19
1805 if nb = 4 then sp =  9
1810 if nb = 5 then sp =  4
1820 if nb = 6 then sp =  9
1830 if nb < 1 or nb > 6 then gosub 14000:goto 1750
1840 print home$:cd = 8:gosub 9000
1850 print "Type in correct information: "
1860 print
1870 gosub 5000:rem input routine
1880 input cinfo$
1890 s$ = cinfo$:gosub 12000:cinfo$ = s$
1900 if nb = 1 then titl$ = left$(cinfo$,23):goto 1600:rem
     ask again
1910 if nb = 2 then auth$ = left$(cinfo$,14):goto 1600:rem
     ask again
1920 if nb = 3 then magz$ = left$(cinfo$,19):goto 1600:rem
     ask again
```

```
1925 if nb = 4 then dte$  = left$(cinfo$,9):goto 1600:rem
     ask again
1930 if nb = 5 then page$ = left$(cinfo$,4):goto 1600:rem
     ask again
1940 if nb = 6 then code$ = left$(cinfo$,9):goto 1600:rem
     ask again
1950 :
1960 :
2000 rem **--file output routine--**
2010 :
2020 rem *-pointer file-*
2030 open 2,8,2,"magazines.ptr,seq,read"
2040 input#2,ptr
2050 close 2
2060 if status = 16 then 3000
2070 ptr = ptr + 1
2080 :
2090 rem *-data file-*
2100 open 15,8,15:rem open command chnl
2110 open  3,8,3,"magazines.rec,l," + chr$(85)
2120 rem l in line 2110 is letter not #
2130 chnl$ = chr$(3):rem channel #
2140 rlow  = ptr:rem low byte of rec.#
2150 rhigh = 0:rem  high byte of rec.#
2160 if rlow > 255 then gosub 15000
2170 rec$  = chr$(rlow) + chr$(rhigh)
2180 :
2190 pztn$ = chr$( 1):rem position
2200 print#15,"p";chnl$;rec$;pztn$
2210 print#3,titl$
2220 :
2230 pztn$ = chr$(25):rem position
2240 print#15,"p";chnl$;rec$;pztn$
2250 print#3,auth$
2260 :
2270 pztn$ = chr$(40):rem position
2280 print#15,"p";chnl$;rec$;pztn$
2290 print#3,magz$
2300 :
2302 pztn$ = chr$(60):rem position
2304 print#15,"p";chnl$;rec$;pztn$
2306 print#3,dte$
2308 :
2310 pztn$ = chr$(70):rem position
2320 print#15,"p";chnl$;rec$;pztn$
2330 print#3,page$
2340 :
2350 pztn$ = chr$(75):rem position
2360 print#15,"p";chnl$;rec$;pztn$
2370 print#3,code$
2380 close 3:close 15
2390 :
2400 :
2410 rem *-update ptr file-*
2420 open 2,8,2,"@0:magazines.ptr,seq,write"
2430 print#2,ptr
```

```
2440 close 2
2450 :
2460 :
2470 goto 4000:rem repeat routine
2480 :
2490 :
3000 rem **--first time use only--**
3010 close 2
3020 open 2,8,2,"magazines.ptr,seq,write"
3030 print#2,"0"
3040 close 2
3050 :
3060 goto 2000:rem begin file routine
3070 :
3080 :
4000 rem **--repeat routine--**
4010 print home$:rem clr/home
4020 cd = 3:rem 3 lines down
4030 gosub 9000:rem crsr down routine
4040 print "Do you want to add more articles?"
4050 print
4060 gosub 18000:rem y/n input routine
4070 if yes$ = "y" then 1000
4080 if yes$ = "n" then 6000
4090 :
4100 :
5000 rem **--input subroutine--**
5010 for i = 1 to sp
5020 print chr$(175);:rem underline
5030 next i
5040 print:print:print
5050 print "Do not go beyond the end of the line!"
5060 rem crsr up 5
5070 print cu$;cu$;cu$;cu$;cu$
5080 return
5090 :
5100 :
6000 rem **--return to inv.menu--**
6010 poke 19,0:rem restore input prompt
6020 print home$:rem clr/home
6030 cd = 5:rem 5 lines down
6040 gosub 9000:rem crsr down routine
6050 print tab(tb)
6060 print rvs$;
6070 print "LOADING THE MAGAZINES MENU"
6080 ^"magazine.menu"
6090 :
6100 :
9000 rem **--cursor down routine--**
9010 for i = 1 to cd
9020 print cd$;
9030 next i
9040 return
9050 :
9060 :
12000 rem **--strip excess underline character--**
12010 s2$ = s$
```

```
12020 i = 1
12030 if mid$(s2$,i,1) = chr$(175) then 12070
12040 i = i + 1
12050 if i > sp then 12070
12060 goto 12030
12070 s$ = left$(s2$,i - 1)
12080 return
12090 :
12100 :
12110 :
14000 rem *-incorrect choice message-*
14010 print:print tab(tb)
14020 print rvs$;"Incorrect Choice!"
14030 print:print tab(tb)
14040 print "Press ";wht$;"RETURN";ylw$;" to continue:";
14050 gosub 19000:rem return key routine
14060 return
14070 :
14080 :
14090 :
15000 rem **--figure rec.# routine--**
15010 rhigh = int(rlow/256)
15020 rlow  = rlow - 256 * rhigh
15030 return
15040 :
15050 :
15060 :
18000 rem **--y/n input routine--**
18010 print "Type a ";wht$;"Y";ylw$;" or ";wht$;"N";ylw$;" :";
18020 poke 19,32:rem disable input ?
18030 input yes$
18040 print
18050 if yes$ = "y" or yes$ = "Y" then yes$ = "y":return
18060 if yes$ = "n" or yes$ = "N" then yes$ = "n":return
18070 print
18080 print rvs$;"Incorrect Choice!";ylw$
18090 print
18100 goto 18000:rem begin again
18110 :
18120 :
18130 :
19000 rem **-return key routine--**
19010 poke 198,0:rem clr kbrd buffer
19020 for i = 631 to 640
19030 poke i,0:rem no value
19040 next i
19050 x = peek(197):rem store key press
19060 if x = 1 then 19080:rem 1 = rtn
19070 goto 19050:rem if not 1 go back
19080 poke 198,1:rem allow for cursor
19090 poke 631,0:rem clr kbrd
19100 nu$ = "":rem clr string variable
19110 poke 19,32:rem disable input ?
19120 return

ready.
```

12 planning a file system

Rather than present another chapter explaining the programming of another system, this chapter will present the procedures involved in conceiving and creating a file system. I will use a Stock Market System as the example. Although shorter than previous chapters, this chapter is no less important.

There are five main steps involved in conceiving and creating a specific data-base system.

1. Know your subject.
2. Plan carefully and organize your thoughts.
3. Make preliminary decisions on the number of main variables, the length of each record, and, if necessary, the lengths of fields within each record.
4. Roughly plan the sequence of the data-base operation and the code for each part of that operation.
5. Begin on the code for the first part of the system.

Some programmers will argue with either the sequence of the steps or the steps themselves. Some may say that such an outline is too limited. All may be right. I am merely trying to give a limited amount of guidance in the development of a specific file system. Some systems analysts are carried away with the precode procedures. But one thing is clear. A certain amount of planning before coding is absolutely necessary!

STOCK MARKET SYSTEM

Results of the previous day's trading activity are printed in most daily newspapers. Normally, these results include such things as: 52-week high and low stock price; stock symbol; latest dividend; a yield figure; P/E ratio; sales; daily high, low, and closing price; and, possibly, the amount of price change from the previous day. This information is available for active issues on the New York and American Stock Exchanges. Less information is given for Over the Counter or NASDAQ issues, option, commodity, and bond trading. There are figures for the various averages: NYSE Index, Dow, Standard & Poors, American Index, NASDAQ Composite and/or Industrials, to name just a few. There are other key items to watch: gold, interest rates, value of the dollar overseas, money supply, President's daily intake of vitamins, and so on. As you might guess, the list is limitless.

Although an investment record may contain more variables than maintaining information on your own library, the principle is the same. You must thoroughly know your subject in order to be able to make decisions concerning the information to be saved. The first step in planning your data base should be deciding which information is of value (*i.e.*, what information to save).

In our Stock Market System, I am going to severely limit the amount of information saved. Individuals may wish to keep additional information they believe to be important. For each issue, we will save the daily high, low, and closing price, plus the day's volume, P/E ratio, and date. In addition, we will save any price that makes either a new high or new low for that issue.

Steps two and three somewhat blend together at this point. In the planning, decisions are made. Most stock prices are under $1000 per share, so I will allow a maximum of three places before the decimal point. Prices are usually given in terms of eighths of a dollar (*i.e.*, 3/8 or 1/2). With a little extra planning and coding, significant disk space can be saved on each issue. If the extreme right figure is always viewed as the decimal portion of the stock price, then four digits will represent all stock prices up to $999 and 7/8 per share. (This price would be saved on the disk as 9997.) Saving the high, low, and close each day already means 15 bytes per issue per day (4 bytes for the number plus one byte for the delimiter for a total of 5 bytes for each high, low, and closing price).

Volume can be handled in somewhat the same way. Most papers indicate the sales volume only in hundreds of shares sold per day. A volume of 2000 shares would be displayed as 20. Since virtually every stock trades under 9,999,900 shares in one day, we can limit the number of places to six (99999 plus one for the carriage return delimiter). All P/E ratios are under 999 for any issue. This necessitates another four bytes for each issue. Finally, we will save the trading date with each record (ten more bytes). That brings the total number of bytes for each issue to 35: 4 for the P/E ratio, 6 for the volume, 5 for the high, 5 for the low, 5 for the close, and 10 for the date. We will save any new high or new low price in a separate sequential file.

Next, we must decide on the number of issues to follow on a daily basis. This is an individual choice and often depends on the time available for closely following the market. A reasonable figure to start out with is ten issues. If a number greater than ten is used, the string array variable chosen for the stock names will need to be dimensioned to the proper number. With the number of stocks determined, we can calculate the maximum number of bytes used for each day's transactions. Ten stocks, each requiring 35 bytes, mean a length of 350 bytes per trading day. Based on approximately 170,000 available bytes on a single-sided diskette, we can store just under 500 days' trading information. That is about a year and a half of stock market activity for ten issues on a single data diskette.

Step four is a rough plan of the sequence of programs and the code within each program. Following the procedures we have used in our previous examples, we need programs that will create the necessary files and daily add to those files. Second, we need programs to display, in a variety of ways, the information either stored in the file or derived from the information stored. Finally, we must have correction programs.

I am going to introduce another method of creating random files. I have included a program that will only be used once for each set of stocks followed. The "stock.menu" program indicates that, when the user chooses the first option, the "stock.add" program is run. The very first time (and only the first time) the "stock.menu" program is run and the number one selection is made, the computer will load a program that is called "stock.add". In reality, this is a program used one time to create the "stock.ptr" (stock pointer) file and the "stock.high/low" file. It also provides the user with some information on the general operation of the Stock Market System. Once these files have been created and the user has indicated that the information has been absorbed, this program renames itself on the diskette so that it now has the program file name "stock.oldadd". Then, it renames a second program from its original "stock.realadd" file name to the necessary "stock.add" file name. Finally, the user is given the choice to either return to the main Stock Menu or to add the first day's trading activity. The "stock.menu" program always runs a program called "stock.add". The first time it runs one program (originally called "stock.add", renamed to "stock.oldadd"), but every time after that, it runs another program (originally called "stock.realadd", renamed to "stock.add"). The different programs share the same file name, "stock.add", but at different times. In summary, the first program is designed to create the necessary files and then rename both itself and the real "stock.add" program. The real "stock.add" (originally "stock.realadd") program is designed to daily update each individual stock's file. The explanation may sound complicated, but the operation itself is surprisingly simple.

Within the file addition program, the sequence of operation is fairly standard. We need to read in: (1) the value of the file pointer (add one to that value), (2) the symbols for the various stocks, and (3) their current high and low price. Next, the previous day's figures must be entered for each issue and checked for accuracy. The previous day's figures must also be compared to the current high and low, and if they exceed those figures, they need to replace the appropriate figure. Finally, all the new information must be written to the disk.

The editing programs should follow a similar pattern but with a few exceptions. The pointer should be determined by an input from the keyboard. The high, low, close, volume, and P/E should come from the disk instead of the keyboard, with corrections coming from the keyboard.

The display programs are more difficult to structure in any absolute manner. The only certain structure is that information comes from the disk and is displayed either on the screen or through the printer. In between, a variety of steps can take place. The information can be used to calculate certain values that may be used to evaluate a particular situation and project the price movement of the stock. Or the disk information may simply be formatted for display on either the screen or the printer. The information may be used to graph the price movement of the stock or compare its movement against that of another stock or average. The display portion of the Stock Market System is the core of the system and is usually not a fixed set of programs. User needs change and require that the display programs change. In the system presented, the display programs will be limited in their scope. We will display individual stock histories, along with some calculated figures, averages, price and volume changes, and the like. We will not get into graphic representation of stock performance in this book. (A future book will deal with graphic representation of data base information, because it is such a broad topic that it requires a book of its own.)

The final step is coding the programs according to the plans established. At the end of this chapter, you will find minimum programs designed according to the structure outlined in this chapter. You are encouraged to take these minimum programs and expand upon them to fit your own interest, or alter them to cover a topic of your own design. It is only by practical experience that you will learn to create Commodore-64 BASIC files.

QUESTIONS

1. *True or False:* Good programmers can just sit down and start writing code.
2. What is the first step in planning a data base system?
3. Give the three main parts to any data base system.
4. Which part must be flexible as user needs change?

ANSWERS

1. False
2. Deciding which information is of value
3. Creation and addition, display, correction
4. Display

Program for STOCK.MENU

```
100 rem ***--stock.menu--***
110 :
120 :
130 rem **--initialization--**
140 home$ = chr$(147):rem clr/home
150 ::cd$ = chr$( 17):rem cursor down
160 ::cu$ = chr$(145):rem cursor up
170 ::cl$ = chr$(157):rem cursor left
180 ::cr$ = chr$( 29):rem cursor right
190 :blk$ = chr$(144):rem black
200 :ylw$ = chr$(158):rem yellow
210 :wht$ = chr$(  5):rem white
220 :rvs$ = chr$( 18):rem reverse video
230 :
240 poke 53280,14:rem border = lt.blue
250 poke 53272,23:rem upper/lower case
260 poke 53281, 9:rem set bkgrd to brn
270 :
280 :
500 rem **--menu--**
510 tb = 10:rem tab value-10 spaces rt.
520 print home$:rem clr/home
530 print wht$;
540 print tab(tb)
550 print rvs$;
560 print "STOCK SYSTEM MENU"
570 print
580 print ylw$
590 print tab(tb)
600 print "1. ADD STOCK INFO."
610 print:print tab(tb)
620 print "2. DISPLAY STOCK INFO."
630 print:print tab(tb)
640 print "3. DISPLAY HI/LOW VALUES"
650 print:print tab(tb)
660 print "4. CORRECT HI/LOW VALUES"
670 print:print tab(tb)
680 print "5. CORRECT STOCK DATA"
690 print:print tab(tb)
700 print "6. DIF TRANSLATION"
710 print:print tab(tb)
720 print "7. LIST OF FILES"
730 print:print tab(tb)
740 print "8. END"
750 print:print tab(tb)
760 poke 19,32:rem disable input ?
770 input "Which Program Number? ";nu$
780 number = val(nu$)
790 :
800 if number = 1 then 1000
810 if number = 2 then 2000
820 if number = 3 then 3000
830 if number = 4 then 4000
```

```
840 if number = 5 then 5000
850 if number = 6 then 6000
860 if number = 7 then 7000
870 if number = 8 then 8000
880 :
890 rem *-incorrect choice message-*
900 print:print:print tab(tb)
910 print rvs$;"Incorrect Choice!"
920 print:print tab(tb)
930 print "Press ";wht$;"RETURN";ylw$;" to continue:";
940 gosub 19030:rem return key routine
950 goto 500:rem menu--check again
960 :
970 :
1000 rem **--stock add program--**
1010 file$ = "STOCK.ADD"
1020 gosub 17000:rem new program routine
1030 ^"stock.add":rem load & run
1040 :
1050 :
2000 rem **--stock display program--**
2010 file$ = "STOCK.DISPLAY"
2020 gosub 17000:rem new program routine
2030 ^"stock.display":rem load & run
2040 :
2050 :
3000 rem **--display hi/low program--**
3010 file$ = "STOCK.DSP HI/LOW"
3020 gosub 17000:rem new program routine
3030 ^"stock.dsp hi/low":rem load & run
3040 :
3050 :
4000 rem **--correct hi/low program--**
4010 file$ = "STOCK.CRT HI/LOW"
4020 gosub 17000:rem new program routine
4030 ^"stock.crt hi/low":rem load & run
4040 :
4050 :
5000 rem **--correct stock program--**
5010 file$ = "STOCK.CORRECT"
5020 gosub 17000:rem new program routine
5030 ^"stock.correct":rem load & run
5040 :
5050 :
6000 rem **--translate stock info--**
6010 file$ = "STOCK.TRANSLATE"
6020 gosub 17000:rem new program routine
6030 ^"stock.translate":rem load & run
6040 :
6050 :
7000 rem **--list of files routine--**
7010 print home$:rem clr/home
7020 @"$"
7030 print cu$;chr$(13):rem 13 = rtn
7040 print "Are you ready to return to the menu?"
7050 print
```

```
7060 gosub 18000:rem y/n input routine
7070 if yes$ = "y" then 500:rem menu
7080 goto 7000:rem check again
7090 :
7100 :
8000 rem **--end routine--**
8010 poke 19,0:rem restore input prompt
8020 print home$:rem clr/home
8030 cd = 5:rem 5 lines down
8040 gosub 9000:rem crsr down routine
8050 print tab(tb - 5)
8060 print rvs$;
8070 print "That's all for this session!"
8080 print:print:print
8090 print tab(tb)
8100 print rvs$;
8110 print "See you next time."
8120 print ylw$
8130 cd = 10:rem 10 lines down
8140 gosub 9000:rem crsr down routine
8150 end
8160 :
8170 :
9000 rem **--cursor down routine--**
9010 for i = 1 to cd
9020 print cd$;
9030 next i
9040 return
9050 :
9060 :
17000 rem **--new program routine--**
17010 print home$:rem clr/home
17020 cd = 2:rem 2 lines down
17030 gosub 9000:rem crsr down routine
17040 print "You have selected the ";file$:print:print
      "program."
17050 print:print:print
17060 print "Is this the program you want?"
17070 print
17080 gosub 18000:rem y/n input routine
17090 if yes$ = "n" then 500:rem menu
17100 print home$:rem clr/home
17110 cd = 5:rem 5 lines down
17120 gosub 9000:rem crsr down routine
17130 print tab(tb - 5)
17140 print rvs$;
17150 print "Please wait!"
17160 print:print:print
17170 print tab(tb)
17180 print rvs$;
17190 print "I'm loading...."
17200 print:print:print
17210 print tab(tb + 8)
17220 print rvs$;
17230 print file$
17240 poke 19,0:rem restore input prompt
```

```
17250 return
17260 :
17270 :
18000 rem **--y/n input routine--**
18010 print "Type a ";wht$;"Y";ylw$;" or ";wht$;"N";ylw$;" :";
18020 poke 19,32:rem disable input ?
18030 input yes$
18040 print
18050 if yes$ = "y" or yes$ = "Y" then yes$ = "y":return
18060 if yes$ = "n" or yes$ = "N" then yes$ = "n":return
18070 print
18080 print rvs$;"Incorrect Choice!";ylw$
18090 print
18100 goto 18000:rem check again
18110 :
18120 :
19000 rem **--return key routine--**
19010 print
19020 print "Press ";wht$;"RETURN";ylw$;" to continue:";
19030 poke 198,0:rem clr kbrd buffer
19040 for i = 631 to 640
19050 poke i,0:rem no value
19060 next i
19070 x = peek(197):rem store key press
19080 if x = 1 then 19100
19090 goto 19070:rem if not 1 go back
19100 poke 198,1:rem allow 1 for cursor
19110 poke 631,0:rem clr kbrd
19120 nu$ = "":rem clr string variable
19130 print home$:rem clr/home
19140 return

ready.
```

■ Program for STOCK.ADD

```
100 rem ***--initalize stock files--***
110 :
120 :
130 rem **--initialization--**
140 home$ = chr$(147):rem clr/home
150 ::cd$ = chr$( 17):rem cursor down
160 ::cu$ = chr$(145):rem cursor up
170 ::cl$ = chr$(157):rem cursor left
180 ::cr$ = chr$( 29):rem cursor right
190 :blk$ = chr$(144):rem black
200 :ylw$ = chr$(158):rem yellow
210 :wht$ = chr$(  5):rem white
220 :rvs$ = chr$( 18):rem reverse video
230 :
240 poke 53280,14:rem border = lt.blue
250 poke 53272,23:rem upper/lower case
260 poke 53281, 9:rem set bkgrd to brn
270 :
280 :
1000 rem **--information--**
1010 print home$:rem clr/home
1020 print "Before you can enter any daily stock"
1030 print
1040 print "information, you must decide which"
1050 print
1060 print "stocks you will be following. This"
1070 print
1080 print "program will ask you to enter the name"
1090 print
1100 print "or symbol of ten stocks and their re-"
1110 print
1120 print "spective values for the high and low"
1130 print
1140 print "prices within the last 12 months. If"
1150 print
1160 print "the high or low values are not known,"
1170 print
1180 print "simply enter a '0'. The high and low"
1190 print
1200 print "values will automatically be updated"
1210 print
1220 :
1230 gosub 19000:rem return key routine
1240 :
1250 print "when daily prices exceed or are less"
1260 print
1270 print "than the values in the HI/LOW file."
1280 print
1290 print "If you need to change any information"
1300 print
1310 print "in the HI/LOW file, choose #4 CORRECT"
1320 print
1330 print "HI/LOW from the main program menu. Once"
```

```
1340 print
1350 print "you have finished entering the infor-"
1360 print
1370 print "mation in this program, you will be"
1380 print
1390 print "given a choice to enter the first"
1400 print
1410 print "day's prices or to return to the main"
1420 print
1430 print "program menu. After this first time,the"
1440 print
1450 print "ADD STOCK INFO. (#1) will not show all"
1460 print
1470 :
1480 gosub 19000:rem return key routine
1490 :
1500 print "this text or require you to update the"
1510 print
1520 print "HI/LOW file. If you want to re-read"
1530 print
1540 print "this information, type a 'Y', if not,"
1550 print
1560 print "type an 'N'."
1570 print
1580 gosub 18000:rem y/n input routine
1590 if yes$ = "y" then 1000
1600 gosub 19000:rem return key routine
1610 :
1620 :
2000 rem **--keyboard input routine--**
2010 for k = 1 to 10
2020 print home$:rem clr/home
2030 print "Type in the name of the stock or its"
2040 print
2050 print "symbol. You will be given a chance to"
2060 print
2070 print "make corrections later."
2080 print
2090 print "Stock #";k;": ";:input stk$(k)
2100 print
2110 gosub 16000:rem remainder routine
2120 print "If you are not sure of the ";wht$;"hi";ylw$;"
     value for"
2130 print
2140 print "the previous 12 months, enter a '0'."
2150 print
2160 print "12 month ";wht$;"hi";ylw$;" value for ";stk$(k);":
     ";:input hi$(k)
2170 gosub 16000:rem remainder routine
2180 print "If you are not sure of the ";wht$;"low";ylw$;"
     value for"
2190 print "the previous 12 months, enter a '0'."
2200 print
2210 print "12 month ";wht$;"low";ylw$;" value for ";stk$(k);":
     ";:input low$(k)
```

```
2220 :
2230 :
3000 rem **--correction routine--**
3010 rem clr/home crsr down 5
3020 print home$:cd = 5:gosub 9000
3030 print
3040 print "1. ";stk$(k)
3050 print
3060 m = val(hi$(k)):gosub 17000:rem convert to fraction
3070 print "2. Hi value  = ";m;" ";f$
3080 print
3090 m = val(low$(k)):gosub 17000:rem convert to fraction
3100 print "3. Low value = ";m;" ";f$
3110 print
3120 print "Is this correct? ";
3130 gosub 18000:rem y/n input routine
3140 print
3150 if yes$ = "n" then 3170
3160 goto 3250:rem next i
3170 input "Which number is wrong? ";nb
3180 print
3190 if nb = 1 then input "Correct stock name or symbol: ";
     stk$(k)
3200 if nb = 2 then input "Correct hi value: ";hi$(k)
3210 if nb = 3 then input "Correct low value ";low$(k)
3220 if nb < 1 or nb > 3 then print "INCORRECT CHOICE!"
3230 goto 3000:rem ask again
3240 print
3250 next k
3260 :
3270 :
4000 rem **--file output routine--**
4010 :
4020 rem *-stock pointer file-*
4030 open 2,8,2,"0:stock.pointer,seq,write"
4040 print#2,"0"
4050 close 2
4060 :
4070 rem *-hi/low data file-*
4080 open 3,8,3,"0:hi/low data,seq,write"
4090 for k = 1 to 10
4100 print#3,stk$(k)
4110 print#3,hi$(k)
4120 print#3,low$(k)
4130 next k
4140 close 3
4150 :
4160 :
5000 rem **--rename files routine--**
5010 @"r:stock.oldadd=stock.add"
5020 @"r:stock.add=stock.real"
5030 rem clr/home crsr down 5
5040 print home$:cd = 5:gosub 9000
5050 print "Do you want to add the first day's"
5060 print
```

```
5070 print "stock prices? ";
5080 gosub 18000:rem y/n input routine
5090 print
5100 if yes$ = "y" then ^"stock.add":rem load & run stock.add
5110 ^"stock.menu":rem load & run menu
5120 :
5130 :
9000 rem **--cursor down routine--**
9010 for i = 1 to cd
9020 print cd$;
9030 next i
9040 return
9050 :
9060 :
16000 rem **--reminder routine--**
16010 print home$:rem clr/home
16020 print tab(8)
16030 print "*****---REMEMBER---*****"
16040 print
16050 print "You must add the fraction as the last"
16060 print "digit! 21 5/8 should be entered as: 215"
16070 print
16080 print "If the number has no fraction, please"
16090 print "enter a '0' after the number! 21 even"
16100 print "should be entered as: 210"
16110 print
16120 print tab(11) "1/8 --------- = 1"
16130 print tab(11) "1/4 --------- = 2"
16140 print tab(11) "3/8 --------- = 3"
16150 print tab(11) "1/2 --------- = 4"
16160 print tab(11) "5/8 --------- = 5"
16170 print tab(11) "3/4 --------- = 6"
16180 print tab(11) "7/8 --------- = 7"
16190 print tab(11) "EVEN -------- = 0"
16200 print
16210 return
16220 :
16230 :
17000 rem **--convert to fraction--**
17010 f = m - int(m/10) * 10
17020 m = int(m/10)
17030 if f = 0 then f$ = ""
17040 if f = 1 then f$ = "1/8"
17050 if f = 2 then f$ = "1/4"
17060 if f = 3 then f$ = "3/8"
17070 if f = 4 then f$ = "1/2"
17080 if f = 5 then f$ = "5/8"
17090 if f = 6 then f$ = "3/4"
17100 if f = 7 then f$ = "7/8"
17110 return
17120 :
17130 :
18000 rem **--y/n input routine--**
18010 print "Type a ";wht$;"Y";ylw$;" or ";wht$;"N";ylw$;" :";
18020 poke 19,32:rem disable input ?
18030 input yes$
```

```
18040 print
18050 if yes$ = "y" or yes$ = "Y" then yes$ = "y":return
18060 if yes$ = "n" or yes$ = "N" then yes$ = "n":return
18070 print
18080 print rvs$;"Incorrect Choice!";ylw$
18090 print
18100 goto 18000:rem check again
18110 :
18120 :
19000 rem **--return key routine--**
19010 print
19020 print "Press ";wht$;"RETURN";ylw$;" to continue:";
19030 poke 198,0:rem clr kbrd buffer
19040 for i = 631 to 640
19050 poke i,0:rem no value
19060 next i
19070 x = peek(197):rem store key press
19080 if x = 1 then 19100
19090 goto 19070:rem if not 1 go back
19100 poke 198,1:rem allow 1 for cursor
19110 poke 631,0:rem clr kbrd
19120 nu$ = "":rem clr string variable
19130 print home$:rem clr/home
19140 return
```

■ Program for STOCK.REAL

```
100 rem ***--add stock information--***
110 :
120 :
130 rem **--initialization--**
140 home$ = chr$(147):rem clr/home
150 ::cd$ = chr$( 17):rem cursor down
160 ::cu$ = chr$(145):rem cursor up
170 ::cl$ = chr$(157):rem cursor left
180 ::cr$ = chr$( 29):rem cursor right
190 :blk$ = chr$(144):rem black
200 :ylw$ = chr$(158):rem yellow
210 :wht$ = chr$(  5):rem white
220 :rvs$ = chr$( 18):rem reverse video
230 :
240 poke 53280,14:rem border = lt.blue
250 poke 53272,23:rem upper/lower case
260 poke 53281, 9:rem set bkgrd to brn
270 :
280 :
290 rem **--variables list--**
300 rem stk$ = stock symbol
310 rem hi$  = current hi price
320 rem low$ = current low price
330 rem dte$ = date
340 rem nh$  = new high
350 rem hl$  = new low
360 rem f$   = fraction
370 rem pe   = p/e ratio
380 rem vol  = sales volume
390 rem h    = daily high price
400 rem low  = daily low price
410 rem c    = daily closing price
420 rem cr   = corrected figure
430 :
440 :
450 rem **--file input routine--**
460 :
470 rem *-pointer file-*
480 open 2,8,2,"stock.pointer,seq,read"
490 input#2,ptr
500 close 2
510 ptr = ptr + 1
520 :
530 rem *-high/low file-*
540 open 3,8,3,"hi/low data,seq,read"
550 for k = 1 to 10
560 input#3,stk$(k)
570 input#3,hi$(k)
580 input#3,low$(k)
590 next k
600 close 3
610 :
620 :
```

```
630 k = 1
640 print ylw$
650 poke 19,32:rem disable input ?
660 :
670 :
1000 rem **--keyboard input routine--**
1010 :
1020 rem *-date information-*
1030 rem clr/home crsr down 5
1040 print home$:cd = 5:gosub 9000
1050 input "Type in today's date: ";dte$
1060 print:print
1070 print "Today's date is ";dte$
1080 print:print
1090 print "Is this correct? ";
1100 gosub 18000:rem y/n input routine
1110 if yes$ = "y" then 1160
1120 print:input "Type in the correct date: ";dte$
1130 goto 1060
1140 :
1150 rem *-stock information-*
1160 print home$:rem clr/home
1170 poke 19,32:rem disable input ?
1180 print tab(5) wht$;stk$(k)
1190 print:print:print tab(5) ylw$;
1200 print stk$(k);"'s ";wht$;"P/E RATIO";ylw$;" for ";dte$;":
     ";:input pe
1210 print:print:print tab(5)
1220 print stk$(k);"'s ";wht$;"VOLUME";ylw$;" for ";dte$;": ";:
     input vol
1230 gosub 16000:rem reminder routine
1240 print stk$(k);"'s ";wht$;"HIGH";ylw$;" for ";dte$;": ";:
     input h
1250 gosub 16000:rem reminder routine
1260 print stk$(k);"'s ";wht$;"LOW";ylw$;" for ";dte$;": ";:
     input low
1270 gosub 16000:rem reminder routine
1280 print stk$(k);"'s ";wht$;"CLOSE";ylw$;" for ";dte$;": ";:
     input c
1290 :
1300 :
2000 rem **--correction routine--**
2010 rem clr/home crsr down 5
2020 print home$:cd = 5:gosub 9000
2030 print
2040 print stk$(k);"'s data for ";dte$
2050 print:print
2060 print "1. P/E ratio ---- ";pe
2070 print "2. Volume ------- ";vol
2080 m = h:gosub 17000:rem convert to fraction
2090 print "3. High --------- ";m;" ";f$
2100 m = low:gosub 17000:rem convert to fraction
2110 print "4. Low ---------- ";m;" ";f$
2120 m = c:gosub 17000:rem convert to fraction
```

```
2130 print "5. Close -------- ";m;" ";f$
2140 print
2150 print "Is this correct? ";
2160 gosub 18000:rem y/n input routine
2170 print
2180 if yes$ = "n" then 2220
2190 :
2200 goto 3000:rem exchange routine
2210 :
2220 input "Which number is wrong? ";nb
2230 if nb < 1 or nb > 5 then print:print "INCORRECT CHOICE!":
     goto 2140
2240 print
2250 input "The correct figure = ";cr
2260 if nb = 1 then pe  = cr
2270 if nb = 2 then vol = cr
2280 if nb = 3 then h   = cr
2290 if nb = 4 then low = cr
2300 if nb = 5 then c   = cr
2310 goto 2000:rem ask again
2320 print
2330 :
2340 :
3000 rem **--exchange hi/low--**
3010 if h > val(hi$(k)) then hi$(k) = str$(h):nh$ = "*"
3020 if low < val(low$(k)) then low$(k) = str$(low):nl$ = "*"
3030 if val(low$(k)) = 0 then low$(k) = str$(low)
3040 :
3050 :
4000 rem **--data file update--**
4010 rem clr/home crsr down 5
4020 print home$:cd = 5:gosub 9000
4030 print tab(11) rvs$;"ONE MOMENT PLEASE!"
4040 print:print:print:print
4050 print tab(10) "Updating ";wht$;stk$(k);"'s";ylw$;" file."
4060 :
4070 cvt$ = stk$(k)
4080 gosub 14000:rem convert to l.c.
4090 stk$ = cvt$
4100 :
4110 open 15,8,15:rem open command chnl
4120 open  3,8,3,stk$ + ".data,l," + chr$(35)
4130 rem l in line 4120 is letter not #
4140 rem 35 in line 4120 is rec.length--not # of records
4150 chnl$ = chr$(3):rem channel #
4160 rlow  = ptr:rem low byte of rec.#
4170 rhigh = 0:rem  high byte of rec.#
4180 if rlow > 255 then 15000:rem rec.# routine
4190 rec$ = chr$(rlow) + chr$(rhigh)
4200 :
4210 pztn$ = chr$( 1):rem position
4220 print#15,"p";chnl$;rec$;pztn$
4230 print#3,dte$
4240 :
4250 ss$=str$(pe):gosub 20000:pe$=ss$
4260 pztn$ = chr$ (11):rem position
```

```
4270 print#15,"p";chnl$;rec$;pztn$
4280 print#3,pe$
4290 :
4300 ss$=str$(vol):gosub 20000:vol$=ss$
4310 pztn$ = chr$ (15):rem position
4320 print#15,"p";chnl$;rec$;pztn$
4330 print#3,vol$
4340 :
4350 ss$=str$(h):gosub 20000:h$=ss$
4360 pztn$ = chr$ (21):rem position
4370 print#15,"p";chnl$;rec$;pztn$
4380 print#3,h$
4390 :
4400 ss$=str$(low):gosub 20000:low$=ss$
4410 pztn$ = chr$ (26):rem position
4420 print#15,"p";chnl$;rec$;pztn$
4430 print#3,low$
4440 :
4450 ss$=str$(c):gosub 20000:c$=ss$
4460 pztn$ = chr$ (31):rem position
4470 print#15,"p";chnl$;rec$;pztn$
4480 print#3,c$
4490 :
4500 close 3:close 15
4510 :
4520 nh$ = "":nl$ = ""
4530 k = k + 1
4540 if k < 11 then 1150:rem next stock
4550 :
4560 :
5000 rem **--hi/low file update--**
5010 open 3,8,3,"@0:hi/low data,seq,write"
5020 for k = 1 to 10
5030 print#3,stk$(k)
5040 print#3,hi$(k)
5050 print#3,low$(k)
5060 next k
5070 close 3
5080 :
5090 :
6000 rem **--pointer file update--**
6010 open 2,8,2,"@0:stock.pointer,seq,write"
6020 print#2,ptr
6030 close 2
6040 :
6050 :
7000 rem **--return to main menu--**
7010 print home$:rem clr/home
7020 cd = 5:gosub 9000:rem crsr down 5
7030 print tab(14)
7040 print rvs$;"PLEASE WAIT!"
7050 print:print:print
7060 print tab(11)
7070 print "LOADING STOCK.MENU"
7080 ^"stock.menu"
7090 :
```

```
7100 :
9000 rem **--cursor down routine--**
9010 for i = 1 to cd
9020 print cd$;
9030 next i
9040 return
9050 :
9060 :
14000 rem **--convert to lowercase--**
14010 nc$ = ""
14020 for cv = 1 to len(cvt$)
14030 x = asc(mid$(cvt$,cv,1))
14040 if x > 192 then x = x - 128
14050 nc$ = nc$ + chr$(x)
14060 next cv
14070 :
14080 cvt$ = nc$
14090 f = asc(left$(cvt$,1))
14100 f = f + 128
14110 nc$ = chr$(f) + right$(cvt$,len(cvt$)- 1)
14120 return
14130 :
14140 rem cvt$ = converted to lowercase
14150 rem  nc$ = 1st letter/uppercase
14160 :
14170 :
15000 rem **--figure rec.# routine--**
15010 rhigh = int(rlow/256)
15020 rlow  = rlow - 256 * rhigh
15030 return
15040 :
15050 :
16000 rem **--reminder routine--**
16010 print home$:rem clr/home
16020 print tab(8)
16030 print "*****---REMEMBER---*****"
16040 print
16050 print "You must add the fraction as the last"
16060 print "digit! 21 5/8 should be entered as: 215"
16070 print
16080 print "If the number has no fraction, please"
16090 print "enter a '0' after the number! 21 even"
16100 print "should be entered as: 210"
16110 print
16120 print tab(11) "1/8 --------- = 1"
16130 print tab(11) "1/4 --------- = 2"
16140 print tab(11) "3/8 --------- = 3"
16150 print tab(11) "1/2 --------- = 4"
16160 print tab(11) "5/8 --------- = 5"
16170 print tab(11) "3/4 --------- = 6"
16180 print tab(11) "7/8 --------- = 7"
16190 print tab(11) "EVEN -------- = 0"
16200 print
16210 return
16220 :
16230 :
```

```
17000 rem **--convert to fraction--**
17010 f = m - int(m/10) * 10
17020 m = int(m/10)
17030 if f = 0 then f$ = ""
17040 if f = 1 then f$ = "1/8"
17050 if f = 2 then f$ = "1/4"
17060 if f = 3 then f$ = "3/8"
17070 if f = 4 then f$ = "1/2"
17080 if f = 5 then f$ = "5/8"
17090 if f = 6 then f$ = "3/4"
17100 if f = 7 then f$ = "7/8"
17110 return
17120 :
17130 :
18000 rem **--y/n input routine--**
18010 print "Type a ";wht$;"Y";ylw$;" or ";wht$;"N";ylw$;" :";
18020 poke 19,32:rem disable input ?
18030 input yes$
18040 print:print
18050 if yes$ = "y" or yes$ = "Y" then yes$ = "y":return
18060 if yes$ = "n" or yes$ = "N" then yes$ = "n":return
18070 print
18080 print rvs$;"Incorrect Choice!";ylw$
18090 print
18100 goto 18000:rem check again
18110 :
18120 :
19000 rem **--return key routine--**
19010 print
19020 print "Press ";wht$;"RETURN";ylw$;" to continue:";
19030 poke 198,0:rem clr kbrd buffer
19040 for i = 631 to 640
19050 poke i,0:rem no value
19060 next i
19070 x = peek(197):rem store key press
19080 if x = 1 then 19100
19090 goto 19070:rem if not 1 go back
19100 poke 198,1:rem allow 1 for cursor
19110 poke 631,0:rem clr kbrd
19120 nu$ = "":rem clr string variable
19130 print home$:rem clr/home
19140 return
19150 :
19160 :
20000 rem **--strip sign routine--**
20010 lgth = len(ss$)
20020 s2$  = right$(ss$,lgth - 1)
20030 ss$  = s2$
20040 return

ready.
```

Program for STOCK.DISPLAY

```
100 rem ***--display hi/low data--***
110 :
120 :
130 rem **--initialization--**
140 home$ = chr$(147):rem clr/home
150 ::cd$ = chr$( 17):rem cursor down
160 ::cu$ = chr$(145):rem cursor up
170 ::cl$ = chr$(157):rem cursor left
180 ::cr$ = chr$( 29):rem cursor right
190 :blk$ = chr$(144):rem black
200 :ylw$ = chr$(158):rem yellow
210 :wht$ = chr$(  5):rem white
220 :rvs$ = chr$( 18):rem reverse video
230 :
240 poke 53280,14:rem border = lt.blue
250 poke 53272,23:rem upper/lower case
260 poke 53281, 9:rem set bkgrd to brn
270 :
280 :
500 rem **--file input routine--**
510 open 2,8,2,"hi/low data,seq,read"
520 for k = 1 to 10
530 input#2,stk$(k)
540 input#2,hi$(k)
550 input#2,low$(k)
560 next k
570 close 2
580 :
590 :
1000 rem **--display routine--**
1010 :
1020 rem *-titles-*
1030 print ylw$
1040 print home$:rem clr/home
1050 print "Stock Symbol";
1060 print tab(18) "Hi Value";
1070 print tab(28) "Low Value"
1080 print
1090 :
1100 rem *-stock name-*
1110 for k = 1 to 10
1120 if k < 10 then print tab(1)
1130 print k;" ";
1140 print stk$(k);
1150 :
1160 rem *-high value-*
1170 m = val(hi$(k))
1180 gosub 17000:rem convert to fraction
1190 hi$(k) = str$(m)
1200 print tab(18)
1210 print hi$(k);" ";f$;
1220 :
1230 rem *-low value-*
```

```
1240 m = val(low$(k))
1250 gosub 17000:rem convert to fraction
1260 low$(k) = str$(m)
1270 print tab(28)
1280 print low$(k);" ";f$
1290 :
1300 next k
1310 :
1320 cd = 5:gosub 9000:rem crsr down 5
1330 gosub 19000:rem return key routine
1340 :
1350 :
2000 rem **--return to main menu--**
2010 print home$:rem clr/home
2020 cd = 5:gosub 9000:rem crsr down 5
2030 print tab(11)
2040 print rvs$;"ONE MOMENT PLEASE!"
2050 print:print:print
2060 print tab(11)
2070 print "LOADING STOCK.MENU"
2080 ^"stock.menu"
2090 :
2100 :
9000 rem **--cursor down routine--**
9010 for i = 1 to cd
9020 print cd$;
9030 next i
9040 return
9050 :
9060 :
17000 rem **--convert to fraction--**
17010 f = m - int(m/10) * 10
17020 m = int(m/10)
17030 if f = 0 then f$ = ""
17040 if f = 1 then f$ = "1/8"
17050 if f = 2 then f$ = "1/4"
17060 if f = 3 then f$ = "3/8"
17070 if f = 4 then f$ = "1/2"
17080 if f = 5 then f$ = "5/8"
17090 if f = 6 then f$ = "3/4"
17100 if f = 7 then f$ = "7/8"
17110 return
17120 :
17130 :
18000 rem **--y/n input routine--**
18010 print "Type a ";wht$;"Y";ylw$;" or ";wht$;"N";ylw$;" :";
18020 poke 19,32:rem disable input ?
18030 input yes$
18040 print
18050 if yes$ = "y" or yes$ = "Y" then yes$ = "y":return
18060 if yes$ = "n" or yes$ = "N" then yes$ = "n":return
18070 print
18080 print rvs$;"Incorrect Choice!";ylw$
18090 print
18100 goto 18000:rem check again
18110 :
```

```
18120 :
19000 rem **--return key routine--**
19010 print
19020 print "Press ";wht$;"RETURN";ylw$;" to continue:";
19030 poke 198,0:rem clr kbrd buffer
19040 for i = 631 to 640
19050 poke i,0:rem no value
19060 next i
19070 x = peek(197):rem store key press
19080 if x = 1 then 19100
19090 goto 19070:rem if not 1 go back
19100 poke 198,1:rem allow 1 for cursor
19110 poke 631,0:rem clr kbrd
19120 nu$ = "":rem clr string variable
19130 print home$:rem clr/home
19140 return
```

■ Program for STOCK.DSP HI/LOW

```
100 rem ***--display stock history--***
110 :
120 :
130 rem **--initialization--**
140 home$ = chr$(147):rem clr/home
150 ::cd$ = chr$( 17):rem cursor down
160 ::cu$ = chr$(145):rem cursor up
170 ::cl$ = chr$(157):rem cursor left
180 ::cr$ = chr$( 29):rem cursor right
190 :blk$ = chr$(144):rem black
200 :ylw$ = chr$(158):rem yellow
210 :wht$ = chr$(  5):rem white
220 :rvs$ = chr$( 18):rem reverse video
230 :
240 poke 53280,14:rem border = lt.blue
250 poke 53272,23:rem upper/lower case
260 poke 53281, 9:rem set bkgrd to brn
270 :
280 :
290 rem **--variables list--**
300 rem stk$ = stock symbol
310 rem hi$  = current hi price
320 rem low$ = current low price
330 rem dte$ = date
340 rem nh$  = new high
350 rem hl$  = new low
360 rem f$   = fraction
370 rem pe   = p/e ratio
380 rem vol  = sales volume
390 rem h    = daily high price
400 rem low  = daily low price
410 rem c    = daily closing price
420 rem w    = temp. stock #
430 rem av   = average volume
440 rem ap   = average price
450 rem cv   = closing price w/o conv.
460 rem c1   = 1st close price
470 rem c2   = last close price
480 rem cd   = diff. between c1 & c2
490 rem z2   = common var. conv.
500 rem m    = common var. conv.
510 :
520 :
530 rem **--program title /msg.--**
540 print home$:rem clr/home
550 cd = 5:gosub 9000:rem crsr down 5
560 print tab(14)
570 print rvs$;"STOCK HISTORY"
580 print:print:print
590 print tab(12) "One Moment Please!"
600 print:print:print
610 print tab( 8) "Loading Stock Information."
620 :
```

```
630 :
1000 rem **--file input routine--**
1010 :
1020 rem *-pointer file-*
1030 open 2,8,2,"stock.pointer,seq,read"
1040 input#2,ptr
1050 close 2
1060 :
1070 rem *-high/low file-*
1080 open 3,8,3,"hi/low data,seq,read"
1090 for k = 1 to 10
1100 input#3,stk$(k)
1110 input#3,hi$(k)
1120 :
1130 m = val(hi$(k))
1140 gosub 17000:rem convert to fraction
1150 hi$(k) = str$(m) + " " + f$
1160 :
1170 input#3,low$(k)
1180 :
1190 m = val(low$(k))
1200 gosub 17000:rem convert to fraction
1210 low$(k) = str$(m) + " " + f$
1220 :
1230 next k
1240 close 3
1250 :
1260 :
1270 tb = 10
1280 print ylw$
1290 poke 19,32:rem disable input ?
1300 :
1310 :
2000 rem **--display stock names--**
2010 rem clr/home crsr down 3
2020 print home$:cd = 3:gosub 9000
2030 print tab(tb) rvs$;"STOCK HISTORY"
2040 print:print
2050 for k = 1 to 10
2060 if k < 10 then print tab(tb + 1) k;" ";stk$(k):goto 2080
2070 print tab(tb) k;" ";stk$(k)
2080 next k
2090 print tab(tb + 1) "11  Stock Menu"
2100 print:print:print tab(tb)
2110 input "Which Number? ";w$
2120 w = val(w$)
2130 if w < 1 or w > 11 then 13000:rem incorrect # routine
2140 if w = 11 then 7000
2150 :
2160 :
3000 rem **--titles--**
3010 print home$:rem clr/home
3020 lgth = len(stk$(w))
3030 print tab((40 - lgth)/2) wht$;stk$(w)
3040 print ylw$
3050 print:print
```

```
3060 print "DATE"; tab(10) "VOL"; tab(15)"HI"; tab(23) "LOW";
     tab(31) "CLOSE"
3070 :
3080 :
4000 rem **--data file input--**
4010 :
4020 cvt$ = stk$(w)
4030 gosub 14000:rem convert to l.c.
4040 stk$ = cvt$
4050 :
4060 open 15,8,15:rem open command chnl
4070 open  3,8,3,stk$ + ".data,l," + chr$(35)
4080 rem l in line 4070 is letter not #
4090 rem 35 in line 4070 is rec.length--not # of records
4100 chnl$ = chr$(3):rem channel #
4110 :
4120 for kx = 1 to ptr
4130 rlow  = kx:rem low byte of rec.#
4140 rhigh = 0:rem  high byte of rec.#
4150 if rlow > 255 then 15000:rem rec. # routine
4160 rec$ = chr$(rlow) + chr$(rhigh)
4170 :
4180 pztn$ = chr$( 1):rem position
4190 print#15,"p";chnl$;rec$;pztn$
4200 input#3,dte$
4210 print dte$;
4220 :
4230 pztn$ = chr$ (11):rem position
4240 print#15,"p";chnl$;rec$;pztn$
4250 input#3,pe$
4260 :
4270 pztn$ = chr$ (15):rem position
4280 print#15,"p";chnl$;rec$;pztn$
4290 input#3,vol$
4300 print tab(10) vol$;
4310 :
4320 pztn$ = chr$ (21):rem position
4330 print#15,"p";chnl$;rec$;pztn$
4340 input#3,h$
4350 :
4360 m = val(h$)
4370 gosub 17000:rem convert to fraction
4380 h = m
4390 for z = 1 to len(h$)
4400 if mid$(h$,z,1) = "*" then nh$ = "*"
4410 next z
4420 print tab(14) h;f$;nh$;
4430 :
4440 pztn$ = chr$ (26):rem position
4450 print#15,"p";chnl$;rec$;pztn$
4460 input#3,low$
4470 :
4480 m = val(low$)
4490 gosub 17000:rem convert to fraction
4500 low = m
```

```
4510 for z = 1 to len(low$)
4520 if mid$(low$,z,1) = "*" then n1$ = "*"
4530 next z
4540 print tab(22) low;f$;n1$;
4550 :
4560 pztn$ = chr$ (31):rem position
4570 print#15,"p";chnl$;rec$;pztn$
4580 input#3,c$
4590 :
4600 c = val(c$)
4610 if kx = 1 then c1 = c:v1 = val(vol$)
4620 if kx = ptr then c2 = c
4630 cv = c
4640 z2 = cv
4650 gosub 12000:rem convert to decimal
4660 cv = z2
4670 m = c
4680 gosub 17000:rem convert to fraction
4690 c = m
4700 print tab(30) c;f$
4710 :
4720 nh$ = "":n1$ = ""
4730 av = av + val(vol$)
4740 ap = ap + cv
4750 :
4760 next kx
4770 :
4780 :
4790 close 3:close 15
4800 gosub 19000:rem return routine
4810 :
4820 :
5000 rem **--display second page--**
5010 print home$:rem clr/home
5020 tc = 5
5030 print tab((40 - lgth)/2) wht$;stk$(w)
5040 print:print ylw$
5050 print tab(tc) "Current P/E ratio  =  ";pe$
5060 print
5070 print tab(tc) "Current high price = ";hi$(w)
5080 print
5090 print tab(tc) "Current low price  = ";low$(w)
5100 print
5110 :
5120 av = av / (kx - 1)
5130 av$ = str$(av)
5140 for q = 1 to len(av$)
5150 if mid$(av$,q,1) = "." then dec = q
5160 next q
5170 print tab(tc) "Average volume     = ";left$(av$,dec + 2)
5180 print
5190 :
5200 ap = ap / (kx - 1)
5210 ap$ = str$(ap)
5220 for q = 1 to len(ap$)
5230 if mid$(ap$,q,1) = "." then dec = q
```

```
5240 next q
5250 print tab(tc) "Average price       = ";left$(ap$,dec + 2)
5260 :
5270 print
5280 print tab(tc) "Last price          = ";c;f$
5290 z2 = c2
5300 gosub 12000:rem convert to decimal
5310 c2 = z2
5320 :
5330 z2 = c1
5340 gosub 12000:rem convert to decimal
5350 c1 = z2
5360 :
5370 cd = c2 - c1
5380 print:print tab(tc) "Price difference"
5390 print tab(tc) "from 1st record     = ";cd
5400 :
5410 :
6000 rem **--another stock--**
6010 gosub 19000:rem return routine
6020 poke 19,32:rem disable input ?
6030 av = 0:ap = 0
6040 goto 2000:rem start again
6050 :
6060 :
7000 rem **--return to main menu--**
7010 print home$:rem clr/home
7020 cd = 5:gosub 9000:rem crsr down 5
7030 print tab(14)
7040 print rvs$;"PLEASE WAIT!"
7050 print:print:print
7060 print tab(11)
7070 print "LOADING STOCK.MENU"
7080 ^"stock.menu"
7090 :
7100 :
9000 rem **--cursor down routine--**
9010 for i = 1 to cd
9020 print cd$;
9030 next i
9040 return
9050 :
9060 :
12000 rem **--convert to decimal--**
12010 z2 = z2 / 10:s3 = int(z2):dc = z2 - s3
12020 dc = (dc * 10)/ 8:z2 = s3 + dc:z2 = int(z2 * 1000 + .5)
      / 1000
12030 return
12040 :
12050 :
13000 rem **--incorrect number routine--**
13010 print:print
13020 print tab(tb) rvs$;"INCORRECT NUMBER!"
13030 gosub 19000:rem return routine
13040 goto 2000:rem dsp menu again
13050 :
```

```
13060 :
14000 rem **--convert to lowercase--**
14010 nc$ = ""
14020 for cv = 1 to len(cvt$)
14030 x = asc(mid$(cvt$,cv,1))
14040 if x > 192 then x = x - 128
14050 nc$ = nc$ + chr$(x)
14060 next cv
14070 :
14080 cvt$ = nc$
14090 f = asc(left$(cvt$,1))
14100 f = f + 128
14110 nc$ = chr$(f) + right$(cvt$,len(cvt$)- 1)
14120 return
14130 :
14140 rem cvt$ = converted to lowercase
14150 rem  nc$ = 1st letter/uppercase
14160 :
14170 :
15000 rem **--figure rec.# routine--**
15010 rhigh = int(rlow/256)
15020 rlow  = rlow - 256 * rhigh
15030 return
15040 :
15050 :
16000 rem **--reminder routine--**
16010 print home$:rem clr/home
16020 print tab(8)
16030 print "*****---REMEMBER---*****"
16040 print
16050 print "You must add the fraction as the last"
16060 print "digit! 21 5/8 should be entered as: 215"
16070 print
16080 print "If the number has no fraction, please"
16090 print "enter a '0' after the number! 21 even"
16100 print "should be entered as: 210"
16110 print
16120 print tab(11) "1/8 --------- = 1"
16130 print tab(11) "1/4 --------- = 2"
16140 print tab(11) "3/8 --------- = 3"
16150 print tab(11) "1/2 --------- = 4"
16160 print tab(11) "5/8 --------- = 5"
16170 print tab(11) "3/4 --------- = 6"
16180 print tab(11) "7/8 --------- = 7"
16190 print tab(11) "EVEN -------- = 0"
16200 print
16210 return
16220 :
16230 :
17000 rem **--convert to fraction--**
17010 f = m - int(m/10) * 10
17020 m = int(m/10)
17030 if f = 0 then f$ = ""
17040 if f = 1 then f$ = "1/8"
17050 if f = 2 then f$ = "1/4"
17060 if f = 3 then f$ = "3/8"
```

```
17070 if f = 4 then f$ = "1/2"
17080 if f = 5 then f$ = "5/8"
17090 if f = 6 then f$ = "3/4"
17100 if f = 7 then f$ = "7/8"
17110 return
17120 :
17130 :
18000 rem **--y/n input routine--**
18010 print "Type a ";wht$;"Y";ylw$;" or ";wht$;"N";ylw$;" :";
18020 poke 19,32:rem disable input ?
18030 input yes$
18040 print:print
18050 if yes$ = "y" or yes$ = "Y" then yes$ = "y":return
18060 if yes$ = "n" or yes$ = "N" then yes$ = "n":return
18070 print
18080 print rvs$;"Incorrect Choice!";ylw$
18090 print
18100 goto 18000:rem check again
18110 :
18120 :
19000 rem **--return key routine--**
19010 print:print
19020 print "Press the ";wht$;"RETURN";ylw$;" key to continue:";
19030 poke 198,0:rem clr kbrd buffer
19040 for i = 631 to 640
19050 poke i,0:rem no value
19060 next i
19070 x = peek(197):rem store key press
19080 if x = 1 then 19100
19090 goto 19070:rem if not 1 go back
19100 poke 198,1:rem allow 1 for cursor
19110 poke 631,0:rem clr kbrd
19120 nu$ = "":rem clr string variable
19130 print home$:rem clr/home
19140 return

ready.
```

■ Program for STOCK.CRT HI/LOW

```
100 rem ***--correct stock info.--***
110 :
120 :
130 rem **--initialization--**
140 home$ = chr$(147):rem clr/home
150 ::cd$ = chr$( 17):rem cursor down
160 ::cu$ = chr$(145):rem cursor up
170 ::cl$ = chr$(157):rem cursor left
180 ::cr$ = chr$( 29):rem cursor right
190 :blk$ = chr$(144):rem black
200 :ylw$ = chr$(158):rem yellow
210 :wht$ = chr$(  5):rem white
220 :rvs$ = chr$( 18):rem reverse video
230 :
240 poke 53280,14:rem border = lt.blue
250 poke 53272,23:rem upper/lower case
260 poke 53281, 9:rem set bkgrd to brn
270 :
280 :
290 rem **--variables list--**
300 rem stk$ = stock symbol
310 rem hi$  = current hi price
320 rem zow$ = current low price
330 rem dte$ = date
340 rem nh$  = new high
350 rem hz$  = new low
360 rem f$   = fraction
370 rem pe   = p/e ratio
380 rem vol  = sales volume
390 rem h    = daily high price
400 rem low  = daily low price
410 rem c    = daily closing price
420 rem cr   = corrected figure
430 rem m    = common var. conv.
440 rem w    = temp. stock #
450 :
460 :
470 rem **--program title /msg.--**
480 print home$:rem clr/home
490 cd = 5:gosub 9000:rem crsr down 5
500 print tab(10)
510 print rvs$;"CORRECT STOCK HISTORY"
520 print:print:print:print
530 print tab(12) "One Moment Please!"
540 print:print:print:print
550 print tab( 8) "Loading Stock Information."
560 :
570 :
1000 rem **--file input routine--**
1010 :
1020 rem *-pointer file-*
1030 open 2,8,2,"stock.pointer,seq,read"
1040 input#2,ptr
```

```
1050 close 2
1060 :
1070 rem *-high/low file-*
1080 open 3,8,3,"hi/low data,seq,read"
1090 for k = 1 to 10
1100 input#3,stk$(k)
1110 input#3,hi$(k)
1120 :
1130 m = val(hi$(k))
1140 gosub 17000:rem convert to fraction
1150 hi$(k) = str$(m) + " " + f$
1160 :
1170 input#3,low$(k)
1180 :
1190 m = val(low$(k))
1200 gosub 17000:rem convert to fraction
1210 low$(k) = str$(m) + " " + f$
1220 :
1230 next k
1240 close 3
1250 :
1260 :
1270 tb = 10
1280 print ylw$
1290 poke 19,32:rem disable input ?
1300 :
1310 :
2000 rem **--display stock names--**
2010 rem clr/home crsr down 1
2020 print home$:cd = 1:gosub 9000
2030 print tab(tb) rvs$;"CORRECT STOCK HISTORY"
2040 print:print
2050 for k = 1 to 10
2060 if k < 10 then print tab(tb + 3) k;" ";stk$(k):goto 2080
2070 print tab(tb + 2) k;" ";stk$(k)
2080 next k
2090 print tab(tb + 3) "11  Stock Menu"
2100 print:print tab(tb + 3)
2110 input "Which Number? ";w$
2120 w = val(w$)
2130 if w < 1 or w > 11 then wr = w:gosub 13000:goto 2000
2140 if w = 11 then 7000
2150 :
2160 rem clr/home crsr down 5
2170 print home$:cd = 5:gosub 9000
2180 print "Which record for ";wht$;stk$(w);ylw$;" (1 to";str$
     (ptr);")? ";
2190 input rk
2200 if rk < 1 or rk > ptr then wr = rk:gosub 13000:goto 2160
2210 :
2220 :
3000 rem **--data file input--**
3010 :
3020 cvt$ = stk$(w)
3030 gosub 14000:rem convert to l.c.
3040 stk$ = cvt$
```

```
3050 :
3060 open 15,8,15:rem open command chnl
3070 open  3,8,3,stk$ + ".data,l," + chr$(35)
3080 rem l in line 3070 is letter not #
3090 rem 35 in line 3070 is rec.length--not # of records
3100 chnl$ = chr$(3):rem channel #
3110 :
3120 rlow  = rk:rem low byte of rec.#
3130 rhigh = 0:rem  high byte of rec.#
3140 if rlow > 255 then 15000:rem rec. # routine
3150 rec$ = chr$(rlow) + chr$(rhigh)
3160 :
3170 pztn$ = chr$( 1):rem position
3180 print#15,"p";chnl$;rec$;pztn$
3190 input#3,dte$
3200 :
3210 pztn$ = chr$ (11):rem position
3220 print#15,"p";chnl$;rec$;pztn$
3230 input#3,pe$
3240 :
3250 pztn$ = chr$ (15):rem position
3260 print#15,"p";chnl$;rec$;pztn$
3270 input#3,vol$
3280 :
3290 pztn$ = chr$ (21):rem position
3300 print#15,"p";chnl$;rec$;pztn$
3310 input#3,h$
3320 :
3330 pztn$ = chr$ (26):rem position
3340 print#15,"p";chnl$;rec$;pztn$
3350 input#3,low$
3360 :
3370 pztn$ = chr$ (31):rem position
3380 print#15,"p";chnl$;rec$;pztn$
3390 input#3,c$
3400 :
3410 :
3420 close 3:close 15
3430 :
3440 pe  = val(pe$)
3450 vol = val(vol$)
3460 h   = val(h$)
3470 low = val(low$)
3480 c   = val(c$)
3490 :
3500 :
4000 rem **--correction routine--**
4010 flag$ = "off":rem info.unchanged
4020 rem clr/home crsr down 5
4030 print home$:cd = 5:gosub 9000
4040 print
4050 print stk$(w);"'s data for ";dte$
4060 print:print
4070 print "1. P/E ratio ---- ";pe
4080 print "2. Volume ------- ";vol
4090 m = h:gosub 17000:rem convert to fraction
```

```
4100 print "3. High --------- ";m;" ";f$
4110 m = low:gosub 17000:rem convert to fraction
4120 print "4. Low ---------- ";m;" ";f$
4130 m = c:gosub 17000:rem convert to fraction
4140 print "5. Close -------- ";m;" ";f$
4150 print
4160 print "Is this correct? ";
4170 gosub 18000:rem y/n input routine
4180 print
4190 if yes$ = "n" then 4240
4200 :
4210 if flag$ = "off" then 2000:rem info not changed & ok
4220 goto 5000:rem file correction
4230 :
4240 input "Which number is wrong? ":nb
4250 if nb < 1 or nb > 5 then print:print "INCORRECT CHOICE!":
     goto 4150
4260 if nb = 1 then info$ = "P/E"
4270 if nb = 2 then info$ = "VOL"
4280 if nb = 3 then info$ = "HI":gosub 16000:rem reminder
     routine
4290 if nb = 4 then info$ = "LOW":gosub 16000:rem reminder
     routine
4300 if nb = 5 then info$ = "CLOSE":gosub 16000:rem reminder
     routine
4310 print
4320 print "The correct ";info$;" figure = ";:input cr
4330 if nb = 1 then pe  = cr
4340 if nb = 2 then vol = cr
4350 if nb = 3 then h   = cr
4360 if nb = 4 then low = cr
4370 if nb = 5 then c   = cr
4380 flag$ = "on":rem info changed
4390 goto 4020:rem ask again
4400 print
4410
4420
5000 rem **--file correction--**
5010 rem clr/home crsr down 5
5020 print home$:cd = 5:gosub 9000
5030 print tab(11) rvs$;"ONE MOMENT PLEASE!"
5040 cd = 7:gosub 9000:rem crsr down 7
5050 print tab(10) "Updating ";wht$;stk$(w);"'s";ylw$;" file."
5060 :
5070 cvt$ = stk$(w)
5080 gosub 14000:rem convert to l.c.
5090 stk$ = cvt$
5100 :
5110 open 15,8,15:rem open command chnl
5120 open  3,8,3,stk$ + ".data,l," + chr$(35)
5130 rem l in line 5120 is letter not #
5140 rem 35 in line 5120 is rec.length--not # of records
5150 chnl$ = chr$(3):rem channel #
5160 rlow  = rk:rem low byte of rec.#
5170 rhigh = 0:rem  high byte of rec.#
```

```
5180 if rlow > 255 then 15000:rem rec.# routine
5190 rec$ = chr$(rlow) + chr$(rhigh)
5200 :
5210 pztn$ = chr$( 1):rem position
5220 print#15,"p";chnl$;rec$;pztn$
5230 print#3,dte$
5240 :
5250 ss$=str$(pe):gosub 20000:pe$=ss$
5260 pztn$ = chr$ (11):rem position
5270 print#15,"p";chnl$;rec$;pztn$
5280 print#3,pe$
5290 :
5300 ss$=str$(vol):gosub 20000:vol$=ss$
5310 pztn$ = chr$ (15):rem position
5320 print#15,"p";chnl$;rec$;pztn$
5330 print#3,vol$
5340 :
5350 ss$=str$(h):gosub 20000:h$=ss$
5360 pztn$ = chr$ (21):rem position
5370 print#15,"p";chnl$;rec$;pztn$
5380 print#3,h$
5390 :
5400 ss$=str$(low):gosub 20000:low$=ss$
5410 pztn$ = chr$ (26):rem position
5420 print#15,"p";chnl$;rec$;pztn$
5430 print#3,low$
5440 :
5450 ss$=str$(c):gosub 20000:c$=ss$
5460 pztn$ = chr$ (31):rem position
5470 print#15,"p";chnl$;rec$;pztn$
5480 print#3,c$
5490 :
5500 close 3:close 15
5510 :
5520 :
6000 rem **--another stock--**
6010 rem clr/home crsr down 5
6020 print home$:cd = 5:gosub 9000
6030 print stk$(w);"'s file has been updated!"
6040 gosub 19000:rem return routine
6050 poke 19,32:rem disable input ?
6060 goto 2000:rem start again
6070 :
6080 :
7000 rem **--return to main menu--**
7010 print home$:rem clr/home
7020 cd = 5:gosub 9000:rem crsr down 5
7030 print tab(14)
7040 print rvs$;"PLEASE WAIT!"
7050 print:print:print
7060 print tab(11)
7070 print "LOADING STOCK.MENU"
7080 ^"stock.menu"
7090 :
```

```
7100 :
9000 rem **--cursor down routine--**
9010 for i = 1 to cd
9020 print cd$;
9030 next i
9040 return
9050 :
9060 :
13000 rem **--incorrect number routine--**
13010 wr$ = str$(wr)
13020 zw = len(wr$)
13030 rem clr/home crsr down 5
13040 print home$:cd = 5:gosub 9000
13050 print right$(wr$,zw - 1);" is not a valid choice."
13060 print
13070 print"Please try again!"
13080 gosub 19000:rem return routine
13090 return
13100 :
13110 :
14000 rem **--convert to lowercase--**
14010 nc$ = ""
14020 for cv = 1 to len(cvt$)
14030 x = asc(mid$(cvt$,cv,1))
14040 if x > 192 then x = x - 128
14050 nc$ = nc$ + chr$(x)
14060 next cv
14070 :
14080 cvt$ = nc$
14090 f = asc(left$(cvt$,1))
14100 f = f + 128
14110 nc$ = chr$(f) + right$(cvt$,len(cvt$)- 1)
14120 return
14130 :
14140 rem cvt$ = converted to lowercase
14150 rem  nc$ = 1st letter/uppercase
14160 :
14170 :
15000 rem **--figure rec.# routine--**
15010 rhigh = int(rlow/256)
15020 rlow  = rlow - 256 * rhigh
15030 return
15040 :
15050 :
16000 rem **--reminder routine--**
16010 print home$:rem clr/home
16020 print tab(8)
16030 print "*****---REMEMBER---*****"
16040 print
16050 print "You must add the fraction as the last"
16060 print "digit! 21 5/8 should be entered as: 215"
16070 print
16080 print "If the number has no fraction, please"
16090 print "enter a '0' after the number! 21 even"
```

```
16100 print "should be entered as: 210"
16110 print
16120 print tab(11) "1/8 --------- = 1"
16130 print tab(11) "1/4 --------- = 2"
16140 print tab(11) "3/8 --------- = 3"
16150 print tab(11) "1/2 --------- = 4"
16160 print tab(11) "5/8 --------- = 5"
16170 print tab(11) "3/4 --------- = 6"
16180 print tab(11) "7/8 --------- = 7"
16190 print tab(11) "EVEN -------- = 0"
16200 print
16210 return
16220 :
16230 :
17000 rem **--convert to fraction--**
17010 f = m - int(m/10) * 10
17020 m = int(m/10)
17030 if f = 0 then f$ = ""
17040 if f = 1 then f$ = "1/8"
17050 if f = 2 then f$ = "1/4"
17060 if f = 3 then f$ = "3/8"
17070 if f = 4 then f$ = "1/2"
17080 if f = 5 then f$ = "5/8"
17090 if f = 6 then f$ = "3/4"
17100 if f = 7 then f$ = "7/8"
17110 return
17120 :
17130 :
18000 rem **--y/n input routine--**
18010 print "Type a ";wht$;"Y";ylw$;" or ";wht$;"N";ylw$;" :";
18020 poke 19,32:rem disable input ?
18030 input yes$
18040 print:print
18050 if yes$ = "y" or yes$ = "Y" then yes$ = "y":return
18060 if yes$ = "n" or yes$ = "N" then yes$ = "n":return
18070 print
18080 print rvs$;"Incorrect Choice!";ylw$
18090 print
18100 goto 18000:rem check again
18110 :
18120 :
19000 rem **--return key routine--**
19010 print:print
19020 print "Press ";wht$;"RETURN";ylw$;" to continue:";
19030 poke 198,0:rem clr kbrd buffer
19040 for i = 631 to 640
19050 poke i,0:rem no value
19060 next i
19070 x = peek(197):rem store key press
19080 if x = 1 then 19100
19090 goto 19070:rem if not 1 go back
19100 poke 198,1:rem allow 1 for cursor
19110 poke 631,0:rem clr kbrd
19120 nu$ = "":rem clr string variable
19130 print home$:rem clr/home
```

```
19140 return
19150 :
19160 :
20000 rem **--strip sign routine--**
20010 lgth = len(ss$)
20020 s2$  = right$(ss$,lgth - 1)
20030 ss$  = s2$
20040 return

ready.
```

■ Program for STOCK.CORRECT

```
100 rem ***--translate stock info.--***
110 :
120 :
130 rem **--initialization--**
140 home$ = chr$(147):rem clr/home
150 ::cd$ = chr$( 17):rem cursor down
160 ::cu$ = chr$(145):rem cursor up
170 ::cl$ = chr$(157):rem cursor left
180 ::cr$ = chr$( 29):rem cursor right
190 :blk$ = chr$(144):rem black
200 :ylw$ = chr$(158):rem yellow
210 :wht$ = chr$(  5):rem white
220 :rvs$ = chr$( 18):rem reverse video
230 :
240 poke 53280,14:rem border = lt.blue
250 poke 53272,23:rem upper/lower case
260 poke 53281, 9:rem set bkgrd to brn
270 :
280 :
290 rem **--variables list--**
300 rem  stk$ = stock symbol
310 rem   hi$ = current hi price
320 rem  zow$ = current low price
330 rem  dte$ = date
340 rem   nh$ = new high
350 rem   hz$ = new low
360 rem    f$ = fraction
370 rem    pe = p/e ratio
380 rem   voz = sales volume
390 rem     h = daily high price
400 rem   zow = daily low price
410 rem     c = daily closing price
420 rem    cr = corrected figure
430 rem     m = common var. conv.
440 rem     w = temp. stock #
450 rem  rlow = low  byte of rec.#
460 rem rhigh = high byte of rec.#
470 rem  file = file # in open cmnd
480 rem  dvic = device # in open cmnd
490 rem  cmnd = command # in open cmnd
500 rem   ptr = pointer for # of recd's
510 rem chnl$ = channel # in open cmnd
520 rem  rec$ = rec.# from rlow & rhigh
530 rem pztn$ = position within record
540 :
550 :
560 rem **--program title /msg.--**
570 print home$:rem clr/home
580 cd = 5:gosub 9000:rem crsr down 5
590 print tab(10)
600 print rvs$;"TRANSLATE STOCK HISTORY"
610 print:print:print:print
620 print tab(12) "One Moment Please!"
```

```
630 print:print:print:print
640 print tab( 8) "Loading Stock Information."
650 :
660 :
1000 rem **--file input routine--**
1010 :
1020 rem *-pointer file-*
1030 open 2,8,2,"stock.pointer,seq,read"
1040 input#2,ptr
1050 close 2
1060 :
1070 rem *-high/low file-*
1080 open 3,8,3,"hi/low data,seq,read"
1090 for k = 1 to 10
1100 input#3,stk$(k)
1110 input#3,hi$(k)
1120 :
1130 z2 = val(hi$(k))
1140 gosub 12000:rem convert to decimal
1150 hi(k) = z2
1160 :
1170 input#3,zow$(k)
1180 :
1190 z2 = val(zow$(k))
1200 gosub 12000:rem convert to decimal
1210 zow(k) = z2
1220 :
1230 next k
1240 close 3
1250 :
1260 :
1270 tb = 10
1280 print ylw$
1290 poke 19,32:rem disable input ?
1300 :
1310 :
2000 rem **--display stock names--**
2010 rem clr/home crsr down 1
2020 print home$:cd = 1:gosub 9000
2030 print tab(tb) rvs$;"TRANSLATE STOCK HISTORY"
2040 print:print
2050 for k = 1 to 10
2060 if k < 10 then print tab(tb + 3) k;" ";stk$(k):goto 2080
2070 print tab(tb + 2) k;" ";stk$(k)
2080 next k
2090 print tab(tb + 3) "11  Stock Menu"
2100 print:print tab(tb + 3)
2110 input "Which Number? ";w$
2120 w = val(w$)
2130 if w < 1 or w > 11 then wr = w:gosub 13000:goto 2000
2140 if w = 11 then 7000
2150 :
2160 :
3000 rem **--dif file setup--**
3010 :
3020 rem clr/home crsr down 5
```

```
3030 print home$:cd = 5:gosub 9000
3040 print tab(5) rvs$;
3050 print "DIF TRANSLATION IN PROGRESS."
3060 print:print:print
3070 print tab(8) rvs$;
3080 print "PLEASE DO NOT TOUCH!!"
3090 :
3100 cvt$ = stk$(w)
3110 gosub 14000:rem convert to l.c.
3120 stk$ = cvt$
3130 :
3140 open 15,8,15:rem open command chnl
3150 open  3,8,3,stk$ + ".data,l," + chr$(35)
3160 rem l in line 3150 is letter not #
3170 rem 35 in line 3150 is rec.length--not # of records
3180 chnl$ = chr$(3):rem channel #
3190 rem nv = number of vectors
3200 rem nt = number of tuples
3210 nv = 8:nt = ptr + 1
3220 q$ = chr$(34):rem quote mark
3230 open 2,8,2,stk$ + ".dif,seq,write"
3240 :
3250 :
4000 rem *-header section-*
4010 :
4020 print#2,"TABLE"
4030 print#2,"0,1"
4040 print#2,q$q$
4050 :
4060 print#2,"VECTORS"
4070 print#2,"0,";nv
4080 print#2,q$q$
4090 :
4100 print#2,"TUPLES"
4110 print#2,"0,";nt
4120 print#2,q$q$
4130 :
4140 print#2,"DATA"
4150 print#2,"0,0"
4160 print#2,q$q$
4170 :
4180 :
5000 rem *-data section-*
5010 :
5020 print#2,"-1,0"
5030 print#2,"BOT"
5040 :
5050 print#2,"1,0"
5060 print#2,stk$(w)
5070 :
5080 print#2,"1,0"
5090 print#2,"52 WK.HI"
5100 :
5110 print#2,"1,0"
5120 print#2,"52 WK.LOW"
5130 :
```

```
5140 print#2,"-1,0"
5150 print#2,"BOT"
5160 :
5170 print#2,"1,0"
5180 print#2," "
5190 :
5200 print#2,"0,";hi(w)
5210 print#2,"V"
5220 :
5230 print#2,"0,";zow(w)
5240 print#2,"V"
5250 :
5260 print#2,"-1,0"
5270 print#2,"BOT"
5280 :
5290 print#2,"1,0"
5300 print#2,q$"DATE"q$
5310 :
5320 print#2,"1,0"
5330 print#2,q$"P/E"q$
5340 :
5350 print#2,"1,0"
5360 print#2,q$"VOL."q$
5370 :
5380 print#2,"1,0"
5390 print#2,q$"HI"q$
5400 :
5410 print#2,"1,0"
5420 print#2,q$"LOW"q$
5430 :
5440 print#2,"1,0"
5450 print#2,q$"CLOSE"q$
5460 :
5470 print#2,"1,0"
5480 print#2,q$"52 WK.HI"q$
5490 :
5500 print#2,"1,0"
5510 print#2,q$"52 WK.LOW"q$
5520 :
5530 :
6000 rem **--read/write data--**
6010 for rk = 1 to ptr
6020 rlow  = rk:rem low byte of rec.#
6030 rhigh = 0:rem  high byte of rec.#
6040 if rlow > 255 then 15000:rem rec. # routine
6050 rec$ = chr$(rlow) + chr$(rhigh)
6060 :
6070 pztn$ = chr$( 1):rem position
6080 print#15,"p";chnl$;rec$;pztn$
6090 input#3,dte$
6100 :
6110 pztn$ = chr$ (11):rem position
6120 print#15,"p";chnl$;rec$;pztn$
6130 input#3,pe$
6140 :
6150 pztn$ = chr$ (15):rem position
```

```
6160 print#15,"p";chnl$;rec$;pztn$
6170 input#3,voz$
6180 :
6190 pztn$ = chr$ (21):rem position
6200 print#15,"p";chnl$;rec$;pztn$
6210 input#3,h$
6220 :
6230 pztn$ = chr$ (26):rem position
6240 print#15,"p";chnl$;rec$;pztn$
6250 input#3,zow$
6260 :
6270 pztn$ = chr$ (31):rem position
6280 print#15,"p";chnl$;rec$;pztn$
6290 input#3,c$
6300 :
6310 pe  = val(pe$)
6320 voz = val(voz$)
6330 h   = val(h$)
6340 zow = val(zow$)
6350 c   = val(c$)
6360 :
6370 print#2,"-1,0"
6380 print#2,"BOT"
6390 :
6400 print#2,"1,0"
6410 print#2,dte$
6420 :
6430 print#2,"0,";pe
6440 print#2,"V"
6450 :
6460 print#2,"0,";voz
6470 print#2,"V"
6480 :
6490 z2 = h
6500 gosub 12000:rem convert to decimal
6510 h = z2
6520 :
6530 print#2,"0,";h
6540 print#2,"V"
6550 :
6560 z2 = zow
6570 gosub 12000:rem convert to decimal
6580 zow = z2
6590 :
6600 print#2,"0,";zow
6610 print#2,"V"
6620 :
6630 z2 = c
6640 gosub 12000:rem convert to decimal
6650 c = z2
6660 :
6670 print#2,"0,";c
6680 print#2,"V"
6690 :
6700 next rk
6710 :
```

```
6720 rem *-all finished-*
6730 :
6740 print#2,"-1,0"
6750 print#2,"EOD"
6760 :
6770 close 2
6780 close 3:close 15
6790 :
6800 print home$:cd = 5:gosub 9000
6810 print tab(14) "ALL FINISHED"
6820 print:print
6830 print tab(8)
6840 rem print "Insert Program Diskette!"
6850 print:print:print
6860 print tab(8) "Press ";wht$;"RETURN";ylw$;" to continue: "
6870 gosub 19030:rem return routine
6880 :
6890 rem *-another stock-*
6900 poke 19,32:rem disable input ?
6910 goto 2000:rem start again
6920 :
6930 :
7000 rem **--return to main menu--**
7010 print home$:rem clr/home
7020 cd = 5:gosub 9000:rem crsr down 5
7030 print tab(14)
7040 print rvs$;"PLEASE WAIT!"
7050 print:print:print
7060 print tab(11)
7070 print "LOADING STOCK.MENU"
7080 ^"stock.menu"
7090 :
7100 :
9000 rem **--cursor down routine--**
9010 for i = 1 to cd
9020 print cd$;
9030 next i
9040 return
9050 :
9060 :
12000 rem **--convert to decimal--**
12010 z2 = z2 / 10:s3 = int(z2):dc = z2 - s3
12020 dc = (dc * 10)/ 8:z2 = s3 + dc:z2 = int(z2 * 1000 + .5)
      / 1000
12030 return
12040 :
12050 :
13000 rem **--incorrect number routine--**
13010 wr$ = str$(wr)
13020 zw = len(wr$)
13030 rem clr/home crsr down 5
13040 print home$:cd = 5:gosub 9000
13050 print right$(wr$,zw - 1);" is not a valid choice."
13060 print
13070 print"Please try again!"
13080 gosub 19000:rem return routine
```

```
13090 return
13100 :
13110 :
14000 rem **--convert to lowercase--**
14010 nc$ = ""
14020 for cv = 1 to len(cvt$)
14030 x = asc(mid$(cvt$,cv,1))
14040 if x > 192 then x = x - 128
14050 nc$ = nc$ + chr$(x)
14060 next cv
14070 :
14080 cvt$ = nc$
14090 f = asc(left$(cvt$,1))
14100 f = f + 128
14110 nc$ = chr$(f) + right$(cvt$,len(cvt$)- 1)
14120 return
14130 :
14140 rem cvt$ = converted to lowercase
14150 rem  nc$ = 1st letter/uppercase
14160 :
14170 :
15000 rem **--figure rec.# routine--**
15010 rhigh = int(rlow/256)
15020 rlow  = rlow - 256 * rhigh
15030 return
15040 :
15050 :
19000 rem **--return key routine--**
19010 print:print
19020 print "Press ";wht$;"RETURN";ylw$;" to continue:";
19030 poke 198,0:rem clr kbrd buffer
19040 for i = 631 to 640
19050 poke i,0:rem no value
19060 next i
19070 x = peek(197):rem store key press
19080 if x = 1 then 19100
19090 goto 19070:rem if not 1 go back
19100 poke 198,1:rem allow 1 for cursor
19110 poke 631,0:rem clr kbrd
19120 nu$ = "":rem clr string variable
19130 print home$:rem clr/home
19140 return

ready.
```

■ Program for STOCK.TRANS

```
100 rem ***--correct hi/low data--***
110 :
120 :
130 rem **--initialization--**
140 home$ = chr$(147):rem clr/home
150 ::cd$ = chr$( 17):rem cursor down
160 ::cu$ = chr$(145):rem cursor up
170 ::cl$ = chr$(157):rem cursor left
180 ::cr$ = chr$( 29):rem cursor right
190 :blk$ = chr$(144):rem black
200 :ylw$ = chr$(158):rem yellow
210 :wht$ = chr$(  5):rem white
220 :rvs$ = chr$( 18):rem reverse video
230 :
240 poke 53280,14:rem border = lt.blue
250 poke 53272,23:rem upper/lower case
260 poke 53281, 9:rem set bkgrd to brn
270 :
280 :
290 rem **--program title /msg.--**
300 print home$:rem clr/home
310 cd = 5:gosub 9000:rem crsr down 5
320 print tab(10)
330 print rvs$;"CORRECT HI/LOW INFO."
340 print:print:print:print
350 print tab(11) "One Moment Please!"
360 print:print:print:print
370 print tab( 7) "Loading Stock Information."
380 :
390 :
400 tb = 10
410 print ylw$
420 flag$ = "off":rem info unchanged
430 :
440 :
450 rem **--file input routine--**
460 :
470 open 2,8,2,"hi/low data,seq,read"
480 for k = 1 to 10
490 input#2,stk$(k)
500 input#2,hi$(k)
510 input#2,low$(k)
520 next k
530 close 2
540 :
550 :
560 rem **--hi/low correct menu--**
570 poke 19,32:rem disable input ?
580 rem clr/home crsr down 3
590 print home$:cd = 3:gosub 9000
600 print tab(tb) rvs$;"CORRECT HI/LOW INFO."
610 print:print
620 print tab(tb - 3) "1. Display HI/LOW Information"
```

```
630 print
640 print tab(tb - 3) "2. Correct HI/LOW Information"
650 print
660 print tab(tb - 3) "3. Return to Main Stock Menu"
670 print:print tab(tb - 3)
680 input "Which Number? ";w$
690 w = val(w$)
700 if w < 1 or w > 3 then wr = w:gosub 13000:goto 560
710 if w = 1 then 1000
720 if w = 2 then 2000
730 if w = 3 and flag$ = "off" then 7000
740 if w = 3 and flag$ = "on" then 4000
750 :
760 :
1000 rem **--display routine--**
1010 :
1020 rem *-titles-*
1030 print ylw$
1040 print home$:rem clr/home
1050 print "Stock Symbol";
1060 print tab(18) "Hi Value";
1070 print tab(28) "Low Value"
1080 print
1090 :
1100 rem *-stock name-*
1110 for k = 1 to 10
1120 if k < 10 then print tab(1)
1130 print k;" ";
1140 print stk$(k);
1150 :
1160 rem *-high value-*
1170 m = val(hi$(k))
1180 gosub 17000:rem convert to fraction
1190 print tab(18)
1200 print str$(m);" ";f$;
1210 :
1220 rem *-low value-*
1230 m = val(low$(k))
1240 gosub 17000:rem convert to fraction
1250 print tab(28)
1260 print str$(m);" ";f$
1270 :
1280 next k
1290 :
1300 cd = 5:gosub 9000:rem crsr down 5
1310 gosub 19000:rem return routine
1320 goto 560
1330 :
1340 :
2000 rem **--display stock names--**
2010 rem clr/home crsr down 1
2020 print home$:cd = 1:gosub 9000
2030 print tab(tb) rvs$;"CORRECT STOCK HISTORY"
2040 print:print
2050 for k = 1 to 10
2060 if k < 10 then print tab(tb + 3) k;" ";stk$(k):goto 2080
```

```
2070 print tab(tb + 2) k;" ";stk$(k)
2080 next k
2090 print tab(tb + 3) "11  Menu"
2100 print:print tab(tb + 3)
2110 input "Which Number? ";w$
2120 w = val(w$)
2130 if w < 1 or w > 11 then wr = w:gosub 13000:goto 2000
2140 if w = 11 then 560
2150 :
2160 :
3000 rem **--correction routine--**
3010 flag$ = "off":rem info unchanged
3020 rem clr/home crsr down 5
3030 print home$:cd = 5:gosub 9000
3040 print
3050 print "1. ";stk$(w)
3060 print
3070 m = val(hi$(w)):gosub 17000:rem convert to fraction
3080 print "2. Hi value  = ";m;" ";f$
3090 print
3100 m = val(low$(w)):gosub 17000:rem convert to fraction
3110 print "3. Low value = ";m;" ";f$
3120 print
3130 print "Is this correct? ";
3140 gosub 18000:rem y/n input routine
3150 print
3160 if yes$ = "n" then 3180
3170 goto 2000:rem another stock
3180 input "Which number is wrong? ";nb
3190 print
3200 if nb = 1 then input "Correct stock name or symbol: ";
     stk$(w)
3210 if nb = 2 then gosub 16000:input "Correct hi value: ";
     hi$(w)
3220 if nb = 3 then gosub 16000:input "Correct low value: ";
     low$(w)
3230 if nb < 1 or nb > 3 then print "INCORRECT CHOICE!"
3240 flag$ = "on":rem info changed
3250 goto 3020:rem ask again
3260 print
3270 :
3280 :
4000 rem **--file output routine--**
4010 :
4020 rem *-hi/low data file-*
4030 open 3,8,3,"@0:hi/low data,seq,write"
4040 for k = 1 to 10
4050 print#3,stk$(k)
4060 print#3,hi$(k)
4070 print#3,low$(k)
4080 next k
4090 close 3
4100 :
4110 :
7000 rem **--return to main menu--**
```

```
7010 print home$:rem clr/home
7020 cd = 5:gosub 9000:rem crsr down 5
7030 print tab(11)
7040 print rvs$;"ONE MOMENT PLEASE!"
7050 print:print:print
7060 print tab(11)
7070 print "LOADING STOCK.MENU"
7080 ^"stock.menu"
7090 :
7100 :
9000 rem **--cursor down routine--**
9010 for i = 1 to cd
9020 print cd$;
9030 next i
9040 return
9050 :
9060 :
13000 rem **--incorrect number routine--**
13010 wr$ = str$(wr)
13020 zw = len(wr$)
13030 rem clr/home crsr down 5
13040 print home$:cd = 5:gosub 9000
13050 print right$(wr$,zw - 1);" is not a valid choice."
13060 print
13070 print"Please try again!"
13080 gosub 19000:rem return routine
13090 return
13100 :
13110 :
16000 rem **--reminder routine--**
16010 print home$:rem clr/home
16020 print tab(8)
16030 print "*****---REMEMBER---*****"
16040 print
16050 print "You must add the fraction as the last"
16060 print "digit! 21 5/8 should be entered as: 215"
16070 print
16080 print "If the number has no fraction, please"
16090 print "enter a '0' after the number! 21 even"
16100 print "should be entered as: 210"
16110 print
16120 print tab(11) "1/8 --------- = 1"
16130 print tab(11) "1/4 --------- = 2"
16140 print tab(11) "3/8 --------- = 3"
16150 print tab(11) "1/2 --------- = 4"
16160 print tab(11) "5/8 --------- = 5"
16170 print tab(11) "3/4 --------- = 6"
16180 print tab(11) "7/8 --------- = 7"
16190 print tab(11) "EVEN -------- = 0"
16200 print
16210 return
16220 :
16230 :
17000 rem **--convert to fraction--**
17010 f = m - int(m/10) * 10
17020 m = int(m/10)
```

```
17030 if f = 0 then f$ = ""
17040 if f = 1 then f$ = "1/8"
17050 if f = 2 then f$ = "1/4"
17060 if f = 3 then f$ = "3/8"
17070 if f = 4 then f$ = "1/2"
17080 if f = 5 then f$ = "5/8"
17090 if f = 6 then f$ = "3/4"
17100 if f = 7 then f$ = "7/8"
17110 return
17120 :
17130 :
18000 rem **--y/n input routine--**
18010 print "Type a ";wht$;"Y";ylw$;" or ";wht$;"N";ylw$;" :";
18020 poke 19,32:rem disable input ?
18030 input yes$
18040 print
18050 if yes$ = "y" or yes$ = "Y" then yes$ = "y":return
18060 if yes$ = "n" or yes$ = "N" then yes$ = "n":return
18070 print
18080 print rvs$;"Incorrect Choice!";ylw$
18090 print
18100 goto 18000:rem check again
18110 :
18120 :
19000 rem **--return key routine--**
19010 print
19020 print "Press ";wht$;"RETURN";ylw$;" to continue:";
19030 poke 198,0:rem clr kbrd buffer
19040 for i = 631 to 640
19050 poke i,0:rem no value
19060 next i
19070 x = peek(197):rem store key press
19080 if x = 1 then 19100
19090 goto 19070:rem if not 1 go back
19100 poke 198,1:rem allow 1 for cursor
19110 poke 631,0:rem clr kbrd
19120 nu$ = "":rem clr string variable
19130 print home$:rem clr/home
19140 return

ready.
```

appendices

Appendix A

CHECKSUM

I developed the following "checksum" program to help readers know if the programs they have entered have been typed in correctly. The checksum program generates cumulative values at specified points within each program. Theoretically, the user should be able to match his/her values with the values published for each program. If the values do not match, then the typist knows that the program has not been entered exactly as given in the book. The location of the incorrect values should give a clue as to the general location of the typing error(s). The process should work something like this:

1. Type in some program published in the book.
2. Save the program out to diskette or tape.
3. Type "new" and then load the program back into the computer. (This step is taken only as a precaution against a number of possible problems.)
4. Type:
   poke 43,peek(45)
   poke 44,peek(46)
5. Load in the "checksum" program:
   /checksum
6. Add the last line number of the program to be checked as a new line number for the "checksum" program and as a part of a data statement for that new instruction. For example, if the last line number in the program you are checking is 19150, you type: 19150 data 19150,0,0. If the last line number you entered was 770, then you type: 770 data 770,0,0

Once this step is done correctly, run the checksum program and observe the values generated and displayed on the screen. If the screen values match the printed values, you can be fairly certain that you have entered the program correctly. If the screen values do not match the printed values, then something has been entered that does not match exactly with the printed listing. (Notice that I did not say that some error had been entered.) It is quite possible to not match the checksum values yet have a correctly operating program by making changes at some noncritical point(s).

Limitations

There are four basic limitations to use of this checksum program:

1. For some people, the process involved may prove too awkward to be useful. If the procedure outlined above is not followed exactly, the program will not work correctly and may generate incorrect values.
2. The checksum program will check to see that everything is included. In order to match the printed values, you must enter programs EXACTLY as given in the book—spaces, rem, etc. Everything must be exactly as shown in the book. One missing space somewhere near the beginning of the program would throw all the generated values off.
3. It is possible for all the values to match yet the program might not work. The checksum program will not catch transposed characters. For example, an instruction line containing "pirnt" has the same characters as "print", and the checksum values for these two words would be the same. But the program containing "pirnt" would not work until the characters "i" and "r" were turned around.
4. If the program to be checked has line numbers below 100, Step 6 above needs to be changed. Instead of entering the last line number as a part of the checksum program, enter all lines you want checked as data statements with line numbers from 90 to 99. For example: 90 data 10, 20, 30; 92 data 40,0,0

For these reasons, I am not certain how useful the checksum values will be. On the hope that some readers might find it easier to locate typing errors, I decided to include these values and the checksum program. Please be certain that you enter the checksum program correctly. Good luck!

■ Program for Checksum

```
10 rem ***--checksum--***
11 :
12 :
13 rem **--information--**
14 input "program name ";file$
15 print chr$(147)
16 print tab(12) file$
17 print chr$(10)
18 print chr$(10)
19 print tab(3) "Line #";
20 print tab(20)"Checksum"
21 print chr$(10)
22 :
23 :
24 rem **--main loop--**
25 x = peek(44)*256 + peek(43)
26 read number
27 for i = 2048 to x - 1
28 z = peek(i)
29 t = t + z
30 if z = 0 then 45
31 next i
32 :
33 :
34 rem **--all finished--**
35 print t
36 poke x,0
37 poke x + 1,0
38 poke 43,1
39 poke 44,8
40 close 4
41 end
42 :
43 :
44 rem **--zero subroutine--**
45 lo = peek(i + 1)
46 ho = peek(i + 2)
47 if i + 3 > x -1 then 50
48 ll = peek(i + 3)
49 hl = peek(i + 4)
50 i = i + 4
51 line = hl * 256 + ll
52 if line = number then 57
53 if line > number then read number:goto 52
54 if flag$ = "on" then print t:flag$ = "off"
55 t = t + lo + ho + ll + hl
56 goto 31
57 if flag$ = "on" then print t:flag$ = "off"
58 t = t + lo + ho + ll + hl
59 if line = 0 then print tab(6) line;:goto 63
60 if line < 1000 then print tab(4) line;
61 if line > 999 and line < 10000 then print tab(3) line;
62 if line > 9999 then print  tab(2) line;
```

```
63 print tab(20)
64 lo = 0:ho = 0:ll = 0:hl = 0
65 flag$ = "on"
66 read number
67 goto 31
68 :
69 :
70 rem **--data statements--**
100 data 100
400 data 400
700 data 700
1000 data 1000
1500 data 1500
2000 data 2000
2500 data 2500
3000 data 3000
3500 data 3500
4000 data 4000
4500 data 4500
5000 data 5000
5500 data 5500
6000 data 6000
6500 data 6500
7000 data 7000
7500 data 7500
8000 data 8000
8500 data 8500
9000 data 9000
9500 data 9500
10000 data 10000
18000 data 18000
19000 data 19000
20000 data 20000
```

Chapter 4

mail.create

Line #	Checksum
100	1517
400	52032
700	109895
3000	148363
5000	162713
8000	165854
9000	187945
9040	191012
0	191012

Chapter 5

mail.reader1

Line #	Checksum
100	1566
400	42856
1000	49872
5000	56396
9000	59627
9040	62410
0	62410

mail.adder1

Line #	Checksum
100	1482
400	83509
700	142134
2000	179895
3000	196160
5000	223483
8000	226495
9000	248103
9040	250786
0	250786

mail.adder2

Line #	Checksum
100	1483
400	83383
700	142266
1000	180264
2000	234798
3000	260960
5000	276470
8000	279331
9000	300767
9040	303554
0	303554

■ *Chapter 6*

mail.menu

Line #	Checksum
100	1388
700	72831
1000	108490
2000	154875
3000	164756
4000	176121
5000	187786
6000	205864
7000	231735
8000	271601
9000	293323
19000	299051
19110	317506
0	317506

shell

Line #	Checksum
100	1114
8000	66710
9000	85255
10000	90070
18000	144881
19000	167918
20000	192950
20080	206793
0	206793

mail.reader2

Line #	Checksum
100	1567
400	66329
700	129154
1000	156490
2000	175714
3000	206069
4000	224078
5000	271545
6000	325186
7000	360128
7500	451365
8000	515118
9000	534018
10000	538750
18000	594532
19000	618214
20000	643214
20080	657841
0	657841

■ *Chapter 7*

mail.correction

Line #	Checksum
100	1845
400	64283
1000	116190
2000	170464
2500	251961
3000	262295
4000	318301
7000	338006
9000	353411
10000	357996
18000	413172
19000	436560
20000	461536
20080	479399
0	479399

mail.menu

Line #	Checksum
100	1388
700	72831
1000	108490
2000	154875
3000	164756
4000	176121
5000	187786
6000	205864
7000	231735
8000	271601
9000	293323
19000	299051
19110	317506
0	317506

mail.create

Line #	Checksum
100	1517
400	52032
700	109895
3000	148363
5000	163511
8000	182233
9000	203578
9040	206337
0	206337

mail.adder2

Line #	Checksum
100	1483
400	83383
700	142266
1000	180264
2000	234798
3000	260960
5000	277268
8000	296565
9000	318275
9040	320754
0	320754

mail.reader2

Line #	Checksum
100	1567
400	66329
700	129154
1000	156490
2000	175714
3000	206069
4000	224078
5000	271545
6000	325186
7000	360128
7500	451365
8000	515118
9000	534018
10000	538750
18000	594532
19000	618214
20000	643214
20080	657841
0	657841

mail.correction

Line #	Checksum
100	1845
400	64283
1000	116190
2000	170464
2500	251961
3000	262295
4000	318301
7000	338006
9000	353411
10000	357996
18000	413172
19000	436560
20000	461536
20080	479399
0	479399

Chapter 8

math.menu

Line #	Checksum
100	1395
700	64675
1000	109181
2000	118345
3000	129179
4000	139787
5000	149913
6000	159762
6500	241781
7000	318096
8000	334120
9000	359711
18000	407170
19000	429663
19140	454250
0	454250

math.add

Line #	Checksum
100	1329
400	70052
700	120224
1000	146056
1500	190994
2000	225689
3000	239130
4000	297619
5000	317277
6000	330121
7000	342793
9000	368016
19000	373345
19110	391827
0	391827

math.subtract

Line #	Checksum
100	1590
400	70187
700	121239
1000	147371
1500	192852
2000	227150
3000	240735
4000	299625
5000	319204
6000	332192
7000	345024
9000	370551
19000	376008
19110	394411
0	394411

math.multiply

Line #	Checksum
100	1817
400	70543
700	121733
1000	148217
1500	193648
2000	228084
3000	241723
4000	300859
5000	320504
6000	333546
7000	346438
9000	371824
19000	377329
19110	395798
0	395798

math.divide

Line #	Checksum
100	1354
400	69367
700	119719
1000	154819
1500	194134
2000	231062
3000	244314
4000	303897
5000	323494
6000	336404
7000	349716
9000	374625
19000	380466
19110	399142
0	399142

math.scores

Line #	Checksum
100	1551
400	59788
700	107941
6000	133834
7000	152241
9000	177683
10000	183191
18000	237923
19000	260978
19150	287502
0	287502

create q & a

Line #	Checksum
100	1461
700	66294
1000	74584
9000	87290
18000	92491
18100	111856
0	111856

drill & practice

Line #	Checksum
100	1813
400	58183
700	101498
1000	110924
6000	126367
7000	145412
9000	170715
10000	176745
18000	232116
19000	254869
19150	281798
0	281798

■ *Chapter 9*

scores.dif

Line #	Checksum
100	1463
400	66157
1000	89608
2000	110865
3000	127906
5000	167513
7000	181427
9000	206600
9040	209539
0	209539

read dif

Line #	Checksum
100	1268
400	63810
1000	89913
5000	96589
7000	109368
9000	134234
9040	137001
0	137001

Chapter 10

random example

Line #	Checksum
100	2077
400	45090
1000	82157
1070	90135
0	90135

medical rec.sys.

Line #	Checksum
100	2228
400	56353
700	115803
1000	139059
1500	238936
2000	326784
2500	397527
3000	422434
3500	509910
4000	577787
4500	670275
5000	681432
6000	699789
9000	725833
10000	731773
18000	909606
19000	933388
20000	958436
20080	970906
0	970906

Chapter 11

homeinv.menu

Line #	Checksum
100	1634
700	68830
1000	114634
2000	125170
3000	136489
4000	148197
5000	160386
6000	171484
7000	182760
8000	198731
9000	224073
18000	271317
19000	293701
19140	318151
0	318151

homeinv.write

Line #	Checksum
100	2194
400	56554
1000	74608
1500	176161
2000	273463
3000	340743
4000	350228
5000	367330
6000	381348
9000	401463
18000	444282
19000	467932
19120	488755
0	488755

homeinv.read

Line #	Checksum
100	2082
400	56386
1000	74004
1500	138059
6000	183423
9000	203277
10000	208849
18000	272562
19000	295904
19120	316718
0	316718

homeinv.search

Line #	Checksum
100	2178
400	56512
700	97490
1000	139251
2000	172053
3000	205286
3500	303638
4000	366286
5000	400214
6000	467297
6500	548214
7000	550555
9000	570587
10000	576083
18000	817237
19000	840881
20000	864990
25150	936205
0	936205

homeinv.correct

Line #	Checksum
100	2079
400	56383
700	98442
1000	122999
1500	220553
2000	228407
3000	304435
5000	324733
6000	373290
7000	426145
9000	440484
18000	484180
19000	507162
19120	527886
0	527886

homeinv.translate

Line #	Checksum
100	2016
400	56260
1000	84409
1500	150698
2000	153766
2500	208751
3000	256893
9000	276581
19000	290770
19120	311479
0	311479

homeinv.copy

Line #	Checksum
100	1761
400	56200
1000	84311
1500	149936
2000	153381
2500	222979
3000	226260
9000	246335
19000	260179
19120	281020
0	281020

magazine.menu

Line #	Checksum
100	1689
700	69525
1000	115441
2000	126247
3000	137848
4000	149595
5000	162090
6000	173506
7000	184602
8000	200749
9000	226124
18000	273163
19000	295500
19140	319919
0	319919

magazine.write

Line #	Checksum
100	2147
400	56507
1000	77783
1500	206902
2000	313941
3000	385783
4000	396109
5000	413825
6000	427998
9000	448024
18000	491734
19000	514668
19120	535533
0	535533

Chapter 12

stock.menu

Line #	Checksum
100	1486
700	73560
1000	118872
2000	128519
3000	140382
4000	152328
5000	164379
6000	175613
7000	187198
8000	202855
9000	228425
18000	275319
19000	297726
19140	322475
0	322475

stock.add

Line #	Checksum
100	2245
400	51019
1000	80695
2000	141724
3000	200146
4000	212699
4500	295836
5000	303604
6000	314659
7000	321560
9000	339336
18000	437539
19000	460271
20000	488338
20040	493315
0	493315

stock.real

Line #	Checksum
100	2258
1000	33873
1500	120219
2000	138560
3000	184516
4000	232862
5000	251233
9000	276304
18000	341085
19000	363886
19140	388412
0	388412

stock.display

Line #	Checksum
100	2302
400	51076
1000	90739
2000	124318
3000	151804
4000	167747
4500	239504
5000	279090
6000	337201
7000	347409
9000	365120
18000	487147
19000	510226
19140	535676
0	535676

stock.dsp hi/low

Line #	Checksum
100	2066
1000	42856
2000	83525
9000	101668
18000	127594
19000	149803
19140	174378
0	174378

stock.crt hi/low

Line #	Checksum
100	2062
400	51510
700	98078
1000	108753
2000	146495
3000	175582
4000	229792
7000	242200
9000	261116
18000	344074
19000	366442
19140	391149
0	391149

stock.correct

Line #	Checksum
100	2080
400	50822
1000	81394
2000	115174
3000	157084
3500	223447
4000	225516
5000	310900
5500	395050
6000	397613
7000	412439
9000	430305
18000	545452
19000	568663
20000	596856
20040	601753
0	601753

stock.trans

Line #	Checksum
100	2238
400	51486
1000	103257
2000	134701
3000	163954
4000	211183
5000	227722
5500	268470
6000	272892
6500	333362
7000	382462
9000	400130
19000	465575
19140	490382
0	490382

Appendix B

PROGRAM LIST

I. MAILING LIST SYSTEM PROGRAMS
   1. MAIL.MENU (Chapters 6 and 7)
   2. MAIL.CREATE (Chapters 4 and 7)
   3. MAIL.ADDER1 (Chapter 5)
   4. MAIL.ADDER2 (Chapters 5 and 7)
   5. MAIL.READER2 (Chapters 6 and 7)
   6. MAIL.CORRECTION (Chapter 7: two programs)
   7. SHELL (Chapter 6)

II. MATH SYSTEM PROGRAMS
   1. MATH.MENU (Chapter 8)
   2. MATH.ADD (Chapter 8)
   3. MATH.SUBTRACT (Chapter 8)
   4. MATH.MULTIPLY (Chapter 8)
   5. MATH.DIVIDE (Chapter 8)
   6. MATH.SCORES (Chapter 8)
   7. SCORES.DIF (Chapter 9)

III. DRILL & PRACTICE PROGRAMS
   1. CREATE Q & A (Chapter 8)
   2. DRILL & PRACTICE (Chapter 8)

IV. DIF PROGRAMS
   1. SCORES.DIF (Chapter 9)
   2. READ.DIF (Chapter 9)
   3. HOMEINV.TRANS (Chapter 11)
   4. STOCK.TRANS (Chapter 12)

V. MEDICAL RECORDS SYSTEM PROGRAM
   1. MEDICAL REC.SYS. (Chapter 10)

VI. HOME INVENTORY SYSTEM PROGRAMS
   1. HOMEINV.MENU (Chapter 11)

2. HOMEINV.WRITE (Chapter 11)
3. HOMEINV.READ (Chapter 11)
4. HOMEINV.SEARCH (Chapter 11)
5. HOMEINV.CORRECT (Chapter 11)
6. HOMEINV.TRANS (Chapter 11)
7. HOMEINV.COPY (Chapter 11)

VII. MAGAZINE CATALOG SYSTEM PROGRAMS

1. MAGAZINE.MENU (Chapter 11)
2. MAGAZINE.WRITE (Chapter 11)

VIII. STOCK MARKET SYSTEM PROGRAMS

1. STOCK.MENU (Chapter 12)
2. STOCK.ADD (Chapter 12)
3. STOCK.REAL (Chapter 12)
4. STOCK.DISPLAY (Chapter 12)
5. STOCK.DSP HI/LOW (Chapter 12)
6. STOCK.CRT HI/LOW (Chapter 12)
7. STOCK.CORRECT (Chapter 12)
8. STOCK.TRANS (Chapter 12)

Appendix C

KEYBOARD VALUES

The following is a list of the values obtained by pressing a key and PEEKing at location 197:

KEY	VALUE
A	10
B	28
C	20
D	18
E	14
F	21
G	26
H	29
I	33
J	34
K	37
L	42
M	36
N	39
O	38
P	41
Q	62
R	17
S	13
T	22
U	30
V	31
W	9
X	23
Y	25
Z	12
1	56
2	59
3	8
4	11
5	16
6	19
7	24
8	27
9	32
0	35
–	43
+	40
P	46
*	49
:	45
;	50
=	53

,	47
.	44
/	55
F1	4
F3	5
F5	6
F7	3
INST/DEL	0
RETURN	1
CRSR RIGHT/LEFT	2
CRSR UP/DOWN	7
CLR/HOME	51
UP ARROW	54
ENG.POUND	48
LEFT ARROW	57
RUN	63
SPACE BAR	60
NO KEY	64

There is a somewhat obscure pattern in the assignment of the keyboard values. Begin at the number 3 key, proceed down to the W key and then to the A key. Jump up to the top row and the number 4 key. Drop to the bottom row and the key in the direct line from the number 4 key (Z). Move up to the key above it (S) and then to the key above that key (E). Drop to the bottom row and the key immediately before the previously used bottom row key. (In this instance, it should be the SHIFT key which comes immediately before the last used bottom row key of Z. The SHIFT key is not actually assigned a value and that is probably why the numbers 15 and 52 are not used.) To begin the cycle over again, jump to the next key on the top row (5) and follow the same sequence of two more keys down, up to the top row, down to the bottom row, up two more keys, complete the cycle by dropping to the bottom row and the key just before the last-used bottom row key. Surprisingly, the sequence even "wraps around" the keyboard and pretty much stays consistent. It would appear that the left arrow key was originally intended to be in the location of the CTRL key but for some reason was moved. This is obviously speculative, but the pattern does suggest that the left arrow key is not where it should be. The values of the keys are given below, this time in numerical order.

VALUE	KEY
0	INST/DEL
1	RETURN
2	CRSR RIGHT/LEFT
3	F7
4	F1
5	F3
6	F5
7	CRSR UP/DOWN
8	3
9	W
10	A
11	4

12	Z
13	S
14	E
15	(NOT USED)
16	5
17	R
18	D
19	6
20	C
21	F
22	X
24	7
25	Y
26	G
27	8
28	B
29	H
30	V
31	V
32	9
33	I
34	J
35	0
36	M
37	K
38	O
39	N
40	+
41	P
42	L
43	-
44	.
45	:
46	P
47	,
48	ENG.POUND
49	*
50	;
51	CLR/HOME
52	(NOT USED)
53	=
54	UP ARROW
55	/
56	1
57	LEFT ARROW
58	(NOT USED)
59	2
60	SPACE BAR
61	(NOT USED)
62	Q
63	RUN
64	NO KEY

Appendix D

RANDOM (RELATIVE) FILES WITHOUT THE POSITION PARAMETER

The problem with random (Commodore's relative) files without the position parameter can be easily demonstrated by slight modification of the "random test" program. The purpose of the modification is to eliminate the position parameter from the position command statements and to bypass those statements that refer to the second field within each record. After starting up the system and loading the DOS Wedge, load the random test program or type it in from the listing given at the end of Chapter 10. Then, make the following changes:

1. Line 180—delete the position parameter (the last chr$ value).
2. Add line 195: 195 goto 220.
3. Line 350—delete the position parameter (the last chr$ value).
4. Line 370—delete the semicolon.
5. Add line 375: 375 goto 410.
6. Line 610—delete the position parameter (the last chr$ value).
7. Add line 575: 575 goto 610.
8. Line 630—delete the tab(15) leaving the statement as: print a$.

When you have finished making these changes, save the program as "random test 2":

```
←random test 2
```

If you are using the same diskette that was used to create the first "random example" file, you should scratch that file or insert another formatted diskette before continuing. We want to be absolutely certain that we will not pick up any extraneous characters. Another possibility would be to change the name of the file in lines 150, 320, and 560 to something other than "random example". When you are certain you have followed all the steps, run the program.

```
@scratch0:random example
run
```

The first part of the program creates a random (relative) file without using the position parameter. Each record should contain the word "record" and the actual number of the record. Since we have not specified a position parameter, it is logical to assume that the "r" in "record" would exist at the first space or byte of each record. It should also be possible to input and display the contents of each record. As we will soon see, both of these assumptions are incorrect. When the disk drive has stopped, the file "random example" should be on the diskette with twenty-five records and each record should be 50 bytes (spaces) in length. The message: Press RETURN to continue: should be displayed on the screen. When you are ready, follow the directions and press the RETURN key. The disk drive should come back on and the screen should display:

```
record 1
record 2
record 3
record 4
record 5
```

After the fifth record is displayed, the disk drive continues to run but no further information is displayed on the screen. In the past, I have waited for as long as five minutes before stopping the program. You do not need to wait. Instead, press the RUN/STOP key and at the same time press the RESTORE key. This combination of keys halts the operation of the computer and eventually stops the disk drive. In order to continue, you will need to manually close the files. Type:

```
close 3
close 2
```

Then, switch back to lower case and type:

```
goto 500
```

By manually closing the files, we are able to go on to the next portion of the program and double-check the apparent problem. The screen should display the question: Which record number? Answer with the number 5. The disk drive should come on and the screen should show:

```
record 5
Which record number?
```

Type the number 7 in response to the request for the next record number. Again, the screen should show:

```
record 7
Which record number?
```

At this point, we know that there is information in records one through five and record seven that we can access with a simple input# statement and without a position parameter. But the computer stopped working the last time when it came to record six. It will also stop when it comes to record 11 and every fifth record thereafter until record 66. At record 66, the problem advances one record and again proceeds for every fifth record. I stopped tracking the pattern at record 100. You can check this out by answering with record numbers on either side of records 6, 11, 16, and 21. Since this test only created 25 records, you cannot go above record 25. But if you answer with record number 6, 11, 16, or 21, the computer will again "hang" with the disk drive continuing to run. In other words, the computer can properly access records with the exception of every fifth record. If you have tried one of the "problem" records, you will need to press the RUN/STOP key and at the same time press the RESTORE key. This combination of keys halts the operation of the computer and eventually stops the disk drive. In order to continue, you will need to manually close the files. Type:

```
close 3
close 2
```

Then, switch back to lower case. This demonstration confirms the existence of a problem with random (relative) files created without the position parameter but does not explain why the problem exists or what the actual problem is. If you are interested in discovering what the problem is, you will need to modify the "random test 2" program further. The following changes need to be made:

1. Add line 505: 505 × = 1
2. Add to the end of line 610: ;chr$(x)
3. Change 620 to: 620 get#3,a$
4. Change 630 to: 630 print "Byte (space)";x;a$
5. Add line 635: 635 × = × + 1
6. Add line 637: 637 if status = 0 then 610
7. Add line 645: 645 × = 1

These changes allow us to "get" and display each byte of the record until we come to the end-of-record marker. We have added a position parameter to line 610 that will start at position 1 and increase by 1 byte until the status variable indicates a value other than zero. In other words, we should be able to see what is in each record beginning at the first byte or space of the record. When all the additions and changes have been made, save the program as "random test 3":

```
←random test 3
```

Then, type:

goto 500

Begin answering the record number question in the same way you did before. Type the number 5. The screen should show:

```
Byte (space) 1 #
Byte (space) 2
Byte (space) 3
Byte (space) 4
Byte (space) 5
Byte (space) 6
Byte (space) 7
Byte (space) 8
Byte (space) 9
Byte (space) 10
Byte (space) 11
Byte (space) 12
Byte (space) 13 r
Byte (space) 14 e
Byte (space) 15 c
Byte (space) 16 o
Byte (space) 17 r
Byte (space) 18 d
Byte (space) 19
Byte (space) 20 5
Byte (space) 21
Byte (space) 22

Which record number?
```

Answer with record number 6. This time the computer will not "hang". Instead, the screen will show:

```
Byte (space)  1 r
Byte (space)  2 e
Byte (space)  3 c
Byte (space)  4 o
Byte (space)  5 r
Byte (space)  6 d
Byte (space)  7
Byte (space)  8 6
Byte (space)  9
Byte (space) 10
```

We now have the answer to what caused the computer to "hang" when it tried to access record number six. Records one through five do not actually have the information beginning with the first byte of each record. As demonstrated when we just now asked for record number five, the "r" in the word "record" did not come until the 13th byte or space of that record. But record number six does begin storing the information in the normal first byte of the record. Therefore, when the file input routine in lines 300 to 450 tried to bring information in from the file, the input#3,a$ statement (line 360) for some reason began reading every record at the 13th byte of that record. But when it came to the sixth record, it did not find any information at the 13th byte of that record. The computer had stored the information where it should have stored all the information in every record—in the first 8 bytes of the record. In other words, when the information was written, the computer stored the information in most of the records in the wrong location. But in those records that appeared to be causing the computer to "hang", the information was actually stored in the correct location. This fact indicates that the operating system has an additional problem because the computer was able to "read" the records that had information stored in the wrong location and was not able to read records that had the information stored in the right location. Yet, as you saw when you ran the first "random test" program in Chapter 10, the process works properly if the position parameter is included at every step. Therefore, until Commodore releases a new version of its DOS operating system, I would not recommend use of undivided random files without a position parameter.

Program for Random Test 2

```
100 rem ***--random file example--***
110 :
120 :
130 rem **--file output routine--**
140 open 2,8,15:rem open command chnl
150 open 3,8,4,"random example,l," + chr$(50)
160 for i = 1 to 25
170 gosub 1000:rem figure rec.# routine
180 print#2,"p";chr$(4);chr$(rlow);chr$(rhigh)
190 print#3,"record";i
195 goto 220
200 print#2,"p";chr$(4);chr$(rlow);chr$(rhigh);chr$(20)
210 print#3,"abcdef";i
220 next i
230 close 3:close 2
240 input "Press 'RETURN' to continue: ";r$
250 :
260 :
300 rem **--file input routine--**
310 open 2,8,15:rem open command chnl
320 open 3,8,4,"random example,l," + chr$(50)
330 for i = 1 to 25
340 gosub 1000:rem figure rec.# routine
350 print#2,"p";chr$(4);chr$(rlow);chr$(rhigh)
360 input#3,a$
370 print a$
375 goto 410
380 print#2,"p";chr$(4);chr$(rlow);chr$(rhigh);chr$(20)
390 input#3,b$
400 print tab(15) b$
410 next i
420 close 3:close 2
430 input "Press 'RETURN' to continue: ";r$
440 :
450 :
500 rem **--random access routine--**
510 input "Which record number";nb$
520 nb = val(nb$)
530 if nb = 0 then 900:rem end
540 if nb > 25 then 510:rem ask again
550 i = nb:gosub 1000:rem figure rec.#
560 open 2,8,15:rem open command chnl
570 open 3,8,4,"random example,l," + chr$(50)
575 goto 610
580 print#2,"p";chr$(4);chr$(rlow);chr$(rhigh);chr$(20)
590 input#3,b$
600 print b$;
610 print#2,"p";chr$(4);chr$(rlow);chr$(rhigh)
620 input#3,a$
630 print a$
640 close 3:close 2
650 goto 510
660 :
```

```
670 :
900 rem **--end routine--**
910 end
920 :
930 :
1000 rem **--figure rec.# routine--**
1010 rlow  = i
1020 rhigh = 0
1030 if rlow > 255 then 1050
1040 return
1050 rhigh = int(rlow/256)
1060 rlow  = rlow - 256 * rhigh
1070 return

ready.
```

■ Program for Random Test 3

```
100 rem ***--random file example--***
110 :
120 :
130 rem **--file output routine--**
140 open 2,8,15:rem open command chnl
150 open 3,8,4,"random example,l," + chr$(50)
160 for i = 1 to 25
170 gosub 1000:rem figure rec.# routine
180 print#2,"p";chr$(4);chr$(rlow);chr$(rhigh)
190 print#3,"record";i
195 goto 220
200 print#2,"p";chr$(4);chr$(rlow);chr$(rhigh);chr$(20)
210 print#3,"abcdef";i
220 next i
230 close 3:close 2
240 input "Press 'RETURN' to continue: ";r$
250 :
260 :
300 rem **--file input routine--**
310 open 2,8,15:rem open command chnl
320 open 3,8,4,"random example,l," + chr$(50)
330 for i = 1 to 25
340 gosub 1000:rem figure rec.# routine
350 print#2,"p";chr$(4);chr$(rlow);chr$(rhigh)
360 input#3,a$
370 print a$
375 goto 410
380 print#2,"p";chr$(4);chr$(rlow);chr$(rhigh);chr$(20)
390 input#3,b$
400 print tab(15) b$
410 next i
420 close 3:close 2
430 input "Press 'RETURN' to continue: ";r$
440 :
450 :
500 rem **--random access routine--**
505 x = 1
510 input "Which record number";nb$
520 nb = val(nb$)
530 if nb = 0 then 900:rem end
540 if nb > 25 then 510:rem ask again
550 i = nb:gosub 1000:rem figure rec.#
560 open 2,8,15:rem open command chnl
570 open 3,8,4,"random example,l," + chr$(50)
575 goto 610
580 print#2,"p";chr$(4);chr$(rlow);chr$(rhigh);chr$(20)
590 input#3,b$
600 print b$;
610 print#2,"p";chr$(4);chr$(rlow);chr$(rhigh);chr$(x)
620 get#3,a$
630 print "Byte (space)";x;a$
635 x = x + 1
637 if status = 0 then 610
```

```
640 close 3:close 2
645 x = 1
650 goto 510
660 :
670 :
900 rem **--end routine--**
910 end
920 :
930 :
1000 rem **--figure rec.# routine--**
1010 rlow  = i
1020 rhigh = 0
1030 if rlow > 255 then 1050
1040 return
1050 rhigh = int(rlow/256)
1060 rlow  = rlow - 256 * rhigh
1070 return

ready.
```

Appendix E

WEDGE COPIER

■ Instructions

1. Type in the program "wedge copier".
2. Save it to a diskette.
3. Run the program and follow the screen directions.
4. At this point, you have two options:
   a. Load the program called "c-64 wedge" from the "test/demo" diskette and save it back out to the diskette containing the copy of the "dos 5.1" wedge. You can save the program under a name easier to type, such as "wedge". Then, in order to institute the wedge, just type: load "wedge",8. Follow with the run command and the "dos 5.1" program will be loaded and initiated.
   b. If you do not want to bother with saving a copy of the "c-64 wedge", then everytime you want the wedge, you will need to type: load "dos 5.1",8,1: sys 52224. The wedge should then become active.

■ Program for Wedge Copier

```
100 rem ***--wedge copier--***
110 :
120 :
130 rem **--read in wedge--**
140 dim a%(1000)
150 i = 1
160 print chr$(147):print:print:print
170 print "Insert TEST/DEMO diskette and press"
180 print:print
190 input "'RETURN' to continue:";w$
200 print chr$(147):print:print:print
210 print tab(5) "READING WEDGE. PLEASE WAIT!"
220 print
230 open 2,8,2,"0:dos 5.1,prg,read"
240 get#2,a$
250 a$ = a$ + chr$(0)
260 a%(i) = asc(a$)
270 print ".";
280 i = i + 1
290 if status = 0 then 240
300 close 2
```

```
310 print:print:print
320 input "Insert new diskette. Press 'RETURN' :";w$
330 :
340 :
350 rem **--write out wedge--**
360 print chr$(147):print:print:print
370 print tab(5) "WRITING WEDGE. PLEASE WAIT!"
380 open 3,8,3,"0:dos 5.1,prg,write"
390 for k = 1 to i - 1
400 print#3,chr$(a%(k));
410 next k
420 close 3
430 :
440 :
450 rem **--end--**
460 print chr$(147):print:print:print
470 print tab(5) "ALL FINISHED!!"
480 end
```

index

D

H

I

K

L

M

N

O

P

Q

R

S

T

U

V

W